The Princeton Review

P9-BYB-432

Cracking the

AP®

U.S. HISTORY EXAM

2014 Edition

Tom Meltzer and Jean Hofheimer Bennett
Updated by Susan Babkes

PrincetonReview.com

Random House, Inc. New York

The Princeton Review, Inc.
111 Speen Street, Suite 550
Framingham, MA 01701
E-mail: editorialsupport@review.com

ISBN: 978-0-307-94624-9
ISSN: 1092-0072

AP and Advanced Placement Program are registered trademarks of the
College Board, which does not sponsor or endorse this product.

The Princeton Review is not affiliated with Princeton University.

Editor: Meave Shelton
Production Editor: Lee Elder
Production Artists: John E. Stecyki, Keren Peysakh

Printed in the United States of America on partially recycled paper.

10 9 8 7 6 5 4 3 2 1

2014 Edition

Editorial
Rob Franek, Senior VP, Publisher
Mary Beth Garrick, Director of Production
Selena Coppock, Senior Editor
Calvin Cato, Editor
Kristen O'Toole, Editor
Meave Shelton, Editor
Alyssa Wolff, Editorial Assistant

Random House Publishing Team
Tom Russell, Publisher
Nicole Benhabib, Publishing Director
Ellen L. Reed, Production Manager
Alison Stoltzfus, Managing Editor

ACKNOWLEDGMENTS

The Princeton Review would like to thank David Stoll, Adam Cadre, and Chris Stobart for their invaluable contributions to this edition, and all of the contributors to previous editions.

Contents

Part I
Using This
Book to Improve
Your AP Score

- Preview: Your Knowledge, Your Expectations
- Your Guide to Using This Book
- How to Begin

PREVIEW: YOUR KNOWLEDGE, YOUR EXPECTATIONS

Your route to a high score on the AP U.S. History Exam depends a lot on how you plan to use this book. Respond to the following questions.

1. Rate your level of confidence about your knowledge of the content tested by the AP U.S. History Exam:

    A. Very confident—I know it all
    B. I'm pretty confident, but there are topics for which I could use help
    C. Not confident—I need quite a bit of support
    D. I'm not sure

2. Circle your goal score for the AP U.S. History Exam:

    5   4   3   2   1   I'm not sure yet

3. What do you expect to learn from this book? Circle all that apply to you.

    A. A general overview of the test and what to expect
    B. Strategies for how to approach the test
    C. The content tested by this exam
    D. I'm not sure yet

YOUR GUIDE TO USING THIS BOOK

This book is organized to provide as much—or as little—support as you need, so you can use this book in whatever way will be most helpful to improving your score on the AP U.S. History Exam.

-   The remainder of **Part I** will provide guidance on how to use this book and help you determine your strengths and weaknesses.

-   **Part II** of this book will:
    o   provide information about the structure, scoring, and content of the AP U.S. History Exam
    o   help you to make a study plan
    o   point you towards additional resources

- **Part III** of this book will explore various strategies:
  - how to attack multiple-choice questions
  - how to write effective essays
  - how to manage your time to maximize the number of points available to you

- **Part IV** of this book covers the content you need for the AP U.S. History Exam.

- **Part V** of this book contains practice tests, answers and explanations, and scoring worksheets to help you grade your practice tests.

You may choose to use some parts of this book over others, or you may work through the entire book. This will depend on your needs and how much time you have. Let's now look at how to make this determination.

HOW TO BEGIN

1. **Take a Test**

   Before you can decide how to use this book, you need to take a practice test. Doing so will give you insight into your strengths and weaknesses, and the test will also help you make an effective study plan. If you're feeling test-phobic, remind yourself that a practice test is a tool for diagnosing yourself—it's not how well you do that matters but how you use information gleaned from your performance to guide your preparation.

   So, before you read further, take Practice Test 1 starting at page 288 of this book. Be sure to do so in one sitting, following the instructions that appear before the test.

2. **Check Your Answers**

   Using the answer key on page 312, count how many multiple-choice questions you got right and how many you missed. Don't worry about the explanations for now, and don't worry about why you missed questions. We'll get to that soon.

3. **Reflect on the Test**

   After you take your first test, respond to the following questions:

   - How much time did you spend on the multiple-choice questions?
   - How much time did you spend on each essay?
   - How many multiple-choice questions did you miss?
   - Do you feel you had the knowledge to address the subject matter of the essays?
   - Do you feel you wrote well organized, thoughtful essays?
   - Circle the content areas that were most challenging for you and draw a line through the ones in which you felt confident/did well.

   Puritanism/Early Colonization
   Colonial Era
   English Oppression and The Revolutionary War
   The U.S. Constitution and Early American Politics
   The Louisiana Purchase and Westward Expansion
   The War of 1812
   Woman's Rights and Suffrage Movement
   Slavery and the Abolitionist Movement
   Manifest Destiny
   Civil War
   Reconstruction
   The Gilded Age (Reconstruction–1900)
   The Industrial Revolution
   World War I
   Prohibition
   The Great Depression and New Deal
   World War II
   The Cold War
   McCarthyism
   The Civil Rights Movement
   Great Society
   Vietnam War

4. **Read Part II of this Book and Complete the Self-Evaluation**

   As discussed in the Goals section above, Part II will provide information on how the test is structured and scored. It will also set out areas of content that are tested.

   As you read Part II, re-evaluate your answers to the questions above. At the end of Part II, you will revisit and refine the questions you answer above. You will then be able to make a study plan, based on your needs and time available, that will allow you to use this book most effectively.

5. **Engage with Parts III and IV as Needed**

Notice the word engage. You'll get more out of this book if you use it intentionally than if you read it passively, hoping for an improved score through osmosis.

Strategy chapters will help you think about your approach to the question types on this exam. Part III will open with a reminder to think about how you approach questions now and then close with a reflection section asking you to think about how/whether you will change your approach in the future.

Content chapters are designed to provide a review of the content tested on the AP U.S. History Exam, including the level of detail you need to know and how the content is tested. You will have the opportunity to assess your mastery of the content of each chapter through test-appropriate questions and a reflection section.

6. **Take Practice Test 2 and Assess Your Performance**

Once you feel you have developed the strategies you need and gained the knowledge you lacked, you should take Practice Test 2, which starts at page 363 of this book. You should do so in one sitting, following the instructions at the beginning of the test.

When you are done, check your answers to the multiple-choice sections. See if a teacher will read your essays and provide feedback.

Once you have taken the test, reflect on what areas you still need to work on, and revisit the chapters in this book that address those deficiencies. Through this type of reflection and engagement, you will continue to improve.

7. **Keep Working**

As we'll discuss in Part II, there are other resources available to you, including a wealth of information on AP Central. You can continue to explore areas that can stand to improve and engage in those areas right up to the day of the test.

Part II
About the
AP U.S.
History Exam

- The Structure of the AP U.S. History Exam
- How the AP U.S. History Exam Is Scored
- Overview of Content Topics
- How AP Exams Are Used
- Other Resources
- Designing Your Study Plan

THE STRUCTURE OF THE AP U.S. HISTORY EXAM

The AP United States History Exam consists of two main sections: a multiple-choice section and an essay questions section. The multiple-choice section is comprised of 80 multiple-choice questions covering the breadth of U.S. history (from Pre-Columbian to the Modern Era). During this time, you will be asked to fill in bubbles (as you likely have done in the past on other exams) corresponding to which of the five letter choices best answers each question being asked. You will be given 55 minutes (or approximately 40 seconds per question) to complete this section.

The essay questions section of the exam comprises a total of three essays to be completed in a total of 2 hours and 10 minutes (130 minutes). One of the essay questions will be a document-based question (DBQ) where you will have to answer a question based on 8 to 12 primary source documents provided. The remaining two essays are free-response questions (FRQ). You will be asked to select one FRQ essay prompt from each of two different pairs of questions. You will be given 15 minutes to read and prepare for your essay prompts and are suggested to spend 45 minutes writing the DBQ and 35 minutes each on the remaining FRQ prompts.

Structure of the AP United States History Exam			
Section	**Description**	**Number of Questions/ Parts**	**Time Allotted**
Section I Multiple Choice	Multiple Choice Questions	80 Questions	55 min
Section II Essay Questions	3 Essays Questions: 1 Document-based Question (DBQ) and 2 Free-Response Questions (FRQ)	1 DBQ and 2 FRQ	2 hr 10 min (total): 15 min (reading) 115 min (writing)

HOW THE AP U.S. HISTORY EXAM IS SCORED

AP U.S. History Exam scoring is based equally on the performance of the multiple-choice and essay questions sections. The raw scores from each section will be weighted and summed to generate an overall AP grade of 1–5. Scoring of the multiple-choice section is based solely on the raw score of the number of correct answers. There is no penalty for guessing.

Overview of AP U.S. History Exam Scoring		
Section	**How Is It Scored?**	**Percentage of Test Grade (of Section)**
Multiple Choice Section	Raw Score of Correct Answers (no penalty for guessing)	50%
Essay Question Section 1 DBQ 2 FRQ	Each Essay is Scored from 0 – 9 (see scoring rubric below)	50% (45%) (27.5% each)

Within the essay questions section, the DBQ will be weighted equal to 45 percent of the total section score (22.5 percent of the overall test score) and the two FRQ essays will each be weighted equal to 27.5 percent of the essay score (13.75 percent of the overall score). According to the College Board, each of the essay prompts will be scored on a scale of 0–9 as described below:

Essay Scoring Rubric	
Grade	**Description of Essay**
8 to 9	Well-developed, focused thesis; in-depth, effective analysis using a substantial number of documents (if applicable); numerous references to outside information; analysis of complexity of issue, acknowledgement of opposing viewpoints; may contain minor errors, but overall well-written and clearly organized.
5 to 7	Consistent thesis; analysis of several documents (if applicable); reference to most documents and to relevant outside information; acceptable organization; clearly written, logical but with flaws.
2 to 4	Limited or undeveloped thesis; describes documents but only achieves superficial treatment of the subject (if applicable); merely paraphrases or briefly cites documents; contains errors; may have major errors and be poorly organized and/or written.
0 to 1	Confused thesis or no thesis at all; inadequate or incorrect understanding of question; little understanding of documents (if applicable); ignores most documents; outside information sparse and often inaccurate; contains major errors; weak writing.

OVERVIEW OF CONTENT TOPICS

The College Board provides a breakdown by era and by general subject matter of the exam's questions. This breakdown is only approximate and will *not* appear in your test booklet. It comes from the preparatory material that the College Board publishes.

Breakdown of Questions by Era		
Era	**Percent of Questions**	**Number of Questions**
Pre-Columbian–1789	~20%	~16
1790–1914	~45%	~36
1915–Present	~35%	~28

The test requires students to know about early and recent history and everything in between. It also emphasizes political and social history more than diplomatic, economic, and cultural history, but the essay choices collectively tend to hit all five of these themes and five different areas. Remember this as you study. You should also note that multiple-choice questions might concern events since 2000, and there have been multiple-choice questions concerning the 1970s, 1980s, and 1990s on recent exams. So brush up on your more recent history, but don't focus on it too much, as none of the essay questions will deal exclusively with the post-1980 era.

Breakdown of Questions by General Subject Matter		
Subject	**Percent of Questions**	**Number of Questions**
Political institutions, behavior, and public policy	~35%	~28
Social change, cultural and intellectual developments	~40%	~32
Diplomacy and international relations	~15%	~12
Economic developments	~10%	~8

Excelling on the AP U.S. History Exam requires a thorough knowledge of the events of American history and their significance. We have provided a review of this material in Part IV of this text. According to the College Board, the specific topics that will be covered on the AP U.S. History Exam and should be reviewed in a course are:

1. Pre-Columbian Societies
2. Transatlantic Encounters and Colonial Beginnings, 1492–1690
3. Colonial North America, 1690–1754
4. The American Revolutionary Era, 1754–1789
5. The Early Republic, 1789–1815
6. Transformation of the Economy and Society in Antebellum America
7. The Transformation of Politics in Antebellum America
8. Religion, Reform, and Renaissance in Antebellum America
9. Territorial Expansion and Manifest Destiny
10. The Crisis of the Union
11. Civil War
12. Reconstruction
13. The Origins of the New South
14. Development of the West in the Late Nineteenth Century
15. Industrial America in the Late Nineteenth Century
16. Urban Society in the late Nineteenth Century
17. Populism and Progressivism
18. The Emergence of America as a World Power
19. The New Era: 1920s
20. The Great Depression and the New Deal
21. The Second World War
22. The Home Front During the War
23. The United States and the Early Cold War
24. The 1950s
25. The Turbulent 1960s
26. Politics and Economics at the End of the Twentieth Century
27. Society and Culture at the End of the Twentieth Century
28. The United States in the Post–Cold War World

HOW AP EXAMS ARE USED

Different colleges use AP exams in different ways, so it is important that you go to a particular college's web site to determine how it uses AP exams. The three items below represent the main ways in which AP exam scores can be used:

- **College Credit.** Some colleges will give you college credit if you score well on an AP exam. These credits count towards your graduation requirements, meaning that you can take fewer courses while in college. Given the cost of college, this could be quite a benefit, indeed.

- **Satisfy Requirements.** Some colleges will allow you to "place out" of certain requirements if you do well on an AP exam, even if they do not give you actual college credits. For example, you might not need to take an introductory-level course, or perhaps you might not need to take a class in a certain discipline at all.

- **Admissions Plus.** Even if your AP exam will not result in college credit or even allow you to place out of certain courses, most colleges will respect your decision to push yourself by taking an AP course or even an AP exam outside of a course. A high score on an AP exam shows mastery of more difficult content than is taught in many high school courses, and colleges may take that into account during the admissions process.

OTHER RESOURCES

There are many resources available to help you improve your score on the AP U.S. History Exam, not the least of which are your teachers. If you are taking an AP class, you may be able to get extra attention from your teacher, such as obtaining feedback on your essays. If you are not in an AP course, reach out to a teacher who teaches U.S. history (or another AP history teacher) and ask if the teacher will review your essays or otherwise help you with content.

Another wonderful resource is **AP Central**, the official site of the AP exams. The scope of the information at this site is quite broad and includes:

- A comprehensive course description, which includes details on what content is covered and sample questions
- Course syllabi, including teacher and student classroom resources
- A free full-length practice test
- Essay prompts, answers, and grading suggestions from previous years
- Several helpful links to websites containing era-specific information
- Past AP U.S. History Exams for purchase through the College Board website
- Updates on future changes to the AP U.S. History Exam

The AP Central home page address is:
http://apcentral.collegeboard.com/apc/Controller.jpf.

The AP U.S. History Exam Course home page address is:
http://apcentral.collegeboard.com/apc/public/courses/teachers_corner/3501.html

Finally, **The Princeton Review** offers tutoring and small group instruction for the AP U.S. History Exam. Our expert instructors can help you refine your strategic approach and add to your content knowledge. For more information, call 1-800-2REVIEW.

DESIGNING YOUR STUDY PLAN

In Part I you identified some areas of potential improvement. Let's now delve further into your performance on Practice Test 1, with the goal of developing a study plan appropriate to your needs and time commitment.

Read the answers and explanations associated with the multiple-choice questions (starting at page 313). After you have done so, respond to the following questions:

- Review the content topics on page 11 and, next to each one, indicate your rank of the topic as follows: "1" means "I need a lot of work on this," "2" means "I need to beef up my knowledge," and "3" means "I know this topic well."

- How many days/weeks/months away is your AP U.S. History Exam?

- What time of day is your best, most focused study time?

- How much time per day/week/month will you devote to preparing for your AP U.S. History Exam?

- When will you do this preparation? (Be as specific as possible: Mondays and Wednesdays from 3 to 4 P.M., for example)

- Based on the answers above, will you focus on strategy (Part III) or content (Part IV) or both?

- What are your overall goals in using this book?

Part III
Test-Taking Strategies for the AP U.S. History Exam

PREVIEW

Review your responses to the questions on page 4 of Part I and then respond to the following questions:

- How many multiple-choice questions did you miss even though you knew the answer?

- On how many multiple-choice questions did you guess blindly?

- How many multiple-choice questions did you miss after eliminating some answers and guessing based on the remaining answers?

- How did you use the 15-minute reading and planning period before writing your essay prompts?

- Did you create an outline before you wrote your DBQ essay?

- How did you approach your FRQ essays?

- Did you find any of the essays easier/harder than the others—and, if so, why?

HOW TO USE THE CHAPTERS IN THIS PART

Before you read the following Strategy chapters, think about what you are doing now. As you read and engage in the directed practice, be sure to appreciate the ways you can change your approach. At the end of Part III, you will have the opportunity to reflect on how you will change your approach.

Chapter 1
How to Approach Multiple-Choice Questions

THE BASICS

The directions for the multiple-choice section of the AP U.S. History Exam are pretty simple. They read:

> **Directions**: Each of the questions or incomplete statements below is followed by five suggested answers or completions. Select the one that is best in each case and then blacken the corresponding space on the answer sheet.

In short, you are being asked to do what you have done on lots of other multiple-choice exams. Pick the right answer, then fill in the appropriate bubble on a separate answer sheet. You will *not* be given credit for answers you record in your test booklet (e.g., by circling them) but not on your answer sheet. The section consists of 80 questions. You will be given 55 minutes to work on the section.

TYPES OF QUESTIONS

The majority of questions on the multiple-choice section of the test are pretty straightforward, like this one:

3. Roger Williams was exiled from the Salem Bay settlement because he

   (A) endangered the colony by negotiating with neighboring Native Americans
   (B) championed the abolition of private property
   (C) questioned Parliament's authority to tax the colonists
   (D) disputed the authenticity of the Mayflower Compact
   (E) argued for the separation of church and state

Sometimes, the College Board makes the questions a little trickier. One way it does this is by phrasing a question so that four answers are correct and one is incorrect. We call these questions "NOT/EXCEPT" questions because they usually contain one of those words (in capital letters, so they're harder to miss). A simple way to handle these types of problems is by treating them as true/false questions. Go through your answer choices labeling them as "true" or "false." The answer choice that is false is correct. Here is an example:

6. The New Deal included programs for achieving all of the following goals EXCEPT

   (A) developing an interstate highway system
   (B) stabilizing agricultural prices
   (C) insuring bank deposits
   (D) eliminating industrial overproduction
   (E) providing employment for the unemployed

A few times during the multiple-choice section, you will be asked to interpret an illustration, often a map or a political cartoon. These are usually pretty easy. The key is *not* to try to read too much between the lines. To save time, read the question first, and then go to the illustration, map, or political cartoon. This way you know what you are looking for!

Here is an example:

*Hanna to McKinley: That Man Clay was an Ass.
It's Better to be President than to be Right!*

45. The political cartoon above implies that

(A) McKinley was the first president to favor big
     business interests openly
(B) by the 1890s, Henry Clay's political approach had
     lost favor with the electorate
(C) McKinley's presidential campaign was
     masterminded by Marcus Hanna
(D) Marcus Hanna single-handedly controlled all three
     branches of the
     federal government
(E) McKinley was too young to be an effective
     president

Finally, there will be a few questions on your test asking you to interpret a graph or chart. Again, these are usually very straightforward, unless they are "EXCEPT" or "NOT" questions. Those tend to be time-consuming, and even strong students should probably do those at the end, if time permits. When you answer one of these chart or graph questions, realize that more than one answer might be valid, but only one will be supported by the information in the chart or graph.

Here's an example:

Average, Highest, and Lowest Approval Ratings, by Percentage of All Eligible Voters, for American Presidents, 1953 to 1974			
	Average	High	Low
Eisenhower	65	79	48
Kennedy	70	83	56
Johnson	55	79	35
Nixon	49	67	24

Source: Gallup Polls

13. Which of the following conclusions can be drawn from the information presented in the chart above?

(A) Eisenhower was the most consistently popular president in the nation's history.

(B) Kennedy received greater congressional support for his programs than did any other president during the period in question.

(C) Nixon's lowest approval rating was the result of the Watergate scandal.

(D) The difference between Johnson's highest and lowest approval ratings was the greatest for any president during the period in question.

(E) Eisenhower and Johnson were equally well-liked by all Americans.

Answers to these and other drill questions appear in the Summary at the end of this chapter.

No Military History and No Trivial Pursuit

Here's some good news: The AP U.S. History Exam doesn't ask about the details of military history, i.e., the military strategy or exact death toll of a specific battle. You will never see a question on the AP exam like the one below:

XX. Union general Ulysses S. Grant was intent on capturing Vicksburg, Mississippi, because

   (A) Vicksburg was the munitions capital of the Confederacy

   (B) whoever controlled the city could control transportation along the Mississippi River

   (C) Grant hoped to use the city as a supply depot for Union troops stationed throughout the South

   (D) the city was poorly defended, and the Union desperately needed a victory for morale purposes

   (E) Vicksburg was controlled by Indians hostile to the Union

Although Grant's siege of Vicksburg in 1863 marked an important moment in the Civil War, you won't be asked about it on the test. The AP U.S. History Exam does not ask about important battles, military strategy, or advances in weapons technology. When it asks about war, the questions concern the political, diplomatic, or social implications of a war or battle, rather than the details of warfare. For example, you might have a question about the significance of the battle of Saratoga in the Revolutionary War. (It helped lead to the French providing direct aid to the colonists.) The correct answer, to the question above, by the way, is (B).

Also, AP U.S. History questions never test rote memorization *only*. While you have to know your facts to do well on this test, the questions always ask for information in the context of larger historical trends. Therefore, you will never see a question like this one:

YY. The treaty that ended the War of 1812 was called the

   (A) Anglo-American Treaty

   (B) Treaty of Versailles

   (C) War of 1812 Treaty

   (D) Jay Treaty

   (E) Treaty of Ghent

The Big Picture

One of the most important characteristics of the AP U.S. History multiple-choice section is that the questions and answers are designed to illustrate **basic principles** of American history. Multiple-choice questions will NOT ask about exceptions to historical trends; the test ignores these, because the test writers are trying to find out whether you have mastered the important generalizations that can be drawn from history. They do not want to know whether you have memorized your textbook (they already know that you haven't). Talk of historical exceptions is welcome in the essay section, though. Students who discuss exceptions in their essays often impress the readers. More on that later.

Overall, you should always keep the **big picture** in mind as you take this exam. Even if you cannot remember the specific event or concept being tested, you should be able to answer the question by remembering the general social and political trends of the era.

Let's look at a couple of illustrative examples:

53. During the Harding and Coolidge administrations, the Federal Trade Commission

    (A) greatly increased the number of court cases it brought against unethical businesses
    (B) controlled the rationing of food, rubber, and gasoline
    (C) generally worked to assist businesses, rather than to regulate them
    (D) was permanently eliminated
    (E) saw its regulatory powers expanded

Here's How to Crack It!

At first glance, this question appears to require you to remember the history of the Federal Trade Commission. It's not that tricky, though. To answer this question correctly, you really only need to remember the big picture. What was the attitude of the Harding and Coolidge administrations toward business? Harding and Coolidge were presidents after the Progressive Era and World War I both ended; the country grew more conservative during their administrations, and both pursued policies favorable to business. Because pro-business governments weaken regulations, you should have been able to eliminate answer choices (A) and (E). Now let's look at the remaining answer choices. Was there rationing during the 1920s? No, rationing occurred during World War II, in the early 1940s. Eliminate answer choice (B). How about answer choice (D)? Is there still a Federal Trade Commission today? Yes; therefore, the FTC wasn't "permanently eliminated." Eliminate answer choice (D). The correct answer is (C), which illustrates a "big picture" principle; the 1920s were a pro-business era.

Let's try one more question:

---

68. "[This legislative body declares] that it views the power
    of the Federal Government as resulting from the com-
    pact to which the states are parties, as limited by plain
    sense and intention of the instrument constituting that
    compact…and that, in case of a deliberate, palpable,
    and dangerous exercise of other powers, not granted
    by the said compact, the states…have the right, and are
    duty bound, to interpose, for arresting the progress of
    the evil, and for maintaining…the authorities, rights,
    and liberties, pertaining to them."

    The quotation above appears in

    (A) The Halfway Covenant
    (B) The Wealth of Nations
    (C) Common Sense
    (D) Virginia Resolutions of 1798
    (E) The Liberator

Here's How to Crack It!

The first thing you may notice is that this question is pretty difficult; the quotation
is one long sentence filled with archaic language and syntax. However, if you key
in on the big picture, this question isn't all that hard, provided you've prepared for
the exam. The central concept of the quotation is that the states have the right to
try to stop the federal government when it tries to exercise too much power (particularly when it exceeds the constitutional limitations on it). Sounds familiar? It's
the doctrine of *nullification*. If you remembered that the source of the doctrine of
nullification was the Virginia and Kentucky Resolutions, you would already be on
your way to the next question. If not, look at the other answer choices. The Halfway Covenant concerns the baptism of Puritans; *The Wealth of Nations* is a treatise
on capitalism; *Common Sense* was written before there even *were* states, let alone
state assemblies; and *The Liberator* was an abolitionist newspaper. Looking at the
big picture, you should realize that only the Virginia Resolutions and *The Liberator* could conceivably be right. If you don't know, guess. A 50-50 shot is pretty
good on question 68. (Only about 30 percent of students taking the test will get
this question right.)

Process of Elimination (POE)

If it seems that we are focusing more on eliminating incorrect answers than on
finding the correct answers, it is because that is the most efficient way to take
a multiple-choice exam. Use **process of elimination** (POE) to whittle down the

answer choices to one on all but the easiest questions (on easy questions, the correct answer will be obvious), because incorrect answers are much easier to identify than correct ones. When you look for the correct answer among the answer choices, you have a tendency to try to justify how each answer *might* be correct. You'll adopt a forgiving attitude in a situation in which tough assertiveness is rewarded. Eliminate incorrect answers. Terminate them with extreme prejudice. Remember that half wrong is all wrong and mark up the test as you do this. You are probably used to teachers telling you not to write on the test. This test, however, is yours to mark up, and that will make it easier for you to decide what to guess. If you have done your job well, only the correct answer will be left standing at the end.

Common Sense Can Help

Sometimes an answer on the multiple-choice section contradicts common sense. Eliminate those answers. Common sense works on the AP U.S. History Exam. Which of the answer choices to the question below don't make common sense?

---

26. Which of the following best explains the most important effect tobacco cultivation had on the development of the Chesapeake Bay settlements during the seventeenth century?

    (A) Because tobacco cultivation requires large tracts of fertile land, it led to the rapid expansion of settled areas in the region.
    (B) The immediate commercial success of tobacco forced the settlers to defend against attacks by Spanish and French settlers, who wanted to take control of the tobacco trade.
    (C) Tobacco provided the settlers a lucrative crop to trade with nearby Native American tribes.
    (D) Dependence on tobacco as their only cash crop brought the settlements to financial ruin in the early 1600s.
    (E) British customs houses established in the region to regulate tobacco trade led to widespread resentment of the British by the colonists.

Here's How to Crack It!

Common sense should allow you to eliminate answer choice (C) immediately. Nearby Native American tribes lived on farmland similar to that held by the Chesapeake Bay settlers; why would they trade for something they could have easily grown themselves? Now let's consider the other answer choices. Did the Spanish or the French attack the Maryland/Virginia region during the seventeenth century? It would have been a pretty big deal if they had, right? You would remember if there had been a war for the control of Virginia in the 1600s, wouldn't you?

You don't remember it because it didn't happen; eliminate answer choice (B). Answer choice (D) gets it all wrong; in the early 1600s, tobacco cultivation *saved* the Chesapeake Bay settlements from financial ruin, as tobacco proved an immediately popular product in England. Answer choice (E) is anachronistic. The period of colonial resentment toward England was still one hundred years away during the seventeenth century. The correct answer is (A).

Context Clues

Some questions contain context clues or vocabulary words that will either lead you to the correct answer or at least help you eliminate an incorrect answer. Look at the question below:

---

60. The Confiscation Act of 1861 authorized the Union to

   (A) divert commercial production in the North toward the war effort

   (B) negotiate a settlement to the Civil War with ambassadors from the Confederacy

   (C) liberate those slaves used by the Confederacy "for insurrectionary purposes"

   (D) stop merchant ships headed for Europe and seize their cargo

   (E) arrest those advocating secession and hold them without a writ of habeas corpus

Here's How to Crack It!

If you don't remember the exact purpose of the Confiscation Act of 1861, the word *"confiscation"* might give you enough of a context clue to answer this question correctly anyway. Which answer choices have nothing to do with confiscation? Clearly, (B). How about (E)? You might think that arresting someone is the same as confiscating the person, but it's not. The dictionary definition of *"confiscation"* is "the seizure of private property." Answer choice (A) seems pretty unlikely, too. It indicates that the government used industry for the war effort, not that it confiscated the factories. Answer choice (D) looks good, except when you ask yourself: For what purpose would the Union be stopping ships headed *away* from the Confederacy? This answer would much more likely be correct if it discussed the confiscation of property headed *for* the Confederacy. The correct answer, choice (C), is a little tricky, because we don't normally think of human beings as private property. Slaves, however, were exactly that: the private property of slave holders. In order to liberate them, the Union had to "confiscate" them.

Summary

o   Don't overextend yourself. If all you want is a final score of 3, don't even try to work through every question on the multiple-choice section. Take your time and work on the first 60 questions only. If you are shooting for a 4, take your time and work on the first 70 questions only. Remember that even if you do not attempt every problem, you need to fill in all the bubbles in the answer sheet before time is up. Doing so can only help you, since there is no penalty for guessing.

o   Familiarize yourself with the different types of questions that will appear on the multiple-choice section. Be aware that you will see many questions about political and social history, some questions about international relations, and relatively few about economic and cultural trends. Tailor your studies accordingly.

o   Look for "big picture" answers. Correct answers on the multiple-choice section confirm important trends in American history. This section will not ask you about weird exceptions that contradict those trends. It also will not ask you about military history featured on the History Channel. You will not be required to perform miraculous feats of memorization; however, you must be thoroughly familiar with all the basics of American history. (And there are a lot of them! See our history review later in the book.)

o   Use process of elimination (POE) on all but the easiest questions. Once you have worked on a question, eliminated some answers (by scratching them out in your packet of questions), and convinced yourself that you cannot eliminate any other incorrect answers, you should guess and move on to the next question.

o   Use common sense. Look for context clues.

o   Finally, here are the answers to the questions that appear in this chapter. 3: (E); 6: (A); 45: (C); 13: (D); XX: (B); YY: (E); 53: (C); 68: (D); 26: (A); 60: (C).

Chapter 2
How to Approach the Document-Based and Free-Response Questions

OVERVIEW

There are two types of essay questions on the AP U.S. History Exam. The first is the document-based question (DBQ), which requires you to answer a question based on eight to 12 primary source documents and your knowledge of the subject and time period. The second are the free-response questions (FRQ), which are more like typical essay questions on any other history exam. The eras addressed in the FRQs shift depending on what era the DBQ covers. Hence, if the DBQ concerns progressivism, then the second pair of essays might concern the road to the Civil War and elections in the late twentieth century. Collectively, the five essay prompts will address five eras throughout United States history. We will discuss each of these question types in greater detail in the next two chapters. First, let's talk about the basics of writing a successful AP essay.

What Are the AP Essay Graders Looking For?

Here is what one AP grader said:

> "My most basic advice to students taking the AP U.S. History Exam would be the same advice I give to college students facing an essay exam: ANSWER THE QUESTION, begin with a thesis, and follow a reasonable outline. Questions usually suggest a basic thesis statement, and a logical outline, so look for them and follow them. The less a writer confuses his or her reader, the better."
> —Pamela Riney-Kehrberg, Illinois State University

In other words, be straightforward. Do not try to fudge your way through the essay; the graders are all experts in history, and you will not be able to fool them into thinking you know more than you actually do.

It is also very important to focus on the phrasing of the question. Some students are so anxious to get going that they start writing as soon as they know the general subject of the question, and many of these students lose points because their essays do not answer the question being asked. Take, for example, an essay question that asks you to discuss the effects of the Great Depression on working-class citizens. The overanxious test taker might start rattling off everything he or she knows about the Depression: its causes, its effect on the presidential election of 1932, the New Deal programs that helped alleviate its effects, etc. No matter how well this essay is written, points are going to be lost for one simple reason—the writer did not answer the question!

Second, a good essay does more than rattle off facts. It reveals an understanding of the general principles or the "big picture" of American history. Professor Keith Edgerton at Montana State University in Billings grades AP essays, and he says:

> "The best essays that I encountered were the ones that wove an understanding of content with some critical analysis. I am impressed with some originality of thought too; so few students possess it these days. Students should be willing to take something of a chance with the essays and not simply provide recitation of the few 'facts' that they have memorized. Longer essays, though not necessarily better, are usually more thorough in their coverage rather than the quick, I-need-to-get-this-done-because-I'm-tired-and-sick-of-this-test essays. It is a cliché, to be sure, but there still is no substitute for hard work. It can be painful and awfully grinding sometimes to learn history well, and it seems that there are not many students who want to devote much time to it. It does not provide instant gratification and cannot be mastered quickly, and it certainly does not happen in 23 minutes with appropriate commercial interruption. Students should read everything they can get their hands on and turn off the television. That is the best advice I can give."

If all this sounds intimidating, read on! There are a few simple things you can do to improve your grade on your AP essays.

Reasons to Be Cheerful

AP graders know that you are given only 130 minutes to plan and write three separate essays. They also know that is not enough time to cover the subject matter tested by the question. The fact is, many very long books have been written about any subject that you might be asked about on the DBQ and the free-response questions. That is why the College Board states:

> "Answers to standard essay questions will be judged on the strength of the thesis developed, the quality of the historical argument, and the evidence offered in support of the thesis."

In other words, expressing good ideas and presenting valid evidence in support of those ideas are important. Making sure you mention every single relevant piece of historical information is not so important, or even possible.

Remember that the graders are not given a lot of time to read your essays. One of them explains the grading experience this way:

> "There were about 545 graders drawn from colleges, universities, high schools, and prep schools. We had about 70 tables of readers. A table leader presides over each group. A typical schedule looks like this: 8:30 a.m. to 10:00 reading; 10:00 to 10:20 break; 10:20 to 12:00 reading; 12:00 to 1:00 lunch; 1:00 to 3:00 reading; 3:00 to 3:20 break; 3:20 to 5:00 reading. We read for six and a half days. Before grading the essays, we read sample packets selected by the table leaders, who arrive a few days before the rest of us. With the sample packets we try to establish standards using a 0 to 9 scale. When the table leader believes we all have 'locked into' the standards, we commence reading. The table leader occasionally samples our finished product in order to ensure accuracy. Also, a computer correlates the essay scores with the grade received on the multiple-choice section. The AP authorities emphasize accuracy rather than speed. In the six and a half days I read 995 essays. I do not know how this rate relates to other readers.... We look for responsiveness to the question. For the DBQ, we seek a clear thesis statement and supporting evidence."
>
> —Charles Quirk, University of Northern Iowa

Think about it. Professor Quirk averaged almost 150 essays a day—a little more than two minutes per essay. True, they are not writing comments, but at any rate, readers cannot look for anything profound or subtle. What they can do is look for evidence that you have something reasonably intelligent to say and that you know how to say it. Furthermore, the graders read many awful essays. (Not everyone, remember, is preparing for this test as well as you are.)

It is true that you can only get the best possible score if you have mastered the material. However, regardless of how well-prepared you are, you can improve your score if you follow the guidelines below. They will tell you how to avoid the mistakes all graders hate and how to use writing and organizational techniques they love.

Before we get to those guidelines, a final word from Darril Wilburn, a high school history teacher in Bardstown, New York. We think it is inspirational:

> "On essay questions I stress two things: using detail and staying positive. You must be able to substantiate your ideas and thoughts with detail (factual, of course). This will go very far in impressing the reader that you do indeed know what you are talking about…. On staying positive, I ask the students not to think of the essay questions (or any part of the exam for that matter) as something you lose points on. Think of each question and each bit of detail and each morsel of fact as an addition to your score; do not think of everything you leave out as being a subtraction from your score. This helps you stay focused and keeps stress levels lower (unless, of course, you do not know anything; then you deserve to be nervous). You can also play a mind game with yourself: 'How many points can I gather on this question?' This also keeps stress low."

Focus on what you know, rather than on what you do not know. Turn the test into a game.

Things That Make Any Essay Better

There are two essential components to writing a successful timed essay. First, plan what you are going to write before you start writing! Second, use a number of tried-and-true writing techniques that will make your essay appear better organized, better thought-out, and better written. This section is about those techniques. Remember: An essay that is better written and better organized usually earns a higher score than an essay that rambles but is packed with facts.

Before You Start Writing

Read the question carefully. Then, brainstorm for one or two minutes. In your test booklet, write down everything that comes to mind about the subject. (There is room in the margins and at the top and bottom of the pages.) Look at your notes and consider the results of your brainstorming session as you decide what point you will argue in your essay; that argument is going to be your thesis. Remember: Your thesis *must* respond to the question. Utilize your notes to prove your thesis, but do not choose an argument that you know is wrong or with which you disagree.

You will be required to write one DBQ and two free-response essays. While there is no choice regarding the DBQ, you will be asked to select one question from each group of free-response questions. Typically, the free-response questions span the curriculum and require that you answer one question from the seventeenth or eighteenth century and another from the late nineteenth or twentieth century. The DBQ requires you to interpret a variety of documents and integrate your interpretation of these documents with your knowledge of the topic or time period. Being familiar with these instructions is useful in preparing you for the exam, but you should re-read all of the instructions very carefully on the actual day you take the exam to ensure that you are doing what is required of you.

Finally, sort the results of your brainstorm. Some of what you wrote down will be "big picture" conclusions, some will be historical facts that can be used as evidence to support your conclusions, and some will be garbage.

Next, make an outline. You should plan to write a body paragraph for each topic in the prompt. If you are not given specific topics in the prompt and must create the categories for the essay, then try to have at least three body paragraphs. You'll want to go into special detail in each of the paragraphs on the DBQ. (Remember, you will have the documents and your outside knowledge to discuss on the DBQ. Plus, you will have more time.) Your first paragraph should contain your thesis statement as the last sentence. Your second, third, and fourth paragraphs (if there are three topics in the prompt) should contain three arguments that support that statement, along with historical evidence to back those arguments. The fifth paragraph should contain your conclusion, and you must specifically answer the question here if you have not already done so.

Before you start to write your outline, you will have to decide what type of argument you are going to make. The following is a list of some classic arguments:

- **Three Good Points**
  This is the simplest strategy. Look at the results of your brainstorming session and pick the three best points supporting your position. Make each of these points the subject of one paragraph, respectively. Make the weakest of the three points the subject of the second paragraph, and save the strongest point for the fourth paragraph. If your three points are interrelated and there is a natural sequence to arguing them, then by all means use that sequence, but otherwise, try to save your strongest point for last. Begin each paragraph with a topic sentence that tells the reader which topic you are going to address in that paragraph. Then spend the rest of the paragraph supporting it. Use specific historical examples whenever possible. Your first paragraph should state what you intend to argue; your final paragraph should explain why you have proven what you set out to prove. Don't forget to use transitions to make your examples and argument more cohesive and stronger.

- **The Chronological Argument**
  Many questions lend themselves to a chronological treatment. Questions about the development of a political, social, or economic trend can hardly be answered any other way. When you make a chronological argument, look for important transitions and use them to start new paragraphs. A five-paragraph essay about the events leading up to the Civil War, for example, might start with an introductory discussion of slavery and regional differences in the early nineteenth century. This is also where you should state your thesis. The second paragraph might then discuss the Missouri Compromise and other efforts to avoid the war. The third paragraph might mention the

expansionism of the Polk era and how it forced the slavery issue, and the fourth paragraph might cover the collapse of the Missouri Compromise and how the events that followed—the Compromise of 1850, the Kansas-Nebraska Act, and the Dred Scott case—led the country into war. Your conclusion in this type of essay should restate the essay question and answer it. For example, if the question asks whether the war was inevitable, you should answer "yes" or "no" in this paragraph. However, remember that simply writing "The Civil War was inevitable" is a thesis.

- **Comparison**
  Some questions, particularly on the free-response section, ask you to compare events, issues, and/or policies. Very often, the way the question is phrased will suggest the best organization for your essay. Take, for example, a question asking you to compare the impact of three events and issues on the United States' decision to enter World War II. This question pretty much requires you to start by setting the historical scene prior to the three events/issues you are about to discuss. Continue by devoting one paragraph to each of the three, and conclude by comparing and contrasting the relative importance of each.

  Other questions will provide options. If you are asked to compare the political philosophies of two presidents, you might use each paragraph to compare and contrast both presidents' views on a single subject. For example, you might compare the two presidents' philosophies regarding the interpretation of the constitution (loose or strict) in one paragraph, their differing approaches to foreign policy in one paragraph, and their ideas about the American economy in another paragraph. In the final paragraph, you can draw your conclusion (e.g., "their similarities were more significant than their differences," or vice versa), but be certain you state your argument in your thesis at the beginning of the essay.

- **The "Straw Dog" Argument**
  In this essay-writing technique, choose a couple of arguments that someone taking the position opposite yours would take. State their arguments, and then tear them down. Remember that proving that your opposition is wrong does not mean that you have proved you are correct; that is why you should choose only a few opposing arguments to refute. Summarize your opponent's arguments in paragraph two, dismiss them in paragraph three, and use paragraph four to make the argument for your side. Or, use one paragraph to summarize and dismiss each of your opponent's arguments, and then make the case for your side in your concluding paragraph. Acknowledging both sides of an argument, even when you choose one over the other, is a good indicator that you understand that historical issues are complex and can be interpreted in more than one way—which teachers and readers like to see.

No matter which format you choose, remember to organize your essay so that the first paragraph addresses the question and states how you are going to answer it. (That is your thesis.) The second, third, and fourth paragraphs should each be organized around a single argument that supports your thesis, and each of these arguments must be supported by historical evidence. Your final paragraph then ties the essay up into a nice, neat package. Your concluding paragraph should also answer the question.

As You Are Writing, Observe the Following Guidelines

- **Keep sentences as simple as possible.** Long sentences get convoluted very quickly and will give your graders a headache, putting them in a bad mood. Do not antagonize your reader! Remember that good writing does not have to be complicated; some great ideas can be stated simply. NEVER use a word if you are unsure of its definition or proper usage. A malapropism might give your graders a good laugh, but it will not earn you any points, and it will probably cost you.

- **Write clearly and neatly.** As long as we are discussing your graders' moods, here is an easy way to put them in good ones. Graders look at a lot of chicken scratch; it strains their eyes and makes them grumpy. Neatly written essays make them happy. When you cross out, do it neatly. If you are making any major edits—if you want to insert a paragraph in the middle of your essay, for example—make sure you indicate these changes clearly.

- **Define your terms.** Most questions require you to use terms that mean different things to different people. One person's "conservative" is another person's "liberal" and yet another person's "radical." What one person considers "expansionism," another might call "colonialism" or "imperialism." The folks who grade the test want to know what you think these terms mean. When you use them, define them. Take particular care to define any such terms that appear in the question. The introductory paragraph is a good place to include any definitions. Almost all official College Board materials stress this point, so do not forget it. Be sure to define any term that you suspect can be interpreted in more than one way.

- **Use transition words between paragraphs and within paragraphs to show where you are going.** When continuing an idea, use words such as furthermore, also, and in addition. When changing the flow of thought, use words such as however and yet. Transition words make your essay easier to understand by clarifying your intentions. Better yet, they indicate to the graders that you know how to make a coherent, persuasive argument.

- **Use structural indicators to organize your paragraphs.** Another way to clarify your intentions is to organize your essay around structural indicators. For example, if you are making a number of related points, number them ("First… Second… And last…"). If you are writing a compare/contrast essay, use the indicators "on the one hand" and "on the other hand."

- **Stick to your outline.** Unless you get an absolutely brilliant idea while you are writing, do not deviate from your outline. If you do, you will risk winding up with an incoherent essay.

- **Try to prove one "big picture" idea per paragraph.** Keep it simple. Each paragraph should make one point and then substantiate that point with historical evidence.

- **Back up your ideas with examples.** Yes, we have said this already, but it bears repeating: Do not just throw ideas out there and hope that you are right (unless you are absolutely desperate). You will score big points if you substantiate your claims with specific, historical examples.

- **Try to fill the essay form.** An overly short essay will hurt you more than one that is overly long. Try to write five solid paragraphs.

- **Make sure your first and last paragraphs directly address the question.** Nothing will cost you points faster than if the graders decide you did not answer the question. It is always a safe move to start your final paragraph by answering the question. If you have written a good essay, that answer will serve as a legitimate conclusion.

CRACKING THE DOCUMENT-BASED QUESTION

The DBQ is an essay question that requires you to interpret a mix of textual and visual *primary source* documents. (There are typically nine documents in a DBQ.) These documents will include many, if not all, of the following: newspaper articles and editorials, letters, diaries, speeches, excerpts from legislation, political cartoons, charts, and graphs. The documents will *not* include excerpts from current textbooks. Occasionally, one or two of the documents will be taken from something "classic" that you may have previously seen, but generally the documents will be new to you. However, they will discuss events and ideas with which you should be familiar. All the documents will pertain to a single subject. The documents are usually between a quarter and a half page long, although occasionally you will see something longer.

The hour-long DBQ is the second part of the AP U.S. History Exam; it is administered immediately after the five to 10 minute break that follows the multiple-choice section. At the beginning of the DBQ, you will be handed a green booklet, in which the essay question and documents are printed, as well as a separate form on which to write your essay. The DBQ session begins with a 15-minute mandatory reading period, during which you are allowed to read the documents and take notes in the DBQ booklet. You may not start recording your essay on the essay form until the 45-minute writing period begins. However, if you finish taking notes and outlining your essay before the reading period is over, you should write a first draft of your opening paragraph in your DBQ booklet; then, when the writing period begins, you can transcribe it into your essay form and continue.

To give you an idea of what you can expect on your DBQ, let's look at what appeared on a recent test. The question asked students to decide whether liberal opponents, conservative opponents, or President Woodrow Wilson bore the responsibility for the Senate's defeat of the Treaty of Versailles. The nine documents included excerpts from the following:

- A speech by a conservative senator, denouncing the League of Nations

- An editorial from the then-liberal magazine The New Republic, criticizing the Treaty of Versailles

- A speech by President Wilson, defending the League of Nations

- A letter from Herbert Hoover to Wilson, urging him to compromise with the Senate

- An editorial cartoon from a newspaper, opposing the League of Nations

- An article by economist John Maynard Keynes, discussing the European victors' opposition to Wilson's Fourteen Points

- A 1920 speech by Wilson, asking voters to support the League of Nations

- A 1921 article by W. E. B. Du Bois, criticizing Wilson for his handling of the treaty negotiations with the Senate

- A 1922 article by Jane Addams, discussing the necessity of the League of Nations

As you can see, a typical DBQ may contain documents you might have seen prior to the exam. (The first Wilson speech, for example, is famous.) However, the DBQ also includes documents you certainly have not seen before. Each of the documents, though, represents a political position you have studied. Many are written by famous people about whom you should know quite a bit (Keynes, Addams, Du Bois, Hoover), even if you do not know precisely how they felt about the Treaty of Versailles before reading the documents. In other words, you will not be starting from square one, even when the documents are new to you. Each document should trigger a memory of some historical figure, event, or trend in U.S. history.

Is There a "Right" Answer to Each DBQ?

No. DBQs are worded in such a way that you can argue any number of positions, and often the question is a historiographical one that historians have been debating for years. In the example above, the documents provide evidence for those who would blame the failure of the Treaty of Versailles on Wilson, liberals, conservatives, or some combination of the three. So long as you support your argument with evidence, you can argue whatever thesis you want. Often, however, the documents will "drive" a particular thesis and it becomes more difficult to try to argue the other side.

Similarly, the College Board claims that there is no "checklist" of facts and ideas against which DBQs are graded. According to their official material:

> Answers to standard essay questions will be judged on the strength of the thesis developed, the quality of the historical argument, and the evidence offered in support of the thesis, rather than on the factual information per se. Unless a question asks otherwise, students will not be penalized for omitting one or another specific illustration.

Readers are supposed to take into account the strength of your argument and the evidence you offer in support of it. In other words, if you forget to mention a good, illustrative historical event but manage to back up your point in some other way, you will not be penalized.

However, in order to earn the most credit for your essay, you must include *outside information*. You will notice that your DBQ contains a phrase that looks something like this:

Use the Documents AND Your Knowledge of the Subject...

"Your knowledge of the subject" is the outside information. It includes historical facts and ideas that are relevant to the question but not mentioned in the DBQ documents. For example, in the Treaty of Versailles DBQ described above, any information offered about the writers' backgrounds would count as outside information, as would information about the war itself. Of course, to receive credit, that information would have to help explain who was responsible for the failure of the Treaty of Versailles in the United States. Some students make the mistake of throwing everything they know about a subject into their essays, whether or not it pertains to the question. That type of information receives partial credit, at best.

GETTING STARTED ON THE DBQ: THE QUESTION

Start by reading the question. This direction may seem obvious, but it obviously is not, given how many students write essays on subjects that are only marginally related to the question being asked. Students miss the question because they get anxious during the exam. They panic. They think they are going too slowly. In an effort to speed up, they read half the question, say to themselves, "A-ha! I know what they're going to ask!" and stop reading. Do NOT make this mistake! The question is probably the shortest thing you have to read on the DBQ. Take your time; savor it. Explore its nuances. Essays that address the question fully earn huge bonuses; essays that ignore parts of the question are doomed to a grade of 5 or lower.

Here's a sample question:

1. "Both the constituencies and the agenda of the Progressive movement of the early 1900s were more similar to those of the reform movements of the 1830s and 1840s than to those of the Populist movement of the 1890s." Using the documents and your knowledge of the periods in question, assess the validity of the statement.

The first question you should ask yourself is: Do I have an opinion about this subject? The second question is: What must I discuss in order to write a successful essay?

Of the two questions, the second is much more important. You can construct a position later, after you have gathered the information you want to include in your essay. First, you need to figure out what issues you must address and what data you will use in your discussion.

To begin with, you should notice that the question asks you to compare three movements—the Progressives, the Populists, and the reformers of the 1830s and 1840s. Your essay will obviously have to mention all three groups. Equally important, the question asks you to consider the constituencies and the agendas of these three groups in drawing your comparisons. Also, you must decide whether the Progressives were more similar to the Populists or to the reformers. Finally, you must include a discussion of the given documents and your outside knowledge in your essay.

Some people find it helpful to circle and underline key elements of an essay question. If you did that, your question probably looked something like this:

1. "Both the constituencies and the agenda of the Progressive movement of the early 1900s were more similar to those of the reform movements of the 1830s and 1840s than to those of the Populist movement of the 1890s." Using the documents and your knowledge of the periods in question, assess the validity of the statement.

However you decide to approach the question, it is essential that you do not rush. Read carefully to make sure that you understand what issues must be addressed in your essay. Then, determine how to organize the information you are going to collect from the documents and from memory for inclusion in the essay.

Organizing Your Essay: Grids and Columns

Many DBQs ask you to draw comparisons. For those questions you can always organize your thoughts in a grid. Drawing a grid helps in seeing all sides of an argument, which is important because DBQ graders will reward you for acknowledging arguments other than your own. Consider the question from earlier; here is how you could grid this question:

	Constituency	Agenda
Antebellum Reformers		
Populists		
Progressives		

As you remember appropriate outside information and as you read the documents, take notes in the appropriate boxes. When it comes time to write your essay, you will find it easier to compare and contrast the three movements because your information will already be organized in a way that makes similarities and differences more obvious.

If you cannot draw a grid for a question, you can instead set up column headings. Because every DBQ can be argued from at least two different positions, you can always set up two (or more) columns, designating one for each position. Consider the DBQ about the Treaty of Versailles, which we discussed at the beginning of the chapter. You could create one column entitled "It was Wilson's fault," one entitled "It was liberals' fault," a third entitled "It was conservatives' fault," and even a fourth for information that you know belongs in your essay but that you cannot yet classify (give that the title "To be classified").

Good essays do not just flow out of your pen by accident. They happen when you know what you are going to say *before you start writing*. Although, given the time constraints, it is difficult (if not impossible) to prepare your entire DBQ essay before you begin writing, pre-organization and a good outline will get you much closer to that goal.

A Sample Question

Let's take a look at another question. Circle and/or underline the key elements of the question, then create a grid (or columns) in which to organize your information.

1.   From the end of World War II through the Eisenhower administration, many Americans feared that communism threatened the existence of the United States. Using BOTH the documents AND your knowledge of the 1940s and 1950s, assess the reasons for and the validity of those fears.

Your question should look something like this:

1.   From the end of World War II through the Eisenhower administration, many Americans feared that communism threatened the existence of the United States. Using BOTH the documents AND your knowledge of the 1940s and 1950s, assess the reasons for and the validity of those fears.

Your thesis must address the reasons for and validity of the Cold War fears, and your essay will have to address the Red Scare, the widespread fear of a communist takeover that Americans experienced during the early Cold War. (Remember that the second Red Scare in the age of McCarthyism during the 1950s followed the first Red Scare in the 1920s.) You will, of course, have to include analysis of both the documents and outside information, and your essay should cover the years between the end of the war and the end of the Eisenhower administration. Last (and what most students miss), you must answer two questions: Why did Americans fear a communist takeover? And, how valid were their fears?

Because the question does not ask you to draw any comparisons, you might want to organize your information in columns titled "Valid reason," "Not a valid reason," and "Maybe valid/maybe not." However, the question naturally lends itself to comparisons among the various perceived and real threats to the United States, which means that you could use a grid instead. Americans feared communist attacks both from communist nations and from subversives in the government. You could, therefore, draw a grid, giving your rows the headings "Threats from other countries" (e.g., the USSR and China), and "Threats from within the United States" (e.g., the Communist Party of the United States of America). This analysis would leave you with a grid that looks like the following:

	Valid	Not valid	Maybe/maybe not
Threats from other countries			
Threats from within the United States			

Once you have created your grid, begin collecting information for your essay. At this point, you are probably anxious to start reading the documents. Resist the temptation. You have one more important job to do before you start reading.

Gather Outside Information

Most students read the DBQ documents first and then try to think of outside information to supplement their essays. This is a mistake. The reason? *The power of suggestion.* Once you have read the documents—a chore that can take six to eight minutes—those documents will be on your mind. If you wait until after you have read them to think of outside information, you will not be able to get the documents out of your head. Invariably, you will think of things you have already read about, rather than things you *have not* read about, which is precisely what outside information means.

Plus, reading and processing the documents is a big task. Once you have accomplished that, you will want to get started right away on organizing and writing your essay while the documents are fresh in your mind. You *do not* want to stop to think of outside information to include in your essay. And you certainly do not want to be trying to come up with outside information *while* you are writing your essay. So, do it *before* you read the documents. The only exception to this strategy is the unlikely event that you are totally unfamiliar with a topic. In that case, the documents might jog your memory.

Look at your grid or columns and brainstorm. In a separate blank space in your green booklet (*not* in your grid/columns), write down everything you can think of that relates to the question. Spend two or three minutes on this task, then look at what you have written, cross out what you know you cannot use, and enter the rest into your grid/columns in the appropriate spaces.

Chances are that some of the outside information you think of will be mentioned in the documents, which means that it will not be outside information anymore. That is no big deal. In fact, you should think of it as something good. If some of what you remembered shows up in the documents, that means you are on the right track toward answering the question!

This is what a brainstorming grid for the communism question might look like:

	Valid	Not valid	Maybe/maybe not
Threats from other countries	–Soviets develop H-bomb –U.S.–Soviet confrontations: containment, Greece, Marshall Plan, Truman Doctrine –Korean War heightens tensions –fall of Cuba		–Chinese revolution –fall of Hungary: Soviet aggression, or Soviets protecting border? –U.S. involvement in Vietnam –Guatemala's ties to USSR
Threats from within the United States	–there was an American Communist party –though small, party was influential in powerful labor unions –some evidence of espionage: the Rosenbergs	–Rosenbergs' punishment too great for crime, shows U.S. paranoia –Loyalty Review Board; McCarthy's list of State Dept. subversives; blacklisting; bomb shelters –postwar affluence made Americans more conservative	–Alger Hiss case

Read the Documents

After you have gathered outside information to include in your essay, you are ready to read the documents. As you read, keep the following things in mind:

- **The order in which documents appear is almost always helpful.** Very often, the documents in the DBQ appear in chronological order. When they do, it often indicates that the College Board wants you to trace the historical development of the DBQ subject. On such questions, you do not have to write an essay that adheres strictly to chronological order, but chronology should play an important part in the development of your thesis. When the documents appear in an order other than chronological, they are usually organized so that you can easily compare and contrast different viewpoints on a particular event or issue. On these questions, one of your main goals should be to draw those comparisons.

- **Watch for inconsistencies within and among the documents.** The documents will not necessarily agree with one another. In fact, they are almost certain to present different viewpoints on issues, and almost as certain to present conflicting accounts of a historical event. Some documents might even contradict themselves! This is intentional. The AP is testing your ability to recognize these contradictions. You are expected to resolve these conflicts in your essay. To do so, you will have to identify the sources of the documents. (See below.)

- **Identify the sources of the documents.** Why do two accounts of the same event contradict each other? Why do two economists, looking at the same data, come up with dissimilar interpretations? It is because the people giving these accounts—the sources of the documents—have different perspectives. Identify the sources and explain why their opinions differ. As you explain these differences, look for the following differences between sources:

    —political ideology
    —class
    —race
    —religion
    —gender

    Consider the question of whether communism posed a serious threat to the United States in the 1940s and 1950s. An urban Northeastern intellectual, a wealthy Midwestern industrialist, and a Chinese immigrant on the West Coast would offer very different answers to that question. The graders will be looking specifically to see if you have tried to explain those differences.

- **Look for evidence that could refute your argument.** Once you have decided what your thesis will be, you will be looking through the documents for evidence to support your argument. Not all the documents will necessarily back you up. Some may appear to contradict your argument. Do not simply ignore those documents! As you read them, try to figure out how you might incorporate them into your argument. Again, let's consider the communism DBQ. Suppose you argue that Americans overreacted to the communist threat. Now suppose that one of the documents presents evidence of subversive communist activity in the United States. You might be tempted to pretend that the document does not exist. However, you will be better off if you incorporate the document into your essay: Acknowledge that America was not immune to communist subversion but that the threat was nowhere near as great as most anti-communists claimed. By doing this, you will be acknowledging that this historical issue, like all historical issues, is complex and multifaceted. This acknowledgment is good. AP readers are instructed to look for evidence that you understand that history has no simple answers, and to reward you for it.

As you read the documents, be aware that each one holds a few morsels of information for your essay. Do not fixate on any one document, as you can't afford to waste the time. Try to use as many documents as possible. Don't panic if you are initially confused by a document. Remember, the AP puts each document in the DBQ to serve one or two purposes, rather than five. Think about it and try to figure out why they've included this document, and you'll have a pretty good idea of why it's in the DBQ and how to fit it into your essay. Unless you are clueless (which is unlikely), you will be able to find a way to include each document in your essay: That's better than leaving it out entirely. However, it is better to leave a document out than to misinterpret it. And be confident: If you're in an AP History course, you're smart enough to figure out why the document has been included in the DBQ. Often, the documents "speak" to one another. You, the historian, should enter that dialogue.

Also, as you read the documents, take note of any outside information that the document reminds you of, scribble it into the margins around the document, and enter it into your grid/columns. Again, don't panic if, after you read the question, you can't think of any outside information. Stay calm; you will remember more after looking at the documents. Even though brainstorming first is best, if you freeze, then you should go to the documents and let the documents get you going on the outside info.

Developing a Thesis

As you finish reading the documents and prepare to formulate your thesis, remember that while you do not have to answer this question by falling squarely on one side or the other of the issue, it's best to lean one way, with a nod to the other side. A safe, effective route to take on your DBQ essay is to indicate that there is evidence to support both sides of the argument. A good lawyer acknowledges there is other evidence, but is confident that there is stronger evidence to support his or her side of the case. Try to develop a case as you write your essay, using the documents and outside knowledge as mounting evidence. "To what extent" questions should prompt you to determine if something is more this way than that way. Most questions can be rephrased as "to what extent" questions, and doing so is often a useful strategy in developing a thesis.

Before you decide on your thesis, GO BACK AND READ THE QUESTION ONE MORE TIME! Make sure that your thesis addresses all the pertinent aspects of the question.

Before the Writing Period Begins…Create an Outline

At this point, you should still have time left in the mandatory 15-minute reading period. Create an outline with one roman numeral for each paragraph. Decide on the subject of each paragraph and on what information you will include in each paragraph. Do not rely on your grid/columns if you do not have to. The grid/columns are good for organizing your information but are less efficient for structuring an essay.

If you *still* have time after writing an outline, write a rough draft of your first paragraph in your green booklet, then transcribe it to your essay form once the writing period starts.

Write Your Essay

Go back and reread the first section in this chapter to review good essay-writing techniques. Follow this advice: Don't write flowery introductions or conclusions—just say what you are going to say. The readers want to get right to the point and see how much you know. Remember to back up your thesis statement with lots of facts, even if you are stretching it, because the graders want to hear solid evidence and not a lot of fluff. Also, make sure to remember what is being asked in the question, and refer to the question several times during the essay writing, as it is easy to wander away from your main point.

Stay confident. Everyone else taking the test, all across the country, is at least as nervous about it as you are.

CRACKING THE FREE-RESPONSE QUESTIONS

The free-response question (FRQ) is a two-part essay section consisting of two groups of questions. The first group asks questions about one era; the second group asks questions about a different era. This chronological shift will depend upon the era addressed in the DBQ. Each group contains two questions; you must choose one question from each group. The essay questions on the tests your AP teacher gives are probably very similar to the free-response questions on the AP test.

The FRQ is the final section of the AP U.S. History Exam. It is administered immediately following the DBQ. (You do not get a break between sections.) The College Board recommends that you set aside 70 of your 130 minutes to plan and write both FRQ essays.

The free-response questions, like the DBQ, have no single correct answer. Unlike the DBQ, though, the free-response questions are not accompanied by any documents; *everything* you include in your free-response answer will be outside information that you come up with. Also, because you have less time to plan and write the free-response essays, these essays can be shorter and less comprehensive than your DBQ essay. Most free-response questions ask you to *analyze*, *assess*, or *evaluate* the causes and effects of a historical subject. A simple, defensible thesis, accompanied by an organized essay filled with strong analysis of the given subject, should earn a top grade. Do not write an essay that is simply descriptive, in which you regurgitate everything you know about the essay prompt. Purely descriptive essays almost never score higher than a 4. A high-scoring essay is one that does indeed analyze, assess, and evaluate the given subject. Here are two examples:

1. Assess the impact of any THREE of the following on the United States' decision to declare war on England in 1812:

    the Napoleonic wars
    the Embargo Act of 1807
    America's desire for Western land
    America's military preparedness

2. Analyze the reasons for Congress's decision to end Reconstruction in 1877.

As you can see, free-response questions are designed to prompt analysis and evaluation of subject matter that you have learned in class. The subjects should be familiar; the questions are straightforward.

The free-response essays are graded on the same 0 to 9 scale as is the DBQ, but the DBQ is worth more to your final grade than each free-response question. When computing your final score, the College Board multiplies your DBQ score by 4.5 and each of your free-response scores by 2.75. Yes, it's confusing, but don't sweat it. All you need to know is the end result: The DBQ is worth 45 percent of your overall grade and each free-response question is worth 27.5 percent.

Which Questions to Choose

Choose the questions about which you know the most, NOT the ones that look easiest at first glance. The more you know about the subject, the better your final grade will be.

How to Write the Essays

Because we have already covered this information, here are brief directions to structure your essay. First, read the question and analyze it. Second, create a grid or columns and take notes. Third, assess your information and devise a thesis. Fourth, write a quick outline. Lastly, write your essay. If any of these instructions are unclear, reread the previous parts of this chapter.

As best you can, *split your time evenly between the two essays*. Too many students spend most of their time on the first essay, then do not have enough time to write a decent second essay. Both essays are worth the same number of points. Treat them equally. Pace yourself, watch the clock, and make sure you are finishing (or, better yet, have finished) your first essay when 35 minutes have passed. Then move directly on to the next essay.

A Final Note

This section is short because we have already discussed what you need to know to write successful AP essays, not because the free-response questions are unimportant. Each free-response question is worth more than one-quarter of your grade; they are VERY important. Many students are tempted to ease up when they finish the DBQ because it is so challenging. Do not make that mistake. Reach down for that last bit of energy, like a long-distance runner coming into the home stretch. When you reach the free-response questions, you only have a little more than an hour to go. *Then* you can take it easy.

Summary

Overview

o Read the questions carefully. You must answer the specific question asked in order to get full credit.

o Do not start writing until you have brainstormed, developed a thesis, and written an outline.

o Follow your outline. Stick to one important idea per paragraph (say, comparisons only or social issues only). Support your ideas with historical evidence.

o Write clearly and neatly. Do not write in long, overly complex sentences. When in doubt, stick to simple syntax and vocabulary.

o Use transition words to indicate continuity of thought and changes in the direction of your argument.

o Proofread your essay to make sure you have answered the question and to catch any errors or omissions. Watch out for any careless errors in names or years. Did you write Theodore Roosevelt when you meant to write Franklin Roosevelt? Did you say that the Declaration of Independence was written in 1876 when you meant to write 1776?

The Document-Based Question

o   The DBQ consists of an essay question
     and eight to 12 historical documents.
     Most likely, you will not have seen most
     of the documents before, but they will
     all relate to major historical events and
     ideas and will remind you of what you
     have learned about this topic. The DBQ
     begins with a 15-minute reading period,
     followed by a 45-minute writing period.

o   There is no single "correct" answer to the
     DBQ. DBQs are framed so that they can
     be successfully argued from many differ-
     ent viewpoints.

o   Read the essay question carefully. Circle
     and/or underline important words and
     phrases. Once you understand the ques-
     tion, create a grid or columns in which to
     organize your notes on the essay.

o   Before you start reading the documents,
     brainstorm about the question. This way
     you will gather the all-important outside
     information before you submerge yourself
     in the documents.

o   Read the documents. Read them in order,
     as there is usually a logic to the order in
     which they are presented. Pay attention
     to contradictions within and among the
     documents, and also to who is speaking
     and what sociopolitical tradition he or she
     represents. If you have already decided
     on a thesis, keep an eye out for informa-
     tion that might refute your thesis, and be
     prepared to address it in your essay.

o   Decide on a thesis, then write an outline
     for your essay.

o   Try to summarize key points from as
     many of the documents as you can in
     your essay. Weave in as much outside
     information as you can.

The Free-Response Questions

o   The free-response section consists of two pairs of
    questions. You must answer one question from
    each of the pairs. The eras covered in the free-
    response section will depend upon what eras were
    covered on your DBQ. Just know that collec-
    tively, the five essay prompts will address five eras
    throughout U.S. history.

o   Choose the questions about which you know the
    most, not the ones that look easiest.

o   Analyze each question you choose. Circle and/
    or underline important words and phrases. Once
    you understand the question, create a grid or
    columns in which to organize your notes on
    the essay.

o   Decide on a thesis, and then write an outline for
    your essay.

o   Follow your outline. Stick to one important idea
    per paragraph. Support your ideas with historical
    evidence.

o   Write clearly and neatly. Do not write in overly
    complex sentences. Toss in a couple of "big"
    words that you know you will not misuse. When
    in doubt, stick to simple syntax and vocabulary.

o   Use transition words to indicate continuity of
    thought and changes in the direction of your
    argument.

Chapter 3
Using Time Effectively to Maximize Points

Very few students stop to think about how to improve their test-taking skills. Most assume that if they study hard, they will test well, and if they do not study, they will do poorly. Most students continue to believe this even after experience teaches them otherwise. Have you ever studied really hard for an exam, then blown it on test day? Have you ever aced an exam for which you thought you weren't well prepared? Most students have had one, if not both, of these experiences. The lesson should be clear: Factors other than your level of preparation influence your final test score. This chapter will provide you with some insights that will help you perform better on the AP U.S. History Exam and on other exams as well.

PACING AND TIMING

A big part of scoring well on an exam is working at a consistent pace. The worst mistake made by inexperienced or unsavvy test takers is that they come to a question that stumps them, and, rather than just skip it, they panic and stall. Time stands still when you're working on a question you cannot answer, and it is not unusual for students to waste five minutes on a single question (especially a question involving a graph or the word EXCEPT) because they are too stubborn to cut their losses. It is important to be aware of how much time you have spent on a given question and on the section you are working. There are several ways to improving your pacing and timing for the test:

- **Know your average pace.** While you prepare for your test, try to gauge how long you take on 5, 10, or 20 questions. Knowing how long you spend on average per question will help you identify how many questions you can answer effectively and how best to pace yourself for the test.

- **Have a watch or clock nearby.** You are permitted to have a watch or clock nearby to help you keep track of time. It is important to remember, however, that constantly checking the clock is in itself a waste of time and can be distracting. Devise a plan. Try checking the clock after every 15 or 30 questions to see if you are keeping the correct pace or whether you need to speed up, this will ensure that your cognizant of the time but will not permit you to fall into the trap of dwelling on it.

- **Know when to move on.** Since all questions are scored equally, investing appreciable amounts of time on a single question is inefficient and can potentially deprive you of the chance to answer easier questions later on. If you are able to eliminate answer choices do so, but don't worry about picking a random answer and moving on if you cannot find the correct answer. Remember, tests are like marathons; you do best when you work through them at a steady pace. You can always come back to a question you don't know. When you do, very often you will find that your previous mental block is gone, and you will wonder why the question perplexed you the first time around (as you gleefully move on to the next question). Even if you still don't know the answer, you will not have wasted valuable time you could have spent on easier questions.

- **Be selective.** You don't have to do any of the questions in a given section in order. If you are stumped by an essay or multiple-choice question, skip it or choose a different one. In the section below, you will see that you may not have to answer every question correctly to achieve your desired score. Select the questions or essays that you can answer and work on them first. This will make you more efficient and give you the greatest chance of getting the most questions correct.

- **Use Process of Elimination on multiple-choice questions.** Many times, one or more answer choices can be eliminated. Every answer choice that can be eliminated increases the odds that you will answer the question correctly. The section on multiple-choice questions will go through strategies to find these incorrect answer choices and increase your odds of getting the question correct.

Remember, when all the questions on a test are of equal value, no one question is that important, your overall goal for pacing is to get the most questions correct. Finally, you should set a realistic goal for your final score. In the next section, we will breakdown how to achieve your desired score and ways of pacing yourself to do so.

GETTING THE SCORE YOU WANT

Depending on the score you need, it may be in your best interest not to try to work through every question. Check with the schools to which you are applying. Do you need a 3 to earn credit for the test? If you get a raw score of 48 (out of 80) on the multiple-choice section and do as well on the essays, you will get a 3.

Since the administration of the May 2011 exam, AP exams in all subjects no longer include a "guessing penalty" of a quarter of a point for every incorrect answer. Instead, students are assessed only on the total number of correct answers. A lot of AP materials, even those you receive in your AP class, may not include this information. It is really important to remember that if you are running out of time, you should fill in all the bubbles before the time for the multiple-choice section is up. Even if you don't plan to spend a lot of time on every question and even if you have no idea what the correct answer is, it is to your advantage to fill something in.

On the 2011 exam, out of 180 points total for the three essays and multiple-choice questions, students needed at least 111 points to get a score of 5, 91 points for a 4, 76 points for a 3, and 57 points for a 2. Because the College Board has not recently released its grading statistics, the following is an approximation of how to pace yourself on the multiple-choice section:

If you want to get a:	Work on this many:
2	45
3	60
4	70
5	80

Below is a table to give you an idea of approximately how many questions you must get right and how you must do on the essays to get the score you need. Realize that these numbers are approximations and will vary from year to year depending upon test performance. From these data, it becomes readily apparent that you must attempt and perform well on the essays to have a chance to score a 4 or 5. As you take practice tests, you can use this information to evaluate how best to get the score you want and what areas of the exam are hindering your progress. You can calculate your own score on the Practice Tests in this book using the worksheets on pages 361 and 410. There are multiple ways to achieve your desired score. It is important to remember that guessing is no longer penalized and that you must put in the energy and effort on the essays to perform well.

How to Get the Score You Want			
Total AP Score Desired	Multiple Choice Correct (out of 80)	Score Needed on DBQ	Average Score Needed on FRQs
5	80	3	2
	70	4	3
	60	5	4
	50	6	5
4	70	2	1
	60	3	2
	50	4	3
	40	7	7
3	60	2	1
	50	2	2
	40	4	3
	30	5	4
2	50	1	1
	40	2	1
	30	3	2
	20	4	3

TEST ANXIETY

Everybody experiences anxiety before and during an exam. To a certain extent, test anxiety *can* be helpful. Some people find that they perform more quickly and efficiently under stress. If you have ever pulled an all-nighter to write a paper and ended up doing good work, you know the feeling.

However, *too much* stress is definitely a bad thing. Hyperventilating during the test, for example, almost always leads to a lower score. If you find that you stress out during exams, here are a few preemptive actions you can take.

- **Take a reality check.** Evaluate your situation before the test begins. If you have studied hard, remind yourself that you are well prepared. Remember that many others taking the test are not as well prepared, and (in your classes, at least) you are being graded against them, so you have an advantage. If you didn't study, accept the fact that you will probably not ace the test. Make sure you get to every question you know something about. Don't stress out or fixate on how much you don't know. Your job is to score as high as you can by maximizing the benefits of what you do know. In either scenario, it is best to think of a test as if it were a game. How can you get the most points in the time allotted to you? Always answer questions you can answer easily and quickly before you answer those that will take more time.

- **Try to relax.** Slow, deep breathing works for almost everyone. Close your eyes, take a few, slow, deep breaths, and concentrate on nothing but your inhalation and exhalation for a few seconds. This is a basic form of meditation, and it should help you to clear your mind of stress and, as a result, concentrate better on the test. If you have ever taken yoga classes, you probably know some other good relaxation techniques. Use them when you can (obviously, anything that requires leaving your seat and, say, assuming a handstand position won't be allowed by any but the most free-spirited proctors).

- **Eliminate as many surprises as you can.** Make sure you know where the test will be given, when it starts, what type of questions are going to be asked, and how long the test will take. You don't want to be worrying about any of these things on test day or, even worse, after the test has already begun.

The best way to avoid stress is to study both the test material and the test itself. Congratulations! By buying or reading this book, you are taking a major step toward a stress-free AP U.S. History Exam.

Chapter 4
Pacing Drills

In this chapter, you'll have the opportunity to use the strategies you've learned. Let's get cracking!

Multiple-Choice Drill

Here is a group of five questions that could have come from the multiple-choice section of the AP U.S. History Exam. As you work through them, try to apply everything you learned in Chapter 1. Make sure you keep the big picture in mind as you consider the answer choices. Use POE. If you can get rid of one or more answer choices and can go no further, guess and move on. Use common sense and context clues. Answers and explanations for these questions follow the drills in this chapter.

33. Between 1836 and 1844, a gag order prevented Congress from

    (A) increasing tariffs
    (B) admitting new states to the Union
    (C) declaring war
    (D) overriding a presidential veto
    (E) considering abolitionist petitions

34. The Wilmot Proviso was most firmly supported by which national political party?

    (A) Federalist
    (B) Whig
    (C) Free-Soil
    (D) Know-Nothing
    (E) Populist

35. The Reconstruction plan approved by Congress included all of the following provisions EXCEPT

    (A) the imposition of martial law in the South
    (B) the implementation of black codes to govern the behavior of freedmen in the South
    (C) a requirement that each Southern state ratify the Fourteenth Amendment before being readmitted to the Union
    (D) the establishment of a government bureau to help relocate, feed, and employ newly liberated blacks
    (E) a mandate that all Southern states rewrite their constitutions and submit them to Congress for approval

36. Theodore Roosevelt's policy toward Cuba reflected his belief that

    (A) any domestic instability in Latin America could justify American intervention
    (B) it was in the United States' best interest to foster democracies in the region, even if those democracies were hostile to the United States
    (C) the United States should avoid all foreign entanglements
    (D) a multinational governing board made up of the United States and all Latin American countries should confer on all crises in the Western Hemisphere
    (E) the Monroe Doctrine was outdated and should be discarded

37. Which of the following best characterizes the purpose of English mercantilist policy in the colonies?

    (A) To develop the colonies' industrial base
    (B) To exploit colonial resources for the benefit of England
    (C) To foster democracy and self-government in the New World
    (D) To establish British military bases in the New World
    (E) To create a new nation to which those who were persecuted at home, such as the Puritans, could be sent

DBQ Drill

Below is a "mini-DBQ" (it has only four documents, instead of the usual eight to 12). Read through the documents, taking notes in the margins and blank spaces.

1. From the end of World War II through the Eisenhower administration, many Americans feared that communism threatened the existence of the United States. Using BOTH the documents AND your knowledge of the 1940s and 1950s, assess the reasons for and the validity of those fears.

Document A

Source: Decoded telegram from a KGB agent, New York to Moscow. Intercepted by U.S. intelligence.

November 14, 1944

To VIKTOR,

LIBERAL has safely carried through the contracting of Kh' YuS. Kh' YuS is a good pal of METR's. We propose to pair them off and get them to photograph their own materials having given them a camera for this purpose... LIBERAL will receive the film from METR for passing on...

OSA has agreed to cooperate with us in drawing in ShMEL'... with a view to ENORMOUS. On summons from KALIER she is leaving on 22 November for the Camp 2 area...

_____

Notes:

VIKTOR = Lt. Gen. P. M. FITIN [KGB Moscow]

LIBERAL = Julius ROSENBERG

Kh' YuS = probably Joel BARR or Alfred SARANT

OSA = Ruth GREENGLASS

ShMEL'/KALIER = David GREENGLASS

ENORMOUS = Atomic Energy Project

Document B

Source: Speech in Congress, Representative John F. Kennedy, January 1949

Mr. Speaker, over this weekend we have learned the extent of the disaster that has befallen China and the United States. The responsibility for the failure of our foreign policy in the Far East rests squarely with the White House and the State Department.

The continued insistence that aid would not be forthcoming unless a coalition government with the Communists was formed, was a crippling blow to the National Government.

So concerned were our diplomats and their advisers…with the imperfection of the democratic system in China… and the tales of corruption in high places that they lost sight of our tremendous stake in a non-Communist China…

This House must now assume the responsibility of preventing the onrushing tide of communism from engulfing all of Asia.

Document C

Source: Speech by President Harry Truman, July 29, 1951

This malicious propaganda has gone so far that on the Fourth of July…people were afraid to say they believed in the Declaration of Independence. A hundred and twelve people were asked to sign a petition that contained nothing except quotations from the Declaration of Independence and the Bill of Rights. One hundred and eleven of these people refused to sign that paper—many of them because they were afraid that it was some kind of subversive document and that they would lose their jobs or be called Communists.

Document D

Source: Advertisement, Civil Defender magazine, 1955

TO: CIVIL DEFENSE AUTHORITIES, EDUCATORS, AND PARENT-TEACHER ASSOCIATIONS

STUDENT IDENTIFICATION DURING AN "ATOMIC" ALERT

NEED: Is Civil Defense needed? If the answer to this question is yes, then we must entertain the thought of evacuation. Since the advent of the Hydrogen Bomb the only safety lies in not being "there."

EVACUATION: Should it be necessary to evacuate the children during school hours, it is also necessary to identify them. Many educators feel that this identification is more necessary for the grades from sixth down through kindergarten.

IDENTIFICATION: Identification must be positive, practical, and nontransferable. Identification most be kept in the school, to be used only during the time of the actual alert or drill. Identification must be inexpensive, since neither the schools nor the Civil Defense people have a lot of money to spend.

How do we of NATIONAL SCHOOL STUDIOS fit into this picture?

We offer the solution to the Identification problem...

We will furnish the Identification Card, chain, and pin (pictured in this ad) for the small sum of sixty cents per student... We will furnish the Identification Card...free of charge if we are permitted to submit our envelopes of pictures to the parents for possible purchase of these envelopes by the parents. Incidentally, this entails absolutely NO OBLIGATION on the part of the parent to purchase the envelope of pictures. We submit the envelope of pictures 100% on speculation...

FRQ Drill

Below is a drill based upon a free-response question. During the actual exam, you will have the option to choose between one of two different questions. Since the free-response questions provide no outside information, you will have to provide all of the relevant outside information you can come up with. Develop an outline and an approach to how you would write an essay to the following question:

1.   Analyze how the role of slavery during the decade of 1850–1860 contributed to the advent of the Civil War.

Explanations for the Multiple-Choice Drill

The five questions in the drill are of medium difficulty. On average, between 50 and 70 percent of those taking the test will get each one right. As we discuss how to take your best guess on the following questions, it should go without saying that, if you know the correct answer to the question, you should simply select it and move on.

Question 33 begins with a good context clue: the phrase *"gag order."* If you know that a gag order prevents discussion of a particular subject, you should have been reasonably certain that (E) was the correct answer. You should also have been thinking about the "big picture" as you worked on this question. Which of these answer choices discusses an important issue of the era? Tariffs were important earlier in the 1830s, so answer choice (A) might seem a reasonable answer. However, tariffs were a "big picture" issue when the "Tariff of Abominations" (passed in 1828) ultimately led to a nullification crisis in 1832, when Congress revised the tariff but still failed to satisfy Southern legislators. This question addresses a period four years later, so (A) is, in fact, an unlikely answer choice. Common sense should tell you that Congress didn't stop admitting states during this period, nor was it about to deny itself the right to declare war or override a presidential veto; both of these privileges are guaranteed to Congress by the Constitution. The answer has to be (E). Slavery is *the* "big picture" issue of the era.

Question 34. If you've forgotten what the Wilmot Proviso was, you should have remembered that it had something to do with the Civil War or the events leading up to the war. From that information you should have eliminated both the Federalists and the Populists, because neither party existed during the period. The Whigs, the Know-Nothings, and the Free-Soilers all existed in roughly the same era, suggesting that one of these choices is the answer. Remember, the national Whig party was split on the slavery issue; the Know-Nothings were a single-issue party, and that issue was the opposition to immigration; and the Free-Soilers were also a single-issue party, but their issue was slavery. Your best guess, the Free-Soilers (C), is the correct answer.

Question 35 asks you to play "one of these things is not like the other." Even if you don't remember that the black codes placed burdensome restrictions on the behavior of the freedmen, you should have realized that answer choices (A), (C), (D), and (E) were all similar in that they clearly indicated a punitive approach toward the South. That would have made (B), the correct answer, your best guess.

Question 36 is an easy one if you remember the "big picture" regarding Roosevelt and his foreign policy. Theodore Roosevelt's administration is associated with imperialism and interventionism, particularly (but not exclusively) in Latin America. That should have led you to choose answer choice (A), the correct answer. Notice that answer choice (E) is a nice distracter; if you remembered that there was a Roosevelt Corollary to the Monroe Doctrine, you might have been tempted to choose this. The corollary, however, was Roosevelt's improvement to the Monroe Doctrine, not a rejection of something he thought was already a pretty good idea.

Question 37 asks about English mercantilism, indicating that the test has returned to the colonial period and that you have moved up to a slightly more difficult set of questions. Again, think "big picture." What did the British want from the colonies? Wealth! By the way, you will very rarely go wrong if you attribute the actions of people and nations to their desire to acquire greater wealth. The correct answer is (B).

Explanation for the DBQ Drill

Document A is a good example of a document that starts out confusing but ends up being pretty straightforward. At first glance, this document makes very little sense; it is just a jumble of words and names. Do not panic; look for familiar elements. First, look at the source information. It is a telegram from a KGB agent. Therefore, it must have something to do with Soviet espionage. Now, look at the notes, and notice that they mention Julius Rosenberg and the Atomic Energy Project. Those references are probably all you need to know to understand why this document is included in the DBQ. It presents evidence that the Soviets were spying on the United States while it was developing the atomic bomb.

When you write your essay, do not fall into the trap of explaining every detail of this telegram. Your job is to analyze the importance of the document, not to describe exactly what it contains. This is true of every document in a DBQ, but it is particularly tempting here. You will be so proud that you have figured out what this document is all about that you might be tempted to spend a paragraph describing your achievement. Forget it. You have bigger fish to fry.

You probably asked yourself why this DBQ starts with a document from 1944, given that the question is about the period from 1945 through 1960. The document is here to demonstrate that there was some foundation for America's anti-communist fears after World War II. You can use this document as a springboard to discuss other reasons for that fear, such as the relative popularity of the American Communist Party (CPUSA) in the 1930s and the party's disproportionate representation in some labor unions. Mentioning unions then allows you to discuss labor problems in the postwar era. (Labor held more than 5,000 strikes in 1946 and 1947, which spurred the anti-union Taft-Hartley Act.)

This document can also be incorporated easily into an "America was too paranoid" essay because it raises the issue of the Rosenberg trial and the controversy over their sentence. Many people believe their execution resulted from anti-communist paranoia, not from reasoned consideration of their alleged crimes. (Albert Einstein testified that the Rosenbergs gave the Soviets nothing that they wouldn't have figured out on their own.) Of course, the Rosenberg trial generated a national debate, which illustrates the nation's preoccupation with communism during this period.

You may have thought of other issues that this document raises. That is good, and it highlights an important point: Most DBQ documents will be adaptable to a discussion of many different events and ideas. Consequently, you have a lot of leeway in your essay. (Remember, there is no single correct answer to the DBQ.) It also means you cannot possibly discuss every event that relates to this question. There is simply too much to discuss. Believe it or not, that is good, too. DBQ topics are so large that no one *expects* you to write the definitive essay on the subject. Hence, you will not be penalized for forgetting one or another event that illustrates your point as long as you back your points with other evidence.

Document B is taken from a speech in Congress by John F. Kennedy, and it raises several important issues. Primarily, it brings up the Chinese Revolution, which gives you an opportunity to discuss the expansion of communist power in other parts of the world. Using Document B as a starting point, you could discuss the Korean War, the crises in Eastern Europe in the 1950s (e.g., Hungary), and the fall of Cuba and other Latin American nations to communist insurgents. All of these events support the position that America's fear of communism was valid, especially if you choose to attribute these events to communist expansionism.

On the other hand, you might argue that this speech shows Kennedy demonstrating the same Cold War paranoia that later inspired the Bay of Pigs fiasco. You might attribute this speech to his political skills and argue that Kennedy is exploiting a sensitive issue for his own political gain. (Remember, many early "Cold Warriors" gained political support by accusing the government of "giving away" China to the Communists.) Interestingly, Kennedy felt it so important to keep China from communist control that he was willing to overlook the flagrant corruption of Chiang Kai-shek's government. If you think he was right, this document justifies American fears; if you argue that he was wrong, you can use it to illustrate how anti-communism distorted America's judgment.

Document C clearly supports the argument that Americans were paranoid about communism and that this paranoia was the result of propaganda. President Truman's reference to people "losing their jobs" opens the door for you to talk about blacklisting during the 1950s and, by extension, McCarthyism and other excesses of this anti-communist era. His description of those citizens who thought that the Declaration of Independence was a "subversive document" illustrates the conservatism of the era.

However, Document C also gives you a chance to discuss Truman's anti-communism. Remember, he established loyalty boards with tremendous power to fire government employees merely on the suspicion of communist tendencies. Plus, his foreign policy initiatives, from containment to the Marshall Plan and the Truman Doctrine, might all be considered the ideas of an overzealous anti-communist. You certainly could argue that those policies antagonized communist countries and therefore exacerbated tensions. You could even say that the growing American-communist tension *resulted* from Truman's policies. As usual, nothing is cut-and-dried in the DBQ, which means that you have many options available to you.

Document D addresses two important issues, the hydrogen bomb and its chilling effect on America. The document is an advertisement that very clearly tries to exploit parents' fears as a means of selling them pictures of their children. While it is exploitative, it also indicates just how far fear of the H-bomb had infiltrated the American psyche. You can use this document as a starting point to discuss air-raid shelters, atomic bomb drills in school, the "Duck and Cover" propaganda campaign, and civil defense organizations. All of these events stem from American fear of the Communists. Most Americans were afraid of the USSR primarily because the USSR had the H-bomb. For many Americans, it was conceivable and even likely that the Soviets would use that bomb against the United States.

That's it for the documents. Now, formulate a thesis. There are any number of positions you can argue on our sample question. The best route, as we just said, would be to attribute America's fear of the Communists to a combination of justifiable and exaggerated reasons. Furthermore, there are a number of ways you can choose to construct an essay that demonstrates this thesis. You might want to argue chronologically, indicating which events caused justifiable alarm and which were blown out of proportion by anti-communist propagandists. You might wish to divide the body of your essay into two large paragraphs, one dealing with the communist threat posed from abroad and the other dealing with the threat posed by American Communists.

Once you've figured out how and where to fit all your information into your argument, create an outline, and write your essay.

Explanation for the FRQ Drill

As you begin to think about this prompt, you realize that the theme and therefore thesis of the essay should focus on the connection between slavery and the start of the war. You should begin by making notes or a set of columns of events related to slavery that occurred specifically during this period preceding the Civil War and how they may have contributed to the war. For instance, you could include the some of the following key events in your essay:

- Compromise of 1850 (admission of California as a free state; popular sovereignty in territories; banning of slave trade in Washington D.C.; Fugitive Slave Law)

- *Uncle Tom's Cabin* by Harriet Beecher Stowe, 1852 (anti-slavery novel, fostered abolitionist sentiment)

- Election of 1852 (slavery was a key issue and caused intra- and interparty conflict)

- Kansas-Nebraska Act, 1854 (popular sovereignty in Kansas/Nebraska territories, negated the Missouri Compromise)

- Bleeding Kansas, 1855 (war between pro- and antislavery factions; Pottawatomie Creek Massacre)

- Election of 1856 (party lines are drawn on views of slavery)

- *Dred Scott v. Sanford*, 1857 (made the Missouri compromise unconstitutional)

- Lincoln–Douglas Debates, 1858 (Lincoln's house divided speech, open discussion on slavery in territories)

- Harper's Ferry Raid, 1859 (attempt to start an armed slave revolt)

- Election of 1860 (split of democratic party over views on slavery, election of pro-abolitionist Lincoln)

After you have assembled your list of events, you will need to evaluate which events share a common theme and can be written together to form paragraphs and the start of an outline. For the example above, you may have noticed that several of the events involve issues related to the stance of political parties. This could become the focus of one of your paragraphs. Two possible additional themes include pre-Civil War armed confrontations (such as Bleeding Kansas and the Harper's Ferry Raid) and the role of Popular Sovereignty in new states and territories. Remember, that as you write essays, you must structure your outline and arguments to a central theme, in this case, the connection between slavery and the start of the Civil War. Since you only have approximately 35 minutes for each FRQ essay to structure and write, your sentences should be succinct and your essay should have a clear thesis supported by your outside information. Be confident, pace yourself and, most importantly, stay on target.

REFLECT

Think about what you've learned in Part III, and respond to the following questions:

- How long will you spend on multiple-choice questions?

- How will you change your approach to multiple-choice questions?

- What is your multiple-choice guessing strategy?

- How much time will you spend on the DBQ? The first FRQ essay? The second?

- What will you do now during the 15-minute reading and planning time?

- How will you change your approach to the essays?

- Will you seek further help, outside of this book (such as a teacher, tutor, or AP Central), on how to approach multiple-choice questions, the essays, or a pacing strategy?

Part IV
Content Review for the AP U.S. History Exam

HOW TO USE THE CHAPTERS IN THIS PART

The history review is meant to serve as a supplement to the textbook you use in class. It is not a substitute for your textbook. However, it does cover all major subjects and terms that are likely to appear on the AP U.S. History Exam. If you are familiar with everything in this review, you should do very well on the AP exam.

In the following content review chapters, you will find a summary of those events and actions that the writers of the AP exam consider important. Because historical events often exemplify ESP trends (economic, social, and political trends), and because that's what makes those events important to historians (and to test writers), this review focuses on those connections. We have tried to make this section as interesting and as brief as possible while remaining thorough.

You may need to come back to these chapters more than once. Your goal is to obtain mastery of the content you are missing, and a single read of a chapter may not be sufficient. At the end of each chapter, you will have an opportunity to reflect on whether you truly have mastered the content of that chapter.

Chapter 5
The Seventeenth and Early Eighteenth Centuries (1600–1750)

NATIVE AMERICANS IN PRE-COLUMBIAN NORTH AMERICA

True or False?
Q: Native American cultures tended to have limited or minimal impact on the environment.

Historians refer to the period before **Christopher Columbus's** arrival in the New World as the **pre-Columbian** era. During this period, North America was populated by **Native Americans**—not to be confused with native-born Americans, a group that includes anyone born in the United States. Recently, the College Board has pushed for an increase in the number of multiple-choice questions involving this era, so it is extremely important to understand the clash of cultures that occurred between the European settlers and the Native Americans, as well as their subsequent conflicts throughout American history.

Most historians believe that Native Americans are the descendants of migrants who traveled from Asia to North America. The migration likely occurred in multiple waves, from as early as 40,000 years ago to as recently as 15,000 years ago. During this period, the planet was significantly colder, and much of the world's water was locked up in vast polar ice sheets, causing sea levels to drop. The ancestors of the Native Americans could therefore simply walk across a **land bridge** from Siberia (in modern Russia) to Alaska. As the planet warmed, sea levels rose and this bridge was submerged, forming the **Bering Strait**. These people and their descendants eventually migrated south, either by boat along the Pacific coast or possibly along an ice-free corridor east of the Rocky Mountains, and went on to populate both North and South America.

At the time of Columbus's arrival, between 1 million and 5 million Native Americans lived in modern Canada and the United States; another 20 million populated Mexico. Native American societies in North America ran the gamut from small groups of nomadic huntergatherers to highly organized urban empires. In the year 1500, the Aztec capital of Tenochtitlan was more populous than any city in Europe, and both the Aztecs and the Maya are noted for their advances in astronomy, architecture, and art. While these civilizations were located in Mesoamerica, the territory that would become the United States was home to urban cultures as well, such as the **Pueblo people** of the desert southwest with their multistory stone houses consisting of hundreds of rooms, or the **Mississippian culture** with their immense earthen mounds. The first Native Americans to encounter Europeans were smaller tribes that lived along the Atlantic Ocean; Columbus, mistakenly believing he had reached the East Indies, dubbed them "Indians," and the name stuck for centuries.

Cahokia

Located near the site of modern-day St. Louis, Cahokia was the largest North American city north of Mexico prior to the arrival of European settlers. In the 13th century its population rivaled or surpassed that of any European city, and while it was abandoned a hundred years before the voyages of Columbus, no American city passed Cahokia's peak population mark until after the United States had achieved its independence. Cahokia was dominated by a huge earthwork known as **Monks Mound**, an artificial hill 100 feet high and covering 17 acres, consisting of soil transported to the site by hand in baskets.

EARLY COLONIALIZATION OF THE NEW WORLD (1492–1650)

The Early Colonial Era: Spain Colonizes the New World

Christopher Columbus arrived in the New World in 1492. He was not the first European to reach North America—the Norse had arrived in modern Canada around 1000—but his arrival marked the beginning of the Contact Period, during which Europe sustained contact with the Americas and introduced a widespread exchange of plants, animals, foods, communicable diseases, and ideas in the **Columbian Exchange**. Unlike Leif Eriksson, Bjarni Herjolfsson, and other Norse explorers, the better-remembered Columbus arrived at a time when Europe had the resources and technology to establish **colonies** far from home. (A *colony* is a territory settled and controlled by a foreign power.) When Columbus returned to Spain and reported the existence of a rich new world with easy-to-subjugate natives, he opened the door to a long period of European expansion and colonialism.

During the next century, Spain was *the* colonial power in the Americas. The Spanish founded a number of coastal towns in Central and South America and in the West Indies, where the **conquistadors** collected and exported as much of the area's wealth as they could. Under Spain's **encomienda** system, the crown granted colonists authority over a specified number of natives; the colonist was obliged to protect those natives and convert them to Catholicism, and in exchange, the colonist was entitled to those natives' labor. If this sounds like a form of slavery, that's because it was. Meanwhile, the strength of Spain's navy, the **Spanish Armada**, kept other European powers from establishing much of a foothold in the New World. In 1588, the English navy defeated the Armada, and consequently, French and English colonization of North America became much easier.

Much of early American history revolves around the conflict between Native Americans and European settlers. Europeans were generally victorious. Why? One seemingly obvious answer is that the Europeans had more advanced technology, but this wasn't actually a major factor. In fact, in many ways the Native Americans' technology was superior: their canoes were far better at navigating North American rivers than any European ship, and their moccasins offered better footing than clumsy European boots. The most important factor, by a wide margin, was disease. Native Americans had never been exposed to European microbes and had never developed immunities to them. Epidemics such as **smallpox** devastated Native American settlements, sometimes killing 95% of the population years before Europeans themselves arrived to mop up the few survivors.

True or False?

A: False! Even Native American societies that hadn't developed much in the way of agriculture often transformed the landscape through the strategic use of fire, which encouraged the growth of useful plants and attracted game animals. Many early European immigrants to North America remarked that the areas they were settling resembled parkland; this wasn't the natural condition of these regions, but reflected the cultivation of the local environment by the Native Americans who had preceded them.

The English Arrive

England's first attempt to settle North America came a year prior to its victory over Spain, in 1587, when **Sir Walter Raleigh** sponsored a settlement on Roanoke Island (now part of North Carolina). By 1590, the colony had disappeared, which is why it came to be known as the **Lost Colony**. The English did not try again until 1607, when they settled **Jamestown**. Jamestown was funded by a **joint-stock company**, a group of investors who bought the right to establish New World plantations from the king. (How the monarchy came to sell the rights to land that it clearly did not own is just the kind of interesting question that this review will not be covering. Sorry, but it is not on the AP!) The company was called the **Virginia Company**—named for Elizabeth I, known as the Virgin Queen—from which the area around Jamestown took its name. The settlers, many of them English gentlemen, were ill-suited to the many adjustments life in the New World required of them. them, and were much more interested in searching for gold than in planting crops. (The only "gold" to be found in Virginia was iron pyrite, a.k.a. "fool's gold," which the ignorant aristocrats blithely gathered up.) Within three months more than half the original settlers were dead of starvation or disease, and Jamestown survived only because ships kept arriving from England with new colonists. **Captain John Smith** decreed that "he who will not work shall not eat," and things improved for a time, but after Smith was injured in a gunpowder explosion and sailed back to England, the Indians of the **Powhatan Confederacy** stopped supplying Jamestown with food. Things got so bad during the winter of 1609-1610 that it became known as "the **starving time**": nearly 90 percent of Jamestown's 500 residents perished, with some resorting to cannibalism. The survivors actually abandoned the colony, but before they could get more than a few miles downriver, they ran into an English ship containing supplies and new settlers.

One of the survivors, **John Rolfe,** was notable in two ways. First, he married Powhatan's daughter **Pocahontas**, briefly easing the tension between the natives and the English settlers. Second, he pioneered the practice of growing **tobacco**, which had long been cultivated by Native Americans, as a cash crop to be exported back to England. The English public was soon hooked, so to speak, and the success of tobacco considerably brightened the prospects for English settlement in Virginia.

Because the crop requires vast acreage and depletes the soil (and so requires farmers to constantly seek new fields), the prominent role of tobacco in Virginia's economy resulted in rapid expansion. The introduction of tobacco would also lead to the development of plantation slavery. As new settlements sprang up around Jamestown, the entire area came to be known as the **Chesapeake** (named after the bay). That area today is comprises Virginia and Maryland.

Many who migrated to the Chesapeake did so for financial reasons. Overpopulation in England had led to widespread famine, disease, and poverty. Chances for improving one's lot during these years were minimal. Thus, many were attracted to the New World by the opportunity provided by **indentured servitude**. In return for free passage, indentured servants typically promised seven years' labor, after which they would receive their freedom. Throughout much of the seventeenth century, indentured servants also received a small piece of property with their freedom, thus enabling them (1) to survive, and (2) to vote. As in Europe, the right to vote was tied to the ownership of property, and indentured servitude in America opened a path to land ownership that was not available to most working class men in populous Europe. However, indenture was extremely difficult, and nearly half of all indentured servants—most of whom were young, reasonably healthy men— did not survive their term of service. Still, indenture was common. More than 75 percent of the 130,000 Englishmen who migrated to the Chesapeake during the seventeenth century were indentured servants.

In 1618, the Virginia Company introduced the **headright system** as a means of attracting new settlers to the region and to address the labor shortage created by the emergence of tobacco farming, which required a large number of workers. A "headright" was a tract of land, usually about 50 acres, that was granted to colonists and potential settlers. Men already settled in Virginia were granted two headrights, totaling about 100 acres of land, while new settlers to Virginia were granted one headright. Wealthy investors could accumulate land by paying the passage of indentured servants and gaining a headright for each servant they sponsored. The headright system became the basis for an emerging aristocracy in colonial Virginia (where land was still the basis of wealth and political power) and was one of the factors that hindered the development of democracy in the region. Furthermore, it must be noted that these land grants infringed upon the rights of Native Americans, whose values regarding the environment and property ownership were vastly different from the values of the Europeans who settled in this region.

In 1619 Virginia established the **House of Burgesses**, in which any property-holding, white male could vote. All decisions made by the House of Burgesses, however, had to be approved by the Virginia Company. That year also marks the introduction of **slavery** to the English colonies. (See the section in this chapter, Slavery in the Early Colonies.)

French Colonization of North America

At first glance, the French colonization of North America appears to have much in common with Spanish and English colonization. While the English had founded a permanent settlement at Jamestown in 1607, the French colonized what is today Quebec City in 1608. Like the Spanish missionaries, the French Jesuit priests were trying to convert native peoples to Roman Catholicism, but were much more likely to spread diseases such as smallpox than to convert large numbers to Christianity. Like colonists from other European countries, the French were exploring as much land as they could, hoping to find natural resources such as gold, as well as a shortcut to Asia.

Unlike the Spanish and English, however, the French colonists had a much lighter impact on the native peoples. Few French settlers came to North America, and those who did tended to be single men, some of whom intermarried with women native to the area. They also tended to stay on the move, especially if they were *coureurs du bois* ("runners in the woods") who helped trade for the furs that became the rage in Europe. True, the French ultimately did play a significant role in the French and Indian War (surprise!) from 1754–1763. However, their chances of shaping the region soon known as British North America were slim from the outset and faded dramatically with the **Edict of Nantes** in 1598. This edict provided for religious tolerance of the **Huguenots** (the French Protestants), who might otherwise have fled their mother country just as the Puritans would flee England during the 1600s.

The four main colonizing powers in North America interacted with the native inhabitants very differently:

- **Spain** tended to conquer and enslave the native inhabitants of the regions it colonized. The Spanish also made great efforts to convert Native Americans to Catholicism. Spanish colonists were overwhelmingly male, and many had children with native women, leading to settlements populated largely by mestizos, people of mixed Spanish and Native American ancestry.

- **France** had significantly friendlier relations with indigenous tribes, tending to ally with them and adopt native practices. The French had little choice in this: French settlements were so sparsely populated that taking on the natives head-on would have been very risky.

- **The Netherlands** attempted to build a great trading empire, and while it achieved great success elsewhere in the world, its settlements on the North American continent, which were essentially glorified trading posts, soon fell to the English. This doesn't mean they were unimportant: one of the Dutch settlements was New Amsterdam, later renamed New York City.

- **England** differed significantly from the three other powers in that the other three all depended on Native Americans in different ways: as slave labor, as allies, or as trading partners. English colonies, by contrast, attempted to exclude Native Americans as much as possible. The English flooded to the New World in great numbers, with entire families arriving in many of the colonies rather than just young men, and intermixing between settlers and natives was rare. Instead, when English colonies grew to the point that conflict with nearby tribes became inevitable, the English launched **wars of extermination**. For instance, the Powhatan Confederacy was destroyed by English "Indian fighters" in the 1640s.

The Pilgrims and the Massachusetts Bay Company

During the sixteenth century, English Calvinists led a Protestant movement called **Puritanism** in England. Its name was derived from its adherents' desire to purify the Anglican church of Roman Catholic practices. English monarchs of the early seventeenth century persecuted the Puritans, and so the Puritans began to look for a new place to practice their faith.

One Puritan group, called **Separatists**—because they thought the Church of England was so incapable of being reformed that they had to abandon it—left England around this time. First they went to the Netherlands, but ultimately decided to start fresh in the New World. In 1620 they set sail for Virginia, but their ship, the *Mayflower*, went off course and they landed in modern-day Massachusetts. Because winter was approaching, they decided to settle where they had landed. This settlement was called **Plymouth**.

While on board, the travelers—called **"Pilgrims"**—signed an agreement establishing a "body politic" and a basic legal system for the colony. That agreement, **the Mayflower Compact**, is important not only because it created a legal authority and an assembly, but also because it asserted that the government's power derives from the consent of the governed and not from God, as some **monarchists** known as **Absolutists** believed.

Like the earlier settlers in Jamestown, the Pilgrims received life-saving assistance from local Native Americans. To the Pilgrims' great fortune, they had happened to land at the site of a Patuxet village that had been wiped out by disease; one inhabitant of that village, a man named Tisquantum, better known as **Squanto**, had been spared this fate because he had been captured years before and brought to Europe as a slave. He wound up in London, where he learned English, then returned to his homeland only to find it depopulated. Shortly thereafter, the Pilgrims arrived, and Squanto became their interpreter and taught them how best to plant in their new home.

In 1629 a larger and more powerful colony called **Massachusetts Bay** was established by **Congregationalists** (Puritans who wanted to reform the Anglican church from within). This began what is known as The Great Puritan Migration, which lasted from 1629 to 1642. Led by Governor **John Winthrop**, Massachusetts Bay developed along Puritan ideals. While onboard the ship *Arabella*, Winthrop delivered a now-famous sermon, "A Model of Christian Charity," urging the colonists to be a **"city upon a hill"**—a model for others to look up to. All Puritans believed they had a **covenant** with God, and the concept of covenants was central to their entire philosophy, in both political and religious terms. Government was to be a covenant among the people; work was to serve a communal ideal, and, of course, the Puritan church was always to be served. This is why both the Separatists and the Congregationalists did not tolerate religious freedom in their colonies, even though both had experienced and fled religious persecution.

The settlers of the Massachusetts Bay Colony were strict **Calvinists**, and Calvinist principles dictated their daily lives. For example, much has been written about the "Protestant work ethic" and its relationship to the eventual development of a market economy. In fact, some historians believe the roots of the Civil War can be traced back to the founding of the Chesapeake region and New England, as a plantation economy dependent on slave labor developed in the Chesapeake and subsequent southern colonies, while New England became the commercial center.

Two major incidents during the first half of the seventeenth century demonstrated Puritan religious intolerance. **Roger Williams**, a minister in the Salem Bay settlement, taught a number of controversial principles, among them that church and state should be separate. The Puritans banished Williams, who subsequently moved to modern-day Rhode Island and founded a new colony. Rhode Island's charter allowed for the free exercise of religion, and it did not require voters to be church members. **Anne Hutchinson** was a prominent proponent of *antinomianism*, the belief that faith and God's grace—as opposed to the observance of moral law and performance of good deeds—suffice to earn one a place among the "elect." Her teachings challenged Puritan beliefs and the authority of the Puritan clergy. The fact that she was an intelligent, well-educated, and powerful woman in a resolutely patriarchal society turned many against her. She was tried for heresy, convicted, and banished.

Puritan immigration to New England came to a near-halt between 1649 and 1660, the years during which **Oliver Cromwell** ruled as Lord Protector of England. Cromwell's reign represented the culmination of the **English Civil Wars**, which the Puritans won. For slightly over a decade, Cromwell ruled England as a republic, complete with a constitution. The death of Cromwell (1658) robbed the Puritans of their best-known and most respected leader, and by 1660 the Stuarts were restored to the throne. During the **Interregnum** (literally "between kings"), Puritans had little motive to move to the New World. Everything they wanted—freedom to practice their religion, as well as representation in the government—was available to them in England. With the restoration of the Stuarts, many English Puritans again immigrated to the New World. Not coincidentally, these immigrants brought with them some of the republican ideals of the revolution.

The lives of English settlers in New England and the Chesapeake differed considerably. Entire families tended to immigrate to New England; in the Chesapeake, immigrants were often single males. The climate in New England was more hospitable, and so New Englanders tended to live longer and have larger families than Chesapeake residents. A stronger sense of community, and the absence of tobacco as a cash crop, led New Englanders to settle in larger towns that were closer to one another; those in the Chesapeake lived in smaller, more spread-out farming communities. While both groups were religious, the New Englanders were definitely *more* religious, settling near meetinghouses.

Other Early Colonies

As the population of Massachusetts grew, settlers began looking for new places to live. One obvious choice was the Connecticut Valley, a fertile region with lots of access to the sea (for trade). The area was already inhabited by the **Pequots**, however, who resisted the English incursions. When the Pequots attacked a settlement in Wakefield and killed nine colonists, members of the Massachusetts Bay Colony retaliated by burning the main Pequot village, killing 400, many of them women and children. The result was the near-destruction of the Pequots in what came to be known as the **Pequot War.**

Several colonies were proprietorships; that is, they were owned by one person, who usually received the land as a gift from the king. **Connecticut** was one such colony, receiving its charter in 1635 and producing the **Fundamental Orders**, usually considered the first written constitution in British North America. **Maryland** was another, granted to Cecilius Calvert, Lord Baltimore. Calvert hoped to create a haven colony for Catholics, who faced religious persecution in Protestant England, but he also hoped to make a profit growing tobacco. In order to populate the colony's land more quickly, Calvert offered religious tolerance for all Christians, and Protestants soon outnumbered Catholics, recreating England's old tension between the faiths. After a Protestant uprising in England against a Catholic-sympathizing king, Maryland's government passed the **Act of Toleration** in 1649 to protect the religious freedom of most Christians, but the law was not enough to keep the situation in Maryland from devolving into bloody religious civil war for much of the rest of the century.

New York was also a royal gift, this time to James, the king's brother. The Dutch Republic was the largest commercial power during the seventeenth century and, as such, was an economic rival of the British. The Dutch had established an initial settlement in 1614 near present-day Albany, which they called New Netherland, and a fort at the mouth of the Hudson River in 1626. This fort would become New Amsterdam and is today New York City. In 1664 Charles II of England waged a war against the Dutch Republic and sent a naval force to capture New Netherland. Already weakened by previous clashes with local Native Americans, the Dutch governor, Peter Stuyvesant, along with 400 civilians, surrendered peacefully. Charles II's brother, James, became the Duke of York, and when James became king in 1685, he proclaimed New York a royal colony. The Dutch were allowed to remain in the colony on generous terms, and made up a large segment of New York's population for many years. Charles II also gave **New Jersey** to a couple of friends, who in turn sold it off to investors, many of whom were Quakers.

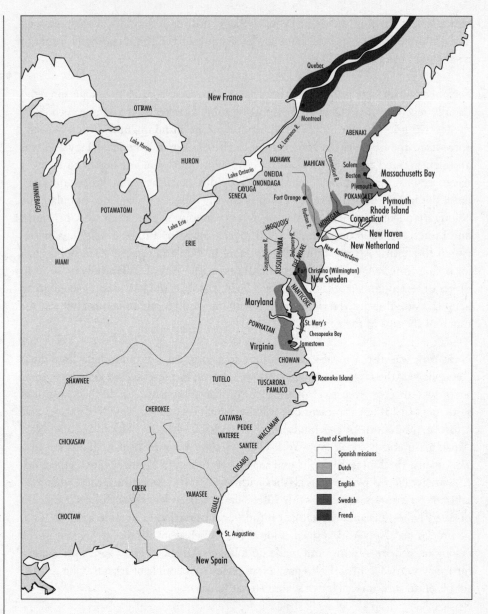

European Settlements in North America, 1650

Ultimately, the Quakers received their own colony. William Penn, a Quaker, was a close friend of King Charles II, and Charles granted Penn what became **Pennsylvania**. Charles, like most Anglicans, perceived the egalitarian Quakers as dangerous radicals, but the two men's friendship (and Charles's desire to export the Quakers to someplace far from England) prevailed. Penn established liberal policies toward religious freedom and civil liberties in his colony. That, the area's natural bounty, and Penn's recruitment of settlers through advertising, made Pennsylvania one of the fastest growing of the early colonies. He also attempted to treat Native Americans more fairly than did other colonies and had mixed results. His attitude attracted many tribes to the area but also attracted many European settlers who bullied tribes off of their land. An illustrative story: Penn made a treaty with the Delawares to take only as much land as could be walked by a man in three days. Penn then set off on a leisurely stroll, surveyed his land, and kept his end of the bargain. His son, however, renegotiating the treaty, hired three marathon runners for the same task, thereby claiming considerably more land.

Carolina was also a proprietary colony, but in 1729 it officially split into **North Carolina**, settled by Virginians as a Virginia-like colony, and **South Carolina**, settled by the descendants of Englishmen who had colonized Barbados. Barbados's primary export was sugar, and its plantations were worked by slaves. Although slavery had existed in Virginia since 1619, the settlers from Barbados were the first Englishmen in the New World who had seen widespread slavery at work. Their arrival truly marked the beginning of the slave era in the colonies.

Eventually, most of the **proprietary** colonies were converted to **royal** colonies; that is, their ownership was taken over by the king, who could then exert greater control over their governments. By the time of the Revolution, only Connecticut, Rhode Island, Pennsylvania, and Maryland were *not* royal colonies.

For an overview of which areas were settled by whom during this period, see the map on the previous page.

Slavery in the Early Colonies

As mentioned above, the extensive use of African slaves in the American colonies began when colonists from the Caribbean settled the Carolinas. Until then, indentured servants and, in some situations, enslaved Native Americans had mostly satisfied labor requirements in the colonies. As tobacco-growing and, in South Carolina, rice-growing operations expanded, more laborers were needed than indenture could provide. Events such as Bacon's Rebellion (see Major Events of the Period for more on this) had also shown landowners that it was not in their best interest to have an abundance of landless, young, white males in their colonies, either.

Enslaving Native Americans was difficult; they knew the land, so they could easily escape and subsequently were difficult to find. In some Native American tribes, cultivation was considered women's work, so gender was another obstacle to enslaving the natives. And as noted, Europeans brought diseases that often decimated the Native Americans, wiping out 85 to 95 percent of the native population. Southern landowners turned increasingly to African slaves for labor. Unlike Native Americans, African slaves did not know the land, and so were less likely to escape. Removed from their homelands and communities, and often unable to communicate with one another because they were from different regions of Africa, black slaves initially proved easier to control than Native Americans. The dark skin of the West Africans who made up the bulk of the enslaved population made it easier to identify slaves on sight, and the English colonists came to associate dark skin with inferiority, rationalizing Africans' enslavement.

The majority of the slave trade, right up to the Revolution, was directed toward the Caribbean and South America. Still, during that period more than 500,000

Geography = Destiny?
Here's a good general guide for remembering which colonies were established for what reasons: The northern colonies were mostly established for religious reasons, the southern for commercial gain.

slaves were brought to the English colonies (of the over 10 million brought to the New World). By 1790, nearly 750,000 blacks were enslaved in England's North American colonies.

The shipping route that brought the slaves to the Americas was called the **Middle Passage** because it was the middle leg of the **triangular trade route** among the colonies, Europe, and Africa. Conditions for the Africans aboard were brutally inhumane, so intolerable that some committed suicide by throwing themselves overboard. Many died of sickness, and others died during insurrections. It was not unusual for one-fifth of the Africans to die on board. Most, however, reached the New World, where conditions were only slightly better. Mounting criticism (primarily in the North) of the horrors of the Middle Passage led Congress to end American participation in the Atlantic slave trade on January 1, 1808. Slavery itself would not end in the United States until 1865.

Slavery flourished in the South. Because of the nature of the land and the short growing season, the Chesapeake and the Carolinas farmed labor-intensive crops such as **tobacco**, **rice**, and **indigo**, and plantation owners there bought slaves for this arduous work. Slaves' treatment at the hands of their owners was often vicious and at times sadistic. While slavery never really took hold in the North the same way it did in the South, slaves were used on farms in New York, New Jersey, and Pennsylvania, in shipping operations in Massachusetts and Rhode Island, and as domestic servants in urban households, particularly in New York City. Although northern states would take steps to phase out slavery following the Revolution, there were still slaves in New Jersey at the outbreak of the Civil War. In both regions, only the very wealthy owned slaves. The vast majority of people remained at a subsistence level.

THE AGE OF SALUTARY NEGLECT (1650–1750)

British treatment of the colonies during the period preceding the **French and Indian War** (also called **the Seven Years' War**) is often described as "**salutary neglect**" or "**benign neglect**." Although England regulated trade and government in its colonies, it interfered in colonial affairs as little as possible. Because of the distance, England set up absentee customs officials and the colonies were left to self-govern, for the most part. England occasionally turned its back to the colonies' violations of trade restrictions. Thus, the colonies developed a large degree of autonomy, which helped fuel revolutionary sentiments when the monarchy later attempted to gain greater control of the New World.

During this century, the colonies "grew up," developing fledgling economies. The beginnings of an American culture—as opposed to a transplanted English culture—took root.

English Regulation of Colonial Trade

Throughout the colonial period, most Europeans who thought about economics at all subscribed to a theory called **mercantilism**. Mercantilists believed that economic power was rooted in a favorable balance of trade (that is, exporting more than you import) and the control of **specie** (hard currency, such as gold coins). Colonies, they felt, were important mostly for economic reasons, which explains why the British considered their colonies in the West Indies that produced sugar and other valuable commodities to be more important than their colonies on the North American continent. The colonies on the North American continent were seen primarily as markets for British and West Indian goods, although they also were valued as sources of raw materials that would otherwise have to be bought from a foreign country.

In order to guarantee a favorable balance of trade, the British government encouraged manufacturing in England and placed **protective tariffs** on imports that might compete with English goods. A number of such tariffs, included in the **Navigation Acts**, were passed between 1651 and 1673. The Navigation Acts required the colonists to buy goods only from England, to sell certain of their products only to England, and to import any non-English goods via English ports and pay a duty on those imports. The Navigation Acts also prohibited the colonies from manufacturing a number of goods that England already produced. In short, the Navigation Acts sought to establish wide-ranging English control over colonial commerce.

The Navigation Acts were only somewhat successful in achieving their goal, as it was easy to smuggle goods into and out of the colonies. Not surprisingly, many merchants did just that. In the 1690s the British took steps to strengthen the Navigation Acts. First, they set up **vice-admiralty courts**—military-style courts, in which defendants were not entitled to a jury—to try violations of the Navigation Acts. The British considered this change necessary because most colonial juries sided with the colonists accused of smuggling, and not with the Crown. Second, the British set up **Boards of Trade** to better regulate colonial commerce. The Boards of Trade also reviewed colonial legislation, revoking laws that conflicted with British law, and administered government appointments. Because the colonists understood and accepted the concept of mercantilism, their protests to the Navigation Acts and Boards of Trade were less strenuous than their protests would later be to the Stamp Act and Townshend Acts. (See the next chapter for details on these acts.) The colonists also did not protest aggressively against the Navigation Acts at the time, because they were entirely dependent on England for trade and for military protection.

Colonial Governments

Despite trade regulations, the colonists maintained a large degree of autonomy. Every colony had a **governor** who was appointed by either the king or the proprietor. Although the governor had powers similar to the king's in England, he was also dependent on colonial **legislatures** for money. Also, the governor, whatever his official powers, was essentially stranded in the New World. His power relied on the cooperation of the colonists, and most governors ruled accordingly, only infrequently overruling the legislatures.

Except for Pennsylvania (which had a unicameral legislature with just one house), all the colonies had **bicameral** legislatures modeled after the British Parliament. The lower house functioned in much the same way as does today's House of Representatives; its members were directly elected (by white, male property holders), and its powers included the "power of the purse" (control over government salaries and tax legislation). The upper house was made up of appointees, who served as advisors to the governor and had some legislative and judicial powers. Most of these men were chosen from the local population. Most were concerned primarily with protecting the interests of colonial landowners.

The British never tried to establish a powerful central government in the colonies. The autonomy that England allowed the colonies helped ease their transition to independence in the following century.

The colonists did make some small efforts toward centralized government. **The New England Confederation** was the most prominent of these attempts. Although it had no real power, it did offer advice to the northeastern colonies when disputes arose among them. It also provided colonists from different settlements the opportunity to meet and to discuss their mutual problems.

Major Events of the Period

Bacon's Rebellion took place on Virginia's western frontier in 1676. With virtually all coastal land having been claimed, newcomers who sought to start their own farms in the region were forced west into the back country. Encroaching on land inhabited by Native Americans made frontier farmers subject to raids. In response, the western settlers sought to band together and drive the native tribes out of the region. In this effort they were stymied by the government in Jamestown, which did not want to risk a full-scale war. Class resentment grew as frontiersmen, many of whom had been indentured servants, began to suspect that eastern elites viewed them as expendable "human shields" serving as a buffer between them and the natives.

The farmers rallied behind **Nathaniel Bacon**, a recent immigrant who, despite his wealth, had arrived too late to settle on the coast. Bacon demanded that Governor **William Berkeley** grant him the authority to raise a militia and attack the nearby tribes. When Berkeley refused, Bacon and his men lashed out at the natives anyway, attacking not only the Susquehannock but also the Pamunkeys, who were actually allies of the English. The rebels then turned their attention to Jamestown, sacking and burning the city. The rebellion dissolved when Bacon suddenly died of dysentery, and the conflict between the colonists and Native Americans was averted with a new treaty, but Bacon's Rebellion is often cited as an early example of a populist uprising in America.

Bacon's Rebellion is significant for other reasons not always discussed in most textbooks. Many disgruntled former indentured servants allied themselves with free blacks who were also disenfranchised—or unable to vote. This alliance along class lines, as opposed to racial lines, frightened many southerners and led to the development of what would eventually become **black codes**. Bacon's Rebellion may also be seen as a precursor to the American Revolution. As colonists pushed westward, in search of land, but away from the commercial and political centers, they experienced a sense of alienation and desire for greater political autonomy. It is important to remember that Berkeley was the royal governor of Virginia, and the backcountry of Virginia was even further from London.

In New England, colonial expansion led to the bloodiest English–Native American conflict of the time. By the 1670s the Wampanoags living in near Narragansett Bay in Rhode Island were surrounded by white settlements, and colonists were attempting to blot out Native American life with English culture and religion. The Wampanoags were led by Metacomet (a man known to the English as King Philip; hence, **King Philip's War**), who led attacks on several settlements in retaliation for this intrusion on Wampanoag territory. Soon after, he formed an alliance with two other local tribes. The alliance destroyed a number of English settlements but eventually ran out of food and ammunition. When Metacomet died, the alliance fell apart and the colonists devastated the tribes, selling many into slavery in the West Indies. King Philip's War marks the end of a formidable Native American presence among the New England colonists.

Insurrections led by slaves did not begin until nearly 70 years later with the **Stono Uprising,** the first and one of the most successful slave rebellions. In September 1739, approximately 20 slaves met near the Stono River outside Charleston, South Carolina. They stole guns and ammunition, killed storekeepers and planters, and liberated a number of slaves. The rebels, now numbering about 100, fled to Florida, where they hoped the Spanish colonists would grant them their freedom. The colonial militia caught up with them and attacked, killing some and capturing most others. Those who were captured and returned were later executed. As a result of the Stono Uprising (sometimes called the **Cato Rebellion**), many colonies passed more restrictive laws to govern the behavior of slaves. Fear of slave rebellions increased, and New York experienced a "witch hunt" period, during which 31 blacks and four whites were executed for conspiracy to liberate slaves.

Speaking of witch hunts, the **Salem Witch Trials** took place in 1692. These were not the first witch trials in New England. During the first 70 years of English settlement in the region, 103 people (almost all women) had been tried on charges of witchcraft. Never before had so many been accused at once, however; during the summer of 1692, more than 130 "witches" were jailed or executed in Salem.

Historians have a number of explanations for why the mass hysteria started and ended so quickly. The region had recently endured the autocratic control of the

Dominion of New England, an English government attempt to clamp down on illegal trade. Massachusetts' charter had been revoked, its assemblies dissolved, and the governor who ruled for two years was granted powers usually exercised only by an absolute monarch. The Dominion of New England came to an end when the **Glorious Revolution** in England overthrew James II and replaced him with William and Mary. In 1691, Massachusetts became a royal colony under the new monarchs, and suffrage was extended to all Protestants; previously only Puritans could vote, so this move weakened Puritan primacy. War against French and Native Americans on the Canadian border (called **King William's War** in the colonies and **the War of the League of Augsburg** in England) soon followed and further heightened regional anxieties.

To top it all off, the Puritans feared that their religion—which they fervently believed was the *only* true religion—was being undermined by the growing commercialism in cities like Boston. Many second- and third-generation Puritans lacked the fervor of the original Pilgrim and Congregationalist settlers, a situation that led to the **Halfway Covenant**, which changed the rules governing Puritan baptisms. (Prior to the passage of the Halfway Covenant in 1662, a Puritan had to experience the gift of God's grace in order for his or her children to be baptized by the church. With so many, particularly men, losing interest in the church, the Puritan clergy decided to baptize all children whose parents were baptized. However—here is the "halfway" part—those who had not experienced God's grace were not allowed to vote.) All of these factors—religious, economic, and gender—historians argue, combined to create **mass hysteria in Salem in 1692**. The hysteria ended when the accusers, most of them teenage girls, accused some of the colony's most prominent citizens of consorting with the Devil, thus turning town leaders against them. Some historians also feel that the hysteria had simply run its course.

As noted above, the generations that followed the original settlers were generally less religious than those that preceded them. By 1700 women constituted the majority of active church members. However, between the 1730s and 1740s the colonies (and Europe) experienced a wave of religious revivalism known as the **Great Awakening**. Two men, Congregationalist minister **Jonathan Edwards** and Methodist preacher **George Whitefield**, came to exemplify the period. Edwards preached the severe, predeterministic doctrines of Calvinism and became famous for his graphic depictions of Hell; you may have read his speech "Sinners in the Hands of an Angry God." Whitefield preached a Christianity based on emotionalism and spirituality, which today is most clearly manifested in Southern **evangelism**. The First Great Awakening is often described as the response of devout people to the **Enlightenment**, a European intellectual movement that borrowed heavily from ancient philosophy and emphasized rationalism over emotionalism or spirituality.

Whitefield was a native of England, where the Enlightenment was in full swing; its effects were also being felt in the colonies, especially in the cities. The colonist who came to typify Enlightenment ideals in America was the self-made and self-educated man, **Ben Franklin**. Franklin was a printer's apprentice who, through his own ingenuity and hard work, became a wealthy printer and a successful and respected intellectual. His ***Poor Richard's Almanack*** was extremely popular and remains influential to this day. (It is the source of such pithy aphorisms as "A stitch in time saves nine" and "A penny saved is a penny earned.") Franklin did pioneering work in the field of electricity. He invented bifocals, the lightning rod, and the Franklin stove, and he founded the colonies' first fire department, post office, and public library. Franklin espoused Enlightenment ideals about education, government, and religion and was, until Washington came along, the colonists' favorite son. Toward the end of his life, he served as an ambassador in Europe, where he negotiated a crucial alliance with the French and, later, the peace treaty that ended the Revolutionary War.

Life in the Colonies

Perhaps the most important development in the colonies during this period was the rate of growth. The population in 1700 was 250,000; by 1750, that number was 1,250,000. Throughout these years the colonies began to develop substantial non-English European populations. Scotch-Irish, Scots, and Germans all started arriving in large numbers during the eighteenth century. English settlers, of course, continued to come to the New World as well. The black population in 1750 was more than 200,000, and in a few colonies (South Carolina, for example) they would outnumber whites by the time of the Revolution.

The vast majority of colonists—over 90 percent—lived in **rural areas**. Life for whites in the countryside was rugged but tolerable. Labor was divided along gender lines, with men doing the outdoor work such as farming, and women doing the indoor work of housekeeping and childrearing. Opportunities for social interaction outside the family were limited to shopping days and rare special community events. Both children and women were completely subordinate to men, particularly to the head of the household, in this patriarchal society. Children's education was secondary to their work schedules. Women were not allowed to vote, own property, draft a will, or testify in court.

Blacks, most of whom were slaves, lived predominantly in the countryside and in the South. Their lives varied from region to region, with conditions being most difficult in the South, where the labor was difficult and the climate less hospitable to hard work. Those slaves who worked on large plantations and developed specialized skills such as carpentry or cooking fared better than did field hands. In all cases, though, the condition of servitude was demeaning. Slaves often developed extended kinship ties and strong communal bonds to cope with the misery of servitude and the possibility that their nuclear families might be separated by sale. In the North, where black populations were relatively small, blacks often had trouble maintaining a sense of community and history.

Conditions in the **cities** were often much worse than those in the country. Because work could often be found there, most immigrants settled in the cities. The work they found generally paid too little, and poverty was widespread. Sanitary conditions were primitive, and epidemics, as of smallpox, were common. On the positive side, cities offered residents much wider contact with other people and with the outside world. Cities served as centers for progress and education.

Citizens with anything above a rudimentary level of education were rare and nearly all **colleges** established during this period served primarily to train ministers.

The lives of colonists in the various regions differed considerably. **New England** society centered on trade. Boston was the colonies' major port city. The population farmed for subsistence, not for trade, and mostly subscribed to rigid Puritanism. The **middle colonies**—New York, Pennsylvania, New Jersey—had more fertile land and so focused primarily on farming (they were also known as the "bread colonies," due to their heavy exports of grain). Philadelphia and New York City, like Boston, were major trade centers. The population of the region was more heterogeneous than was that of New England. The **lower South** (the Carolinas) concentrated on such cash crops as tobacco and rice. Slavery played a major role on plantations, although the majority of Southerners were subsistence farmers who had no slaves. Blacks constituted up to half the population of some Southern colonies. The colonies on the **Chesapeake** (Maryland and Virginia) combined features of the middle colonies and the lower South. Slavery and tobacco played a larger role in the Chesapeake than in the middle colonies, but like the middle colonies, the Chesapeake residents also farmed grain and thus diversified their economies. The development of major cities in the Chesapeake region also distinguished it from the lower South, which was almost entirely rural.

Thus, the colonies were hardly a unified whole as they approached the events that led them to rebel. How then did they join together and defeat the most powerful nation in the world? The answer to this and other exciting questions awaits you in the next chapter.

Chapter 5 Drill

See Chapter 13 for answers and explanations.

1. Which of the following statements about indentured servitude is true?

   (A) Indentured servitude was the means by which most Africans came to the New World.
   (B) Indentured servitude never attracted many people because its terms were too harsh.
   (C) Approximately half of all indentured servants died before earning their freedom.
   (D) Indenture was one of several systems used to distinguish house slaves from field slaves.
   (E) Indentured servants were prohibited from practicing religion in any form.

2. The Mayflower Compact foreshadows the U.S. Constitution in which of the following ways?

   (A) It posits the source of government power in the people rather than in God.
   (B) It ensures both the right to free speech and the separation of church and state.
   (C) It limits the term of office for all government officials.
   (D) It establishes three branches of government in order to create a system of checks and balances.
   (E) It grants equal rights to all residents regardless of race or gender.

3. The first important cash crop in the American colonies was

   (A) cotton
   (B) corn
   (C) tea
   (D) tobacco
   (E) pineapples

4. The philosophy of mercantilism holds that economic power resides primarily in

   (A) surplus manpower and control over raw materials
   (B) control of hard currency and a positive trade balance
   (C) the ability to extend and receive credit at favorable interest rates
   (D) domination of the slave trade and control of the shipping lanes
   (E) the ability to compete successfully in free markets

5. The Age of Salutary Neglect drew to a close with

   (A) the Boston Tea Party
   (B) the formation of the Republic of Texas
   (C) the Salem Witch Trials
   (D) Bacon's Rebellion
   (E) the end of the French and Indian War

6. Colonial vice-admiralty courts were created to enforce

   (A) Puritan religious edicts
   (B) prohibitions on anti-monarchist speech
   (C) import and export restrictions
   (D) travel bans imposed on Native Americans
   (E) border disputes among the colonies

7. All of the following are examples of conflicts between colonists and Native American tribes EXCEPT

   (A) Bacon's Rebellion
   (B) the Pequot War
   (C) the Stono Uprising
   (D) King Philip's War
   (E) King William's War

8. Which of the following statements about cities during the colonial era is NOT true?

   (A) Poor sanitation left colonial cities vulnerable to epidemics.
   (B) Religious and ethnic diversity was greater in colonial cities than in the colonial countryside.
   (C) Most large colonial cities grew around a port.
   (D) Cities served as the cultural centers of the American colonies.
   (E) The majority of colonists lived in urban areas.

9. Colleges and universities during the colonial period were dedicated primarily to the training of

(A) medical doctors
(B) scientists
(C) political leaders
(D) the clergy
(E) farmers

10. Which of the following is the best explanation for why the British did not establish a powerful central government in the American colonies?

(A) The British cared little how the colonists lived so long as the colonies remained a productive economic asset.
(B) Britain feared that the colonists would rebel against any substantial government force that it established.
(C) Few members of the British elite were willing to travel to the colonies, even for the opportunity to govern.
(D) Britain gave the colonies a large measure of autonomy as a first step in transitioning the region to independence.
(E) The British were philosophically opposed to the concept of a powerful central government, either at home or abroad.

REFLECT ACTIVITY

Respond to the following questions:

- For which content topics discussed in this chapter do you feel you have achieved sufficient mastery to answer multiple-choice questions correctly?

- For which content topics discussed in this chapter do you feel you have achieved sufficient mastery to discuss effectively in an essay?

- For which content topics discussed in this chapter do you feel you need more work before you can answer multiple-choice questions correctly?

- For which content topics discussed in this chapter do you feel you need more work before you can discuss effectively in an essay?

- What parts of this chapter are you going to re-review?

- Will you seek further help, outside of this book (such as a teacher, tutor, or AP Central), on any of the content in this chapter—and, if so, on what content?

Chapter 6
The Road to Independence (1750–1781)

In 1754 the colonists still considered themselves English subjects. Very few could have imagined circumstances under which they would leave the British Empire. The events that led from almost universal loyalty to rebellion are frequently tested on the AP U.S. History Exam. Here is what you need to know:

Albany Plan of Union

In 1754 representatives from seven colonies met in Albany, New York to consider the **Albany Plan of Union**, developed by Benjamin Franklin. The plan provided for an intercolonial government and a system for collecting taxes for the colonies' defense. At that meeting, Franklin also tried to negotiate a treaty with the Iroquois. Franklin's efforts to unite the colonies failed to gain the approval of a single colonial legislature. The plan was rejected because the colonists did not want to relinquish control of their right to tax themselves, nor were they prepared to unite under a single colonial legislature. Franklin's frustration was well publicized in one of the first American political cartoons—his drawing of a snake broken into pieces, under which lie the words "Join or Die."

The Seven Years' War (1754–1763)

Yes, the Seven Years' War lasted for nine years. It is also called the **French and Indian War**, which is almost equally confusing because the French and Indians fought on the same side, not against each other. The Seven Years' War was the British name for the war. The colonists called it the "French and Indian War" because that's who they were fighting. It was actually one of several "wars for empire" fought between the British and the French, and the Americans got stuck in the middle. This was arguably the first world war.

The war was the inevitable result of colonial expansion. (It was also caused by a number of inter-European power struggles, which is how Spain, Austria, Sweden, Prussia, and others got involved, but that is on the European history test, so you can worry about it some other time.) As English settlers moved into the Ohio Valley, the French tried to stop them by building fortified outposts at strategic entry spots. The French were trying to protect their profitable fur trade and their control of the region. A colonial contingent led by **George Washington** attacked a French outpost and lost badly. Washington surrendered and was allowed to return to Virginia, where he was welcomed as a hero. Other skirmishes and battles ensued, and in 1756 England officially declared war on France. Most Native Americans in the region, choosing the lesser of two evils, allied themselves with the French who had traditionally had the best relations with Native Americans of any of the European powers and whom, based on Washington's performance, they expected to win the war. The war dragged on for years before the English finally gained the upper hand. When the war was over, England was the undisputed colonial power of the continent. The treaty gave England control of Canada and almost everything east of the Mississippi Valley. The French only kept two sugar islands, underscoring the impact of mercantilism since the French prioritized two small but highly profitable islands over the large landmass of Canada.

During the Seven Years' War, many Americans served in the English army and, for the first time, came into prolonged contact with English soldiers. The English did not make a good impression, both in how they treated their own soldiers and in how the soldiers behaved themselves. These contacts sowed the first seeds of **anti-British sentiment** in the colonies, particularly in New England, where much of the fighting took place and where most of the colonial soldiers came from.

The English victory spelled trouble for Native Americans, who had previously been able to use French and English disputes to their own advantage. They negotiated their allegiances in return for land, goods, and the right to be left alone. The Native Americans particularly disliked the English, however, because English expansionism was more disruptive to their way of life. The French had sent few colonists, and many of those colonists were fur trappers who did not settle anywhere permanently. In the aftermath of the war, the English raised the price of goods sold to the Native Americans (they now had a monopoly, after all) and ceased paying rent on their western forts. In response, Ottawa war chief **Pontiac** rallied a group of tribes in the Ohio Valley and attacked colonial outposts. The attacks and resultant wars are known as **Pontiac's Rebellion** (or **Pontiac's Uprising**).

In response to the initial attacks, the British government issued the **Proclamation of 1763**, forbidding settlement west of the rivers running through the Appalachians. The proclamation came too late. Settlers had already moved west of the line. The proclamation did have one effect, however. It agitated colonial settlers, who regarded it as unwarranted British interference in colonial affairs.

Pontiac's Rebellion was, in part, a response to the colonists expanding into the Ohio River Valley and encroaching on the Native Americans' lands. (Recall similar events such as the Pequot War and Bacon's Rebellion.) The British were forced to quell this rebellion at great cost in addition to the costs of fighting the French. They used germ warfare, in the form of smallpox-infected blankets, to help defeat the Ottawa. The resulting Proclamation of 1763 is significant for a number of reasons. 1763 is often viewed as a turning point in British-colonial relations in that it marks the end of salutary neglect. The Proclamation of 1763 may be viewed as the first in a new series of restrictions imposed on the colonists by the British Parliament, and in that way, it marks the first step on the "road to revolution." Furthermore, it established a pattern of demarcating "Indian Territory," a pattern that would be adopted and pursued by the United States government long after the colonists gained their independence. (See for example the **Indian Removal Act,** 1830.)

The Sugar Act, the Currency Act, and the Stamp Act

One result of the Seven Years' War was that in financing the war the British government had run up a huge debt. The new king, **George III**, and his prime minister, **George Grenville**, felt that the colonists should help pay that debt. After all, they reasoned, the colonies had been beneficiaries of the war; furthermore, their tax burden was relatively light compared to that of taxpayers in England, even on the same goods. Meanwhile, the colonists felt that they had provided so many soldiers that they had fulfilled their obligation.

Accordingly, Parliament imposed new regulations and taxes on the colonists. The first was the **Sugar Act** of 1764, which established a number of new duties and which also contained provisions aimed at deterring molasses smugglers. Although Parliament had previously passed other acts aimed at controlling colonial trade and manufacturing, there was little colonial resistance prior to the decade leading up to the Revolutionary War. There were benefits to being part of the vast British Empire and most Americans accepted regulations of trade such as the **Navigation Acts** as part of **mercantilism**. Furthermore, although laws such as the Molasses Act of 1733 were on the books, smuggling was common practice and little revenue from taxes was actually collected. Some historians have gone so far as to suggest that Parliament never intended the Molasses Act to raise revenue, but merely to function as a protective tariff aimed against French imports. Parliament was quite shrewd in passing the Sugar Act of 1764 in that this new act actually *lowered* the duty on molasses coming into the colonies from the West Indies. What angered the colonists the most was that this new regulation was to be more strictly enforced: duties were to be collected. It became more difficult for colonial shippers to avoid committing even minor violations of the Sugar Act. Furthermore, violators were to be arrested and tried in vice-admiralty courts, courts where a single judge issued a verdict without the deliberation of a jury. It was this last provision of the Sugar Act that suggested to some colonists that Parliament was overstepping its authority and violating their rights as Englishmen.

Another Parliamentary act, the **Currency Act**, forbade the colonies to issue paper money. Collectively, the Sugar Act, Currency Act, and Proclamation of 1763 caused a great deal of discontent in the colonies, whose residents bristled at what they correctly viewed as British attempts to exert greater control. These acts signaled a clear end to Britain's long-standing policy of salutary neglect. That these acts came during a postwar economic depression further aggravated the situation. Colonial protest to these acts, however, was uncoordinated and ineffective.

That all changed when Parliament passed the **Stamp Act** the following year, 1765. The Stamp Act included a number of provocative elements. First, it was a tax specifically aimed at raising revenue, thus awakening the colonists to the likelihood that even more taxes could follow. The Stamp Act demonstrated that the colonies' tradition of self-taxation was surely being unjustly taken by Parliament, much to the dismay of many colonists. Second, it was a broad-based tax, covering all legal documents and licenses. Not only did it affect almost everyone, but it particularly affected a group that was literate, persuasive, and argumentative—namely, lawyers. Third, it was a tax on goods produced within the colonies.

Reaction to the Stamp Act built on previous grievances, and consequently was more forceful than any protest preceding it. A pamphlet by James Otis, called *The Rights of the British Colonies Asserted and Proved*, laid out the colonists' argument against the taxes and became a bestseller of its day. Otis put forward the "No taxation without representation" argument that later became a rallying cry of the Revolution. Because the colonists did not elect members to Parliament, he argued, they were not obliged to pay taxes (following the accepted precept that no Englishman could be compelled to pay taxes without his consent). Otis did *not* advocate secession; rather, he argued for either representation in Parliament or a greater degree of self-government for the colonies. Neither the British nor the colonists had much interest in creating a colonial delegation to Parliament. The British scoffed at the notion, arguing that the colonists were already represented in Parliament. Their argument was rooted in the theory of **virtual representation**, which stated that members of Parliament represented all British subjects regardless of who elected them. The colonists, for their part, knew that their representation would be too small to protect their interests and so never pushed the issue. What they wanted, and what the British were refusing to give them, was the right to determine their own taxes.

Opponents of the Stamp Act united in the various colonies. In Virginia, Patrick Henry drafted the Virginia Stamp Act Resolves, protesting the tax and asserting the colonists' right to a large measure of self-government. (The Virginia legislature removed Henry's most radical propositions before passing the resolves.) In Boston, mobs burned the customs officers in effigy, tore down a customs house, and nearly destroyed the governor's mansion. Protest groups formed throughout the colonies, calling themselves **"Sons of Liberty."** The opposition was so effective that, by the time the law was supposed to take effect, not one of the Crown's appointed duty collectors was willing to perform his job. In 1766 Parliament repealed the Stamp Act. Just as important, George III replaced Prime Minister Grenville, whom the colonists now loathed, with Lord Rockingham, who had opposed the Stamp Act. Rockingham oversaw the repeal but also linked it to the passage of the **Declaratory Act**, which asserted the British government's right to tax and legislate in all cases anywhere in the colonies. Thus, although the colonists had won the battle over the stamp tax, they had not yet gained any ground in the war of principles over Parliament's powers in the colonies.

The Townshend Acts

Rockingham remained prime minister for only two years. His replacement was William Pitt. Pitt, however, was ill, and the dominant figure in colonial affairs came to be the minister of the exchequer, Charles Townshend. Townshend drafted the eponymous **Townshend Acts**. The Townshend Acts, like the Stamp Act, contained several antagonistic measures. First, they taxed goods imported directly from Britain—the first such tax in the colonies. Mercantilism approved of duties on imports from other European nations but not on British imports. Second, some of the tax collected was set aside for the payment of tax collectors, meaning that colonial assemblies could no longer withhold government officials' wages in order to get their way. Third, the Townshend Acts created even more vice-admiralty courts and several new government offices to enforce the Crown's will in the colonies. Fourth, they suspended the New York legislature because it had refused to comply with a law requiring the colonists to supply British troops.

Last, these acts instituted *writs of assistance*, licenses that gave the British the power to search any place they suspected of hiding smuggled goods.

The colonists got better at protesting with each new tax, and their reaction to the Townshend Acts was their strongest yet. The Massachusetts Assembly sent a letter (called the **Massachusetts Circular Letter**, written by Samuel Adams in 1768) to all other assemblies asking that they protest the new measures in unison. The British fanned the flames of protest by ordering the assemblies *not* to discuss the Massachusetts letter, virtually guaranteeing it to be all anyone *would* talk about. Governors of colonies where legislatures discussed the letter dissolved those legislatures, which, of course, further infuriated colonists. The colonists held numerous rallies and organized boycotts, and for the first time sought the support of "commoners" (previously such protests were confined largely to the aristocratic classes), making their rallies larger and much more intimidating. The boycotts were most successful because they affected British merchants, who then joined the protest. Colonial women were essential in the effort to replace British imports with "American" (New England) products. After two years, Parliament repealed the Townshend duties, although not the other statutes of the Townshend Acts, and not the duty on tea.

The Quartering Act of 1765 stationed large numbers of troops in America and made the colonists responsible for the cost of feeding and housing them. Even after the Townsend duties were repealed, the soldiers remained—particularly in Boston. Officially sent to keep the peace, these soldiers in fact heightened tensions. For one thing, the detachment was huge—4,000 men in a city of only 16,000. To make matters worse, the soldiers sought off-hour employment and so competed with colonists for jobs. Numerous confrontations resulted, with the most famous on March 5, 1770, when a mob pelted a group of soldiers with rock-filled snowballs. The soldiers fired on the crowd, killing five; hence, the **Boston Massacre**. The propaganda campaign that followed suggested that the soldiers had shot into a crowd of innocent bystanders. Interestingly, John Adams defended the soldiers in court, helping to establish a tradition of giving a fair trial to all who are accused.

Non-consumption and Non-importation

There were no police departments in colonial America. Communities were self-policing. If a man was beating his wife, groups of neighbors would gather and threaten him with dire consequences if he didn't stop. Patriot leaders leveraged this practice in organizing resistance to the Townshend and other duties. The colonists' only recourses were **non-consumption** and **non-importation**—in other words, to boycott British goods—but such a policy could only be effective if everyone participated. So it was that New England newspapers printed pleas to women in particular, who generally managed the family budget, not to buy British linen and tea, and exposed importers, such as one William Jackson who ran a shop called the Brazen Head. If these methods proved ineffective, then, yes, Patriot leaders would deploy thugs to get the point across. A few painful and humiliating tar-and-featherings went a long way, and imports from Britain dropped 40 percent by 1770.

The Calm, and Then the Storm

Oddly enough, for the next two years, nothing major happened. The Boston Massacre shocked both sides into de-escalating their rhetoric, and an uneasy status quo fell into place during this period. Colonial newspapers discussed ways in which the relationship between the mother country and the colonies might be altered so as to satisfy both sides, but still, nobody except a very few radicals suggested independence.

Things picked up in 1772 when the British implemented the part of the Townshend Acts that provided for colonial administrators to be paid from customs revenues (and not by the colonial legislatures). The colonists responded cautiously, setting up groups called **Committees of Correspondence** throughout the colonies to trade ideas and inform one another of the political mood. The committees also worked to convince more citizens to take an active interest in the conflict.

Not long after, the British granted the foundering East India Tea Company a monopoly on the tea trade in the colonies as well as a portion of new duties to be collected on tea sales. The result was cheaper tea for the colonists, but the colonists saw a more important issue: Parliament was once again imposing new taxes on them. In Boston, the colonists refused to allow the ships to unload their cargo, and the governor refused to allow them to leave the harbor. On December 16, 1773, a group of Sons of Liberty, poorly disguised as Mohawks, boarded a ship and dumped its cargo into Boston Harbor. It took them three hours to jettison the approximately £10,000 worth of tea. The incident is known as the **Boston Tea Party.**

The English responded with a number of punitive measures, known collectively as the **Coercive Acts** (also called the "**Intolerable Acts**"). One measure closed Boston Harbor to all but essential trade (food and firewood) and declared that it would remain closed until the tea was paid for. Several measures tightened English control over the Massachusetts government and its courts, and a new, stricter Quartering Act put British soldiers in civilian homes. The Coercive Acts convinced many colonists that their days of semi-autonomy were over and that the future held even further encroachments on their liberties by the Crown. To make matters worse, at the same time Parliament passed the Coercive Acts, it also passed the **Quebec Act**, which, to the colonists' chagrin, (1) granted greater liberties to Catholics, whom the Protestant colonial majority distrusted, and (2) extended the boundaries of the Quebec Territory, thus further impeding westward expansion.

The colonists met to discuss their grievances. All colonies except Georgia sent delegates to the **First Continental Congress,** which convened in late 1774. All perspectives were represented—Pennsylvania's delegation included conservatives such as Joseph Galloway, while Virginia sent two radicals, Richard Henry Lee and **Patrick Henry.** The goals of the meeting were to enumerate American grievances, to develop a strategy for addressing those grievances, and to formulate a colonial position on the proper relationship between the royal government and the colonial governments. The Congress came up with a list of those laws the colonists wanted repealed and agreed to impose a boycott on British goods until their grievances were redressed. The delegates also agreed to form a **Continental Association**, with towns setting up committees of observation to enforce the boycott; in time these committees became their towns' de facto governments. Perhaps most important, the Congress formulated a limited set of parameters within which it considered Parliamentary interference in colonial affairs justified; all other spheres, the delegates agreed, should be left to the colonists themselves. This position represented a major break with British tradition and, accordingly, a major step toward independence.

Throughout the winter of 1774 and the spring of 1775, the committees of observation expanded their powers. In many colonies they supplanted the British-sanctioned assemblies. They led acts of insubordination by collecting taxes, disrupting court sessions, and, most ominously, organizing militias and stockpiling weapons. As John Adams would later comment about the period: "The Revolution was effected before the war commenced. The Revolution was in the minds and hearts of the people.... This radical change in the principles, opinions, sentiments, and affections of the people was the real American Revolution."

The Shot Heard 'Round the World

The British underestimated the strength of the growing pro-revolutionary movement. Government officials mistakenly believed that if they arrested the ringleaders and confiscated their arsenals, violence could be averted. To that end, the English dispatched troops to confiscate weapons in Concord, Massachusetts in April 1775. The troops had to first pass through Lexington, where they confronted a small colonial militia, called "**minutemen**" because they reputedly could be ready to fight on a minute's notice. Someone, probably one of the minutemen, fired a shot, which drew British return fire. When the **Battle of Lexington** was over, the minutemen had suffered eighteen casualties, including eight dead. The British proceeded to **Concord**, where a much larger contingent of minutemen awaited them. The Massachusetts militia inflicted numerous casualties on the British "**redcoats**" and forced them to retreat. That a contingent of colonial farmers could repel the army of the world's largest empire was monumental, which is why the **Battle of Concord** is sometimes referred to as "the shot heard 'round the world." The two opponents dug in around Boston, but during the next year only one major battle was fought. The two sides regrouped and planned their next moves.

For the colonists, the period provided time to rally citizens to the cause of independence. Not all were convinced. Among those remaining loyal to the Crown—such people were called "**Loyalists**"—were government officials, devout Anglicans (members of the Church of England), merchants dependent on trade with England, and many religious and ethnic minorities who feared persecution at the hands of the rebels. Many slaves believed their chances for liberty were better with the British than with the colonists, a belief strengthened when the royal governor of Virginia offered to free those slaves who escaped and joined the British army. The pre-Revolutionary War era saw an increase in the number of slave insurrections, dampening some Southerners' enthusiasm for revolution. The **patriots** were mostly white Protestant property holders and gentry, as well as urban artisans, especially in New England, where Puritans had long shown antagonism toward Anglicans. Much of the rest of the population just hoped the whole thing would blow over. The Quakers of Pennsylvania, for example, were pacifists and so wanted to avoid war.

The **Second Continental Congress** convened during this period, just weeks after the battles of Lexington and Concord. Throughout the summer, the Congress prepared for war by establishing a **Continental Army**, printing money, and creating government offices to supervise policy. The Congress chose **George Washington** to lead the army because he was both well-liked and a Southerner (thus bolstering support in an area with many loyalists). There is a lot of interesting military history about Washington's command, but because the AP ignores military history, so too does this review.

Big Man on Campus
Washington's future vice president, John Adams, once griped that "Washington was always selected by deliberative bodies to lead, whatever the cause, because he was always the tallest man in the room."

Not all delegates thought that war was inevitable, and many followed John Dickinson, who was pushing for reconciliation with Britain using the **Olive Branch Petition**. Adopted by the Continental Congress on July 5, 1775 following the skirmish at Breed's Hill, often known as Bunker Hill, the Olive Branch petition was a last-ditch attempt to avoid armed conflict. King George III, however, was hardly interested in the proposal since he considered the colonists to be in open rebellion given their boycotts, attacks on royal officials, and resistance at Lexington and Concord. Still, it is worth noting that just one year before the adoption of the Declaration of Independence, the colonial leaders were trying to reconcile with the mother country.

The Declaration of Independence

The rebels were still looking for the masterpiece of propaganda that would rally colonists to their cause. They got it in ***Common Sense***, a pamphlet published in January of 1776 by an English printer named **Thomas Paine**. Paine not only advocated colonial independence, he also argued for the merits of republicanism over monarchy. The pamphlet was an even bigger success than James Otis's *The Rights of the British Colonies Asserted and Proved*. Though literacy rates in New England were somewhat higher, thanks to the Puritan legacy of teaching children to read the Bible, most of the nation's two million inhabitants could not read. Nevertheless, Paine's pamphlet sold more than 100,000 copies in its first three months alone, the proportional equivalent of selling 13 million downloads today. The secret to Paine's success was that *Common Sense* stated the argument for independence in plainspoken language accessible to colonists who couldn't always keep up with the lofty Enlightenment-speak of the Founding Fathers. It helped swing considerable support to the patriot cause among people who had worried about the wisdom of attacking the powerful mother country.

In June, the Congress was looking for a rousing statement of its ideals, and it commissioned **Thomas Jefferson** to write the **Declaration of Independence.** He did not let them down. The Declaration not only enumerates the colonies' grievances against the Crown, but it also articulates the principle of individual liberty and the government's fundamental responsibility to serve the people. Despite its obvious flaws—most especially that it pertained only to white, propertied men—it remains a work of enormous power. With the document's signing on July 4, 1776, the Revolutionary War became a war for independence.

Chronology of Events Leading to Revolutionary War	
1763	–French and Indian War ends –Pontiac's Rebellion –Proclamation of 1763
1764	–Sugar Act –Currency Act
1765	–Stamp Act –Stamp Act crisis –Sons of Liberty formed
1766	–Grenville replaced by Rockingham as prime minister –Stamp Act repealed –Declaratory Act
1767	–Townshend Acts
1770	–Townshend duties repealed (except tea tax) –Boston Massacre
1772	–parts of Townshend Acts implemented –Committees of Correspondence formed
1773	–British give the Dutch East India Tea Company monopoly on tea in colonies –Boston Tea Party
1774	–Coercive ("Intolerable") Acts –Quebec Act –First Continental Congress meets –Continental Association forms
1775	–Battles of Lexington and Concord –Second Continental Congress meets
1776	–Declaration of Independence

After several years of fighting, the British surrendered at Yorktown in October of 1781. You should remember a few other facts about the war. The Continental Army (as opposed to local militias) had trouble recruiting good soldiers. Eventually, the Congress recruited blacks, and up to 5,000 fought on the side of the rebels (in return, most of those who had been slaves were granted their freedom). The **Franco-American Alliance**, negotiated by **Ben Franklin** in 1778, brought the French into the war on the side of the colonists, after the battle of Saratoga. This was hardly surprising given the lingering resentment of the French toward the English after the French and Indian War. It would be three years before French troops landed in America, but the alliance buoyed American morale, and with the help of militia units, especially in the South, the colonists kept up a war of attrition until support could arrive from France. By then, much like the United States in Vietnam almost two centuries later, the British found themselves outlasted and forced to abandon an unpopular war on foreign soil. The **Treaty of Paris**, signed at the end of 1783, granted the United States independence and generous territorial rights. (This Treaty of Paris is not to be confused with the Treaty of Paris that ended the French and Indian War or the Treaty of Paris that ended the Spanish-American War in 1898. Paris was all the rage as a treaty name, apparently.)

Neither the Declaration of Independence, with its bold statement that "all men are created equal," nor the revolution with its republican ideology, abolished slavery. These events also did not bring about a more egalitarian society. Like blacks, many women played a significant role in the Revolutionary War, either as "camp followers" or by maintaining households and businesses while the men were off fighting the Revolution. It would take another war to end slavery (the Civil War) and centuries of hard work toward progress to help bring about greater political and economic equality for women.

George Washington vs. Volunteer Militias

George Washington was one of the wealthiest men in America, and to a great extent his involvement with the independence movement grew out of his dissatisfaction with the mercantile system, which he felt was keeping him from expanding his fortune as much as he might have liked. The tobacco he sent to Britain never fetched the price he wanted, and the goods he received in return were too expensive and of shoddy quality. He wanted relief from British taxes and the freedom to sell to and buy from whomever he liked. The American Revolution was fueled in large part by libertarian sentiments such as these.

But after becoming commander of the Continental Army, Washington found that libertarian ideals sound terrific when you're a rich planter trying to fill your coffers, but don't work so well when you're trying to build a country or win a war. Washington pressed for a professional standing army, and demanded that the states raise money to pay the troops, but the libertarian-dominated Continental Congress replied that those ideas were precisely what they were fighting against, and that Washington would have to make do with volunteers who paid their own way.

Chapter 6 Drill

See Chapter 13 for answers and explanations.

1. The Albany Plan of Union failed because

   (A) the plan required the Northeastern colonies to contribute a disproportionate share of the necessary troops and money
   (B) no political leader with national stature was willing to support the plan
   (C) there was no legitimate executive power to enforce it
   (D) none of the colonies was willing to share tax-collecting powers with a national entity
   (E) the Nation of Iroquois campaigned aggressively against it

2. The American colonists objected to the policies imposed by Parliament after the French and Indian War for all of the following reasons EXCEPT

   (A) the new restrictions would hinder New England trade
   (B) their rights as Englishmen were being violated
   (C) they resented quartering British troops now that the French threat was removed
   (D) they believed they should be represented in Parliament if they were subjected to mercantilist restrictions
   (E) they believed that only their colonial assemblies had the power to tax them, not the British Parliament

3. According to the theory of virtual representation,

   (A) colonists were represented in Parliament by virtue of their British citizenship
   (B) slaves were represented in Congress by virtue of the fact that their owners were voters
   (C) paper money has value by virtue of the fact that it is backed by the full faith and credit of the government
   (D) the best interests of criminal defendants are represented by their attorneys
   (E) it should be illegal to desecrate the flag because the flag represents the nation and its ideals

4. The Stamp Act Congress of 1765 was historically significant in that it

   (A) represented a first step in colonial unity against Britain
   (B) demonstrated Parliament's determination to tax its American colonies
   (C) represented New England's determination to go to war against England
   (D) demonstrated the colonists' political and philosophical disagreement among themselves
   (E) threatened England's mercantilist policies

5. Thomas Jefferson relied on the ideas of John Locke in writing the American Declaration of Independence in all of the following ways EXCEPT Locke's belief that

   (A) man is born free and equal
   (B) man must submit to the General Will to protect his natural rights
   (C) governments get their authority from the people, not God
   (D) the purpose of government is to protect man's natural rights
   (E) people can overthrow a government that violates man's natural rights

REFLECT ACTIVITY

Respond to the following questions:

- For which content topics discussed in this chapter do you feel you have achieved sufficient mastery to answer multiple-choice questions correctly?

- For which content topics discussed in this chapter do you feel you have achieved sufficient mastery to discuss effectively in an essay?

- For which content topics discussed in this chapter do you feel you need more work before you can answer multiple-choice questions correctly?

- For which content topics discussed in this chapter do you feel you need more work before you can discuss effectively in an essay?

- What parts of this chapter are you going to re-review?

- Will you seek further help, outside of this book (such as a teacher, tutor, or AP Central), on any of the content in this chapter—and, if so, on what content?

Chapter 7
Creating a Functioning Government (1777–1824)

The Articles of Confederation

The colonies did not wait to win their independence from England before setting up their own governments. As soon as the Declaration of Independence was signed, states began writing their own constitutions. In 1777 the Continental Congress sent the **Articles of Confederation**, the first national constitution, to the colonies for ratification. The colonists intentionally created little to no central government since they were afraid of ridding themselves of Britain's imperial rule only to create their own tyrannical government. The articles contained several major limitations, as the country would soon learn. For one, it did not give the national government the power to tax or to regulate trade. Furthermore, amendments to the articles required the unanimous consent of all the states, creating a situation in which one state could hold the others hostage to its demands. The Articles of Confederation were clearly more concerned with prohibiting the government from gaining too much power than with empowering it to function effectively.

With the end of the war, the colonies had other issues to confront as well. The decrease in England's power in the region opened a new era of relations with Native Americans. This new era was even more contentious than the previous one because a number of tribes had allied themselves with the Crown. Second-class citizens and noncitizens—namely, women and blacks—had made sacrifices in the fight for liberation, and some expected at least a degree of compensation. **Abigail Adams** wrote a famous letter to her husband pleading the case for women's rights in the new government; she reminded John to "remember the ladies and be more generous and favorable to them than your ancestors." The number of free blacks in the colonies grew during and after the war, but their increased presence among free whites was also accompanied by a growth of racist publications and legislation. Such conditions led to the early "ghettoization" of blacks and, for similar reasons, other minorities.

Translate the answer choice:
(E) imposed high duties on foreign goods
Translation: *made it more expensive to buy stuff from other countries*

The problems with the Articles of Confederation became apparent early on. The wartime government, unable to levy taxes, tried to finance the war by printing more money, which led, naturally, to wild inflation. After the war, the British pursued punitive trade policies against the colonies, denying them access to West Indian markets and dumping goods on American markets. The government, unable to impose tariffs, was helpless. A protective tariff would impose duties on imported goods; the additional cost would be added to the selling price, thereby raising the cost of foreign products. By making domestic products cheaper than imports, most tariffs protected American manufacturers. Having just fought a war in part caused by taxes imposed by a central authority, the newly independent Americans were reluctant to give this power to their new federal government. In fact, the first protective tariff in United States history wasn't passed until 1816. The issue of the tariff exposed another source of tension within the new country—economic sectionalism—a major conflict that eventually led the new nation to civil war and continues to play a role in partisan politics to this very day.

Furthermore, when state governments dragged their heels in compensating loyalists for lost property, the British refused to abandon military posts in the States, claiming that they were remaining to protect the loyalists' rights. The government, again, was powerless to expel them. Perhaps the rudest awakening came in the form of **Shays's Rebellion**. Lasting from August 1786 to January 1787, it started when an army of 1,500 farmers from western Massachusetts marched on Springfield to protest a number of unfair policies, both economic and political. They were armed and very angry, and they gave the elite class the wake-up call that the revolution might not be over yet. As with the earlier **Bacon's Rebellion** and later **Whiskey Rebellion**, this rebellion revealed lingering resentment on the part of the backcountry farmers toward the coastal elite—and such rebellions were the focus of an FRQ in 2007. One thing that especially worried the wealthy, though, was that the Articles of Confederation had created a national government that was essentially powerless to stop such rebellions.

The government under the Articles was not totally without its successes, though. Its greatest achievements were the adoption of ordinances governing the sale of government land to settlers. Best known is the **Northwest Ordinance of 1787**, which also contained a bill of rights guaranteeing trial by jury, freedom of religion, and freedom from excessive punishment. It abolished slavery in the Northwest territories (northwest of the Ohio River and east of the Mississippi River, up to the Canadian border), and also set specific regulations concerning the conditions under which territories could apply for statehood. Thus, the ordinance is seen as a forerunner to the Bill of Rights and other progressive government policies. It was not so enlightened about Native Americans, however; in fact, it essentially claimed their land without their consent. War ensued, and peace did not come until 1795 when the United States gained a military advantage over the Miami Confederacy, its chief Native-American opponent in the area. The Northwest Ordinance remained important long after the Northwest territories were settled, because of its pertinence to the statehood process and to the issue of slavery.

A New Constitution

By 1787 it was clear that the federal government lacked sufficient authority under the Articles of Confederation. **Alexander Hamilton** was especially concerned that there was no uniform commercial policy and feared for the survival of the new republic. Hamilton convened what came to be known as the **Annapolis Convention**, but only five delegates showed up! Subsequently, Congress consented to a "meeting in Philadelphia" the following May for the sole purpose of "revising the Articles of Confederation." This meeting would eventually become the now-famous Constitutional Convention, comprising delegates from all states except Rhode Island, which met throughout the long, hot summer of 1787.

Much has been written about the framers of the Constitution. There were fifty-five delegates: all men, all white, many of whom were wealthy lawyers or landowners, many of whom owned slaves. They came from many different ideological backgrounds, from those who felt the Articles needed only slight adjustments to those who wanted to tear them down and start from scratch. **The New Jersey Plan** called for modifications, and it also called for equal representation from each state. **The Virginia Plan**, largely the brainchild of James Madison, called for an entirely new government based on the principle of **checks and balances** and for the number of representatives for each state to be based upon the population of the state, giving some states an advantage.

The convention lasted for four months, over the course of which the delegates hammered out a bundle of compromises, including the **Great Compromise** (also known as the **Connecticut Compromise**), which blended the Virginia Plan and the New Jersey plan to have a bicameral legislature, and the **Constitution**. This bicameral legislature included a lower house (the House of Representatives) elected by the people and the upper house (the Senate) elected by the state legislatures. (Direct election of senators, believe it or not, is a twentieth-century innovation.) The president and vice president were to be elected by the electoral college, not the citizens themselves.

The Constitution also laid out a method for counting slaves among the populations of Southern states for "proportional" representation in Congress, even though those slaves would not be citizens. This became known as the Three-Fifths Compromise, because each slave counted as three-fifths of a person. It also established three branches of government—the **executive**, **legislative**, and **judicial**—with the power of checks and balances on each other. Only three of the 42 delegates who remained in Philadelphia to the end refused to sign the finished document (two because it did not include a bill of rights).

Ratification of the Constitution was by no means guaranteed. Opposition forces portrayed the federal government under the Constitution as an all-powerful beast. These opponents, known as **Anti-Federalists**, tended to come from the backcountry and were particularly appalled by the absence of a bill of rights. Their position rang true in many of the state legislatures where the Constitution's fate lay, and some held out for the promise of the immediate addition of the **Bill of Rights** upon ratification. The **Federalist** position was forcefully and persuasively argued in **the Federalist Papers**, anonymously authored by **James Madison**, **Alexander Hamilton**, and **John Jay**. The Federalist Papers were published in a New York newspaper and were later widely circulated. They were critical in swaying opinion in New York, a large and therefore politically important state. (Virginia, Pennsylvania, and Massachusetts were the other powerhouses of the era.) The **Constitution** went into effect in 1789; the **Bill of Rights** was added in 1791.

The Bill of Rights in a Nutshell

1. Freedom of religion, speech, press, assembly, and petition

2. Right to bear arms in order to maintain a well-regulated militia

3. No quartering of soldiers in private homes

4. Freedom from unreasonable search and seizure

5. Right to due process of law, freedom from self-incrimination, double jeopardy (being tried twice for the same crime)

6. Rights of accused persons; for example, the right to a speedy and public trial

7. Right of trial by jury in civil cases

8. Freedom from excessive bail and from cruel and unusual punishment

9. Rights not listed are kept by the people

10. Powers not listed are kept by the states or the people

The Washington Presidency

The electoral college unanimously chose **George Washington** to be the first president. Washington had not sought the presidency, but as the most popular figure in the colonies, he was the clear choice, and he accepted the role out of a sense of obligation.

Knowing that his actions would set precedents for those who followed him in office, Washington exercised his authority with care and restraint. He determined early on to use his veto only if he was convinced that a bill was unconstitutional. He was comfortable delegating responsibility and so created a government made up of the best minds of his time. Although the Constitution does not specifically grant the president the duty or even the power to create a cabinet, every president since George Washington has had one. The cabinet is made up of the heads of the various executive departments, which have grown in number over the years, and it functions as the president's chief group of advisors.

Prominent among his cabinet selections were **Thomas Jefferson** as secretary of state and **Alexander Hamilton** as secretary of the treasury. These two men strongly disagreed about the proper relationship between the federal government and state governments. Hamilton favored a strong central government and weaker state governments. Jefferson, fearing the country would backslide into monarchy, or tyranny, favored a weaker federal government empowered mainly to defend the country and regulate international commerce. All other powers, he thought, should be reserved to the states.

Their argument was not a mere intellectual exercise. The new government was still defining itself, and each man had a vision of what this nation was to become. The debate came to the forefront when Hamilton proposed a **National Bank** to help regulate and strengthen the economy. Both houses of Congress approved Hamilton's plan, but Washington, uncertain of the bank's constitutionality, considered a veto. In the debate that followed, the two main schools of thought on constitutional law were established. On one side were the **strict constructionists**, led by Jefferson and **James Madison**. They argued that the Constitution allowed Congress only those powers specifically granted to it or those "necessary and proper" to the execution of its **enumerated powers**. While a bank might be "desirable" and perhaps beneficial, they argued, it was not "necessary," and thus its creation was beyond the powers of the national government. Hamilton took the opposing viewpoint, framing the **broad (loose) constructionist** position. He argued that the creation of a bank was an **implied power** of the government because the government already had explicit power to coin money, borrow money, and collect taxes. Hamilton put forward that the government could do anything in the execution of those enumerated powers—including create a bank—that was not explicitly forbidden it by the Constitution. Washington agreed with Hamilton and signed the bill.

Hamilton's tenure at treasury was a busy and successful one. Among his achievements was his successful handling of the **national debt** accrued during the war. Hamilton's financial plan called for the federal government to assume the states' debts (further increasing the federal government's power over them) and to repay those debts by giving the debt holders land on the western frontier. The plan

One often hears grumbling about the national debt, but Hamilton considered the creation of a sizable national debt a very good thing. The government regularly borrows money by various means, such as offering bonds for sale, and the national debt is simply the amount the government owes on those loans. Hamilton's logic was that if the government racked up a national debt—that is, if it owed money to its wealthiest citizens—then those citizens would be invested in the success of the government, for only if the government survived could they hope to be paid back.

clearly favored Northern banks, many of which had bought up debt certificates at a small portion of their worth. Northern states also had more remaining debt than Southern states, another reason why the plan drew accusations that Hamilton was helping the monied elite at the expense of the working classes. (Some issues are perennials of American politics; this is one of them. Opposition to tax increases is another.) Hamilton was able to strike a political deal to get most of his plan implemented. His concession was a Southern location for the nation's capital. In 1800, the capital was moved to **Washington, D.C.,** a city created to become the seat of government.

The **French Revolution** took place during the Washington administration, and it too caused considerable debate. Jefferson wanted to support the revolution and its republican ideals. Hamilton had aristocratic leanings and so disliked the revolutionaries, who had overthrown the French aristocracy. The issue came to the forefront when France and England resumed hostilities. The British continued to be America's primary trading partner after the war, a situation that nudged the United States toward neutrality in the French–English conflict. Even Jefferson agreed that neutrality was the correct course to follow. When French government representative **Citizen Edmond Genêt** visited America to seek its assistance, Washington declared the U.S. intention to remain "friendly and impartial toward belligerent powers." This was called the **Neutrality Proclamation**. Genêt's visit sparked large, enthusiastic rallies held by American supporters of the revolution.

Historians cite the differences between Hamilton and Jefferson as the origins of our two-party system. Those favoring a strong federal government came to be known as **Federalists** (not to be confused with the Federalists who supported ratification of the Constitution, even though they were often the same people), while the followers of Jefferson called themselves the Republicans, later known as **Democratic-Republicans** to avoid confusion with members of the Republican Party created in the 1850s, a very different group which still survives today. The development of political parties troubled the framers of the Constitution, most of whom regarded parties as factions and dangerous to the survival of the Republic.

Our First Party System		
	Federalists	Democratic-Republicans
Leaders	Hamilton, Washington, Adams, Jay, Marshall	Jefferson, Madison
Vision	Economy based on commerce	Economy based on agriculture
Governmental Power	Strong federal government	Stronger state governments
Supporters	Wealthy, Northeast	Yeoman farmers, Southerners
Constitution	Loose construction	Strict construction
National Bank	Believed it was "necessary"	Believed it was merely "desirable"
Foreign Affairs	More sympathetic toward Great Britain	More sympathetic toward France

Note: The Federalist party would die out after the **Hartford Convention**, following the War of 1812. Hamilton's vision and programs would be carried out by the nationalist program and **Henry Clay's American System** during the **Era of Good Feelings**. The **Second Party System** would emerge during the presidency of **Andrew Jackson** and would consist of the **Whigs**, who embraced many Federalist principles and policies, and the **Jacksonian Democrats**, who saw themselves as the heirs of the Jeffersonian Republicans.

Hamilton's financial program not only stirred controversy in Congress and helped to create our two-party system but also instigated the **Whiskey Rebellion,** which began in western Pennsylvania when farmers resisted an excise tax on whiskey. As part of his financial program, Hamilton imposed the tax in an attempt to raise revenue to defray the debt incurred by the Revolution. Washington, determined not to let his new government tolerate armed disobedience, dispatched the militia to disperse the rebels. After the opposition was dispelled, the rebels went home, and although there were some arrests and two convictions, Washington eventually pardoned both men. The Whiskey Rebellion is significant because, like Bacon's Rebellion and Shays's Rebellion before it, the uprising demonstrated the lasting class tensions between inland farmers and the coastal elites who ran the new government. But while Shays's Rebellion demonstrated that the national government of the time had lacked the power to respond, Americans noted that the new government had power it wasn't afraid to use. Some saw fairness in Washington's actions; others saw the makings of tyranny. James Madison, among others, would retreat from his support of the Federalists to back Jefferson's camp of Democratic-Republicans.

During his second term, Washington sent John Jay to England to negotiate a treaty concerning the evacuation of the British from the Northwest Territory, as stipulated in the Treaty of Paris that concluded the Revolutionary War, as well as to discuss British violations of free trade. Although Jay's Treaty prevented war with Great Britain, opponents of the treaty believed Jay made too many concessions toward the British, who in essence were not respecting our rights as a sovereign nation (the treaty also involved paying some war debts). Jay's Treaty is often considered to be the low point of Washington's administration, and Jay himself was burned in effigy in the streets of New York.

At the same time, Washington sent Thomas Pinckney to Spain to negotiate use of the Mississippi River, duty-free access to world markets, and the removal of any remaining Spanish forts on American soil. During this mission, Pinckney was able to extract a promise from Spain to try and prevent attacks on Western settlers from Native Americans. The **Treaty of San Lorenzo**, also known as **Pinckney's Treaty**, was ratified by the U.S. Senate in 1796 and is often considered to be the high point of Washington's administration. The next year, however, Congress attempted to withhold funding to enforce the treaty. The House of Representatives asked Washington to submit all documents pertinent to the treaty for consideration. Washington refused, establishing the precedent of **executive privilege** (the right of the president to withhold information when doing so would protect national security, e.g., in the case of diplomatic files and military secrets).

The end of Washington's presidency was as monumental as its beginning. Wishing to set a final precedent, Washington declined to run for a third term. In his famous **farewell address**, composed in part by Alexander Hamilton, he warned future presidents to "steer clear of permanent alliances with any portion of the foreign world." Washington's call for **neutrality** defined American foreign policy from 1800 until the late 1890s (at which point the United States pursued a policy of **imperialism**), and then again from the end of World War I until 1941.

Republican Motherhood

During the 1790s, women's roles in courtship, marriage, and motherhood were all reevaluated in light of the new republic and its ideals. Although women were largely excluded from political activity, they had an important civil role and responsibility. They were to be the teachers and producers of virtuous male citizens.

While public virtue had been a strictly masculine quality in the past, *private* virtue emerged as a very important quality for women, who were given the task of inspiring and teaching men to be good citizens through romance and motherhood. The idea here is that a woman should entertain only suitors with good morals, providing more incentive for men to be more ethical. Women also held a tremendous influence on their sons, leading advocates for female education to speak out, arguing that educated women would be better mothers, who would produce better citizens. Even though the obligations of women had grown to include this new political meaning, traditional gender roles were largely unchanged as the education of women was meant only in service to husbands and family.

The Adams Presidency

The electoral college selected **John Adams**, a Federalist, as Washington's successor. Under the then-current rules, the second-place candidate became vice president, and so Adams's vice president was the Democratic–Republican Thomas Jefferson.

Following the Washington era, Adams's presidency was bound to be an anticlimax. Adams, argumentative and elitist, was a difficult man to like. He was also a hands-off administrator, often allowing Jefferson's political rival **Alexander Hamilton** to take charge. The animosity between Jefferson and Hamilton and the growing belligerence between the Federalists and Democratic-Republicans set the ugly, divisive tone for Adams's term.

Perhaps Adams's greatest achievement was avoiding war with France. After the United States signed the Jay Treaty with Britain, France began seizing American ships on the open seas. Adams sent three diplomats to Paris, where French officials demanded a huge bribe before they would allow negotiations even to begin. The diplomats returned home, and Adams published their written report in the newspapers. Because he deleted the French officials' names and replaced them with the letters X, Y, and Z, the incident became known as the **XYZ Affair**. As a result, popular sentiment did a complete turnaround; formerly pro-French, the public became vehemently anti-French to the point that a declaration of war seemed possible. Aware of how small the American military was, Adams avoided the war (a war Hamilton wanted) and negotiated a settlement with a contrite France.

The low point of Adams's tenure was the passage and enforcement of the **Alien and Sedition Acts**, which allowed the government to forcibly expel foreigners and to jail newspaper editors for "scandalous and malicious writing." The acts were purely political, aimed at destroying new immigrants'—especially French immigrants'—support for the Democratic-Republicans. Worst of all, the Sedition Act, which strictly regulated anti-government speech, was a clear violation of the First Amendment. In a scenario almost unimaginable today, Vice President Jefferson led the opposition to the Alien and Sedition Acts. Together with Madison, he drafted the **Virginia and Kentucky Resolutions** (which were technically anonymous), which argued that the states had the right to judge the constitutionality of federal laws. The resolutions went on to exercise this authority they claimed, later referred to as **nullification**, by declaring the Alien and Sedition Acts void. Virginia and Kentucky, however, never prevented enforcement of the laws. Rather, Jefferson used the laws and the resolutions as key issues in his 1800 campaign for the presidency.

The "Revolution of 1800"

By 1800 the Federalist party was split, clearing the way to the presidency for the Democratic-Republicans. Two men ran for the party nomination: **Thomas Jefferson** and **Aaron Burr**. Each received an equal number of votes in the electoral college, which meant that the Federalist-dominated House of Representatives was required to choose a president from between the two. It took 35 ballots, but Jefferson finally won. Alexander Hamilton swallowed hard and campaigned for Jefferson, with whom he disagreed on most issues and whom he personally disliked, because he believed Burr to be "a most unfit and dangerous man." Burr later proved Hamilton right by killing him.

The election was noteworthy for two reasons. For the second time in as many elections, a president was saddled with a vice president he did not want. That problem was remedied in 1804 with the **Twelfth Amendment** to the Constitution, which allowed electors to vote for a **party ticket**. The other, more important reason the election was significant is that in America's first transfer of power—from the Federalists to the Democratic-Republicans—no violence occurred, a feat practically unprecedented for the time. Jefferson referred to his victory and the subsequent change-over as "the bloodless revolution."

THE JEFFERSONIAN REPUBLIC (1800–1823)

Note: The next two sections primarily review political history. They are followed by a review of social and economic history between 1800 and 1860 because many of the important socioeconomic trends of the era developed over the course of several decades. The economic and social conditions of this period also played a major role in bringing about the Civil War, and the AP exam often tests them in this context. That's why we'll review them as we get closer, chronologically, to the Civil War.

Jefferson's First Term

The transition of power from the Federalists to the Democratic-Republicans may have been a bloodless one, but it was not a friendly one. Adams was so upset about the election that he left the capital before Jefferson took office in order to avoid attending the inauguration ceremony. Before he left town, however, he made a number of **"midnight appointments,"** filling as many government positions with Federalists as he could. Jefferson's response was to refuse to recognize those appointments. He then set about replacing as many Federalist appointees as he could. He dismissed some, pressured others to retire, and waited out the rest. By his second term, the majority of public appointees were Democratic-Republicans.

Jefferson's refusal to accept Adams's midnight appointments resulted in a number of lawsuits against the government. One, the case of ***Marbury v. Madison,*** reached the Supreme Court in 1803. William Marbury, one of Adams's last-minute appointees, had sued Secretary of State James Madison for refusing to certify his appointment to the federal bench. Chief Justice **John Marshall** was a Federalist, and his sympathies were with Marbury, but Marshall was not certain that the court could force Jefferson to accept Marbury's appointment. Marshall's decision in the case established one of the most important principles of the Supreme Court: **judicial review.** The court ruled that Marbury did indeed have a right to his judgeship, but that the court could not enforce his right. Why? Although the power to do so had been granted to the Supreme Court in the Judiciary Act of 1789, Marshall now declared it unconstitutional. In one fell swoop, Marshall had handed Jefferson the victory he wanted while simultaneously claiming a major role for the Supreme Court: the responsibility for reviewing the constitutionality of Congressional acts. Throughout the rest of his tenure, Marshall worked to strengthen that doctrine and, thus, the court.

The major accomplishment of Jefferson's first term was the **Louisiana Purchase**. When Spain gave New Orleans to the French in 1802, the government realized that a potentially troublesome situation was developing. The French, they knew, were more likely to take advantage of New Orleans' strategic location at the mouth of the Mississippi, almost certainly meaning that American trade along the river would be restricted. In hopes of averting that situation, Jefferson sent James Monroe to France. Monroe's mandate was to buy New Orleans for $2 million. Monroe arrived at just the right time. Napoleon was gearing up for war in Europe, and a violent slave revolt in Haiti against the French further convinced him to abandon French interests in the New World. The French offered to sell Monroe the whole Louisiana territory for $15 million.

Thomas Jefferson was now faced with a dilemma. As secretary of state under Washington, he had argued for a strict interpretation of the Constitution, thus limiting the power of the federal government to those powers specifically stated in the Constitution. Nowhere did the Constitution authorize the president to purchase land, yet clearly Jefferson could not pass up this opportunity to double the size of the United States. Ultimately, Jefferson resolved the issue by claiming his presidential power to negotiate treaties with foreign nations. His decision to purchase Louisiana without Congressional approval was not unanimously applauded: some Federalists derided the deal as too expensive (though the land was three cents per acre). Some Republicans, led by John Randolph of Virginia, criticized Jefferson for violating Republican principles. This group became known as the Quids.

Jefferson sent explorers, among them **Lewis and Clark**, to investigate the western territories, including much of what was included in the Louisiana territory. All returned with favorable reports, causing many pioneers to turn their attentions westward in search of land, riches, and economic opportunities. Those early explorers also reported back to Jefferson on the presence of British and French forts that still dotted the territory, garrisoned with foreign troops that had been (deliberately?) slow to withdraw after the regime changes of the previous half-century.

In 1804 Jefferson won reelection in a landslide victory. During the 1804 elections, Aaron Burr ran for governor of New York. Again, Alexander Hamilton campaigned against Burr. When Burr lost, he accused Hamilton of sabotaging his political career and challenged him to a **duel** in which he killed Hamilton. Afterward, Burr fled to the Southwest, where he plotted to start his own nation in parts of the Louisiana Territory. He was later captured and tried for treason but was acquitted because of lack of evidence.

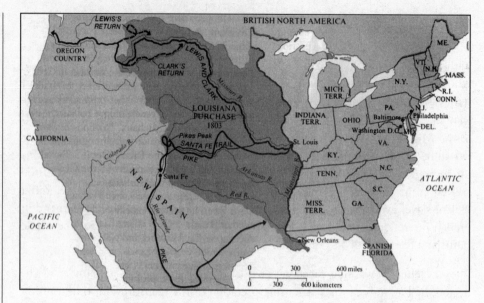

The Louisiana Purchase and the Lewis and Clark Expedition

Jefferson's Second Term

Jefferson's second term did not go nearly as smoothly as his first. During these years, the United States got caught in the middle of yet another French–English dispute. The situation eventually led to the **War of 1812**.

In 1805 the British and French were at war and at a stalemate. In an effort to gain an advantage, each side began blockading the other's trade routes. The United States, dependent on both as trade partners, suffered greatly from the blockades. To add insult to injury, the British began stopping American ships and **impressing** sailors: that is, they declared, often with little or no proof, that those sailors had deserted from the British navy, and forced them back into it. Unfortunately, the English were not as particular about whom they "reenlisted" as the Americans would have liked them to be. Tensions mounted, then boiled over, when a British frigate attacked an American ship in American waters. Jefferson was at a loss. He couldn't go to war against the British because the U.S. Navy was no match for England's forces. So, Jefferson responded with a boycott, biding his time while increasing military and naval appropriations.

Because both the British and the French continued to harass American ships, Jefferson lobbied for and won passage of the **Embargo Act of 1807**. The law basically shut down America's import and export business, with disastrous economic results. New England's economy collapsed, and smuggling became widespread. The **Non-Intercourse Act of 1809** reopened trade with most nations, but it still officially banned trade with the two most significant trade partners, Britain and France. In the end, Jefferson decided, as had Washington before him, that two terms as president were enough. He endorsed his secretary of state, **James Madison**, who handily defeated the ever-weakening Federalists.

Madison's Presidency and the War of 1812

Madison sought a solution to America's trade problems, and Congress responded with **Macon's Bill No. 2**, a bill that reopened trade with both France and England. However, Madison promised that if either country renounced its interference with American trade, he would cut off trade with the other one. Napoleon made that promise, forcing the United States to cut off trade with England, but France then continued to harass American ships. The British, angry at the new embargo, stepped up their attacks on American ships, making a bad situation even worse. These developments helped build pro-war sentiments in the United States. Particularly anxious for a confrontation with the British were the Southern and Western **War Hawks**, who saw war as an opportunity to grab new territories to the west and southwest. Their leaders were **Henry Clay** and **John C. Calhoun**. Madison held out as long as he could but finally relented and asked Congress to declare war in 1812.

You should know several important points about the **War of 1812**. Once again, Native Americans aligned themselves with the British. The great chief **Tecumseh** unified area tribes in an effort to stop American expansion into Indiana and Illinois, both before and during the war. Meanwhile, his brother Tenskwatawa, also known as **the Prophet,** led an extensive revival of traditional Native American culture and religion. Tecumseh's coalition fell apart after he was killed in battle.

> Effects of the War of 1812
> - First and foremost, it represented the end of Native Americans' ability to stop American expansion.
>
> - The American economy, by necessity, became less reliant on trade with Britain.
>
> - It made Andrew Jackson into a celebrity and paved the way to his presidency.
>
> - The victory in New Orleans led to national euphoria.
>
> - The popularity of the war destroyed the Federalists, who had opposed it, and taught American politicians that objecting to going to war could be hazardous to their careers.

American forces were ill-prepared for the war, and much of the fighting went badly. The British captured Washington, D.C. in 1814 and set the White House on fire. However, in most battles America was able to fight to a stalemate. When English–French hostilities ended (with Napoleon's defeat), many of the issues that had caused the war evaporated, and the British soon negotiated peace. Unaware that the Treaty of Ghent had been signed and the war was over, General Andrew Jackson fought and won the Battle of New Orleans, the only clear-cut U.S. victory of the war. The Federalists, opposed to the war because it disrupted trade and unaware that its end was coming, met in Hartford, Connecticut, to consider a massive overhaul of the Constitution or, failing that, secession. When the war ended soon after, most people considered the Federalists to be traitors, and their national party dissolved soon after the Hartford Convention (although the party continued to exert influence in some states through the next decade).

The war had one clear positive result: It spurred **American manufacturing**. Cut off from trade with Europe, the states became more self-sufficient by necessity. New England became America's manufacturing center during the war, and after the war, the United States was less dependent on imports than it had been previously. (For more information on economic developments of the period, see pages 133–138.)

Throughout the rest of his tenure, Madison worked to promote national growth. At the same time, he remained true to his Democratic–Republican principles, and so extended federal power only cautiously. Madison championed a combination of programs that included protective tariffs on imports, improvements to interstate roads (including expansion of the **National Road** from Maryland to Ohio), and the re-chartering of the National Bank after the first National Bank's charter had expired. The programs were known collectively as the **American System**, sometimes referred to as the Nationalist Program. Speaker of the House **Henry Clay** lobbied for them so aggressively that many history books refer to "Henry Clay's American System."

Monroe's Presidency

The demise of the Federalists briefly left the United States with only one political party. This period of unity is referred to as the **Era of Good Feelings**, although the term belies the growing tension created by economic development and increased sectionalism. During this period, Chief Justice John Marshall's rulings continued to strengthen the federal government and its primacy. For example, he ruled in *McCulloch v. Maryland* that the states could not tax the National Bank, thus establishing the precedence of national law over state law.

The good feelings nearly came to an abrupt end in 1819 when a financial scare called the **Panic of 1819** threw the American economy into turmoil. The panic followed a period of economic growth, inflation, and land speculation, all of which had destabilized the economy. When the National Bank called in its loans, many borrowers couldn't repay them. The consequences included numerous mortgage foreclosures and business failures. Many people were thrown into poverty. Nonetheless, no nationally organized political opposition resulted from the panic, and Monroe easily won reelection in 1820.

The postwar period had also ushered in a new wave of westward expansion. As secretary of state under Monroe, **John Quincy Adams**, son of former president John Adams, deftly negotiated a number of treaties that fixed U.S. borders and opened new territories. The United States acquired Florida from the Spanish by the Adams-Onis Treaty in 1819. Adams also had to handle international tensions caused by a series of revolutions in Central America and South America, as the inhabitants of those regions won their independence from Spain. Ultimately, events compelled Monroe and Adams to recognize the new nations. At the same time, they decided that America should assert its authority over the Western Hemisphere. The result was the **Monroe Doctrine**, a policy of mutual noninterference. You stay out of the Americas, Monroe told Europe, and we'll stay out of your squabbles. The Monroe Doctrine also claimed America's right to intervene anywhere in its own hemisphere, if it felt its security was threatened. No European country tried to intercede in the Americas following Monroe's declaration, and so the Monroe Doctrine *appeared* to work. No one, however, was afraid of the American military; Spain, France, and others stayed out of the Western Hemisphere because the powerful British navy made sure they did.

The Monroe Doctrine is the first of several "doctrines" you should know for the AP exam. In general, these doctrines were presidential statements that became foreign policy. For example, in 1823, President Monroe warned European nations that the Western Hemisphere was closed to future colonization. This policy, together with the advice given in Washington's Farewell Address, secured American neutrality all the way until World War I. (The **Truman Doctrine**, issued at the end of World War II, is especially important, but you should also familiarize yourself with the Eisenhower Doctrine, the Nixon Doctrine and, most recently, the Bush Doctrine).

The new period of expansion resulted in a national debate over slavery, as would every period of expansion to follow until the Civil War resolved the slavery question. In 1820 the Union consisted of 22 states. Eleven allowed slavery; 11 prohibited it. Missouri was the first state to be carved out of the Louisiana Purchase, and its application for statehood threatened the balance, particularly in the U.S. Senate. Henry Clay brokered the **Missouri Compromise**, which (1) admitted Missouri as a slave state, (2) carved a piece out of Massachusetts—Maine—and admitted Maine as a free state, (3) drew a line along the 36°30′ parallel across the Louisiana Territory, and (4) established the southern border of Missouri as the northernmost point at which slavery would then be allowed in the western territories of the United States, except of course for Missouri itself, which in a way violated the Missouri Compromise since it was north of the line. The compromise was the first in a series of measures forestalling the Civil War. It also split the powerful Democratic–Republican coalition, ending its 20-year control of national politics.

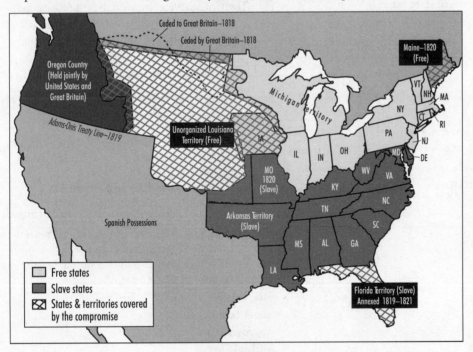

Missouri Compromise, 1820

Chapter 7 Drill

See Chapter 13 for answers and explanations.

1. Historians often cite Shays's Rebellion (1786–1787) as a significant event in U.S. history because it

   (A) demonstrated the strength, yet fairness, of the newly-created federal government
   (B) made many Americans realize that slavery could not last
   (C) made Americans realize that excessive taxation often leads to violence
   (D) demonstrated the weakness of the federal government under the Articles of Confederation
   (E) demonstrated class antagonism, despite the absence of a landed aristocracy

2. Under the Articles of Confederation, the national government had which of the following powers?

   I. The power to collect taxes.
   II. The power to negotiate treaties.
   III. The power to supercede state law.

   (A) I only
   (B) II only
   (C) I and III only
   (D) II and III only
   (E) I, II, and III

3. George Washington established the principle of executive privilege in a dispute with Congress over the

   (A) Alien and Sedition Acts
   (B) legality of political parties
   (C) Jay Treaty
   (D) Whiskey Rebellion
   (E) Louisiana Purchase

4. Which of the following best summarizes the strict constructionist position on the establishment of the National Bank?

   (A) All matters not clearly reconciled by the Constitution, such as the establishment of a national bank, must be arbitrated by the federal judiciary.
   (B) The establishment of the National Bank is necessary to strengthen the United States economy and therefore must be allowed even if it is technically unconstitutional.
   (C) The decision on whether to establish a National Bank, like all important governmental decisions, should be left in the hands of a powerful executive branch.
   (D) The Constitution allows the establishment of the bank, because it allows Congress to take any action necessary to exercise its enumerated powers.
   (E) The Constitution forbids the establishment of the bank, because creating a bank is not among Congress's enumerated powers.

5. Although the Supreme Court was the weakest of the three branches of government in the early days of the new republic, John Marshall strengthened the Court by

   (A) establishing the principle of federalism, giving federal courts the power to declare laws unconstitutional
   (B) declaring the Virginia and Kentucky Resolutions, which asserted the right of states to nullify federal laws, unconstitutional
   (C) establishing the principle of judicial review in the case of *McCulloch v. Maryland*
   (D) establishing the principle of judicial review in the case of *Marbury v. Madison*
   (E) exercising loose construction

6. The Louisiana Purchase was an important factor in the development of U.S. trade because it

(A) opened new markets among the western Indian nations
(B) gave the country complete control of the Mississippi River
(C) added numerous French factories in the Louisiana Territory to the U.S. economy
(D) facilitated the immediate completion of the transcontinental railroad
(E) allowed the United States to develop ports on the Pacific coast

7. As a result of the Hartford Convention following the War of 1812,

(A) the Federalist party lost credibility and eventually died out
(B) the Constitution was amended to limit the president to two terms in office
(C) the New England states threatened to secede
(D) Congress passed the War Powers Act, limiting future presidents from gaining too much power during wartime, as Madison had
(E) the British finally acknowledged American independence

REFLECT ACTIVITY

Respond to the following questions:

- For which content topics discussed in this chapter do you feel you have achieved sufficient mastery to answer multiple-choice questions correctly?

- For which content topics discussed in this chapter do you feel you have achieved sufficient mastery to discuss effectively in an essay?

- For which content topics discussed in this chapter do you feel you need more work before you can answer multiple-choice questions correctly?

- For which content topics discussed in this chapter do you feel you need more work before you can discuss effectively in an essay?

- What parts of this chapter are you going to re-review?

- Will you seek further help, outside of this book (such as a teacher, tutor, or AP Central), on any of the content in this chapter—and, if so, on what content?

Chapter 8
Beginnings of Modern American Democracy (1824–1844)

POLITICAL EVENTS AND SOCIAL DEVELOPMENTS

The Election of 1824 and John Quincy Adams's Presidency

The **election of 1824** marked a major turning point in presidential elections. Prior to 1824, electors, who selected the president in the electoral college, had been chosen by a variety of methods. State legislatures chose many electors, although with each election the number of states using this method decreased. By 1824, a majority of states allowed voters to choose their presidential electors directly. In earlier elections, **congressional caucuses**, or groups of U.S. Congressmen, had chosen their parties' nominees, and electors, often chosen by those same congressmen or by their friends, had not challenged the choices. With more people voting directly for presidential electors, however, there was less and less voter support for the candidates nominated by party leaders in this era before primaries and caucuses. When the Democratic–Republican caucus chose William H. Crawford in 1824, others—among them John Quincy Adams, Henry Clay, and Andrew Jackson—decided to challenge the nomination. Their opposition, along with their accusations that the party caucuses were undemocratic, brought about the **demise of the caucus system**. Of the four, Andrew Jackson received the greatest number of popular votes and electoral votes; however, as none of the four had won a majority, the election was decided in the House of Representatives. There, Speaker of the House Clay threw his support to Adams, thereby handing Adams the victory. Adams subsequently named Clay secretary of state, a position whose previous holders included Adams, Monroe, and Jefferson and that was therefore considered the gateway to the presidency. Jackson and other opponents of Clay's appointment alleged that Adams and Clay had struck a **"corrupt bargain"** and immediately vowed to see both removed in the election of 1828.

Adams's presidency was impeded by a contrary Congress. (Remember, more congressmen had initially supported Jackson than Adams.) He had also been a Federalist congressman and was the son of a Federalist president, and every effort he made to strengthen the central government was thus viewed with deep suspicion. Jackson's supporters strongly favored **states' rights** and thwarted all of Adams's efforts to initiate improvements through the federal government. His proposals to impose new protective tariffs, build interstate highways, and establish federal schools and research centers were all met with steep opposition, though he did go on to found a naval college and become an influential congressman.

John Quincy Adams and Postmillennialism

Postmillennialism was a belief, widespread among 19th-century Christians, that Jesus would only return after a thousand-year golden age brought about by humankind. It was therefore a major progressive force in America, with adherents such as John Quincy Adams. Here is our sixth president calling for the U.S. to adopt the metric system—in the 1820s!

"But if man upon earth be an improvable being; if that universal peace, which was the object of a Saviour's mission, which is the desire of the philosopher, the longing of the philanthropist, the trembling hope of the Christian, is a blessing to which the futurity of mortal man has a claim of more than mortal promise; if the Spirit of Evil is, before the final consummation of things, to be cast down from his dominion over men, and bound in the chains of a thousand years, the foretaste here of man's eternal felicity, then this system of common instruments to accomplish all the changes of social and friendly commerce, will furnish the links of sympathy between the inhabitants of the most distant regions; the metre will surround the globe in use, as well as in mutiplied extension; and one language of weights and measures will be spoken from the equator to the poles."

The Jackson Presidency and Jacksonian Democracy

Despite the political incorrectness of his policies by today's standards and reevaluation of Andrew Jackson by modern-day historians, the era of Jackson as president is an important period in American history. There are always more than a few multiple-choice questions on this material, and often one of the essay questions pertains to Jackson's administration or the concept of Jacksonian democracy.

Furious that he had been denied the presidency in 1824 despite winning a plurality of the vote (more votes than any other candidate, but short of a majority), Jackson put together a support network to assure wide popular support. A coalition of state political organizations, newspaper publishers, and other community leaders rallied around the campaign. That group became the present-day **Democratic** party. The campaign was vicious. While the candidates themselves stayed out of the fray—no presidential candidate would campaign on his own behalf until Stephen Douglas in 1860—their surrogates showed no restraint in slinging mud. Jackson's men accused Adams of being a corrupt career politician, while Adams's men accused Jackson of being a stupid and violent drunkard. Jackson was particularly infuriated by accusations that his wife was a bigamist—which was technically true, as she had married Jackson before her divorce was final. The **Coffin Handbill** accused Jackson of murdering his enlisted men during the Indian Wars. Those who consider today's smear campaigns unprecedented haven't studied much American history.

In 1828 Jackson won the election by a large margin; in so doing, he became the first president who wasn't either born in Virginia or named Adams. He was considered to have the interests of the West in mind, and was seen as the epitome of a self-made man. Among his first acts, he dismissed numerous government officials and replaced them with political supporters. While almost every one of his predecessors had done exactly the same thing, because Jackson was the first true outsider-president, administration jobs that had previously circulated among a relatively insular circle of political supporters fell into new hands. Those who lost power criticized Jackson, but so too did the public, who noticed for the first time the cronyism already inherent in their government. Trading jobs for political favors came to be known as the "**spoils system.**"

Jackson's popularity ushered in the age of **Jacksonian democracy**, which replaced Jeffersonian republicanism. Jefferson had conceived of a nation governed by middle- and upper-class educated property holders, in which the government would be only as large as necessary to provide an acceptable level of services. Jefferson also envisioned a nation of yeoman farmers—farmers who owned their land—whose liberty would be protected by limiting the power of the central government. Jacksonian democracy, on the other hand, benefited from **universal white manhood suffrage**, meaning the extension of voting rights to all white males, even those who did not own property.

A strong presidency also characterized Jacksonian democracy. Jackson parlayed his wide popularity into a mandate to challenge both Congress and the Supreme Court in a way that none of his predecessors had. You should note that, unlike Jeffersonian republicanism, Jacksonian democracy is *not* a coherent vision of how a government should function. Jacksonian Democrats saw themselves as champions of liberty, but they did not always act as such. Jackson was not as great a thinker as Jefferson, the Enlightenment scholar.

No policy of Jackson's has received more criticism by modern scholars than Jackson's treatment of the Cherokees with the **Indian Removal Act,** passed by Congress in 1830. This in some ways represented a natural continuation of policy toward American Indians. Originally, it had been the British who established the concept that Native Americans were "foreign nations," and as such, the government could go to war and make treaties with them. Often these treaties established what the British termed "Indian territory," as was the case with the **Proclamation of 1763** issued at the close of the **French and Indian War.**

When the Americans gained their independence, the U.S. government continued the treatment of Native Americans that had been established by the British. Some Americans, however, among them Thomas Jefferson, suggested assimilation into American culture as a solution to the "Indian Problem." Jefferson and others believed that if the Native Americans gave up their "hunting and gathering" lifestyle and adopted American farming techniques and culture—in essence, "learned to live on less land"—then the Americans and Native Americans might coexist peacefully.

By the time of Jackson's presidency, there were "Five Civilized Tribes" living in the South in the area east of the Mississippi River, among those the Cherokee nation. The Cherokees had developed a written language, converted to Christianity, and embraced agriculture as a way of life. Some Cherokees even owned slaves. (How much more "civilized" could these Native Americans become?!) The Cherokees had developed their own government and deemed themselves to be an independent republic within the state of Georgia. The problem arose when gold was discovered on Cherokee land and the citizens of Georgia demanded that the Cherokees comply with the provisions of the Indian Removal Act, a policy suggested by Monroe but enacted during Jackson's tenure in office. This act demanded that the Native Americans resettle in Oklahoma, which had been deemed Indian territory. Jackson, for his part, argued that moving away from white society was the best was to protect themselves from white encroachment and maintain their traditional customs. The Cherokees refused and brought their case to the Supreme Court. Although John Marshall, Chief Justice at the time, sided with the Cherokees in two cases, *Cherokee Nation v. Georgia* (1831) and *Worcester v. Georgia* (1832), Andrew Jackson refused to comply with the Court's decision and is reputed to have sneered, "John Marshall has made his decision, now let him enforce it." Between 1835 and 1838, thousands of Cherokees walked to Oklahoma under the supervision of the U.S. Army in what has come to be known as the "Trail of Tears." Thousands died of sickness and starvation along the way.

One of the major issues of Jackson's presidency focused on **nullification**. The doctrine of nullification, first expressed by Jefferson and Madison in the Virginia and Kentucky Resolutions, holds that the individual states have the right to disobey federal laws if they find them unconstitutional. John Marshall had established that only the Supreme Court had the power of **judicial review,** in the landmark decision of *Marbury v. Madison* (1803). The **Tariff of 1828**, also known as the **Tariff of Abominations**, was passed during the Adams administration, but it almost turned into a national crisis during Jackson's administration. In 1828, **John C. Calhoun**, a South Carolinian who was Jackson's vice president, anonymously published "The South Carolina Exposition and Protest," arguing that states who felt the 50 percent tariff was unfairly high could nullify the law. By 1830, southern states were openly discussing nullification, as such protectionist tariffs cut into the trade with Britain on which the South relied to sell its cotton and buy British wools and certain other raw materials in return. Jackson, though a strong supporter of states' rights, thought nullification endangered the Union and was thus too extreme. After the **Tariff of 1832** failed to lower rates to an acceptable level, South Carolina nullified the tariff. Jackson had Congress authorize a **Force Bill**, threatening to call in troops to enforce the tariff, but Calhoun and Henry Clay (remember the Missouri Compromise?) brokered a behind-the-scenes compromise, lowering the tariff and diffusing tensions. Although the crisis subsided and South Carolina accepted the compromise tariff, no resolution was reached on the legality of nullification, and it would continue to be an issue until the Civil War.

Jackson's economic policies demonstrated his distrust of both big government and Northeastern power brokers. He spent much of his two terms "downsizing" the federal government and strengthening the office of the presidency through his extensive use of the presidential veto. He fought against the **reform** movements of the time that called for increased government activism against social and economic problems. He saw to it that the **Second Bank of the United States (BUS)** failed by vetoing Congress's attempt to recharter the bank and by withdrawing federal funds and depositing them in state **"pet" banks**. He felt that the BUS protected Northeastern interests at the expense of the West. Jackson argued that the bank was an unconstitutional monopoly, but the Supreme Court ruled against him using a loose interpretation of the commerce clause (*McCulloch v. Maryland*, 1819). He was also suspicious of paper money, preferring "hard currency" such as gold or silver. His **Specie Circular**, which ended the policy of selling government land on

The Bank of the United States

In the 19th century, paper money was issued not by the government but by private banks. If you went to a bank for a $100 loan, the bank would print up some money for you. It didn't necessarily have to have $100 worth of gold in its vaults to do this. If it had $10,000 worth of gold in its vaults, a bank might issue $100,000 in paper money—and as long as no more than 10 percent of that money was cashed in at the same time, the bank would be fine.

What kept such a bank from printing up a million dollars, or a trillion? The main answer was that people could pay their taxes with paper money, and that paper collected at the Bank of the United States. Fear that the Bank would attempt to cash in a huge amount of paper at once kept smaller banks from overusing the printing presses. Once Andrew Jackson killed the Bank of the United States, however, **wildcat banks** did indeed spring up and issue paper money with abandon. Add the fact that the government stopped accepting paper money in payment for land, and people realized that all their paper money was now nearly worthless—a recipe for a major depression.

With only gold and silver now considered to have value, the stage was set for the late 19th century, when arguments over these metals would dominate the debate over economic policy.

credit (buyers now had to pay "hard cash"), caused a money shortage and a sharp decrease in the treasury, and helped trigger the **Panic of 1837**. Congress overturned the circular in the final days of Jackson's final term.

Slavery grew to be an ever more controversial issue during the time of Jacksonian Democracy. As the Northern abolition movement grew stronger, the South experienced several slave revolts, which resulted in the use of more brutal disciplinary measures by slaveholders. The most famous of the insurrections was **Nat Turner's Rebellion**. Turner, a well-read preacher, had a vision, and he took this vision as a sign from God that a black liberation movement would succeed. As a result, he rallied a gang that proceeded to kill and then mutilate the corpses of 60 whites. In retaliation, 200 slaves were executed, some with no connection at all to the rebellion. Fearful that other slaves would hear of and emulate Turner's exploits, Southern states passed a series of restrictive laws, known as **black codes**, prohibiting blacks from congregating and learning to read. Other state laws even prevented whites from questioning the legitimacy of slavery. After Turner's Rebellion, Virginia's House of Burgesses debated ending bondage, but did not pass a law.

The Election of 1836 and the Rise of the Whigs

Jackson's Democratic party could not represent the interests of all its constituencies (Northern abolitionists, Southern plantation owners, Western pioneers), and inevitably, an opposition party, the **Whigs**, was formed. By 1834 almost as many congressmen supported the Whig Party as the Democratic Party. The Whigs were a loose coalition that shared one thing in common: opposition to one or more of the Democrats' policies. For example, while the Democrats favored limited federal government, many Whigs believed in government **activism**, especially in the case of social issues. Many Whigs were also deeply religious and supported the temperance movement and enforcement of the Sabbath. Still, the defining characteristic of the Whigs was their opposition to the Democrats.

In the election of 1836, Jackson supported his second vice president, Democrat **Martin Van Buren**. Van Buren had the misfortune to take over the presidency just as the country was entering a major economic crisis (the Panic of 1837). Van Buren made the situation worse by continuing Jackson's policy of favoring hard currency, thereby insuring that money would be hard to come by. The economic downturn lasted through Van Buren's term, practically guaranteeing that he would not be reelected.

In 1841 former military hero **William Henry Harrison** became the first Whig president. He died of pneumonia a month after taking office. His vice president, **John Tyler**, a former Democrat, assumed the presidency and began championing states' rights, much to his own party's chagrin. Tyler vetoed numerous Whig bills, which alienated Whig leadership; eventually his entire cabinet resigned in protest. Tyler is often referred to as the "president without a party," and his presidency lasted only one term.

ECONOMIC HISTORY (1800–1860)

This section discusses economic developments in the United States during the first part of the nineteenth century. These developments played an important role in the political events that led to the Civil War, and helped to determine the different characteristics of the country's regions. Along with social developments (discussed in the next section), these economic factors laid the foundation for issues that would be important to American society for the following century (such as abolitionism, women's suffrage, and temperance).

Beginnings of a Market Economy

From the time they first arrived until the Revolutionary War era, most settlers in the United States raised crops for subsistence, rather than for sale at market. Most people made their own clothing and built their own furniture and homes, and got by without many other conveniences. Cash transactions were relatively rare. Instead, people used ledgers to keep track of who owed what to whom, and typically settled accounts when someone moved away or died.

Developments in manufacturing and transportation changed all that, however. By making it possible to mass produce goods and transport them across the country cheaply, a **market economy** began to develop. In a market economy, people trade their labor or goods for cash, which they then use to buy other people's labor or goods. Market economies favor those who specialize. For example, farmers who grow a single crop (monoculture) usually do better in a market economy than those who produce many different crops: One-crop farmers can offer buyers more of what they want. These farmers also do not have to look for different buyers for their many products. The trade-off, of course, is that these farmers are no longer self-sufficient. Instead, they become dependent on the market to provide some necessities. Furthermore, such farmers sometimes fall victim to overproduction, resulting in an unexpected, unwelcome drop in the price of their crop.

Market economies grow more quickly and provide more services than subsistence economies, and they also make people more interdependent. However, they are also much more prone to change. Any number of factors can halt a period of prosperity and throw the economy into a skid like the panics of 1819 and 1837. These changes are referred to as "**boom-and-bust cycles.**" During the first decades of the nineteenth century, the United States made a rapid transition from a subsistence economy to a market economy.

As stated earlier, the **War of 1812** and the events leading up to it forced the United States to become less dependent on imports, and, consequently, to develop a stronger national economy. Two key advances, both developed by **Eli Whitney**, also played a major part in the process. The **cotton gin**, invented in 1793, revolutionized Southern agriculture by making it much easier to remove the seeds from cotton plants. (The machine was 5,000 percent more efficient than a human being.) The cotton gin made it easier and cheaper to use cotton for textiles, and as a result, the demand for cotton grew very rapidly into the early 1800s. As demand grew, so did cotton production in the South. Because cotton farming is labor intensive, the spread of cotton as the region's chief crop also intensified the South's dependence on slave labor.

Whitney's second innovation was the use of **interchangeable parts** in manufacturing. Whitney originally struck upon the idea while mass-producing rifles for the U.S. Army. Prior to Whitney's breakthrough, manufacturers had built weapons (and other machines) by hand, custom fitting parts so that each weapon was unique. The process was costly, time-consuming, and inconvenient, because replacing broken parts was extremely difficult. Whitney demonstrated the practicality of his invention to Thomas Jefferson and James Madison by disassembling a number of rifles, scrambling the parts, and then reassembling the rifles from whichever parts he picked out of the pile. Whitney's demonstration was a huge success, and soon his idea was being applied to all aspects of manufacturing.

Interchangeable parts gave birth to the **machine-tool industry**, which produced specialized machines for such growing industries as textiles and transportation. (Without interchangeable parts, such machines would have been impractical because they would have been too expensive to build and too difficult to fix.) Whitney's advances also helped promote the development of **assembly line production**. On an assembly line, products are constructed more efficiently by dividing the labor into a number of tasks and assigning each worker one task. Prior to assembly lines, each worker would create a product in its entirety. The result was a product that took longer to produce and was less uniform in quality.

The North and the Textile Industry

The above-mentioned developments first benefited the textile industry. Advances in machine technology, coupled with a U.S. embargo on British goods prior to and during the War of 1812—England was then America's chief source of textiles—spurred the development of textile mills in New England. During the first decade of the nineteenth century, mills produced thread and hired local women to weave the thread into cloth at home. The mills would then buy the finished cloth and sell it on the open market. The invention of the first **power loom**, in 1813, meant that textile manufacturers could produce both thread and finished fabric in their own factories, and do so quickly and efficiently. The resulting product was both of high quality and inexpensive—so much so that women who had previously woven their own fabrics at home started to buy cloth.

The rapid growth of the textile industry resulted in a shortage of labor in New England. Consequently, textile manufacturers had to "sweeten the pot" to entice laborers (almost all of whom were women from nearby farms) to their factories. The most famous worker-enticement program was called the "**Lowell system**" (or "**Waltham system**"), so named after the two Massachusetts towns in which many mills were located. The Lowell system guaranteed employees housing in respectable, chaperoned boardinghouses; cash wages; and participation in cultural and social events organized by the mill. The system, widely copied throughout New England, lasted until great waves of Irish immigration in the 1840s and 1850s made factory labor plentiful. Later, as working conditions started to deteriorate, workers began to organize **labor unions** to protect their interests. These early unions in the mid-1800s met with strong, frequently violent opposition from industry. Still, they ultimately succeeded. (We'll discuss labor unions in much more detail later, when we discuss the Gilded Age in the late 1800s and the Progressive era in the early 1900s.)

Other industries inevitably sprung up around the textile industry. **Clothing manufacturers**, also located primarily in the Northeast, transformed the textiles into finished products. **Retailers** sold the clothing and other manufactured products in their stores. **Brokers** acted as middlemen, buying and selling raw and finished products and trafficking them among manufacturers and retailers. **Commercial banks** lent money to everyone so that the wheels of commerce stayed well greased. Most significant, the **transportation industry** grew as a result of the need to ship these and other products across the country.

Transportation: Canals, Railroads, Highways, and Steamships

Prior to the 1820s, travel and shipping along east–west routes was difficult, and most trade centered on the north–south routes along the Ohio and Mississippi Rivers. The construction of the **National Road** from Maryland to West Virginia (and ultimately to central Ohio) made east–west travel easier, but the big change came with the completion of the **Erie Canal** in 1825. Funded entirely by the state of New York, the Erie Canal linked the Great Lakes region to New York and, thus, to European shipping routes. Suddenly, it became lucrative for a Midwestern merchant or farmer to sell his products to Eastern buyers, and as a result the Northeast soon established itself as the United States' center of commerce. The Erie Canal was so successful that, by 1835, its width and depth had to be nearly doubled to handle the traffic. Other regions tried to duplicate the Erie Canal's success, and during the 1830s thousands of miles of canals were constructed throughout the Northeast and Midwest. None performed as well as the Erie Canal, and a number of those canals failed. Meanwhile, the railroads developed into a convenient means of transporting goods; by 1850, the **canal era** had ended.

The end of this era, however, did not mark the end of shipping as an important industry. The invention of the steam engine allowed for **steamships**, which traveled faster than sailing vessels. Steamships became important freight carriers and replaced sailing ships for long sea voyages. By 1850 passengers could travel by steamship from New York to England in ten days; by sail the same trip had taken more than a month. Steamships were not without their problems though; exploding boilers, burning ships, and other disasters accompanied the technological advances.

Similarly, railroads redefined land travel. America's first **railroads** were built during the 1830s, the first typically connecting only two cities. As the nation's rail network grew, a major problem arose: Different railroad lines could not be connected to one another because the width, or **gauge**, of their tracks was different. As a result, rail development proceeded slowly. When different railways converted to compatible systems, the government often paid the bill even though the railroads were privately owned. This hastened progress, and by 1853, New York and Chicago were linked by rail, as were Pittsburgh and Philadelphia. (Southern rail development was much slower, and superior rails gave the North a huge advantage during the Civil War.) We'll discuss the railroads further in the post–Civil War period, during which railroad construction really "picked up steam."

The increase in travel and shipping was helped considerably by the invention of the **telegraph**, which allowed immediate long-distance communication for the first time. The telegraph was like a primitive telephone, except that people communicated in **Morse code** rather than by speaking to one another. Americans quickly understood the benefits of telegraphic communications, and widespread use followed its invention almost immediately. Transatlantic telegraph cables, however, would not be successfully laid until 1866, after the Civil War.

Developments in transportation and communication during the first half of the nineteenth century revolutionized American commerce and culture, but favored the Northeast and the West (today known as the Midwest). Products, people, and ideas traveled much faster in 1850 than they had in 1800.

The transportation revolution

By 1855, the cost to send things across America had fallen to one-twentieth of what it had cost in 1825—and they arrived in one-fifth the time.

Farming

Although American manufacturing grew at a rapid pace, agriculture remained by far the most common source of livelihood throughout the first half of the nineteenth century. Mechanization revolutionized farming during the period, as many machines came into common use during this time, including the mechanical plow, sower, reaper, thresher, baler, and cotton gin. The growth of the market economy also changed farming. In 1820 about one-third of all the food grown in the United States went to market. (The rest was kept for personal consumption.) By 1860 that fraction had doubled.

Farming continued in the Northeast, but not without difficulties. The region's rocky, hilly terrain was unsuitable to many of the machines that were making farming on the plains easier and cheaper. Furthermore, much of the farmland in the region had been over farmed, and as a result, the quality of the soil had grown poor. Unable to compete with Midwestern grain farmers, some New England farmers quit cultivating grain and started raising livestock and growing fruits and vegetables. Others quit farming entirely and headed to the cities to take manufacturing jobs.

As mentioned above, the Midwest became America's chief source of grains, such as wheat and corn. Midwestern farms—much larger than New England farms—were also much more adaptable to the new technology that allowed farmers to nearly double production. Banks sprang up to lend farmers the capital necessary to buy modern equipment, and the trade routes created by rail and ship provided access to the markets these farmers needed to sell their crops in order to pay off their loans. The system worked well, except during the various financial crises of the first half of the century. The panics of 1819 and 1837 resulted in bank foreclosures on mortgages and other business loans, not just in the Midwest but all across the country. Not surprisingly, many people were thrown into poverty.

In the South, plantations focused primarily on cotton, especially in the Deep South; tobacco continued to be a major cash crop in the Upper South. The majority of Southerners owned small farms and did not own slaves. (In 1860 approximately one-quarter of white Southern families owned slaves.)

Westward Expansion

The Louisiana Purchase removed one major obstacle to U.S. western settlement, and the resolution of the War of 1812 removed another by depriving Native Americans of a powerful ally in Great Britain. By 1820 the United States had settled the region east of the Mississippi River and was quickly expanding west. Americans began to believe that they had a God-given right to the Western territories, an idea that came to be known as America's **Manifest Destiny**. Some took the idea of Manifest Destiny to its logical conclusion and argued that Canada, Mexico, and even all of the land in the Americas eventually would be annexed by the United States.

Western settlement was dangerous. The terrain and climate could be cold and unforgiving, and these settlers from the East were moving into areas that rightfully belonged to Native Americans and Mexicans, none of whom were about to cede their homes without a fight.

Texas presents a good case in point. When Mexico declared its independence from Spain in 1821, the new country included what is now Texas and much of the Southwest, including California. The Mexican government established liberal land policies to entice settlers, and tens of thousands of Americans (many of them cattle ranchers) flooded the region. In return for land, the settlers were supposed to become Mexican citizens, but they rarely did. Instead, they ignored Mexican law, including—and especially—the one prohibiting slavery. When Mexico attempted to regain control of the area, the settlers rebelled and declared independence from Mexico. It was during this period that the famous battle at the **Alamo** was fought (1836). For a while Texas was an independent country, called the "**Republic of Texas**." The existence of slavery in the area guaranteed a Congressional battle over statehood, and Texas was not admitted to the Union until 1845.

Farther west and north, settlers were also pouring into the **Oregon Territory**. During the early 1840s, thousands of settlers traveled to the Willamette Valley, braving a six-month journey on the Oregon Trail. Again, the Americans were not the first ones in; not only was there a large Native American population, but the British were also there, claiming the territory for Canada. The Russians also staked a claim, and both the British and the Americans saw them as a threat. The Polk administration eventually settled the territorial dispute by signing a treaty with England.

By the late 1840s, though, those heading along the Oregon Trail had a new destination—**California**. In 1848 the discovery of gold in the California mountains set off the **Gold Rush**, attracting more than 100,000 people to the Golden State in just two years. Most of these people did not strike it rich, but they settled the area after discovering that it was very hospitable to agriculture. Its access to the Pacific Ocean allowed major cities such as San Francisco to develop as important trade centers.

Economic Reasons for Regional Differences

Throughout the first half of the nineteenth century, three different sections of the country—North, South, and West, including what is today known as the Midwest—developed in very different directions. Accordingly, they did not see eye to eye on many issues; thus, historians often refer to **sectional strife** during this period.

The **North**, as mentioned earlier, was becoming industrialized. Technological advances in communications, transportation, industry, and banking were helping it become the nation's commercial center. Farming played less of a role in the Northeastern economy than it did elsewhere in the country, and legal slavery became increasingly uncommon in this region's states throughout the early 1800s.

The **South**, meanwhile, remained almost entirely agrarian. Its chief crops—tobacco and cotton—required vast acreage, and so Southerners were constantly looking west for more land. Anxious to protect slavery, which the large landholders depended on, Southerners also looked for new slave territories to include in the Union in order to strengthen their position in Congress and protect slavery from Northern legislators, who in ever-increasing numbers sought to make slavery illegal.

Western economic interests were varied but were largely rooted in commercial farming, fur trapping, and real-estate speculation. Westerners generally distrusted the North, which they regarded as the home of powerful banks that could take their land away. They had little more use for the South, whose rigidly hierarchical society was at odds with the egalitarianism of the West. Most Westerners wanted to avoid involvement in the slavery issue, which they regarded as irrelevant to their lives. Ironically, Western expansion was the core of the most important conflicts leading up to the Civil War.

> Remember these generalizations about the different regions of the United States, because by using them and some common sense, you can often answer specific AP questions. Take, for example, a question dealing with a specific tariff. Even if you do not remember the details of the tariff—and chances are you will not—you should remember that the North, as a commercial and manufacturing center, would probably support it because a tariff makes imports more expensive and therefore reduces competition with American goods. Southerners would probably oppose it, because a tariff reduces competition and therefore raises prices. (Also, tariffs helped the North, and Southerners did not like the North.) Likewise, as the nineteenth century turned to the twentieth, Republicans tended to support a high tariff and the Democrats a lower one, so pay attention to who's in office, i.e., McKinley, Teddy Roosevelt, or Wilson. Note: The AP test asks about events that illustrate important general trends in American history. If there was a nineteenth-century tariff that the South supported and the North opposed, the test would not ask about it!

SOCIAL HISTORY, 1800–1860

The growth of the American economy in the early nineteenth century brought about numerous social changes. The invention of the cotton gin, coupled with the advent of the Industrial Revolution in England, altered Southern agriculture, resulting in the region's increased reliance on slave labor. The development of commerce led to a larger middle class, especially in the North but also in Southern and Midwestern cities. Industrialization resulted in bigger cities with large (and often impoverished) migrant and immigrant neighborhoods. Westward migration created a new frontier culture as pioneers dealt with the uniqueness of the West's landscape and climate. Each of these sets of circumstances influenced people's attitudes and ambitions and set the scene for the social and political events of the era.

The North and American Cities

As we discussed previously, the North became the nation's industrial and commercial center during the first half of the nineteenth century. Accordingly, it became home to many of the nation's major cities. In their early years, American cities faced numerous problems, chiefly the lack of powerful urban governments to oversee their rapid expansion. Modern waste disposal, plumbing, sewers, and incineration were still a long way off, and as a result, cities could be extremely toxic environments. The proximity in which people lived and worked, coupled with sanitation problems, made epidemics not only likely but inevitable.

City life was not, however, without its benefits. First, cities meant jobs. Many Northern farmers, unable to compete with cheaper produce carted in from the West and South by steamship and rail, moved to cities to work in the new factories. Craftsmen, such as tailors, cobblers, and blacksmiths, also found it easier to make a living in cities. Second, cities offered more opportunities for social advancement. In the 1830s and 1840s, as municipal governments grew, cities began to provide important services, such as public schooling. Labor unions began to form; although it would be many decades until they would come close to matching the power of business management, these unions still fought to bring about improvements in the lives of working people, even though they had quite limited success. Middle- and upper-class Americans in cities formed clubs and associations through which they could exert more influence on government and in society. Finally, cities provided a wide variety of leisure-time options, such as theater and sports.

Still, as in the South, there was a great disparity in the **distribution of wealth** in Northern cities. An elite few controlled most of the personal wealth and led lives of power and comfort. Beneath them was the **middle class**, made up of tradesmen, brokers, and other professionals. They worked to reach the plateau at which the women in their families could devote themselves to homemaking instead of wage earning. (Many middle-class women in their teens and early twenties worked—as sales clerks, teachers, and such—before settling down to marriage.) As wage-earning labor was more often performed away from the home, in factories and offices, the notion developed that men should work while women kept house and raised children. That notion, known as the **cult of domesticity**, was supported by popular magazines and novels that glorified home life. The middle classes also constituted much of the market for luxury goods such as housewares and fine furniture. Members of the middle class often rose from the **working class**. In working-class families, men often worked in factories or at low-paying crafts; women often worked at home, taking in sewing. Others worked as domestic servants, and most worked throughout their lives. Such families lived just above the poverty level, and any calamity—loss of a job, injury, sickness, or a death in the family—could plunge them irretrievably into debt. Those in **poverty** were most often recent immigrants. Their numbers swelled in the 1840s and 1850s when the great **immigration waves** from **Ireland** (to the cities in the North) and then **Germany** (to the West) reached the United States. These immigration waves met with hostility, especially from the working classes, who feared competition for low-paying jobs. The Irish, in particular, were subject to widespread bias, directed in part at their Catholicism and because their education level was generally lower than that of the Germans.

Occasionally tensions would boil over, and American cities were frequently the sites of riots. Particularly in the 1830s and 1840s, religious, ethnic, and/or class strife could escalate to violence and even result in fatalities. Such disturbances were largely responsible for the formation of municipal police departments, which replaced privately run security companies in enforcing the peace.

The South and Rural Life

There were few major urban centers in the South. The majority of Southerners lived instead in rural areas in near isolation. In 1860, the population density of Georgia was 18 people per square mile. Family, not surprisingly, played a dominant role in social life. After family came the church, and after the church, little else. There simply were not enough people around to support organized cultural and leisure events.

With almost no major cities, the South also had few centers of commerce, and while the North developed extensive networks of canals, railroads, and highways, the South's infrastructure remained fairly limited. The major city of the South, New Orleans, relied almost completely on waterways for its trade routes, and therefore grew much more slowly than did Northern cities such as New York and Boston. Consequently, the South did not develop a strong market economy, as did the North; many more Southerners made and grew most of their necessities for survival.

The wealthiest Southern citizens formed an aristocracy of plantation owners. As in the North, the wealthy made up a small minority, but in the South, this group dominated Southern society politically, socially, and economically. Less than one percent of the population owned more than 100 slaves. In fact, more than three-quarters of white Southerners owned no slaves. Of the rest, half owned five or fewer slaves. Only 10 percent of actual slaveholders—fewer than about 2 percent of the white population—held 20 or more slaves.

Plantation owners grew cotton throughout the Deep South and tobacco in the Middle Atlantic, alongside the crops they needed to support their families and slaves. Most convinced themselves that the slave system benefited all of its participants, *including* the slaves. This attitude, called **Southern paternalism**, relied on the perception of blacks as childlike and unable to take care of themselves. Many slaves discovered that life became easier for them when they reinforced such paternalistic instincts, and adopted a submissive and grateful demeanor (which will be familiar to you if you've ever seen old Hollywood movies about this period). Slave owners almost always converted their slaves to Christianity, again convinced that they were serving the slaves' best interests. The slaves, in turn, adapted Christianity to their cultures and incorporated their own religions and traditions into their new faith.

Slaves lived in a state of subsistence poverty. They were usually housed in one-room cabins with their families, and often with another family. Conditions were overcrowded and unsanitary. Although work conditions varied from region to region and farm to farm, most worked extremely long hours at difficult and tedious labor, and conditions tended to be worse in the Deep South. (Any concern that slaveholders had for their slaves' welfare could arguably be attributed to the fact that importing African slaves was banned in 1808, making it essential to keep one's slaves alive and reproducing. In addition, the purchase price of a slave remained fairly high or even increased.) Moreover, most slaves lived in fear that their families would be broken up by the sale of one or more of them, or that they would be sold "down river." Many were subjected to the abuses of vicious overseers.

Most slaves survived the physical and psychological degradation of slavery by developing a unique culture that tended to blend aspects of their African roots with elements of Christianity. Likewise, although slave revolts were rarely successful, many slaves developed subtle methods of resistance that enabled them to maintain an aspect of their dignity. This might include violating a local slave code and sneaking out at night to meet a loved one or managing to learn to read and write despite codes forbidding them to do so.

The majority of Southerners farmed smaller tracts of land. Planters (those with 20 or more slaves) were in the minority—the remaining landholders were **yeomen**, who sometimes had a few slaves but often none at all, working their small tracts of land with their families. Most were of Scottish and Irish descent and farmed in the hills, which were unsuitable for plantation farming. They grew subsistence crops, raised livestock, and sometimes produced a few cash crops, though limited access to Northern markets hindered profit making. Less fortunate were **landless whites**, who either farmed as tenants or hired themselves out as manual laborers. Elevation from this social stratum to the level of yeoman proved very difficult.

The South was also home to more than 250,000 **free blacks**, the descendants of slaves freed by their owners or freed for having fought in the Revolutionary War. Black codes prevented them from owning guns, drinking liquor, and assembling in groups of more than three (except in church). Prejudice was a constant fact of life. Some owned land or worked at a trade, but most worked as tenant farmers or day laborers. Some were "mulattoes" (biracial individuals), some of whom led lives of relative luxury and refinement in the Deep South, particularly in and around New Orleans.

The West and Frontier Living

During this period, the frontier's boundaries constantly changed. In 1800, the frontier lay east of the Mississippi River. By 1820, nearly all of this eastern territory had attained statehood, and the frontier region consisted of much of the Louisiana Purchase. Settlers also moved to Texas, then a part of Mexico, in the late 1820s and 1830s. By the early 1840s the frontier had expanded to include the Pacific Northwest. In 1849 the Gold Rush drew numerous settlers, **Forty-Niners**, to California.

The United States government actively encouraged settlers to move west. It gave away, or sold at reduced rates, large tracts of land to war veterans. The government also loaned money at reduced rates to civilians so that they too could move west. Some settlers, called **squatters**, ignored the requirement to buy land and simply moved onto and appropriated an unoccupied tract as their own.

Settlers in the Ohio Valley and points west soon found that the area was hospitable to grain production and dairy farming. As previously discussed, much of the area was flat and could easily be farmed by new farm implements such as mechanical plows and reapers. Transportation advances made shipping produce easier and more profitable, and soon the Midwest came to be known as "the nation's breadbasket."

Fur trading was another common commercial enterprise on the frontiers. Fur traders were also called "over-mountain men." They were often the first pioneers in a region, and constantly moved west, one step ahead of farming families. When they reached Oregon, they ran out of places to go. Furthermore, they had hunted beaver to near extinction. A group of former trappers formed the first American government in the Oregon Territory and began lobbying for statehood. The western frontier was also home to **cattle ranchers** and **miners**.

Frontier life was rugged, to say the least. To survive, settlers constantly struggled against the climate, elements, and Native Americans who were not anxious for the whites to settle, having heard about their treatment of Eastern tribes. Still, the frontier offered pioneers opportunities for wealth, freedom, and social advancement—opportunities that were less common in the heavily populated, competitive East and the aristocratic South. Those women who could handle the difficulties of frontier life found their services in great demand, and many made a good living at domestic work and, later, running boardinghouses and hotels. Because of the possibilities for advancement and for "getting a new start in life," the West came to symbolize freedom and equality to many Americans.

Religious and Social Movements

The nineteenth century saw the beginnings of true social reform in the United States, and much of the impulse to improve the lives of others came from citizens' religious convictions. In fact, early social reform movements grew out of the **Second Great Awakening**, which, like the first, was a period of religious revival, mainly among Methodists, Presbyterians, and Baptists. The Second

Great Awakening began in the **"burned-over district"** of western New York and then spread throughout the country, sparking an intense period of evangelicalism in the South and West. The burned-over district was a place so heavily evangelized, so burned over by the metaphorical fires of religious revival, that there were no more people left to convert. Numerous churches formed in places where previously there had been only occasional religious meetings (called **revivals**, or camp meetings). A few reform societies sprang up in the South and West, but in the Northeast, the Second Great Awakening gave birth to numerous societies dedicated to the task of saving humanity from its own worst impulses. Much of the language of reform had a religious tone. For example, drinking and poverty were considered social evils.

Usually, the most active members of reform groups were women, particularly those of the middle and upper classes. **Temperance societies**, some of which tried to encourage people to sign the pledge not to drink and some of which sought outright prohibition of liquor, formed and remained powerful until the adoption of the Eighteenth Amendment in 1919 provided for nationwide prohibition. (Not coincidentally, prohibition finally succeeded at the same time it became evident to politicians that women would soon gain the right to vote.) These groups battled other vices as well, particularly **gambling**. By 1860 every state in the Union had outlawed **lotteries**, and many had prohibited other forms of gambling. Many Northern states also prohibited the manufacture or purchase of alcoholic beverages during this period. A group called "The Female Moral Reform Society" led the battle against **prostitution** in the cities, focusing not only on eliminating the profession but also on rehabilitating those women involved in it.

> ## Connections
> Where was the burned-over district? Western New York. What else happened in western New York during the same period? The Erie Canal was built. Remember that the First Great Awakening was a reaction against the Enlightenment; some historians contend that, similarly, the Second Great Awakening was a reaction against the rise of market capitalism, and no region was being transformed by market capitalism like western New York. We have put economic history and religious history in separate sections for thematic consistency, but they were intimately interconnected—and these sorts of connections are more the rule than the exception in history.

Reform societies also helped bring about **penitentiaries**, **asylums**, and **orphanages** by popularizing the notion that society is responsible for the welfare of its least fortunate. Asylums, orphanages, and houses of refuge for the poor were built to care for those who would previously have been imprisoned or run out of town. With leadership from Dorothea Dix, penitentiaries sought to rehabilitate criminals (rather than simply isolate them from society, as prisons do) by teaching them morality and a "work ethic."

Before we discuss the abolition movement, we need to mention a few other important movements of the period. **The Shakers**, a utopian group that splintered from the Quakers, believed that they and all other churches had grown too interested in this world and too neglectful of their afterlives. Shakers, followers of Mother Ann Lee, isolated themselves in communes where they shared work and its rewards; they also granted near-equal rights to women, even allowing them to attain priesthood. Believing the end of the world was at hand and that sex was an instrument of evil, the Shakers practiced celibacy; their numbers, not surprisingly, diminished. The Shaker revival ended during the 1840s and 1850s. Other Utopian groups included the Oneida community in New York and the New Harmony community in Indiana.

Perhaps the most well known of these experimental communities was Brook Farm, established near Roxbury, Massachusetts in 1841. Brook Farm was home to the Transcendentalists, a group of nonconformist Unitarian writers and philosophers who drew their inspiration from European romanticism. Transcendentalists believed that humans contained elements of the divine, and thus they had faith in man's, and ultimately society's, perfectibility. The most famous of these writers were Nathaniel Hawthorne, author of *The Scarlet Letter*; Ralph Waldo Emerson; and Henry David Thoreau. Thoreau is most noted for his publication of *Walden*, an account of the two years he spent living alone in a cabin on Walden Pond outside Concord, Massachusetts. Perhaps not as well known, but equally significant, was Thoreau's demonstration of civil disobedience. Thoreau refused to pay taxes to a government that waged war against Mexico and subsequently enacted a Fugitive Slave Act as part of the **Compromise of 1850** (see separate section on this in the next chapter).

Another important group involved in this American Renaissance was the Hudson River School painters, the first distinct school of American art. Their goal was to create a specific vision for American art, and they mostly painted landscapes that seemed to portray an awe for the wilderness and beauty of wild America. Like Thoreau and Emerson, the painters were influenced by European romanticism.

The **Mormons**, on the other hand, continue to thrive today. Joseph Smith formed the Church of Jesus Christ of Latter-Day Saints in 1830. Smith's preaching, particularly his acceptance of polygamy, drew strong opposition in the East and Midwest, culminating in his death by a mob while imprisoned in Illinois. The Mormons, realizing that they would never be allowed to practice their faith in the East, made the long, difficult trek to the Salt Lake Valley, led by Brigham Young. There, they settled and transformed the area from desert into farmland through extensive irrigation. The Mormons' success was largely attributable to the settlers' strong sense of community. Through their united efforts, they came to dominate the Utah territory.

The Second Great Awakening was only one source of the antebellum reform movements. By the 1820s and '30s, most of the Founding Fathers were dead, but they left a legacy of freedom and equality, expressed in part in the Declaration of Independence as well as the Preamble to the Constitution. In the 1830s, "We, the People" still meant white males. Many women were active in the abolitionist movement, and it was their exclusion from participation at a worldwide anti-slavery convention held in London in 1840 that convinced women like Elizabeth Cady Stanton and Lucretia Mott to hold the first women's rights convention in 1848 in Seneca Falls in upstate New York (in the same Burned over District from the Second Great Awakening). Stanton and Mott, along with other reformers, published the *Declaration of Rights and Sentiments of Women*, which they modeled after the American Declaration of Independence. The Declaration began, "We hold these truths to be self-evident, that all men *and women* are created equal...." Four years later, Stanton would team up with Susan B. Anthony, with whom she founded the **National Woman Suffrage Association** in 1869.

Finally, **Horace Mann** was instrumental in pushing for public education and education reform in general. He lengthened the school year, established the first "normal school" for teacher training, and used the first standardized books in education (*McGuffey's Reader* was used by 80 percent of public schools). Mann is noted for his belief that "Education is the great equalizer."

The Abolition Movement

Before the 1830s, few whites fought aggressively for the liberation of the slaves. The Quakers believed slavery to be morally wrong and argued for its end. Most other antislavery whites, though, sought gradual abolition, coupled with colonization, a movement to return blacks to Africa. The religious and moral fervor that accompanied the Second Great Awakening, however, persuaded more and more whites, particularly Northerners, that slavery was a great evil. As in other reform movements, women played a prominent role.

White abolitionists divided into two groups. Moderates wanted emancipation to take place slowly and with the cooperation of slave owners. **Immediatists**, as their name implies, wanted emancipation at once. Most prominent among white immediatists was **William Lloyd Garrison,** who began publishing a popular abolitionist newspaper called the *Liberator* in 1831 and helped found the **American Antislavery Society** in 1833. His early subscribers were mostly free blacks, but as time passed, his paper caught on with white abolitionists as well.

Garrison fought against slavery and against moderates as well, decrying their plans for black resettlement in Africa as racist and immoral. Garrison's persistence and powerful writing style helped force the slavery issue to the forefront. His message, as you may imagine, did not go over well everywhere; some Southern states banned the newspaper, and others prohibited *anyone* from discussing emancipation. When congressional debate over slavery became too heated, Congress adopted a **gag rule** that automatically suppressed discussion of the issue. It also prevented Congress from enacting any new legislation pertaining to slavery. The rule, which lasted from 1836 to 1844, along with Southern restrictions on free speech, outraged many Northerners and convinced them to join the abolition movement.

The abolition movement existed prior to 1830, but it had been primarily supported by free blacks. Abolition associations formed in every large black community to assist fugitive slaves and publicize the struggle against slavery; these groups met at a national convention every year after 1830 to coordinate strategies. In the 1840s, **Frederick Douglass** began publishing his influential newspaper *The North Star.* Douglass, an escaped slave, gained fame as a gifted writer and eloquent advocate of freedom and equality; his *Narrative of the Life of Frederick Douglass* is one of the great American autobiographies. Other prominent black abolitionists included **Harriet Tubman**, who escaped slavery and then returned south repeatedly to help more than 300 slaves escape via the **underground railroad** (a network of hiding places and "safe" trails); and **Sojourner Truth**, a charismatic speaker who campaigned for emancipation and women's rights.

Abolitionists' determination and the South's inflexibility pushed the issue of slavery into the political spotlight. Westward expansion, and the question of whether slavery would be allowed in the new territories, forced the issue further. Together, they set in motion the events that led up to the Civil War.

The AP and retrospect
Abolitionism is an important topic on every AP U.S. History test. But it is worth noting that, right up to the Civil War, abolitionists were widely considered extremists. Far and away the leading reform movement *of the time* was the temperance movement. Nearly all abolitionists believed in temperance; few supporters of temperance were abolitionists. But as the abolition movement succeeded (slavery is now illegal) while the success of the temperance movement was short-lived (Prohibition only lasted from 1920 to 1933), you'll find a lot more questions about the former than about the latter.

"We can see nothing, touch nothing, have no measures proposed, without having this pestilence thrust before us. Here it is, this black question, forever on the table, on the nuptial couch, everywhere!"
—Sen. Thomas Hart Benton of Missouri

Chapter 8 Drill

See Chapter 13 for answers and explanations.

1. Andrew Jackson accused Henry Clay of using his influence to broker the "corrupt bargain" of 1824 (which cost Andrew Jackson the election) because Clay

   (A) was promised a cabinet position if John Quincy Adams was elected president
   (B) was promised the vice presidency if Jackson was defeated
   (C) knew Jackson did not support his "American System"
   (D) feared Jackson's pro-slavery stance on states' rights
   (E) knew Jackson would veto the Second National Bank when its charter came up for renewal

2. The controversy over the tariff during the late 1820s and early 1830s demonstrated that

   (A) New Englanders were more radical than Southerners, as they had been since the days of the American Revolution
   (B) Andrew Jackson favored states' rights over federal supremacy
   (C) the system of checks and balances was flawed
   (D) economic sectionalism was a serious threat to national unity
   (E) the Southern states were gaining political and economic power

3. Andrew Jackson's positions on the Second National Bank and the American System typified his

   (A) distrust of large national government programs
   (B) abhorrence of the spoils system
   (C) tendency to favor the interests of the Northeast
   (D) commitment to developing a national economy
   (E) belief that the executive branch should be the weakest of the government's three branches

4. The Cherokee of Georgia were forced off their land because

   (A) they refused to assimilate to the "American" way of life
   (B) gold was discovered in their territory and Georgians demanded that the Indian Removal Act be enforced
   (C) the Supreme Court refused to hear their cases
   (D) the Seminole tribe, their traditional enemy, conquered their territory
   (E) Georgia refused to obey President Jackson's request that they allow the Cherokee to keep their land

5. Brook Farm in Massachusetts, the Oneida Community in upstate New York, and New Harmony in Indiana were similar in that they

   (A) were religious communities inspired by the Second Great Awakening
   (B) demonstrated the attraction of communism to many Americans
   (C) failed because they practiced political and social equality within their own communities
   (D) were stops along the Underground Railroad that aided fugitive slaves
   (E) were utopian communities designed to ameliorate the effects of a growing commercial society

REFLECT ACTIVITY

Respond to the following questions:

- For which content topics discussed in this chapter do you feel you have achieved sufficient mastery to answer multiple-choice questions correctly?

- For which content topics discussed in this chapter do you feel you have achieved sufficient mastery to discuss effectively in an essay?

- For which content topics discussed in this chapter do you feel you need more work before you can answer multiple-choice questions correctly?

- For which content topics discussed in this chapter do you feel you need more work before you can discuss effectively in an essay?

- What parts of this chapter are you going to re-review?

- Will you seek further help, outside of this book (such as a teacher, tutor, or AP Central), on any of the content in this chapter—and, if so, on what content?

Chapter 9
Toward the Civil War and Reconstruction (1845–1877)

POLITICAL AND JUDICIAL ACTIVITY BEFORE THE WAR

The election of 1844 pitted **James Polk** against Whig leader Henry Clay. Though the differences between the Whig and Democratic platforms may seem hazy by modern standards, and there was more than a little overlap, in one respect the two parties were sharply opposed. Above all else, the Whigs stood for a policy of **internal improvements**: building bridges, dredging harbors, digging canals, and in short civilizing the lands the United States already possessed. Democrats tended to be expansionists, set on pushing the nation's borders ever outward. They also felt that it was not the government's place to do anything with newly added land, and that it should instead be kept in private hands, even if that meant living in a country of meandering dirt roads instead of railways. Compare Whig-dominated New England, dotted with bustling towns and busy factories, to the heavily Democratic South with its isolated plantations, and you have a sense of the two parties' disparate visions for America. The election was close, but Polk won.

The Polk Presidency

Polk took office with four goals, and having pledged to serve only one term, had only four years in which to accomplish them. The first goal was to restore the practice of keeping government funds in the Treasury; Andrew Jackson had kept them in so-called "**pet banks**," and the results had been disastrous. The second was to reduce tariffs. Both of these were accomplished by the end of 1846.

In the last days of his administration, President Tyler had proposed the annexation of Texas. Northern congressmen were alarmed: Texas was huge and lay entirely south of the Missouri Compromise line, raising the prospect that it might end up being divided into as many as five slave states. They demanded that Polk maintain the balance by demanding the entirety of the Oregon Country, which stretched from the Mexican territory of Alta California at 42° north up to the Russian territory of Alaska at 54°40′ north. "54°40′ or Fight," they demanded—yes, this was *not* Polk's slogan, but one directed *at* him—but Polk recognized that the United States could hardly afford to fight two territorial wars at the same time, particularly if one was against Great Britain, the other claimant to the Oregon Country. Consequently, he conceded on demands for expansion deep into Canada and set about instead to negotiate a more reasonable American–Canadian border. The **Oregon Treaty**, signed with Great Britain in 1846, allowed the United States to acquire peacefully what is now Oregon, Washington, and parts of Idaho, Wyoming, and Montana. It also established the current northern border of the region.

Reasonably certain that war in the Northwest could be avoided, Polk concentrated on efforts to claim the Southwest from Mexico. He tried to buy the territory, and when that failed, he challenged Mexican authorities on the border of Texas, provoking a Mexican attack on American troops. Mexico was already agitated over the annexation of Texas, which had gained its independence from Mexico in 1836 (remember the Alamo?). Polk then used the border attack to argue for a declaration of war.Congress granted the declaration, and in 1846 the **Mexican-American War** began. Whigs such as first-term member of the House of Representatives Abraham Lincoln questioned Polk's claim that the Mexicans had fired first, but Congress declared war anyway.

The Mexican-American War did not have universal support from the American public. Northerners feared that new states in the West would become slave states, thus tipping the balance in Congress in favor of proslavery forces. Opponents argued that Polk had provoked Mexico into war at the request of powerful slaveholders, and the idea that a few slave owners had control over the government became popular. Those rich Southerners who allegedly were "pulling the strings" were referred to as the **Slave Power** by suspicious Northerners. The **gag rule** in 1836 raised suspicions of a Slave Power, and the defeat of the **Wilmot Proviso**, a congressional bill prohibiting the extension of slavery into any territory gained from Mexico, reinforced those suspicions. The main thing to remember about the Wilmot Proviso is the outcome of the vote:

Naturally, abolitionists were opposed to the expansion of slavery. But, as noted, abolitionists were a small group with very little political power. The primary opposition to the expansion of slavery came from white farmers and workers who didn't care about the welfare of slaves, but who didn't want to have to compete with slave labor: after all, it's hard to get a decent price for your crops when plantations have flooded the market, and it's hard to get hired for a decent wage when your employer can instead purchase slaves and force them to do the job for free. It's worth noting that many free states barred *all* African-Americans from entering, not only slave but free ones as well.

Wilmot Proviso House vote	Whigs	Democrats
Northern	all in favor	all in four in favor
Southern	all but two opposed	all opposed

As you can see, the vote fell along not *party* lines but *sectional* ones, an ominous sign. Over the course of the next decade, the Democrats would become even more Southern-dominated than before, while the Whigs would split between the anti-slavery, Northern "Conscience Whigs" and the pro-slavery, Southern "Cotton Whigs," and would thus follow the Federalists into extinction. New parties would rise to take its place, the first of which was the **Free-Soil Party**, a regional, single-issue party devoted to the goals of the Wilmot Proviso.

While debate raged on, so too did the Mexican War, which went very well for American forces. The United States prevailed so easily in Texas that Polk ordered troops south to Mexico, but also across the Southwest and into California, hoping to grab the entire region by war's end. When the United States successfully invaded Mexico City, the war was over. In the **Treaty of Guadalupe Hidalgo** (1848), Mexico handed over almost all of the modern Southwest: Arizona, New Mexico, California, Nevada, and Utah. This is known as the **Mexican Cession**. The United States, in return, paid $15 million for the land.

The addition of this new territory greatly increased the nation's potential wealth, especially when gold was found at Sutter's Mill during the year that the treaty was signed. However, it also posed major problems regarding the status of slavery. The chief problem was this. By an accident of geography, it just so happened that, east of the Mississippi, the territory of the United States was divided even between lands suited for plantation agriculture, where slavery flourished, and those that were not, and where slavery died out shortly after independence. Now the country extended all the way to the Pacific—but even south of the Missouri Compromise line, lands west of the Mississippi were not to grow cotton, or tobacco, or any of the traditional plantation crops. Southerners saw a future in which slavery was confined, not to the *southern half* of the country, but to the *southeastern quarter* of it, and where they would therefore be greatly outvoted should free-soil advocated decide to ban slavery everywhere. Southerners therefore decided that the time had come to rip up the Missouri Compromise and attempt to open up more areas to slavery. Their first step was to introduce the concept of **popular sovereignty**. Popular sovereignty meant that the territories themselves would decide, by vote, whether to allow slavery within their borders.

The Compromise of 1850

Sectional strife over the new territories started as the ink was drying on the Treaty of Guadalupe Hidalgo. During the Gold Rush, settlers had flooded into California, and the populous territory wanted statehood. Californians had already drawn up a state constitution. That constitution prohibited slavery, and so, of course, the South opposed California's bid for statehood. At the very least, proslavery forces argued, southern California should be forced to accept slavery, in accordance with the boundary drawn by the Missouri Compromise of 1820. The debate grew so hostile that Southern legislators began to discuss openly the possibility of secession.

Democrat **Stephen Douglas** (not to be confused with black abolitionist Frederick Douglass) and Whig Henry Clay hammered out what they thought to be a workable solution, known as the **Compromise of 1850**. When presented as a complete package, the compromise was defeated in Congress. Douglas, however, realized that different groups supported different parts of the compromise, and so he broke the package down into separate bills. He managed to organize majorities to support each of the component bills, and thus ushered the entire compromise through Congress. Together, the bills admitted California as a free state, at the price of the enactment of a stronger **fugitive slave law**. They also created the territories of Utah and New Mexico, but left the status of slavery up to each territory to decide only when it came time for each to write its constitution, thus reinforcing the concept of **popular sovereignty**. The Compromise of 1850 abolished the slave *trade*, not slavery itself, in Washington, D.C. Proponents of this provision argued that it was immoral to "buy and sell human flesh in the shadow of the nation's capitol."

Instituting popular sovereignty and a new fugitive slave law posed serious problems: The definition of popular sovereignty was so vague that Northerners and Southerners could interpret the law entirely differently so as to suit their own positions. The fugitive slave law, meanwhile, made it much easier to retrieve escaped slaves, but it required citizens of free states to cooperate in their retrieval. Abolitionists considered it coercive, immoral, and an affront to their liberty.

Antislavery sentiments in the North grew stronger in 1852 with the publication of ***Uncle Tom's Cabin***, a sentimental novel written by a then-obscure writer named Harriet Beecher Stowe. Stowe, a Northerner, based her damning depictions of plantation life on information provided her by abolitionist friends. She wisely avoided political preaching, instead playing on people's sympathies. The book sold more than a million copies and was adapted into several popular plays that toured America and Europe. Like Thomas Paine's *Common Sense* during the Revolutionary War era, it was an extremely powerful piece of propaganda, awakening antislavery sentiment in millions who had never before given the issue much thought.

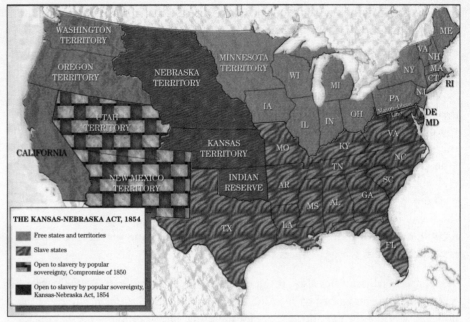

Kansas-Nebraska Act, 1854

The Kansas-Nebraska Act and "Bleeding Kansas"

After California, no new states would be admitted to the Union until 1858. However, the contentious status of the new territories proved increasingly problematic. Settlers entering the Kansas and Nebraska territories found no established civil authority. Congress also wanted to build railways through the territory, but they needed some form of government to impose order, secure land (a task that included driving out Native Americans), and supervise construction.

Stephen Douglas sought to address these issues with the **Kansas-Nebraska Act of 1854**. Again, Douglas formulated and ushered through Congress a law that left the fate of slavery up to residents without specifying *when* or *how* they were to decide. To make matters worse, by opening the two territories to slavery, the Kansas-Nebraska Act repealed the Missouri Compromise, thus further destabilizing the political situation. Northerners considered the new law a betrayal, regarding it as further evidence of the Slave Power's domination of government. In response, many Northern states passed laws weakening the fugitive slave act. These laws, called **personal liberty laws**, required a trial by jury for all alleged fugitives and guaranteed them the right to a lawyer. Southerners, who thought the fugitive slave law would be the final word on the issue, were furious.

The Kansas-Nebraska Act also drove the final stake into the heart of the Whig party. Anti-slavery Whigs, growing more impassioned about the issue and more convinced that the national party would never take a strong stand, joined Northern Democrats and former Free-Soilers (whose single issue was effectively defeated by Kansas-Nebraska) to form a new party, the **Republicans**. Though not abolitionist, the Republicans were dedicated to keeping slavery out of the territories. They also championed a wide range of issues, including the further development of national roads, more liberal land distribution in the West, and increased protective tariffs. As a result, the Republicans appealed to a wider constituency than the Free-Soilers had. Midwestern merchants and farmers, Western settlers, and Eastern importers all found something to like in the Republican platform. The Republican party grew quickly in the North, where it won a majority of congressional seats in 1854.

Another new party formed during this period. The **American** party, often called the **Know-Nothings** because they met privately and remained secretive about their political agenda, rallied around a single issue: hatred of foreigners (**nativism**), a perennial favorite in U.S. politics. The party grew quickly and dominated several state legislatures. It also spread some ugly anti-Irish, anti-German, and anti-Catholic propaganda. For a while it appeared that the Know-Nothings, and not the Republican party, would become the Democrats' chief competition. Yet before it could reach that pinnacle, the party self-destructed, primarily because its Northern and Southern wings disagreed over slavery.

The Kansas-Nebraska Act also provoked violence in the territories. Both abolitionists and proslavery groups rushed into the territories, planning to form governments in hopes of winning the two future states for their side. Just prior to the election for Kansas's legislature, thousands of proslavery Missourians (called **Border Ruffians**) temporarily relocated in Kansas, resulting in rival constitutions being sent to Washington: an anti-slavery one from Topeka and a pro-slavery one from Lecompton. President Franklin Pierce, a "doughface" (as Northerners with who supported pro-Southern policies were called), recognized the Lecompton Constitution and promptly declared Kansas a slave territory. Proslavery forces took Pierce's recognition as a license to expel the free-soilers, and they demolished the free-soil city of Lawrence. In retaliation, radical abolitionist **John Brown** led a raid on a proslavery camp, murdering five. After that, the gloves *really* came off, as gangs from both sides roamed the territory and attacked the opposition. More than 200 people died in the conflict, which is how Kansas came to be known as **Bleeding Kansas**, or **Bloody Kansas**, during this period.

The events in Kansas further polarized the nation. The passions raised were even reflected in Congress when Preston Brooks, nephew of proslavery Senator **Andrew Butler**, savagely beat abolitionist Senator Charles Sumner on the head with a cane for a speech in which Sumner attacked the South and Butler using lewd metaphors about slavery. The crisis destroyed Pierce's political career, and the Democrats chose **James Buchanan** as their 1856 candidate. Buchanan's greatest political asset was that he had been out of the country for the previous four years and so could avoid blame for the disastrous results of the Kansas-Nebraska Act. In a sectional vote, Buchanan won the election, carrying the South, while the North split between Buchanan and Republican John Frémont. The Know-Nothings ran Millard Fillmore, who won 20 percent of the vote. It was the Know-Nothings' last hurrah.

Buchanan, Dred Scott, and the Election of 1860

As president, **James Buchanan** tried to maintain the status quo. He worked to enforce the fugitive slave act and opposed abolitionist activism in the South and West. Like many of the nation's leaders at the time, he was at a loss when it came to a permanent solution to the question of slavery. He hoped merely to maintain the Union until a solution presented itself.

Two days after Buchanan took office, the crisis over slavery escalated when the Supreme Court ruled in ***Dred Scott v. Sandford***. Scott, a former slave whose master had taken him to territories where slavery was illegal, declared himself a free man and sued for his freedom. Scott won the case, then lost the appeal, and the case finally wound up in the Supreme Court where Scott lost. At a time when many wanted to ignore the big questions surrounding slavery, Chief Justice Roger Taney (who wrote the majority decision) chose to attack them head-on. Taney's one-sided, proslavery decision declared that slaves were property, not citizens, and further, that no black person could ever be a citizen of the United States. Because blacks were not citizens, Taney argued, they could not sue in federal courts, as Scott had done. Moreover, he ruled that Congress could not regulate slavery in the territories, as it had done in passing the Northwest Ordinance in 1787 under the Articles of Confederation government and again in 1820 with the Missouri Compromise. This part of the decision not only nullified the now obsolete Missouri Compromise, but also the Kansas-Nebraska Act, and it ruled out any hope of reviving the Wilmot Proviso, which was still championed by many Northerners and abolitionists.

In exercising judicial review and declaring the Missouri Compromise unconstitutional, Taney and the Court were in essence saying that slavery could go anywhere; the Republicans' goal of preventing the spread of slavery into the new territories was destroyed by the Court's ruling. The *Dred Scott* decision was thus a major victory for Southerners and a turning point in the "decade of crisis."

In the North, the Supreme Court decision was viciously denounced. Even those who lacked strong abolitionist sentiments feared that the decision tilted the balance of power too far in the South's favor. Many, including the press, regarded the decision as further proof of a Slave Power that, if left unchecked, would soon dominate the entire country, perhaps even forcing slavery on those states that did not want it. Meanwhile, the Democratic party was dividing along regional lines, raising the possibility that the Republicans might soon control the national government.

1858 was an off-year election, and it was in this politically charged atmosphere that the famous Lincoln-Douglas debates took place. Students often think the debates were for the presidential election, but they weren't. Douglas faced stiff competition for his Illinois Senate seat from **Abraham Lincoln**, a rising star in the newly formed Republican party. The race for Illinois's Senate seat gained national attention in part because of the railroad and telegraph. Stephen Douglas was viewed as the leading Democrat in the United States Senate, while Lincoln had gained his reputation as a Whig opposed to the Mexican War and Kansas-Nebraska Act.

In many ways, the Lincoln-Douglas debates gave voice to the issues and concerns that divided a nation heading for civil war. It was in this campaign that Lincoln delivered his famous "House Divided" speech ("this nation cannot exist permanently half slave and half free"), while Douglas destroyed his political career in his attempt to defend popular sovereignty in what became known as the **Freeport Doctrine**. Douglas tried to depict Lincoln as an abolitionist, but Lincoln skillfully backed Douglas into a corner when he pushed him to reconcile popular sovereignty with the *Dred Scott* decision. Douglas suggested that slavery could not exist where local laws did not protect it. In essence, he contended, voters and residents of a territory could exclude slavery simply by not protecting a man's "property." Douglas alienated both Northern and Southern voters by his ambiguous stance on popular sovereignty and effectively destroyed any chance he might have had for winning the presidency in 1860.

Adding fuel to the secessionist fire was **John Brown**'s raid on **Harper's Ferry** in 1859. Brown hoped to spark a slave revolt but failed. After his execution, news spread that Brown had received financial backing from Northern abolitionist organizations. Brown became a martyr for the cause, celebrated throughout the North.

When it came time for the Democrats to choose their 1860 presidential candidate, their convention split. Northern Democrats backed Douglas; Southerners backed John Breckinridge. The election showed that the nation itself was on the brink of fracture. In the North, the contest was between Douglas and Republican nominee Abraham Lincoln. In the South, Breckinridge faced off against Constitutional Union Party nominee John Bell; Lincoln didn't even appear on Southern ballots. But the North held the majority of the electoral votes, so when Lincoln achieved a clean sweep there, he won the election. The response in Southern legislatures was to propose bills of secession.

Immediately after the election, Southern leaders who wanted to maintain the Union tried to negotiate and came up with the Crittendon Compromise. All hope of resolution died, however, when Lincoln refused to soften the Republican demand that slavery not be extended to the territories. Lincoln probably had no other political option, as to do otherwise would have been to abandon the principles of those who had supported his election. Lincoln and other Northern leaders were banking on the hope that the South was bluffing and would not secede.

In December 1860, three months before Lincoln's inauguration, South Carolina seceded from the Union. Within months six other states had joined South Carolina to form the **Confederate States of America**; the states chose **Jefferson Davis** to lead the Confederacy. Cautiously, Lincoln decided to maintain control of federal forts in the South while waiting for the Confederacy to make a move. On April 12, 1861 it did, attacking and capturing **Fort Sumter**. No one died in this first battle of America's bloodiest war, the **Civil War**.

THE CIVIL WAR AND RECONSTRUCTION (1860–1877)

For many people of the era, the Civil War was not solely (or even explicitly) about slavery. It is worth noting that Missouri, Kentucky, Maryland, and Delaware, the **Border States**, were slave states that fought for the Union. Except for active abolitionists, most Northerners believed they were fighting to preserve the Union. Most Southerners described their cause as fighting for their **states' rights** to govern themselves. But slavery was the issue that had caused the argument over states' rights to escalate to war. Lincoln's views on slavery evolved throughout the 1850s and the Civil War, but as late as 1862, Lincoln stated: "If I could save the Union without freeing any slaves I would do it, and if I could save the union by freeing all the slaves I would do it…. What I do about slavery, and the colored race, I do because I believe it helps to save the Union."

The Civil War took place not only on the battlefields but also in political, economic, and social realms. Although you do not need to know the military details of any specific battles for the AP exam, you should know the political or diplomatic consequences of battles like Gettysburg or Antietam, and you do need to know how political, social, and economic conditions influenced the outcome of the war.

The Civil War and the Confederacy

Ironically, as the Southern states fought to maintain the right to govern themselves locally, the Confederate government brought them under greater central control than they had ever experienced. Jefferson Davis understood the North's considerable advantages in population, transportation, and economics, and he knew that the weak, poorly organized state governments of the South could not mount an effective defense. Davis took control of the Southern economy, imposing taxes and using the revenues to spur industrial and urban growth; he took control of the railroads and commercial shipping; and he created a large government bureaucracy to oversee economic developments. Davis, in short, forced the South to compensate quickly for what it had lost when it cut itself off from Northern commerce. When Southerners opposed his moves, he declared martial law and suspended the writ of *habeas corpus*, a traditional protection against improper imprisonment, in order to maintain control. Lincoln was upsetting Northerners with some of the exact same steps, but the use of the presidential power chafed especially badly in the Confederacy, where many believed they had seceded precisely to avoid the federal government commanding too much power.

Davis had some success in modernizing the Southern economy, but the Confederacy lagged too far behind in industrialization to catch up to the Union. Rapid economic growth, furthermore, brought with it rapid **inflation**. Prices rose so quickly that paychecks and payments for crops became worthless almost as soon as they were made, plunging many Southerners into poverty. In 1862 the Confederacy imposed **conscription** (a military draft), requiring many small farmers to serve in the Confederate Army. This act caused even greater poverty in the country, as many families could not adequately tend their farms without their men.

Confederate conscription also created class conflict. The government allowed the wealthy to hire surrogates to perform military service in their place and exempted anyone who owned more than twenty slaves from military service (on the grounds that the large plantations these men ran fed the Confederacy and its army). In effect, the wealthy did not have to serve, while the poor had no choice. As a result, **class tensions** increased, leading ultimately to widespread desertions from the Confederate Army. Toward the end of the war, it also led many Southerners in small towns to ignore the government and try to carry on as if there was no war. Many resisted when asked to feed, clothe, or house passing troops.

The Civil War and the Union

The Northern economy received a boost from the war as the demand for war-related goods, such as uniforms and weapons, spurred manufacturing. The loss of Southern markets harmed the economy at first, but soon the war economy brought about a boom period. A number of entrepreneurs became extremely wealthy; many succumbed to the temptations of greed, overcharging the government for services and products (**war profiteering**). Some sold the Union government worthless, shoddy food and clothing while government bureaucrats looked the other way for the price of a bribe. Corruption was fairly widespread, eventually prompting a yearlong congressional investigation.

Like the South, the North experienced a period of accelerated inflation, although Northern inflation was nowhere as extreme as its Southern counterpart. (In the North, prices rose between 10 and 20 percent annually; in the South, the inflation rate was well over 300 percent.) Workers, worried about job security in the face of mechanization and the decreasing value of their wages, formed **unions**. Businesses, in return, blacklisted union members, forced new employees to sign contracts in which they promised not to join unions, and used violence to break strikes. The Republican Party, then (as now) believing that government should help businesses but regulate them as little as possible, supported business in its opposition to unions.

Lincoln, like Davis, oversaw a tremendous increase in the power of the central government during the war. He implemented economic development programs without waiting for congressional approval, championed numerous government loans and grants to businesses, and raised tariffs to protect Union trade. He also suspended the writ of *habeas corpus* in the border states, to make it easier to arrest secessionists, especially in Maryland. During the war, Lincoln initiated the printing of a **national currency**. Lincoln's able treasury secretary, Salmon P. Chase, issued **greenbacks**, government-issued paper money that was a precursor to modern currency.

Emancipation of the Slaves

As previously stated, neither the Union nor the Confederacy initially declared the Civil War to be a war about slavery. The Constitution protected slavery where it already existed, so many opponents (including Republicans) were opposed to the *extension* of slavery into the new territories. As a presidential candidate, Lincoln had argued for gradual emancipation, compensation to slaveholders for liberated slaves, and the colonization of freed slaves somewhere outside the United States, perhaps in Africa. When the Union dissolved and the South left Congress, Lincoln was faced with a legislature much more progressive in its thoughts on slavery than he was. The **Radical Republican** wing of Congress wanted immediate emancipation. To that end, the radicals introduced the **confiscation acts** in Congress. The first (1861) gave the government the right to seize any slaves used for "insurrectionary purposes." The second (1862) was much wider in scope, allowing the government to liberate any slave owned by someone who supported the rebellion, even if that support was limited to paying taxes to the Confederate government. The second confiscation act, in effect, gave the Union the right to liberate all slaves. This act had little effect, however, because Lincoln refused to enforce it.

Soon after, however, Lincoln took his first cautious steps toward emancipation. The primary reason was pretty simple: slaves indirectly supported the Southern war effort. They grew the crops and cooked the meals that kept the rebel troops fed. Therefore any strategy the Union army adopted had to include capturing slaves as a key element. But what to do with them once they were captured? Lock them up somewhere and return them to their owners after the war? They had to be freed, or the government of the United States would become the world's biggest slaveholder. And there were other advantages of making the freedom of the slaves one of the side effects of Union victory. One was that it kept Britain and France out of the war. Jefferson Davis had hoped that these countries would support the Confederacy in order to keep receiving shipments of Southern cotton, but once Lincoln made it explicit that Union victory would mean freedom for the slaves, European governments dared not attempt to come to the aid of the rebels for fear of being quickly toppled by an outraged public. Another advantage was that emancipation would provide a new source of troops for the Union side: "The bare sight of fifty thousand armed and drilled black soldiers on the banks of the Mississippi would end the rebellion at once," Lincoln mused. But he dared not make this move until after a Northern victory, lest it appear like a desperate response to the defeats skilled Southern generals were inflicting upon the Union. The moment came in September 1862, with the Union victory at Antietam.

In the aftermath of the battle, Lincoln issued the **Emancipation Proclamation**. Note that the Emancipation Proclamation, for all intents and purposes, actually freed no slaves. Instead, it stated that on January 1, 1863, the government would liberate all slaves residing in those states still "in rebellion." Throughout the war, Lincoln refused to acknowledge secession and insisted on referring to the Confederate states as "those states in rebellion." The Proclamation did not liberate the slaves in the border states such as Maryland, nor did it liberate slaves in Southern counties already under the control of the Union Army. Again, legally, Lincoln had no power to abolish slavery in areas governed by the U.S. Constitution. Abolitionists complained that the Proclamation liberated slaves only where the Union had no power to enforce emancipation and maintained slavery precisely where it could liberate the slaves. The Proclamation also allowed Southern states to rejoin the Union *without* giving up slavery. On the positive side, the Emancipation Proclamation finally declared that the Civil War was, for the Union, a war against slavery, and thus changed the purpose of the war, much as the Declaration of Independence had changed the purpose of the Revolutionary War.

Not until two years later, while campaigning for reelection, did Lincoln give his support to complete emancipation. Just before the Republican convention, Lincoln lobbied for a party platform that called for a constitutional amendment prohibiting slavery; the result was the **Thirteenth Amendment**. After his reelection, Lincoln considered allowing defeated Southern states to reenter the Union and to vote on the Thirteenth Amendment. He tried to negotiate a settlement with Southern leaders along those lines at the **Hampton Roads Conference**. Lincoln also offered a five-year delay on implementing the amendment if it passed, as well as $400 million in compensation to slave owners. Jefferson Davis's commitment to complete Southern independence scuttled any chance of compromise.

The Election of 1864 and the End of the Civil War

As the 1864 presidential election approached, popular opinion in both the North and South favored an end to the war. Lincoln's opponent, General George McClellan, campaigned on a peace platform. In the South, citizens openly defied the civil authority.

It should be reemphasized that less than one percent of the Southern population owned more than 100 slaves, and as the war dragged on, many small, non-slave-holding farmers resented the Confederacy and the war, which they now believed was being waged merely to protect the planter aristocracy's lifestyle. In the North, some "War Democrats" conceded that the war was necessary to preserve the Union. Others, called the **Copperheads**, accused Lincoln of instigating a national social revolution and criticized his administration's policies as a thinly disguised attempt to destroy the South. Nowhere, however, was opposition to the war more violent than in New York City, where racial, ethnic, and class antagonisms exploded into draft riots in July of 1863. Irish immigrants, mostly the poor working-class who were already victims of **nativism**, resented being drafted into a war being fought to end slavery. Many immigrants feared that once freed, former slaves would migrate into Northern cities and compete with them for low-paying labor jobs. And yet, both sides fought on.

Just when a stalemate might have forced an end to the war, things began improving for the North. Victories throughout the summer of 1864 played a large part in helping Lincoln gain reelection. By the early spring of 1865, a Union victory was virtually assured, and the government established the **Freedman's Bureau** to help newly liberated blacks establish a place in postwar society. The Bureau helped with immediate problems of survival (food, housing) and developed social institutions, such as schools. Some historians see the Freedman's Bureau as the first federal, social welfare program in U.S. history. In April 1865 the Confederate leaders surrendered. John Wilkes Booth assassinated Lincoln just five days later, with devastating consequences for the reunited nation.

The Civil War was fought at enormous cost. More than 3 million men fought in the war, and of them, more than 500,000 died. At least as many were seriously wounded. Both governments ran up huge debts during the war, and much of the South was ravaged by Union soldiers. During **Sherman's March** from Atlanta to the sea in the fall of 1864, the Union Army burned everything in its wake (to destroy Confederate morale and deplete the South's material resources), foreshadowing the wide- scale warfare of the twentieth century. From a political perspective, the war permanently expanded the role of government. On both sides government grew rapidly to manage the economy and the war.

Reconstruction and Johnson's Impeachment

At war's end, three major questions faced the reunited nation. First, under what conditions would the Southern states be readmitted to the Union? Second, what would be the status of blacks in the postwar nation? Black leaders hoped that their service in the military would earn blacks equal rights. The newly liberated slaves, called freedmen, were primarily interested in the chance to earn wages and own property. And third, what should be done with the rebels?

Reconstruction may be seen as both a time period and a process. As a time period, Reconstruction usually refers to the years between 1865 and 1877, that is, from the end of the Civil War until the end of military reconstruction when the Union army withdrew from the South. The *process* of reconstruction, however, was complicated and complex, and some argue it continues to this day. Reconstruction involved readmitting the Southern states that had seceded from the Union; physically reconstructing and rebuilding Southern towns, cities, and property that had been destroyed during the war; and finally, integrating newly freed blacks into American society. It is this last process that has proven to be most difficult.

The process of reconstruction had begun even before the Civil War ended, although not without controversy. As president of the United States and commander-in-chief of the armed forces, Lincoln had claimed that he had the authority to determine the conditions under which the Southern states might be readmitted to the Union. Lincoln had no intention of punishing the South and wanted to end the war and reunite the nation quickly and painlessly, as his immortal words from his second inaugural address indicate: "With malice toward none, with charity for all, with firmness in the right, as God gives us to see the right, let us strive on to finish the work we are in, to bind up the nation's wounds, to care for him who shall have borne the battle and for his widow and his orphan, to do all which may achieve and cherish a just and lasting peace among ourselves and with all nations."

Lincoln's plan is usually referred to as the **Ten-Percent Plan** and simply required that 10 percent of those voters who had voted in the 1860 election swear an oath of allegiance to the Union and accept emancipation through the Thirteenth Amendment. These men would then reorganize their state government and reapply for admission into the Union. Congress had another vision, however. It viewed the Southern states as "conquered territory" and as such, **Radical Republicans** in Congress argued, were under the jurisdiction of Congress, not the President. Most Republicans agreed that Lincoln's plan was too lenient and enacted the **Wade-Davis Bill** in July of 1864. This act provided that former Confederate states be ruled by a military governor and required 50 percent of the electorate to swear an oath of allegiance to the United States. A state convention would then be organized to repeal their ordinance of secession and abolish slavery within their state.

It should be noted that neither Lincoln's Ten-Percent Plan nor the Wade-Davis Bill made any provisions for black suffrage. Lincoln pocket-vetoed the Wade-Davis Bill, effectively destroying it. (A pocket veto can only occur at the end of a congressional session. If the president does not sign a bill within 10 days and Congress adjourns within those 10 days, the bill dies and must be reintroduced when Congress reconvenes. Unlike a regular veto, which requires the president to explain his objections to a bill and can subsequently be overridden, a pocket veto does not need to be explained nor is it subject to another congressional vote. It cannot be overridden.) Lincoln was assassinated the following year.

With Lincoln's assassination, Vice President **Andrew Johnson** assumed the presidency. Johnson, a Southern Democrat, had opposed secession and strongly supported Lincoln during his first term. In return, Lincoln rewarded Johnson with the vice presidency. When the war ended, Congress was in recess and would not reconvene for eight months. That left the early stages of Reconstruction entirely in Johnson's hands.

Johnson had lifted himself from poverty and held no great love for the South's elite planters, and at first he seemed intent on taking power away from the old aristocracy and giving it to the yeomen. **Johnson's Reconstruction Plan**, which was based on a plan approved by Lincoln, called for the creation of provisional military governments to run the states until they were readmitted to the Union. It also required all Southern citizens to swear a **loyalty oath** before receiving amnesty for the rebellion. However, it barred many of the former Southern elite (including plantation owners, Confederate officers, and government officials) from taking that vow, thus prohibiting their participation in the new governments. According to this plan, the provisional governments would hold state constitutional conventions, at which time the states would have to write new constitutions eliminating slavery and renouncing secession. Johnson did not require the states to enfranchise blacks by giving them the vote.

The plan did not work, mostly because Johnson **pardoned** many of the Southern elite who were supposed to have been excluded from the reunification process. After the states drafted new constitutions and elected new governments, former Confederate officials were again in positions of great power. Furthermore, many of their new constitutions were only slight revisions of previous constitutions. Southern legislators also passed new black codes limiting freedman's rights to assemble and travel, instituting curfews, and requiring blacks to carry special passes. In the most egregious instances, state legislatures simply took their old slave codes and replaced the word *slaves* with *freedmen*. When Congress reconvened in December 1865, the new Southern senators included the vice president of the Confederacy and other Confederate officials. Northern congressmen were not pleased. Invoking its constitutional right to examine the credentials of new members, Congress voted not to seat the new Southern delegations. Then, it set about examining Johnson's Reconstruction plan.

Congress was divided among conservative Republicans, who generally agreed with Johnson's plan; moderates, who were a large enough contingent to swing a vote in one or the other direction; and Radical Republicans. The Radical Republicans wanted to extend democracy in the South. Following the Civil War, most important political positions were held by appointees; very few officials were directly elected. (Of course, women could not vote and black men could vote only in a few northern states at this time.) The most radical among the Radical Republicans advocated a reconstruction program that punished the South for seceding. Historians of the time suggested that revenge was the real motivation behind the passage of the Thirteenth Amendment, although contemporary historians have dismissed this idea. Under General Sherman's **Special Field Order No. 15**, land seized from the Confederates was to be redistributed among the new freedmen, but President Andrew Johnson rescinded Sherman's order, and the idea of giving freedmen "**40 acres and a mule**" never regained much ground.

All Republicans agreed that Johnson's Reconstruction needed some modification, but Johnson refused to compromise. Instead, he declared Reconstruction over and done with, vetoing a compromise package that would have extended the life of the Freedman's Bureau and enforced a uniform civil rights code on the South. Congress overrode Johnson's vetoes, which only increased tension between the two branches of the federal government.

In response, the radicals drew up the plan that came to be known as **Congressional Reconstruction**. Its first component was the **Fourteenth Amendment** to the Constitution. The amendment (1) stated that if you are born in the United States, you are a citizen of the United States and you are a citizen of the state where you reside; (2) prohibited states from depriving any citizen of "life, liberty, or property without due process of law"; (3) prevented states from denying any citizen "equal protection of the law"; (4) gave states the choice either to give freedmen the right to vote or to stop counting them among their voting population for the purpose of congressional apportionment; (5) barred prominent Confederates from holding political office; and (6) excused the Confederacy's war debt.

The first three points remain the most significant, to this very day, and are the basis for most lawsuits involving discrimination and civil rights. In fact, through a series of cases over the years, most of the first ten amendments have been extended to the states through the due process clause of the Fourteenth Amendment. It is helpful to remember that the Bill of Rights protects the individual from the federal government, while the Fourteenth Amendment protects you from the state government. The Fourteenth Amendment was intended to clarify the status of newly freed slaves, address the issue of citizenship raised by the Dred Scott decision, and limit the effects of the black codes. The radicals hoped to force states to either extend suffrage to black men or lose power in Congress. In the "**Swing Around the Circle**" public speaking tour, Johnson campaigned against the amendment and lost. In the congressional election of 1866, the North voted for a Congress more heavily weighted toward the radical end of the political spectrum.

The new Congress quickly passed the **Military Reconstruction Act of 1867**. It imposed martial law on the South; it also called for new state constitutional conventions and forced the states to allow blacks to vote for convention delegates. The act also required each state to ratify the Fourteenth Amendment and to send its new constitution to Congress for approval. Aware that Johnson would oppose the new Reconstruction, Congress then passed a number of laws designed to limit the president's power. As expected, Johnson did everything in his power to counteract the congressional plan. The conflict reached its climax when the House Judiciary Committee initiated **impeachment proceedings** against Johnson, ostensibly for violating the Tenure of Office Act (which stated that the president had to secure the consent of the Senate before removing his appointees once they'd been approved by that body; Johnson had fired Secretary of War Edwin Stanton, a Radical Republican) but really because he was getting in the way of Reconstruction. Johnson was acquitted by one vote in the Senate, but the trial rendered Johnson politically impotent, and he served the last few months of his presidency with no hope of re-election.

With a new president, **Ulysses S. Grant**, in office, Congress forged ahead in its efforts to remake the South. The **Fifteenth Amendment**, proposed in 1869, finally required states to enfranchise black men. (Women's suffrage would have to wait another half-century.) Ironically, the Fifteenth Amendment passed only because Southern states were required to ratify it as a condition of reentry into the Union; a number of Northern states opposed the amendment.

The Failure of Reconstruction

Reconstruction had its share of successes while the North occupied the South. New state constitutions officially allowed all Southern men to vote (previous constitutions had required voters to own property) and replaced many appointed government positions with elected positions. New Southern governments, directed mostly by transplanted Northern Republicans, blacks, and Southern moderates, created public schools and those social institutions such as orphanages popularized in the North during the reform movement of the 1830s. The new governments also stimulated industrial and rail development in the South through loans, grants, and tax exemptions. The fact that blacks were serving in Southern governments represented a huge step forward, given the seemingly insurmountable restrictions placed on blacks only a few years earlier, though it would prove to be only a temporary victory.

However, ultimately, Reconstruction failed. Although government industrialization plans helped rebuild the Southern economy, these plans also cost a lot of money. High tax rates turned public opinion, already antagonistic to Reconstruction, even more hostile. Opponents waged a propaganda war against Reconstruction, calling Southerners who cooperated **scalawags** and Northerners who ran the programs **carpetbaggers**. (The name came from the suitcases they carried, implying they had come to the South merely to stuff their bags with ill-gotten wealth.) Many who participated in Reconstruction were indeed corrupt, selling their votes for money and favors.

It should be noted that Northerners were just as guilty as Southerners of corruption. The period following the Civil War is also known as "The Gilded Age," to suggest the tarnish that lay beneath the layer of gold. This is the era of political machines and "bosses," which will be discussed in a later chapter. Political scandal was not new at the time, and in fact, Grant's administration was wracked with political scandals and intrigue; Grant himself was supposedly innocent and oblivious to the goings on in his administration. Grant had no political experience when he became president; in fact, he was elected because he was a popular war hero, not an experienced political leader. Like Jackson, Grant appointed his friends and supporters to governmental positions, not necessarily those men most qualified, let alone those with the most integrity.

Unfortunately, although Grant was honest, his friends were not. A series of scandals broke out in the early 1870s, and while you don't need to know the details to do well on the AP test, the sheer length of the list should get the idea across:

> **Black Friday, 1869**
> **Credit Mobilier scandar, 1872**
> **New York Custom House ring, 1872**
> **Star Route frauds, 1872-1876**
> **Sanborn incident, 1874**
> **Pratt & Boyd scandal, 1875**
> **Whiskey Ring, 1875**
> **Delano affair, 1875**
> **Trading post scandal, 1876**
> **Alexander Cattell & Co. scandal, 1876**
> **Safe burglary, 1876**

These scandals diverted the public's attention away from the postwar conditions in the South.

Though the Civil War was officially over, a war of intimidation began, spearheaded by insurgent groups ranging from secretive terrorist groups such as the **Ku Klux Klan**, who focused on murdering freedmen, to openly operating paramilitary forces such as the **White League**, who focused on murdering Republicans. "These combinations amount to war," declared attorney general Amos Akerman, who had been posted to the Carolinas to try to speed trials of Klansmen along—a problem because local judges tended to be Klansmen as well. In some towns the entire adult male population was engaged in battle against Reconstruction. Southern officials explained their failure to do anything to protect blacks and Republicans by complaining that if they obeyed their orders to round up insurgents, there would be mass starvation because nobody would be left to work.

Also, because Reconstruction did nothing to redistribute the South's wealth or guarantee that the freedmen would own property, it did very little to alter the basic power structure of the region. Southerners knew that when the Northerners left, as they inevitably would, things would return to a condition much closer to the way they were before Reconstruction. As early as 1869, the federal government began sending signals that it would soon ease up restrictions. President Grant enforced the law loosely, hoping to lessen tensions and thereby hasten an amicable reunion. Worse, throughout the 1860s and 1870s, the Supreme Court consistently restricted the scope of the Fourteenth and Fifteenth Amendments. In the *Slaughter-House* cases, the court ruled that the Fourteenth Amendment applied only to the federal

"A portion of our southern population hate the government of the United States, because they understand it emphatically to represent northern sentiment, and hate the negro because he has ceased to be a slave and has been promoted to be a citizen and a voter, and hate those of the southern whites who are looked upon as in political friendship with the north, with the United States Government and with the negro. These persons commit the violence that disturbs many parts of the south."
—Attorney General Amos Akerman

government, not to state governments, an opinion the court strengthened in *United States v. Cruikshank*. In *United States v. Reese*, the court cleared the way for "grandfather clauses," poll taxes, literary tests, property requirements, and other restrictions on voting privileges. Soon nearly all Southern states had restrictive laws that effectively prevented blacks from voting. Finally, because Grant's administration was so thoroughly corrupt, it tainted everything with which it was associated, including Reconstruction.

During the 1872 election, moderates calling themselves Liberal Republicans abandoned the coalition that supported Reconstruction. Angered by widespread corruption, this group hoped to end federal control of the South. Although their candidate, Horace Greeley, did not defeat Grant, they made gains in congressional and state elections. As a result, Grant moved further away from the radical position and closer to conciliation. Several congressional acts, among them the Amnesty Act of 1872, pardoned many of the rebels, thus allowing them to reenter public life. Other crises, such as the financial Panic of 1873, drew the nation's attention away from Reconstruction. By 1876 Southern Democrats had regained control of most of the region's state legislatures. These Democrats called themselves "**Redeemers**," and their use of the word redemption suggested they intended to reverse Republican reconstruction policies as they returned to power.

The election of 1876 was one of the more infamously contested elections in American history, with both political parties accusing the other of fraud. Samuel J. Tilden, then governor of New York and a political reformer who had gone after "**Boss**" **Tweed**, the most notorious among the political bosses of the time, won the popular vote by a small margin but needed to win the electoral vote to gain the presidency. (Remember that according to the Constitution, if no one candidate receives a majority of electoral votes, the election is thrown into the House of Representatives. You should remember, for example, that Andrew Jackson lost the presidency to John Quincy Adams through a "corrupt bargain" in 1824.) Republicans challenged the election returns that favored Tilden in South Carolina, Louisiana, and Florida. Congress eventually stepped in to resolve the disputed election and created a special bipartisan electoral commission consisting of senators, representatives, and Supreme Court justices. Through a series of informal negotiations, a deal was struck that has come to be known as the **Compromise of 1877**. It was agreed that if Rutherford B. Hayes won the presidential election, he would end military reconstruction and pull federal troops out of South Carolina and Louisiana, thereby enabling Democrats to regain control of those states. Military reconstruction was thus ended, and it was business as usual in the South. Many historians feel that the federal government dropped the ball in 1877, for in many ways, life for blacks got worse, and it would take almost another 100 years for the federal government to live up to the ideal expressed in the Declaration of Independence: "that all men are created equal."

Southern Blacks During and After Reconstruction

At the end of the Civil War, the former slaves were thrust into an ambiguous state of freedom. Most reacted cautiously, remaining on plantations as sharecroppers where they had been relatively well treated but fleeing from those with cruel overseers. Many set out in search of family members from whom they had been separated. The Freedman's Bureau helped them find new jobs and housing and provided money and food to those in need. The Freedman's Bureau also helped establish schools at all levels for blacks, among them Fisk University and Howard University. Unfortunately, the Freedman's Bureau was terribly underfunded and had little impact once military reconstruction came to an end.

When it became evident that the government would not redistribute land, blacks looked for other ways to work their own farms. The Freedman's Bureau attempted to establish a system in which blacks contracted their labor to whites, but the system failed. Instead, blacks preferred **sharecropping**, in which they traded a portion of their crop in return for the right to work someone else's land. The system worked at first, but unscrupulous landowners eventually used the system as a means of keeping poor farmers in a state of near slavery and debt. Abuses of the sharecropping system grew more widespread at the end of Reconstruction, at which point no court would fairly try the case of a sharecropper against a landowner. Sharecropping existed well into the middle of the twentieth century and actually included more whites than blacks.

Disenchantment with white society led many freedmen to found communities as far removed from the sphere of whites as possible. Black churches continued to serve as another means by which the black community could bond and gain further autonomy. When Reconstruction ended, many blacks anticipated the fate that awaited them in the South and left. The **Great Migration** into Northern cities like Chicago and Detroit would not take place, however, until World War I.

Chapter 9 Drill

See Chapter 13 for answers and explanations.

1. As a result of the Mexican-American War, all of the following became part of the United States EXCEPT

   (A) California
   (B) Nevada
   (C) New Mexico
   (D) Texas
   (E) Utah

2. "Bleeding Kansas" was a direct result of the doctrine of

   (A) judicial review
   (B) imperialism
   (C) containment
   (D) Manifest Destiny
   (E) popular sovereignty

3. As a result of the Emancipation Proclamation,

   (A) all slaves in the Union and the Confederacy were declared free
   (B) nearly 200,000 free blacks and escaped slaves joined the Union Army
   (C) Maryland seceded from the Union
   (D) African-Americans in the United States received the right to vote
   (E) millions of African-Americans left the South and moved to Northern cities

4. Andrew Johnson was impeached because

   (A) he refused to carry out Lincoln's plan for reconstruction
   (B) he vetoed the Wade-Davis Bill
   (C) Congress was controlled by Republicans and he was a Democrat
   (D) he violated the Tenure of Office Act by firing Secretary of War Stanton
   (E) he refused to adequately fund the Freedmen's Bureau because he had vetoed the bill that established it

5. The dispute over electoral votes in the election of 1876

   (A) was similar to the election of 2000 in that the Supreme Court ultimately had to step in and decide the election
   (B) was resolved by a special bipartisan commission and resulted in the end of military reconstruction
   (C) led many members of Congress to push for a Constitutional amendment to abolish the electoral college
   (D) was resolved when Samuel J. Tilden conceded the election to Rutherford B. Hayes
   (E) led to a congressional dispute between the House of Representatives and the Senate as to who had the authority to determine the outcome of the election

REFLECT ACTIVITY

Respond to the following questions:

- For which content topics discussed in this chapter do you feel you have achieved sufficient mastery to answer multiple-choice questions correctly?

- For which content topics discussed in this chapter do you feel you have achieved sufficient mastery to discuss effectively in an essay?

- For which content topics discussed in this chapter do you feel you need more work before you can answer multiple-choice questions correctly?

- For which content topics discussed in this chapter do you feel you need more work before you can discuss effectively in an essay?

- What parts of this chapter are you going to re-review?

- Will you seek further help, outside of this book (such as a teacher, tutor, or AP Central), on any of the content in this chapter—and, if so, on what content?

Chapter 10
The Machine Age
(1877–1900)

THE AGE OF INVENTION AND ECONOMIC GROWTH

In 1876, **Thomas A. Edison** built his workshop in Menlo Park, New Jersey and proceeded to produce some of the most important inventions of the century. Edison's greatest invention was the **light bulb**. Edison's pioneering work in the development of **power plants** also proved immensely important. His advances allowed for the extension of the workday, which previously ended at sundown, and the wider availability of electricity. With that wider availability, Edison and other inventors began to create new uses for electricity, both for industry and the home. The last quarter of the nineteenth century is often called the **Age of Invention** because so many technological advances like Edison's were made. These advances, in turn, generated greater opportunities for **mass production**, which then caused the economy to grow at a tremendous rate. Not surprisingly, the people known as the "captains of industry" to their fans (and the "robber barons" to others), who owned and controlled the new manufacturing enterprises, became extremely rich and powerful during this period.

Industrialization, Corporate Consolidation, and the Gospel of Wealth

As more and faster machines became available to manufacturers, businessmen discovered that their cost per unit decreased as the number of units they produced increased. The more raw product they bought, the cheaper the suppliers' asking price. The closer to capacity they kept their new, faster machines running, the less the cost of labor and electricity per product. The lower their costs, the cheaper they could sell their products. The cheaper the product, the more they sold. That, simply put, is the concept of **economies of scale**.

The downside of this new business practice was that it required employees to work as efficiently, and repetitively, as machines. **Assembly line production** had begun to take hold when Eli Whitney developed interchangeable parts, but reached a whole new level in Ford's plants in the early twentieth century. This type of production required workers to perform a single task over and over, often (before labor reform) for 12 to 14 hours a day. Factories were dangerous; machine malfunctions and human error typically resulted in more than 500,000 injuries to workers per year.

The overriding concern for businessmen, however, was that profits continued to increase by huge margins. Although government made some efforts to regulate this rapid growth, these were tentative. Furthermore, the government remained uncertain as to how to enforce regulations, and widespread corruption existed among those bureaucrats charged with enforcing the regulations. Finally, the courts of the era (especially the Supreme Court) were extremely pro-business. With almost no restraint, businesses such as railroad companies followed the path that led to greater economies of scale, which meant larger and larger businesses. This was known as **corporate consolidation**.

One new form of business organization was called a **holding company**. A holding company owned enough stock in various companies to have a controlling interest in the production of raw material, the means of transporting that material to a factory, the factory itself, and the distribution network for selling the product. The logical conclusion is a **monopoly**, or complete control of an entire industry. One holding company, for example, gained control of 98 percent of the sugar refining plants in the United States. While the company did not control the entire sugar industry, it did control one very important aspect of it.

The most common forms of business consolidation at the end of the nineteenth century were **horizontal** and **vertical integration**. One is legal; one is not; both were practiced by "captains of industry" during the Gilded Age. For all intents and purposes, horizontal integration created monopolies within a particular industry, the best-known example being Standard Oil, created by John D. Rockefeller. In horizontal integration, several smaller companies within the same industry are combined to form one, larger company, either by being bought out legally or by being destroyed through ruthless business practices such as cutthroat competition or pooling agreements. Many of these business practices are illegal today because of antitrust legislation passed at the turn of the last century. Vertical integration remains legal, however, provided the company does not become either a trust or a holding company, but rather allows other companies in the same industry to survive and compete in the marketplace. In vertical integration, one company buys out all the factors of production, from raw materials to finished product. For example, Swift Premium might control the stockyards, the slaughterhouse, and the processing and packaging plants but still compete with Oscar Mayer or Hebrew National.

Numerous problems arose because of this consolidation of power. First, rapid growth required lots of money. Businessmen borrowed huge sums, and when their businesses occasionally failed, bank failures could result. During the last quarter of the nineteenth century, the United States endured one major financial panic per decade. Although irresponsible investors caused the panics, the lower classes suffered the most, as jobs and money became scarce. Second, monopolies created a class of extremely powerful men whose interests clashed with those of the rest of society. As these businessmen grew more powerful, public resentment increased, and the government responded with laws to restrict monopolies (which the courts, in turn, weakened). The back-and-forth battle among the public, the government, and the courts is best exemplified by the **Sherman Antitrust Act of 1890**. Public pressure led to the passage of this law forbidding any "combination...or conspiracy in the restraint of trade."

Unfortunately, the wording of the Sherman Antitrust Act was ambiguous enough to allow the pro-business Supreme Court at the time to interpret the law as it saw fit. For example, in 1895 the Court ruled that E. C. Knight, a company that controlled 98 percent of the sugar refining plants in the United States, did not violate the Sherman Antitrust Act because local manufacturing was not subject to congressional regulation of interstate commerce. (*U.S. v. E. C. Knight Co.*, 1895.) On the other hand, labor unions were often found to be "in restraint of free trade" and declared illegal. This loophole was closed during Wilson's administration in 1914 with the passage of the Clayton Antitrust Act, which made allowances for collective bargaining.

Another response to public pressure for reform came from industrialists themselves. Steel mogul **Andrew Carnegie** promoted a philosophy based on the work of Charles Darwin. Using Darwin's theory of evolution as an analogy, Carnegie argued that in business, as in nature, unrestricted competition allowed only the "fittest" to survive. This theory was called **Social Darwinism**. Aside from the fact that Carnegie's analogy to Darwin's theory was at best dubious, it also lacked consistency; while Carnegie argued against government regulation, he supported all types of government assistance to business (in the form of tax abatements, grants, tariffs, etc.). Carnegie further argued that the concentration of wealth among a few was the natural and most efficient result of capitalism. Carnegie also asserted that great wealth brought with it social responsibility. Dubbing his belief the **Gospel of Wealth**, he advocated philanthropy, as by building libraries and museums or funding medical research, but not charity. Some of his peers were as generous; others were not.

Factories and City Life

Manufacturers cut costs and maximized profits in every way they could imagine. They reduced labor costs by hiring **women** and **children**. In cities, where most factories were located, manufacturers hired the many newly arrived **immigrants** who were anxious for work. Because manufacturers paid as little as possible, the cities in which their employees lived suffered many of the problems associated with poverty, such as crime, disease, and the lack of livable housing for a rapidly expanding population. As mentioned before, factories were dangerous, and many families had at least one member who had been disabled at work. Insurance and workmen's compensation did not exist then, either.

The poverty level in cities also rose because those who could afford it moved away from the city center. As factories sprung up, cities became more dirty and generally less healthy environments. Advances in **mass transportation**, such as the expansion of railroad lines, streetcars, and the construction of subways, allowed the middle class to live in nicer neighborhoods, including bedroom communities in the suburbs, and commute to work. (The growing middle class was made up of managers, secretaries, bureaucrats, merchants, and the like.) As a result, immigrants and migrants made up the majority of city populations. Starting around 1880, the majority of immigrants arrived from southern and eastern Europe. (Prior to 1880 most immigrants to America came from northern and western Europe.) Prejudice against the new arrivals was widespread, and many immigrants settled in **ethnic neighborhoods** usually in **tenements**. Worse off still were **black** and **Latino** migrants. Many employers refused them any but the worst jobs.

Municipal governments of the era were not like those of today. In fact, such governments were practically nonexistent. Most Americans expected churches, private charities, and ethnic communities to provide services for the poor. However, many of those services were provided instead by a group of corrupt men called **political bosses**. Bosses helped the poor find homes and jobs; they also helped them apply for citizenship and voting rights. They built parks, funded auxiliary police and fire departments, and constructed roads and sewage lines. In return, they expected community members to vote as they were instructed. Occasionally, they also required "donations" to help fund community projects. Political bosses—whose organizations were called **political machines**—rendered services that communities would not otherwise have received. However, because the bosses resorted to criminal means to accomplish their goals, the cost of their services was high. The most notorious of these bosses was "Boss" Tweed of Tammany Hall in New York City (mentioned in Chapter 9).

Widespread misery in cities led many to seek changes. Labor unions formed to try to counter the poor treatment of workers. Unions were considered radical organizations by many, and the government was wary of them; businesses and the courts were openly hostile to them. Hired goons and, in some cases, federal troops often broke strikes. Before the Civil War, the few unions that existed were small, regional, or local and represented workers within a specific craft or industry. One of the first national labor unions was the **Knights of Labor**, founded in 1869 by Uriah Stephens, a Philadelphia tailor.

The Knights organized skilled and unskilled workers from a variety of crafts into a single union. Their goals included: (1) an eight-hour workday; (2) equal pay for equal work for men and women (this would not become a federal law until 1963); (3) child labor laws, including the prohibition of working under the age of 14; (4) safety and sanitary codes; (5) a federal income tax (not enacted until the ratification of the Sixteenth Amendment in 1913); and (6) government ownership of railroad and telegraph lines.

> ## Identification
> One important shift during the 19th century was that from vertical identification to horizontal identification. For example, in 1800, an apprentice shoemaker would likely to think of himself as belonging to a class with journeyman shoemakers and master shoemakers. By 1850, he would be much more likely to think of himself as belonging to a class with apprentice tailors and apprentice blacksmiths.

Although the Knights advocated arbitration over strikes, they became increasingly violent in efforts to achieve their goals. By the 1880s, after a series of unsuccessful strikes under the leadership of **Terrence Powderly**, the popularity of the Knights began to decline. The American public began to associate unions with violence and political radicalism. Propagandists claimed that unions were subversive forces—a position reinforced in public opinion by the **Haymarket Square Riot**. During an 1886 labor demonstration in Chicago's Haymarket Square, a bomb went off, killing police. Many blamed the incident on the influence of radicals within the union movement, although no one knew who set off the bomb.

Many early unions did indeed subscribe to utopian and/or socialist philosophies. Later on, the **American Federation of Labor**, led by **Samuel Gompers**, avoided those larger political questions, concentrating instead on such "bread and butter" issues as higher wages and shorter workdays, an approach that proved successful. Gompers also realized that his union could gain more power if it excluded unskilled workers; the AFL was formed as a confederation of **trade unions** (i.e., unions made up exclusively of workers within a single trade). The history of early unions is marred by the fact that most refused to accept immigrants, blacks, and women among their memberships.

Charitable middle-class organizations, usually run by women, also made efforts at urban reform. These groups lobbied local governments for building-safety codes, better sanitation, and public schools. Frustrated by government's slow pace, their members also founded and lived in **settlement houses** in poor neighborhoods. These houses became community centers, providing schooling, childcare, and cultural activities. In Chicago, for example, **Jane Addams** founded Hull House to provide such services as English lessons for immigrants, day care for children of working mothers, childcare classes for parents, and playgrounds for children. Addams also campaigned for increased government services in the slums. She was awarded the Nobel Peace Prize for her life's work in 1931.

While the poor suffered, life improved for both the wealthy and the middle class. Increased production and wealth meant greater access to luxuries and more leisure time. Sports, high theater, vaudeville (variety acts), and, later, movies became popular diversions. It was also during this period that large segments of the public began to read **popular novels** and **newspapers**. The growth of the newspaper industry was largely the responsibility of **Joseph Pulitzer** and **William Randolph Hearst**, both of whom understood the commercial value of bold, screaming headlines and lurid tales of scandal. (Prior to Pulitzer and Hearst, papers were stodgy and looked like the *Wall Street Journal*.) This new style of sensational reporting became known as "**yellow journalism.**"

Jim Crow Laws and Other Developments in the South

Most of the advances made during the machine age affected primarily Northern cities. In the South, agriculture continued as the main form of labor. The industrialization programs of Reconstruction did produce some results, however. Textile mills sprang up around the South, reducing cotton farmers' reliance on the North. Tobacco processing plants also employed some workers. Still, the vast majority of Southerners remained farmers.

Postwar economics forced many farmers to sell their land, which wealthy landowners bought and consolidated into larger farms. Landless farmers, both black and white, were forced into **sharecropping**. The method by which they rented land was called the **crop lien system**; it was designed to keep the poor in constant debt. Because these farmers had no cash, they borrowed what they needed to buy seed and tools, promising a portion of their crop as collateral. Huge interest rates on their loans and unscrupulous landlords pretty much guaranteed that these farmers would never overcome their debt, forcing them to borrow further and promise their *next* crop as collateral. In this way landlords kept the poor, both black and white, in a state of virtual slavery.

The advent of **Jim Crow laws** made matters worse for blacks. As the federal government exerted less influence over Southern states, towns and cities passed numerous discriminatory laws. The Supreme Court assisted the states by ruling that the Fourteenth Amendment did not protect blacks from discrimination by privately owned businesses and that blacks would have to seek equal protection from the states, not from the federal government. In 1883 the Court also reversed the Civil Rights Act of 1875, thus opening the door to legal (*de jure*) segregation. In 1896 the Supreme Court ruled in **Plessy v. Ferguson** that "separate but equal" facilities for the different races was legal. In so doing, the Court set back the civil rights gains made during Reconstruction.

In this atmosphere integration and equal rights for blacks seemed to most a far-off dream. **Booker T. Washington** certainly felt that way. A Southern black born into slavery, Washington harbored no illusions that white society was ready to accept blacks as equals. Instead, he promoted economic independence as the means by which blacks could improve their lot. To pursue that goal he founded the Tuskegee Institute, a vocational and industrial training school for blacks. Some accused Washington of being an **accommodationist** because he refused to press for immediate equal rights. Others believed that Washington simply accepted the reality of his time when he set his goals. In his "Atlanta Exposition," a famous speech delivered in Atlanta, Georgia, in 1895, Washington outlined his view of race relations. Washington's more aggressive rival W. E. B. Du Bois (see Chapter 11) referred to the speech, which he deemed submissive, as "The Atlanta Compromise."

The Railroads and Developments in the West

On the western frontier, **ranching** and **mining** were growing industries. Ranchers drove their herds across the western plains and deserts, ignoring property rights and Native American prerogatives to the land. Individual miners lacked the resources to mine and cart big loads, so mostly they prospected; when they found a rich mine, they staked a claim and sold their rights to a mining company.

In the second year of the Civil War, Lincoln issued a challenge to America not unlike Kennedy's 1961 pledge to reach the Moon—that before the decade was out, America would have a Transcontinental Railroad connecting one side of the country to the other. From 1863 to 1869, former farmers, immigrants, freed slaves, and Civil War veterans worked to make Lincoln's vision a reality. The railroad's arrival changed the West in many ways. The railroads, although owned privately, were built largely at the public's expense, through direct funding and substantial grants of land to the railroads. Both federal and local governments were anxious for rails to be completed and so provided substantial assistance. Although the public had paid for the rail system, rail proprietors strenuously objected to any government control of their industry, and it took years for railroad rates to come under regulation. Until they were regulated the railroads would typically overcharge wherever they owned a monopoly and undercharge in competitive and heavily trafficked markets. This practice was particularly harmful to farmers in remote areas.

As railroad construction crawled across the nation, rail companies organized massive hunts for buffalo (considered a nuisance). Railroad bounty hunters hunted the herds to near extinction, destroying a resource upon which local Native Americans had depended. Some tribes, such as the Sioux, fought back, giving the government an excuse to send troops into the region. While Native Americans won some battles (notably at **Little Big Horn**, where George Custer met his death), the federal army ultimately overpowered them.

The railroads brought other changes as well. Rails quickly transformed depot towns into vital cities by connecting them to civilization. Easier, faster travel meant more contact with ideas and technological advances from the East. Developments in railroad technology had applications in other industries and so accelerated the industrial revolution. In addition, "railroad time," by which rail schedules were determined, gave the nation its first standardized method of time telling with the adoption of time zones.

As the rails pushed the country westward, settlers started filling in the territory. By 1889 North Dakota, South Dakota, Washington, and Montana were populous enough to achieve statehood; Wyoming and Idaho followed in 1890. The result of the 1890 census prompted the Progressive historian Frederick Jackson Turner to declare that the American frontier was gone, and with it the first period of American history. Turner argued that the frontier was significant in: (1) shaping the American character, (2) defining the American spirit, (3) fostering democracy, and (4) providing a safety valve for economic distress in urban, industrial centers by providing a place to which people could flee. Historians refer to these ideas collectively as the **Turner** or **Frontier Thesis**.

In the Great Plains, farming and ranching constituted the main forms of employment. New farm machinery and access to mail (and mail-order retail) made life on the plains easier, but it was still lonely and difficult. The government, realizing the potential of the region as the nation's chief agricultural center, passed two significant pieces of legislation in 1862—the **Homestead Act** and the **Morrill Land Grant Act**. Anxious to attract settlers to develop the West, the federal government offered 160 acres of land to anyone who would "homestead" it (cultivate the land, build a home, and live there) for five years. Of course, the government was giving away land that belonged to Native Americans. Furthermore, private speculators and railroad companies often exploited the law for their own personal economic gain. The Morrill Land Grant Act set aside land and provided money for agricultural colleges. Eventually, agricultural science became a huge industry in the United States.

The big losers in this expansionist era, of course, were Native Americans. At first, pioneers approached the tribes as sovereign nations. They made treaties with them, which the settlers or their immediate successors broke. The result was warfare, leading the government to try another approach. The new tack was to force Native Americans onto reservations, which typically were made up of the least desirable land in a tribe's traditional home region. The reservation system failed for a number of reasons, including the inferiority of the land, the grouping of incompatible tribes on the same reservation, and the lack of autonomy granted the tribes in managing their own affairs. Moreover, some Westerners simply ignored the arrangement and poached on reservation lands. Helen Hunt Jackson's book *A Century of Dishonor* detailed the injustices of the reservation system and inspired reformers to push for change, which came in 1887 in the form of the **Dawes Severalty Act**.

The Dawes Severalty Act broke up the reservations and distributed some of the land to the head of each Native American family. Similar to the Homestead Act, the allotment was 160 acres of land. This time, however, it was required that the family live on the land for 25 years, after which time the land was legally theirs. And the grand prize was American citizenship! The Dawes Act was intended as a humanitarian solution to the "Indian problem"; its main goal was to accelerate the assimilation of Native Americans into Western society by integrating them more closely with whites. Native Americans, naturally, resisted. Furthermore, poverty drove many to sell their land to speculators, leaving them literally homeless. By the time the policy set by Dawes was reversed in 1934, the Native American nations were decimated.

National Politics

Mark Twain dubbed the era between Reconstruction and 1900 the **Gilded Age** of politics. Gilded metals have a shiny, gold-like surface, but beneath lies a cheap base. America looked to have entered a period of prosperity, with a handful of families having amassed unprecedented wealth, but the affluence of a few was built on the poverty of many. Similarly, American politics looked like a shining example of representative democracy, but just beneath the surface lay crass corruption and patronage. Political machines, not municipal governments, ran the cities. Big business bought votes in Congress, then turned around and fleeced consumers. Workers had little protection from the greed of their employers because the courts turned a deaf ear to worker complaints. In other words, Twain was right on the money.

The presidents of this era were generally not corrupt. They were, however, relatively weak. (The president is only as powerful as his support allows him to be; thus popular presidents, such as Andrew Jackson and Franklin Roosevelt, were able to accomplish so much.) Don't expect too many questions about the presidents of this period, but for the record, **Rutherford B. Hayes, James Garfield**, and **Chester A. Arthur** concerned themselves primarily with civil service reform (see the accompanying box), while **Grover Cleveland** believed that government governed best which governed least. **Benjamin Harrison** took the opposite tack, and he and his allies in the Capitol passed everything from the nation's first meat inspection act to the banning of lotteries to the purchase of several battleships. Much of the legislation we have discussed, from the Sherman Antitrust Act to the second Morrill Land-Grant Colleges Act, was passed under Harrison's watch. But the public's discomfort with the activism of Harrison and the "**Billion-Dollar Congress**" of 1890 led to Grover Cleveland's return to the White House.

In response to the outcry over widespread corruption, the government made its first stabs at regulating itself and business. Many states imposed **railroad regulations** because railroads were engaging in price gouging. In 1877 the Supreme Court upheld an Illinois state law regulating railroads and grain elevators in the case of *Munn v. Illinois*. This was a surprising decision, given that railroads crossed state

Civil Service Reform

The "spoils system" pioneered by Andrew Jackson meant that every time a new president took office, thousands of government jobs opened up, and it was the president's responsibility to fill them. This is what the presidents of the mid-19th century did with their days. For instance, even as the Civil War raged, Abraham Lincoln spent morning, afternoon, and evening dealing with the job applicants who lined up outside his office, the line winding through the White House and out the door onto Pennsylvania Avenue.

Within the Republican Party, who dominated control of the White House following the Civil War, a split developed between "**Stalwarts**," who believed that all government jobs should go to loyal Republicans, and "**Half-Breeds**," who thought that qualified Democrats should be able to keep their jobs even after a Republican was elected. When a frustrated job-seeker assassinated President Garfield, it became clear that something had to be done about the way government employment was handled. His successor, Chester Arthur, had been a Stalwart, but he signed the **Pendleton Civil Service Reform Act** that began the dismantling of the old spoils system.

lines and only Congress can regulate interstate commerce. The Court argued that states had the power to regulate private industry that served the "public interest." Although the Supreme Court would reaffirm Congress's authority nine years later in the *Wabash* case, when it ruled that states could *not* establish rates involving interstate commerce, an important precedent for regulating business in the public's interest had been established.

In 1887, just one year after the *Wabash* decision, Congress passed the first federal regulatory law in U.S. history. The **Interstate Commerce Act** set up the Interstate Commerce Commission (ICC) to supervise railroad activities and regulate unfair and unethical practices. (The ICC wasn't disbanded until the 1980s under the Reagan administration, when, in attempts to save money, the federal government deregulated many forms of transportation.)

It was also during this period that **women's suffrage** became an important political issue. **Susan B. Anthony** led the fight, convincing Congress to introduce a suffrage amendment to the Constitution. The bill was introduced every year and rarely got out of committee, but the fight had begun in earnest. Meanwhile, organizations such as the **American Suffrage Association** fought for women's suffrage amendments to state constitutions. By 1890 they had achieved some partial successes, gaining the vote on school issues. (Women finally gained the right to vote with the ratification of the Nineteenth Amendment in 1920, fifty years after male suffrage became universal.)

The Silver Issue and the Populist Movement

In the period after the Civil War, production on all fronts—industrial and agricultural—increased. Greater supply accordingly led to a drop in prices. For many farmers, lower prices meant trouble, as they were locked into long-term debts with fixed payments. Looking for a solution to their problem, farmers came to support a more generous money supply. An increase in available money, they correctly figured, would make payments easier. It would also cause inflation, which would make the farmers' debts (held by Northern banks) worth less. Not surprisingly, the banks opposed the plan, preferring for the country to use only gold to back its money supply.

The farmers' plan called for the liberal use of silver coins, and because silver was mined in the West, this plan had the added support of Western miners along with that of Midwestern and Southern farmers. Thus, the issue had a regional component. Because it pitted poor farmers against wealthy bankers, it also had elements of class strife. Although a complicated matter, the money issue was potentially explosive.

The "silver vs. gold" debate provided an issue around which farmers could organize. They did just that. First came the **Grange Movement**, which, founded in 1867, boasted more than a million members by 1875. The Grangers started out as cooperatives, with the purpose of allowing farmers to buy machinery and sell crops as a group and, therefore, reap the benefits of economies of scale. Soon, the Grangers endorsed political candidates and lobbied for legislation. The Grangers ultimately died out due to lack of money, but they were replaced by **Farmers' Alliances**. The Farmers' Alliances were even more successful than the Grange movement, and they soon grew into a political party called the **People's Party**, the political arm of the **Populist** movement.

The People's Party held a convention in 1892. (The platform it drew up presented many of the ideas that would later be championed by the Progressives.) Aside from supporting the generous coinage of silver, the Populists called for government ownership of railroads and telegraphs, a graduated income tax, direct election of U.S. senators, and shorter workdays. Although their 1892 presidential candidate, James Weaver, came in third, he won more than 1 million votes, awakening Washington to the growing Populist movement.

As Cleveland took office in 1893, the country entered a four-year financial crisis. Hard economic times made Populist goals more popular, particularly the call for easy money. (Most people at the time, after all, had no money at all.) Times got so bad that even more progressive (some would say radical) movements gained popularity; in 1894 the **Socialists**, led by **Eugene V. Debs**, gained support. By 1896 the Populists were poised for power. They backed Democratic candidate **William Jennings Bryan** against Republican nominee **William McKinley**, and Bryan ran on a strictly Populist platform; he based his campaign on the call for **"free silver."** He is probably best remembered for his "Cross of Gold" speech (a typical multiple-choice question). He argued that an easy money supply, though inflationary, would loosen the control that Northern banking interests held over the country. He lost the campaign; this, coupled with an improved economy, ended the Populist movement.

An easy way to remember the Populists is through the book *The Wizard of Oz* by L. Frank Baum. The novel is reportedly a political allegory, with Dorothy representing the common man, her silver shoes (the movie changed them into ruby slippers) representing the silver standard, the scarecrow representing the farmer, and the Tin Man representing the industrial worker. William Jennings Bryan was said to be the model for the Cowardly Lion.

Foreign Policy: The Tariff and Imperialism

Before the Civil War most Americans earned their living by farming. By 1900, however, the United States had become the leading industrial power in the world. It is difficult for us to imagine the enormous controversy surrounding the issue of the tariff throughout U.S. history. Remember that there was no federal income tax until the Sixteenth Amendment was adopted in 1913. Clearly, the most infamous tariff was the **Tariff of Abominations** (1828). This ultimately triggered the nullification crisis during Jackson's first administration. Following the Civil War, the tariff came to dominate national politics, as industrialists competing in an international market demanded high tariffs to protect domestic industries. Farmers and laborers, on the other hand, were hurt by high tariffs. Generally, Democrats supported lower tariffs while Republicans advocated high, protective tariffs.

In 1890 Congress enacted the McKinley Tariff, which raised the level of duties on imported goods almost 50 percent. Certain products, however, such as unprocessed sugar, sugar were put on a duty-free list. Then, in 1894, Congress passed the Wilson-Gorman Tariff, which essentially resembled the schedule established by the **McKinley Tariff**, despite heated debate between members of the House of Representatives and the Senate. The tariff issue not only dominated congressional debate, it also had a tremendous impact on foreign relations (see below). For example, the Wilson-Gorman Tariff is usually considered one of the causes of the **Spanish-American War**.

Throughout the machine age, American production capacity grew rapidly. As we have already discussed, not every American had enough money to buy the products he or she made at work. America began looking overseas to find **new markets**. Increased **nationalism** also led American business to look for new markets. America's centennial celebration in 1876 heightened national pride, as did awareness that the country was becoming a world economic power. As Americans became more certain that their way of life was best, they hoped to spread that around the globe. This philosophy led American influence to expand into a number of new arenas.

First, **William H. Seward**, secretary of state under Lincoln and Johnson, set the precedent for increased American participation in any and all doings in the Western Hemisphere. In particular, Seward engineered the purchase of Alaska and invoked the Monroe Doctrine to force France out of Mexico. In the following decade, American businesses began developing markets and production facilities in Latin America, and gradually they gained political power in the region.

As long as America moved into regions to do business, it was practicing **expansionism**, which most Americans supported. When the United States took control of another country, however, it was exercising **imperialism**, a more controversial practice. A book by naval Captain Alfred T. Mahan, called *The Influence of Sea Power Upon History* (1890), piqued the government's interest in imperialism. Mahan argued that successful foreign trade relied on access to foreign ports, which in turn required overseas colonies, and colonies in turn required a strong navy. The book popularized the idea of the **New Navy**, and after the United States invested in upgrading its ships, it turned its attention to foreign acquisitions.

The search for a port along the trade route to Asia attracted the United States to **Hawaii**. Foreign missionaries had arrived in Hawaii in the early 1800s, but significant U.S. involvement there began in the 1870s, when American sugar producers started trading with the Hawaiians. Due in large part to American interference, the Hawaiian economy collapsed in the 1890s. The United States had allowed Hawaii tariff-free access to American markets. Then, when Hawaii became dependent on trade with the United States, the government imposed high tariffs (the McKinley Tariff mentioned above), thereby greatly diminishing Hawaiian exports. The white minority overthrew the native government, and, eventually, the United States annexed Hawaii. Japan was outraged; more than 40 percent of Hawaii's residents were of Japanese descent. That anger would resurface during World War II.

Another opportunity for American expansion arose when Cuban natives revolted against Spanish control. The revolution in **Cuba**, like the Hawaiian revolution, was instigated by U.S. tampering with the Cuban economy (by imposing high import tariffs, as discussed above). A violent Cuban civil war followed, reported in all its gory detail in the sensational Hearst newspaper (see "yellow journalism," earlier in this chapter). When an American warship, the *Maine*, exploded in the Havana harbor under circumstances that remain a mystery, the drumbeats for war grew deafening. In the ensuing war the United States not only drove Spain out of Cuba, but also sent a fleet to the Spanish-controlled **Philippines** and drove the Spanish out of there too. In the **Treaty of Paris**, Spain granted Cuba independence and ceded the Philippines, Puerto Rico, and Guam to the United States. Remember that Hawaii was annexed the same year, but not because of the Spanish-American War. Also, note that this was the third Treaty of Paris that matters in U.S. history. The first ended the French and Indian War in 1763, while the second ended the Revolutionary War in 1783.

Despite the Teller Amendment, in which the United States claimed it would not annex Cuba after Spain's departure from the island in 1898, U.S. troops remained in Cuba for another few years. Then, in 1901, Cuba was compelled to include a series of provisions in its new constitution. The United States made it quite clear that its troops would not leave unless Cuba agreed to these provisions, collectively known as the **Platt Amendment.** The United States was basically given control over Cuba's foreign affairs. Under the guise of protecting Cuba's political and social stability and thus its independence, the following terms were established: (1) Cuba was not permitted to sign any foreign treaty without the consent of the United States, (2) the United States could intervene in Cuban domestic and foreign affairs, and (3) the United States was granted land on which to build a naval base and coaling station. The Platt Amendment was ultimately repealed in 1934 during **FDR**'s administration as part of his **Good Neighbor Policy.** The United States continues to operate a naval station at Guantanamo Bay, however. (Yes, *that* Guantanamo Bay.)

Control of the Philippines raised a tricky question: Should the United States annex the Philippines, or should it grant the country the independence its people sought? Proponents of annexing the Philippines argued that if the United States granted Filipinos their independence, the archipelago would simply be conquered by another European nation, with the only result being that the United States would lose a valuable possession. Perhaps most compelling, and certainly the best-known rationale for U.S. annexation of the Philippine Islands, was the belief that the United States had a moral obligation to "Christianize and civilize" the Filipinos, who were already overwhelmingly Christian—albeit Catholic, which didn't count for some Protestant imperialists—and preferred to achieve "civilization" in their own way. The notion that people not of European extraction were unfit to rule themselves came to be known as the "white man's burden," from the title of a poem written by Rudyard Kipling in response to the United States' annexation of the Philippines. Opponents felt that the United States should promote independence and democracy, both noble national traditions. To control the Philippines, they argued, would make the United States no better than the British tyrants they overthrew in the Revolutionary War. In the end the Senate voted to annex the Philippines. Filipino nationalists responded by waging a guerrilla war against the United States. Although the United States eventually gained control of the country, the Philippines remained a source of controversy for decades. The United States granted the Philippines independence in 1946.

As the United States acquired an overseas empire, a fundamental question arose as to the legal status of the native population living in these territories: "Does the Constitution follow the flag?" In other words, were colonial subjects entitled to the same protections and privileges granted to U.S. citizens by the Constitution?

The Supreme Court settled this issue by a series of rulings known collectively as the **Insular Cases** (1901–1903). The Court ruled that the Constitution did *not* follow the flag; Congress was free to administer each overseas possession as it chose, depending on the particular situation in any given foreign territory.

Finally, America hoped to gain entry into Asian markets. To that end McKinley sought an **Open Door Policy** for all Western nations hoping to trade with Asia. The European nations that had colonized China were not so keen on the idea; to their way of thinking, they fought for those markets and planned to keep them. When Chinese nationalists (known as the Boxers) rose against European imperialism and besieged the Beijing legation quarter, the United States sent troops to help suppress the rebels. In return, Germany, France, and England grew more receptive to America's foreign policy objectives.

American imperialism would continue through Theodore Roosevelt's administration. We'll discuss that period in the next chapter.

Chapter 10 Drill

See Chapter 13 for answers and explanations.

1. The scalawags were

   (A) another name for the Redeemers, who refused to accept the fact that the South had lost the Civil War
   (B) Northern politicians who traveled to the South after the Civil War to exploit the political and economic instability for their own personal gain
   (C) advocates of civil rights for the newly freed slaves
   (D) the opponents of the Radical Republicans who controlled Congress after the Civil War
   (E) white Southerners who supported Republican policies during Reconstruction

2. Which of the following statements about Supreme Court decisions during the latter part of the nineteenth century is most accurate?

   (A) They reduced federal power over the states by narrowly defining the applicability of the Constitution to state law.
   (B) They cleared the way for the liberal reforms of the twentieth century by broadly interpreting constitutional guarantees of individual rights.
   (C) They had little practical effect because the executive branch consistently refused to enforce the Court's rulings.
   (D) They used the Fourteenth Amendment to create numerous environmental regulations and human rights, stifling American business growth.
   (E) The Court avoided cases where its decisions would profoundly impact the country and, as a result, the Court did little to shape the era.

3. The term vertical integration refers to

   (A) Reconstruction-era efforts to assimilate newly freed slaves into all social strata of American society
   (B) an architectural movement that sought to blend urban skyscrapers with the natural landscape surrounding them
   (C) the industrial practice of assigning workers a single, repetitive task in order to maximize productivity
   (D) control of all aspects of an industry, from production of raw materials to delivery of finished goods
   (E) the belief that wealthy citizens have a moral obligation to engage in philanthropic acts

4. The passage of the Pendleton Act was a direct result of the

   (A) assassination of Abraham Lincoln
   (B) failure of Reconstruction
   (C) assassination of James A. Garfield
   (D) Supreme Court decision in *Plessy v. Ferguson*
   (E) assassination of William McKinley

5. The Haymarket Affair represented a major setback for the

   (A) women's suffrage movement
   (B) civil rights movement for African-Americans
   (C) Knights of Labor
   (D) Temperance movement
   (E) Populist movement

6. Japan was outraged by the American annexation of Hawaii in 1898 primarily because

   (A) Japan depended heavily on trade with Hawaii to support its economy
   (B) the United States had signed a treaty with Japan granting Japan rights to Hawaii
   (C) the Japanese were committed to the principle of self-rule throughout the Pacific
   (D) the annexation contradicted the U.S. policy of non-interference in the Eastern Hemisphere
   (E) nearly half of Hawaii's residents were of Japanese descent

REFLECT ACTIVITY

Respond to the following questions:

- For which content topics discussed in this chapter do you feel you have achieved sufficient mastery to answer multiple-choice questions correctly?

- For which content topics discussed in this chapter do you feel you have achieved sufficient mastery to discuss effectively in an essay?

- For which content topics discussed in this chapter do you feel you need more work before you can answer multiple-choice questions correctly?

- For which content topics discussed in this chapter do you feel you need more work before you can discuss effectively in an essay?

- What parts of this chapter are you going to re-review?

- Will you seek further help, outside of this book (such as a teacher, tutor, or AP Central), on any of the content in this chapter—and, if so, on what content?

Chapter 11
The Early Twentieth Century (1900–1945)

THE PROGRESSIVE ERA AND WORLD WAR I (1900–1920)

The Populist movement dissipated, but not before raising the possibility of reform through government. The Populists' successes in both local and national elections encouraged others to seek change through political action. Building on Populism's achievements and adopting some of its goals (e.g., direct election of senators, opposition to monopolies), the **Progressives** came to dominate the first two decades of twentieth-century American politics. While the Populists were mainly aggrieved farmers who advocated radical reforms, the Progressives were urban, middle-class reformers who wanted to increase the role of government in reform while maintaining a capitalist economy.

The Progressive Movement

One of the reasons Populism failed is that its constituents were mostly poor farmers whose daily struggle to make a living made political activity difficult. The **Progressives** achieved greater success in part because theirs was an urban, middle-class movement. Its proponents started with more economic and political clout than the Populists. Furthermore, Progressives could devote more time to the causes they championed. Also, because many Progressives were Northern and middle class, the Progressive movement did not intensify regional and class differences, as the Populist movement had.

The roots of Progressivism lay in the growing number of associations and organizations at the turn of the century. The National Woman Suffrage Association, the American Bar Association, and the National Municipal League are some of the many groups that rallied citizens around a cause or profession. Most of these groups' members were educated and middle class; the blatant corruption they saw in business and politics offended their senses of decency, as did the terrible plight of the urban poor.

Progressivism got a further boost from a group of journalists who wrote exposés of corporate greed and misconduct. These writers, dubbed "**muckrakers**" by Theodore Roosevelt, revealed widespread corruption in urban management (**Lincoln Steffens**'s *The Shame of the Cities*), oil companies (**Ida Tarbell's** *History of Standard Oil*), and the meatpacking industry (**Upton Sinclair's** *The Jungle*). Their books and news articles raised the moral stakes for Progressives.

Over the course of two decades, Progressives achieved great successes on both the local and national levels. They campaigned to change public attitudes toward education and government regulation in much the same way reformers of the previous century had campaigned for public enlightenment on the plight of orphans, prostitutes, and the mentally infirm.

New groups arose to lead the fight against discrimination but met with mixed success. **W. E. B. Du Bois** headed the **National Association for the Advancement of Colored People** (**NAACP**) in the quest for racial justice, an uphill battle so strenuous that, after a lifelong struggle, Du Bois abandoned the United States and moved to Africa. Meanwhile, women's groups continued to campaign for suffrage. The adamant, conservative opposition they faced gave birth to the **feminist** movement. One early advocate, **Margaret Sanger**, faced wide opposition for promoting the use of contraceptives (illegal in most places). The movement's greatest success was in winning women the right to vote, granted by the **Nineteenth Amendment** in 1920.

Wisconsin governor **Robert La Follette** led the way for many Progressive state leaders. Under his leadership Wisconsin implemented plans for direct primary elections, progressive taxation, and rail regulation. Many states extended greater power to voters by adopting the **ballot initiative**, through which the voters could propose new laws; the **referendum**, which allowed the public to vote on new laws; and the **recall election**, which gave voters the power to remove officials from office before their terms expired. Working-class Progressives also won a number of victories on the state level, including limitations on the length of the work day, minimum-wage requirements, child labor laws, and urban housing codes. Many states adopted progressive income taxes (taxes that charge higher percentages for people with higher incomes), which served partially to redistribute the nation's wealth.

The most prominent Progressive leader was President **Theodore Roosevelt**. McKinley was a conservative president, and Roosevelt was expected to emulate his policies, though rumors had begun to circulate that Roosevelt harbored progressive sympathies. After he convincingly won the 1904 election on the strength of his handling of Latin American affairs, Roosevelt began boldly enacting a progressive agenda. He was the first to successfully use the **Sherman Antitrust Act** against monopolies, and he did so repeatedly during his term, earning the nickname "the Trustbuster." Among Roosevelt's other progressive achievements were tightening food and drug regulations, creating national parks, and broadening the government's power to protect land from overdevelopment. (Roosevelt, an avid outdoorsman, was a particularly impassioned conservationist.) Presidents Taft and Wilson continued to promote Progressive ideals. **William Howard Taft** spearheaded the drive for two constitutional amendments, one that instituted a national income tax (the Sixteenth Amendment) and another that allowed for the direct election of senators (the Seventeenth Amendment). He pursued monopolies even more aggressively than Roosevelt.

The Progressive Era is a turning point in American history because it marks the ever-increasing involvement of the federal government in our daily lives. It's no coincidence that Prohibition took effect during this era. The third Progressive president was **Woodrow Wilson**, a Democrat who had to distinguish himself from Teddy Roosevelt, who ran for reelection (after Taft's one term) on the Bull Moose ticket in 1912. While Roosevelt's policies are often referred to as **New Nationalism**, Wilson referred to his ideas and policies as **New Freedom**. Thomas Jefferson had suggested limiting the power of the federal government in order to protect individual liberty, but Wilson now argued that the federal government had to assume greater control over business to protect man's freedom. For Roosevelt there were "good trusts and bad trusts." For Wilson trusts were monopolies, which violated freedom for workers and consumers. Wilson was committed to restoring competition through greater government regulation of the economy and lowering the tariff.

Double Duty

William Howard Taft is the only former president to also sit on the Supreme Court of the United States. He was the tenth Chief Justice, serving from 1921 to 1930.

Wilson created the **Federal Trade Commission**, lobbied for and enforced the **Clayton Antitrust Act of 1914**, and helped create the **Federal Reserve System**, which gave the government greater control over the nation's finances.

Progressivism lasted until the end of World War I, at which point the nation, weary from war and from the devastating **Spanish Flu** outbreak of 1918,, stepped back from its moral crusade. The war had torn apart the Progressive coalition; pacifist Progressives opposed the war while others supported it. A "Red Scare," heightened by the Russian Revolution, further split the Progressive coalition by dividing the leftists from the moderates. Moreover, the Progressive movement had achieved many of its goals, and as it did, it lost the support of those interest groups whose ends had been met. Some say that the Progressive movement was brought to an end, at least in part, by its own success.

Foreign Policy and U.S. Entry into World War I

Roosevelt differed from his predecessor on domestic policy, but he concurred with his foreign policy. Roosevelt was, if anything, an even more devout imperialist than McKinley had been. In 1903 the Roosevelt administration strong-armed Cuba into accepting the **Platt Amendment**, which essentially committed Cuba to American control. Under Platt's stipulations Cuba could not make a treaty with another nation without U.S. approval, and the United States had the right to intervene in Cuba's affairs if domestic order dissolved. A number of invasions and occupations by the Marines resulted. For 10 of the years between 1906 and 1922, the American military occupied Cuba, arousing anti-American sentiments on the island.

Roosevelt's actions were equally interventionist throughout Central America. During his administration, the country set its sights on building a canal through the Central American isthmus, because a canal would greatly shorten the sea trip from the East Coast to California. Congress approved a plan for a canal through **Panama**, at the time a province of Colombia. Because Colombia asked for more than the government was willing to spend, the United States encouraged Panamanian rebels to revolt, then supported the revolution. Not surprisingly, the new Panamanian government gave the United States a *much* better deal. Because American commercial interests were so closely tied to the canal's successful operation, the United States military became a fixed presence throughout the region. During the next 20 years, troops intervened repeatedly, claiming that Latin American domestic instability constituted a threat to American security. This assertion came to be known as the **Roosevelt Corollary to the Monroe Doctrine** and is often referred to as the Big Stick Policy.

American foreign policy continued to adhere to the Monroe Doctrine, which asserted America's right to assume the role of an international police force and intervene anywhere in the Western Hemisphere where it felt its national security was at stake. It also stated that the United States wanted no part of Europe's internal disputes. American commitment to that aspect of the Monroe Doctrine would soon be tested, as Europe started down the path leading to **World War I**. Complicating matters was the fact that the United States and England were quickly forming a close alliance. To America's benefit, England had not opposed its many forays into

Central American politics, although it could have. The British were not merely being friendly; they were trying to line up the United States as a potential ally in their ongoing rivalry with Germany, the other great European power of the era.

Fortunately, you do not need to know the tangled series of events that led Europe into war in 1914. You do, however, have to know about the United States' initial efforts to stay out of the war and the events that ultimately drew it into the conflict. Woodrow Wilson won the election of 1912, a three-way race in which the third-party candidate, Theodore Roosevelt, outpolled Taft, the Republican incumbent. Wilson entered office with less than a commanding mandate—only 40 percent of the electorate voted for him. However, with regard to the simmering European conflict, he and the electorate were of the same mind: The United States should stay out of it.

When war broke out in Europe in August 1914, Wilson immediately declared the U.S. policy of **neutrality**. Neutrality called for America to treat all the belligerents fairly and without favoritism. It was Wilson's hope that the United States would help settle the conflict and emerge as the world's arbiter. However, the neutrality policy posed several immediate problems, owing to America's close relationship with England and relatively distant relationship with Germany and Austria-Hungary. A number of Wilson's advisors openly favored the Allies (led by the British).

The situation quickly grew more complicated. England's strategic location and superior navy allowed it to impose an effective **blockade** on shipments headed for Germany, particularly those coming from United States. Protests proved futile; the British government impounded and confiscated American ships. They then paid for the cargo, reducing the pressure that American merchants would otherwise have put on the U.S. government to take action against the blockade.

Germany attempted to counter the blockade with **submarines**, or **U-boats**. According to contemporaneous international law, an attacker had to warn civilian ships before attacking. Submarines could not do this, because doing so would eliminate their main advantage. Furthermore, when the Germans attacked civilian ships, it was usually because those ships were carrying military supplies. The Germans announced that they would attack any such ship, but that did not satisfy Wilson, who believed that the Germans should adhere to the strict letter of international law. Thus, when the German submarines sank the passenger ship *Lusitania* in 1915 (killing 1,198 passengers, including 128 Americans), the action provoked the condemnation of both the government and much of the public. That the *Lusitania* was carrying tons of ammunition to the British was a fact that received much less public attention than did the loss of 1,198 innocent lives.

The sinking of the *Lusitania*, and the bad publicity it generated, led the Germans to cease submarine warfare for a while. Britain made steady gains, however, and as the U-boats were Germany's most effective weapon, the Germans resumed their use. In 1916, while Wilson was campaigning for reelection on the slogan "He kept us out of war," Germany sank another passenger liner, the *Arabic*. In response, Wilson, while still maintaining neutrality, asked Congress to put the military into a state of "**preparedness**" for war, just in case. While most Americans wanted to stay out of the war, popular support for entry was beginning to grow.

Then, in early 1917, the British intercepted a telegram from German Foreign Minister Zimmerman. The telegram, imaginatively called the **Zimmerman telegram**, outlined a German plan to keep the United States out of the European war. The telegram stated that *if* Mexico were to declare war on the United States, Germany would provide Mexico help in regaining the lands lost in the Mexican War. The telegram also suggested that Germany would help Japan if they, too, wanted to go to war against America. Published in newspapers around the country, the telegram convinced many Americans that Germany was trying to take over the world. Although the public was by no means universally behind the idea of war, the balance had shifted enough so that within a month, America would declare war on Germany.

World War I and Its Aftermath

As is often the case during wartime, the government's power expanded greatly during the three years America was involved in World War I. The government took control of the telephone, telegraph, and rail industries, and a massive bureaucracy arose to handle these new responsibilities. The **War Industry Board**, created to coordinate all facets of industrial and agricultural production, sought to guarantee that not only the United States but also the rest of the Allies would be well supplied. (European production had been drastically cut by the war.) The WIB had mixed success; like most large bureaucracies, it was slow and inefficient.

The government also curtailed individual civil liberties during the war. In response to the still-sizable opposition to U.S. involvement, Congress passed the **Espionage Act** in 1917 and the **Sedition Act** in 1918. The Espionage Act prohibited anyone from using the U.S. mail system to interfere with the war effort or with the draft that had been instituted under the **Selective Service Act of 1917** upon America's entry into the war. The Sedition Act made it illegal to try to prevent the sale of war bonds or to speak disparagingly of the government, the flag, the military, or the Constitution. Like the Alien and Sedition Acts in the late 1790s, both laws violated the spirit of the First Amendment but were worded vaguely, giving the courts great leeway in their interpretation.

In 1919 the Supreme Court upheld the Espionage Act in three separate cases, the most notable being *Schenck v. United States*. Schenck was a prominent socialist and ardent critic of American capitalism, who was arrested and convicted for violation of the Espionage Act when he printed and mailed leaflets urging men to resist the draft. Schenck argued that the draft was a blatant violation of the Thirteenth Amendment, whose ratification in 1865 had abolished slavery; the wording of the amendment, however, did not mention slavery but rather prohibited "involuntary servitude." Justice Oliver Wendell Holmes ruled that one's freedom of speech, and other civil liberties, were not absolute and could in fact be curtailed if one's actions posed a "clear and present danger" to others or the nation. In essence, you cannot yell "FIRE!" in a crowded theater if there is no fire.

These laws soon became useful tools for the suppression of anyone who voiced unpopular ideas. A mood of increased paranoia pervaded the era, heightened by the **Russian Revolution** in 1917, which placed Russia under Bolshevik control.

Suddenly, Americans began to fear a communist takeover. Radical labor unions, such as the International Workers of the World, were branded enemies of the state, and their leaders were incarcerated. Eugene Debs, the Socialist leader, was also imprisoned for criticizing the war. A new government agency, the **Federal Bureau of Investigation**, was created to prevent radicals from taking over; **J. Edgar Hoover** headed the nascent agency (and continued to run it until the 1970s). Business assumed greater power, while unions lost power. Under the pretext of stamping out radicalism, businesses increased their use of strikebreakers and other forceful tactics against unions. The government helped: In the **Palmer Raids** in early 1920, the government abandoned all pretext of respecting civil liberties as its agents raided union halls, pool halls, social clubs, and residences to arrest 4,000 suspected radicals. Six hundred were eventually deported, some for no other crime than their expression of sympathy for the communist movement.

The government helped create this frenzied atmosphere through its wartime propaganda arm, the **Committee on Public Information** (**CPI**). As the war progressed, the CPI's messages grew more sensational. At lectures and movie theaters, in newspapers and magazines, the CPI created the image of the Germans as cold-blooded, baby-killing, power-hungry Huns. During this period, Americans rejected all things German; for example, they changed the name of sauerkraut to "liberty cabbage." More serious were the many acts of violence against German immigrants and Americans of German descent.

Wartime also presented new opportunities for women. Although the number of women in the workforce did not increase greatly during the war, their means of employment did change. Many women quit domestic work and started working in factories; at one point, 20 percent of factory-floor manufacturing jobs were held by women. (The symbol of Rosie the Riveter, however, belongs to World War II.) These workplace advances ended with the war, as veterans returned home and reclaimed their jobs.

Southern blacks, realizing that wartime manufacturing was creating jobs in the North, undertook a **Great Migration** to the big cities, like New York, Chicago, St. Louis, and Detroit. During the war, more than 500,000 blacks left the South in search of work. Many blacks joined the army; W. E. B. Du Bois encouraged blacks to enlist, hoping that military service would provide an inroad to social equality. Sadly, the army segregated blacks and assigned them mostly to menial labor. Fearful of the effects of integration, the army assigned black combat units to French command.

American participation in the war tipped the balance in the Allies' favor, and two years after America's entry, the Germans were ready to negotiate a peace treaty. Wilson wanted the war treaty to be guided by his **Fourteen Points**, his plan for world peace delivered to Congress in January of 1918, before the end of the war. The Fourteen Points called for free trade through lower tariffs and freedom of the seas; a reduction of arms supplies on all sides; and the promotion of self-determination, both in Europe and overseas—in other words, the end of colonialism. The plan also called for the creation of the League of Nations, a mechanism for international cooperation much like today's United Nations. Wilson's Fourteen Points served as a basis for initial negotiations, but the negotiations soon took a different direction.

The European Allies wanted a peace settlement that punished Germany, and ultimately they got it. Under the **Treaty of Versailles**, Germany was forced to cede German and colonial territories to the Allies, to disarm, to pay huge reparations, and to admit total fault for the war, despite other nations' roles in starting it. Most historians agree that by leaving Germany humiliated and in economic ruin, the Treaty of Versailles helped to set the stage for World War II. Although much of Wilson's plan was discarded, the Treaty of Versailles did create the League of Nations. Wilson hoped that the League would ultimately remedy the peace settlement's many flaws, but when he returned home, a rude surprise awaited him. According to the Constitution, the president has the power to negotiate treaties with foreign nations, but these treaties are subject to Senate ratification. This illustrates the principles of **separation of powers** and **checks and balances**.

At the center of the conflict was the debate over the League of Nations, particularly Article X of the League's covenant, which many people believed curtailed America's ability to act independently in foreign affairs, specifically Congress's power to declare war. The Senate split into three groups: Democrats, who sided with Wilson and were willing to accept America's entrance into the League of Nations; a group of Republicans who were totally opposed to the League and were known as the Irreconcilables; and the Reservationists, a group of Republicans led by **Henry Cabot Lodge**, Chairman of the Senate Foreign Relations Committee and Wilson's political nemesis and intellectual rival.

Much has been made of Wilson's stubbornness and inability to compromise, and in particular, his refusal to accept what were known as the Lodge Reservations. Ultimately, the Democrats and Irreconcilables joined forces and defeated the treaty, which had been amended to include the changes suggested by Henry Cabot Lodge and the Reservationists. Thus, the United States was not only not a signatory of the Treaty of Versailles, but also never joined the League of Nations, an international organization envisioned by an American President to maintain world peace. Weary of war, America was receding into a period of isolationism. The public wanted less interaction with Europe, not more, as the League would have required. Wilson tried to muster popular support for the treaty. However, while campaigning, Wilson suffered a major stroke, thereby ending whatever chance the treaty may have had for ratification. Many people wonder whether the League of Nations would have been more successful in preventing World War II had the United States been a member.

THE JAZZ AGE AND THE GREAT DEPRESSION (1920–1933)

After World War I the American economy went through a brief slump and then started to grow rapidly. By 1922 America was hitting new peaks of prosperity every day. The invention of a practical electric motor was largely responsible for the economic boom; like computers in the 1990s, electric motors became essential to work and home environments, driving industrial machines and household appliances. With the new prosperity, other industries arose to serve the growing middle class in its search for the trappings of affluence.

Pro-Business Republican Administrations

As the age of progressive reform ended, many Americans became more comfortable with the idea of large, successful businesses. Some of these businesses, such as department stores, offered both convenience and reasonable prices. Others, like the automobile industry, offered products that made life more convenient and conferred status on their owners.

The government, which had worked closely with business leaders as part of the war effort, also grew to be more **pro-business** during the era. Government regulatory agencies (such as the Federal Trade Commission) more often assisted business than regulated it. Labor unions fell further out of public favor, particularly when they struck against industries necessary to keeping industrial America running smoothly. Unions striking for higher wages and safer work conditions in the steel, coal, and railroad industries were suppressed by federal troops. The Supreme Court overturned a minimum wage law for women and nullified child labor restrictions.

All three of the era's presidents—**Warren Harding**, **Calvin Coolidge**, and **Herbert Hoover**—pursued pro-business policies and surrounded themselves with like-minded advisors. Like Grant, Harding had the misfortune of surrounding himself with corrupt advisors; several of his cabinet members wound up in prison. The most infamous incident of his administration was the **Teapot Dome Scandal**, in which oil companies bribed the secretary of the interior in order to drill on public lands. Conservative on economic issues, Harding proved more liberal than his predecessor Wilson on issues of civil liberty. He supported anti-lynching laws and tried to help farmers (who were benefiting less from the new economy than were middle-class city dwellers) by providing more money for farm loans. Harding died in office, and Coolidge, his vice president, assumed the presidency. When Coolidge ran for the presidency in 1924, he turned the election into a debate on the economy by running on the slogan "Coolidge prosperity." Coolidge won easily and, following his mandate, continued Harding's conservative economic policies. He also pushed for lower income-tax rates. We will discuss Hoover's presidency later, when we discuss the causes of the Great Depression.

> ## Wilson and Race
> For all his progressivism in other areas, Woodrow Wilson was an outspoken white supremacist. He issued executive orders to segregate the federal government, struck a clause on racial equality from the Covenant of the League of Nations, wrote admiringly of the Ku Klux Klan, and told racist jokes at Cabinet meetings.

The pro-business atmosphere of the era led to a temporary decline in the popularity of labor unions; membership levels dropped throughout the decade. Also contributing to this drop were the efforts of businesses to woo workers with pension plans, opportunities for profit sharing, and company parties and other events designed to foster a communal spirit at work. Businessmen hoped that, if they offered some such benefits, they could dissuade workers from organizing and demanding even more. Such practices were often referred to as **welfare capitalism**.

Modern Culture

No consumer product better typified the new spirit of the nation than the **automobile**. At first, automobiles were expensive conveniences, affordable only to the extremely wealthy; then, Henry Ford perfected the assembly line and mass production, which lowered the cost of automobiles. By the end of the decade, most middle-class families could afford a car. The automobile allowed those who worked in the cities to move farther away from city centers, thus giving birth to the **suburbs**, which, in turn, transformed the automobile from a convenience to a necessity. The impact of the automobile on the 1920s was tremendous, forcing areas to quickly develop roadways and the means of policing traffic. In 1929, with the population topping 100 million in the most recent census, more than 23 million automobiles were registered in the United States.

The **radio** followed automobiles in changing the nation's culture. Ten million families owned radios, and in cities it was not unusual for several families to gather at the home of a radio owner and settle in for the evening. As more houses gained access to electric power, household appliance sales boomed as well. The **advertising industry** grew up during the decade to hype all these new products. Although advertisements from that era look pretty goofy to us now, they were quite effective at convincing people to buy stuff they did not really need—not too different from today!

All this consumerism required money, and as single-earner households often couldn't afford to "keep up with the Joneses," more women entered the working world. While the vast majority of married women continued to stay at home, more than ever—about 15 percent—entered the work force. Women continued, as they had in the past, to work in predominantly female-dominated professions (often called "pink collar jobs"), such as school teaching or office-assistant work, and to earn much less than men.

Despite the persistence of traditional roles for women, a new image of American women emerged and became a symbol of the Roaring Twenties—the **flapper**. World War I, the allure of the "big city," the right to vote, and new attitudes brought about by the ideas of Sigmund Freud (whose ideas were just beginning to circulate in the United States during the 1920s) opened up a whole new world for this new generation of emancipated women. They discarded the corset, layers of petticoats and long, dark dresses worn by their Victorian grandmothers, in favor of waistless dresses worn above the knee (shocking!), flesh-colored silk stockings (brought back from Paris), cute little hats, strings of long beads, a wrist full of bracelets, and ruby-red lips. Many flappers risked ruining their reputation by smoking cigarettes; drinking in public (despite Prohibition); and dancing the tango, the lindy, and the shimmy.

The rapid modernization of American society was reflected in the way it entertained itself. **Movies** grew tremendously popular during the decade, reflecting back at the nation its idealized self-image; on movie screens, young, independent-minded, gorgeous heroes and heroines defied all odds to succeed in romance and—at the same time—strike it rich. Sports grew more popular as well, especially baseball, whose greatest player of the era, Babe Ruth, was idolized by millions. In literature America gained international prominence through such world-class authors as **F. Scott Fitzgerald**, **Ernest Hemingway**, and playwright **Eugene**

O'Neill. Ironically, many of these writers moved to Europe, where they chronicled their alienation from the modern era, which explains why they came to be known as the **lost generation**.

In the largest black neighborhood of New York City, theaters, cultural clubs, and newspapers sprang up—a development called the **Harlem Renaissance**. W. E. B. Du Bois opened writers' centers, and his prominence helped draw attention to Harlem's cultural movement. Among the great figures of the Harlem Renaissance were the poets **Langston Hughes**, **Countee Cullen**, and **Zora Neale Hurston**. Another major black cultural development was the popularization of **jazz**. Because jazz featured improvisation and free-spiritedness, it came to be seen as emblematic of the era (which is how the decade came to be known as the **Jazz Age**). Probably the most popular and most gifted of the era's jazz musicians was trumpeter **Louis Armstrong**.

Backlash Against Modern Culture

Not all Americans were excited about the rapid transition into the modern age, and the 1920s were also a time of considerable reactionary backlash and renewed nativism. Most prominently, the **Ku Klux Klan** grew to more than 5 million members and widened its targets, attacking blacks, Jews, urbanites, and anyone whose behavior deviated from the Klan's narrowly defined code of acceptable Christian behavior. Anti-immigration groups grew in strength as well, targeting the growing number of southern and eastern European immigrants. Accusations that America's newcomers were dangerous subversives intensified when two Italian immigrant anarchists, **Sacco and Vanzetti**, were arrested on charges of murder. (Their trial immediately became a cause célèbre for the political left, as the evidence against them was inconclusive. Nonetheless, they were convicted and executed.) At the start of the decade, the United States started setting limits and quotas to restrict immigration. The **Emergency Quota Act of 1924** set immigration quotas based on national origins and discriminated against the "new immigrants" who came from southern and eastern Europe. These limits were set to reduce "foreign influence" on the country.

Another famous trial also illustrated the societal tensions of the decade. In 1925 Tennessee passed a law forbidding teachers to teach the theory of evolution. **John Thomas Scopes** broke that law, and his trial (dubbed the **Scopes Monkey Trial**) drew national attention, due in part to the two prominent attorneys arguing the case—**Clarence Darrow** and **William Jennings Bryan**, who, you may recall, ran for president in 1896, 1900, and 1908. The case also captivated the nation because, for many, it encapsulated the debate over whether to stick with tradition or abandon it for progress's sake.

Nineteenth-century morals played a part in the institution of **Prohibition**, which banned the manufacture, sale, and transport of alcoholic beverages. The Prohibition movement had its roots in the reform campaigns of the 1830s and remained a mainstay of women's political agendas until, on the eve of women's enfranchisement (1917), the **Eighteenth Amendment** outlawed the American liquor industry. Many people soon came to resent the government's intrusion in what they considered a private matter. Prohibition was further weakened by the effectiveness of organized crime in producing and selling liquor, especially in the cities. Open warfare between competing gangs and between criminals and law enforcement earned this period the title of the "**gangster era,**" which inspired many movies and television series. Prohibition was repealed by the Twenty-first Amendment in 1933.

Herbert Hoover and the Beginning of the Great Depression

In 1928 the Republicans nominated **Herbert Hoover.** Like Coolidge, Hoover was able to parlay a strong economy into an easy victory. During his campaign, Hoover predicted that the day would soon come when no American would live in poverty. He turned out to be very wrong.

In October 1929 the bottom fell out of the stock market, and this was one of the reasons for the Great Depression, but not the main reason. Prices dropped, and no matter how far they dropped, nobody wanted to buy. Hoover and his advisers underestimated the damage that the stock market crash would eventually cause. Convinced that the economy was sound, Hoover reassured the public that only stock traders would be hurt because of their irresponsible speculation. (Traders had been allowed to buy on margin, which meant that they might only have to put up 10 or 20 percent of the cost of each stock, allowing them to borrow against future profits that might or might not materialize. Margin buying is a destabilizing practice that was made illegal soon after the crash.) Unfortunately, among those speculators were huge banks and corporations, which suddenly found themselves on the verge of bankruptcy and unable to pay employees or guarantee bank deposits.

Other factors contributed to plunging the nation into a deep depression. Immediately following World War I, the carnage of the conflict, along with Germany's disastrous attempts to satisfy its reparations obligations under the Treaty of Versailles, had put Europe's economy, and much of the rest of the world's, into a depression. Domestically, though, manufacturers and farmers had been overproducing for years, creating large inventories. This led factories to lay off workers and made the farmers' crops worth much less on the market. Furthermore, production of new consumer goods was outstripping the public's ability to buy them. Supply so exceeded demand for so many goods, that this might be the main underlying cause for the Great Depression, ultimately leading to deflation, unemployment, and business failures. Finally, government laxity in regulating large businesses had led to the concentration of wealth and power in the hands of a very few businessmen. When their businesses failed, many people were thrown out of work.

The Depression had a calamitous effect on tens of millions of Americans. People lost their jobs as their employers went bankrupt or, to avoid bankruptcy, laid off the majority of workers. People lost their life savings as thousands of banks failed, and many lost their homes when they could not keep up with mortgage payments. The homeless built shantytowns, sarcastically called "**Hoovervilles.**" In rural areas farmers struggled to survive as produce prices dropped more than 50 percent. Furthermore, a prolonged drought afflicted the Great Plains area of the Midwest, turning the region into a giant **Dust Bowl.** The situation encouraged agrarian unrest; farmers fought evictions and foreclosures by attacking those who tried to enforce them. Farmers also conspired to keep prices at farm auctions low, then returned the auctioned property to its original owner. In addition, they formed the **Farmers' Holiday Association**, which organized demonstrations and threatened a nationwide walkout by farmers in order to raise prices.

At first Hoover opposed any federal relief efforts because he believed they violated the American ideal of "rugged individualism," but as the Depression worsened, he initiated a few farm assistance programs and campaigned for federal works projects (such as the Hoover Dam and the Grand Coulee Dam) that would create jobs. He hoped that raising tariffs would help American business, but the **Hawley-Smoot Tariff** actually worsened the economy. The Hawley-Smoot Tariff was the highest protective tariff in U.S. history, and it was enacted during one of the worst economic depressions ever.

Hoover's most embarrassing moment came in 1932 when Congress considered early payment of benefits to World War I veterans. Tens of thousands of impoverished veterans and their families, calling themselves the **Bonus Expeditionary Force**, came to Washington to lobby for the bill. When the bill was narrowly defeated, many refused to leave. They squatted in empty government offices or built shanties and stayed through the summer. In July Hoover ordered the Army to expel them, which Douglas MacArthur chose to do with excessive force. Employing the cavalry and attacking with tear gas, Army forces drove the veterans from D.C., then burned their makeshift homes. One hundred people died during the attack, including two babies who suffocated from exposure to tear gas.

News of the Army attack on the BEF killed any chance Hoover had for reelection, partly because he had taken the heat for MacArthur's actions. Nonetheless, by the summer of 1932, he had already secured the Republican nomination. He ran a campaign stressing his traditional conservative values. (His main concession was to accept the repeal of Prohibition; Hoover had opposed repeal during his first term.) His opponent, New York Governor **Franklin D. Roosevelt**, argued for a more interventionist government. Roosevelt also promised relief payments to the unemployed, which Hoover had opposed throughout his term. Roosevelt won the election easily.

THE NEW DEAL AND WORLD WAR II (1934–1945)

In his inaugural address, Roosevelt declared war on the Depression, and he asked the country to grant him the same broad powers that presidents exercise during wars against foreign nations. He also tried to rally the public's confidence. In the most famous line of the speech, Roosevelt declared, "The only thing we have to fear is fear itself—nameless, unreasoning, unjustified fear." A powerful presidency and the people's confidence in Roosevelt both played a large part in the implementation of his sweeping reforms, called the **New Deal**.

The First New Deal

Early in 1933 Roosevelt summoned an emergency session of Congress to work out the details of his recovery plan. The period that followed is often called the **First Hundred Days** because (1) that's how long it lasted, and (2) it was during this time that the government implemented most of the major programs associated with the **First New Deal**. (The **Second New Deal** began two years later.)

Roosevelt first sought to reestablish America's confidence in its banking system. The **Emergency Banking Relief Bill** put poorly managed banks under the control of the Treasury Department and granted government licenses (which functioned as seals of approval) to those that were solvent. In the first of many **fireside chats** broadcast over the radio, Roosevelt reassured the public that the banks were once again secure. More than 60 million Americans listened, and they obviously took Roosevelt at his word. The following week, millions redeposited the savings they had withdrawn during the bank failures of the previous years. American banks, once on the verge of ruin, were again healthy and could begin to contribute to the economic recovery. Later during the first hundred days, the government passed the **Banking Act of 1933**, which created the **Federal Deposit Insurance Corporation (FDIC)** to guarantee bank deposits, which was a big deal since people used to lose all of the money in their accounts if a bank went bankrupt. Roosevelt also instituted a number of intentionally inflationary measures in order to artificially raise prices (to get more money flowing into the economy).

Roosevelt then set out to provide relief for the rural poor. At the time, farmers were overproducing. They hoped that by growing more they could make up for falling produce prices, but their efforts were futile; the more they produced, the further prices fell, just as they had in the 1800s during the time of the Populists. Roosevelt's solution was the **Agricultural Adjustment Act**, referred to as the **AAA**. (So many of Roosevelt's new agencies were referred to by their acronyms that the entire group became known as the "**alphabet agencies**.") The AAA provided payments to farmers in return for their agreement to cut production by up to one-half; the money to cover this program came from increased taxes on meat packers, millers, and other food processors. A month later, Congress passed the **Farm Credit Act**, which provided loans to those farmers in danger of foreclosure.

Several other New Deal programs established government control over industry. The **National Industrial Recovery Act (NIRA)** consolidated businesses and coordinated their activities with the aim of eliminating overproduction and, by so doing, stabilizing prices. The NIRA also established the **Public Works Administration (PWA)**, which set aside $3 billion to create jobs building roads, sewers, public housing units, and other civic necessities. At the same time, the **Civilian Conservation Corps (CCC)** provided grants to the states to manage their own PWA-like projects. In one of the New Deal's most daring moves, the government took over the **Tennessee Valley Authority (TVA)**. Under government control the TVA (which provided energy to the Tennessee Valley region) expanded its operations greatly, which led to the economic recovery of the region.

In June 1933 Congress adjourned, ending the First Hundred Days. Most of the programs that made up the First New Deal were in place, although others, such as the creation of both the **National Labor Relations Board (NLRB)**—which mediated labor disputes—and the **Securities and Exchange Commission (SEC)**—which regulated the stock market—were not implemented until 1934. The First New Deal was an immediate success, both politically and economically; the unemployment rate fell and wages rose. In the midterm elections of 1934, the Democrats increased their majorities in both houses.

The Second New Deal

Not everyone, however, was enamored of the New Deal. In fact, both ends of the political spectrum criticized Roosevelt. **Conservatives** opposed the higher tax rates that the New Deal brought; they also disliked the increase in government power over business, and they complained that relief programs removed the incentive for the poor to lift themselves out of poverty. Additionally, the government had to borrow to finance all of its programs, and its **deficit spending** was also anathema to conservatives. **Leftists** complained that the AAA policy of paying farmers *not* to grow was immoral, given that many Americans were still too poor to feed themselves. They also felt that government policy toward businesses was too favorable; they wanted more punitive measures as many on the left blamed corporate greed for the Depression. The despair caused by the Depression provided fodder for a more radical left, and the **Socialists** (and, to a lesser extent, the **Communist Party of America**) were gaining popularity by calling for the nationalization (that is, a takeover by the government) of businesses.

Then, in 1935, the Supreme Court started to dismantle some of the programs of the First New Deal in a series of cases, one of which came to known as the "sick chicken case." *Schechter Poultry Corp. v. United States* invalidated sections of the NIRA on the grounds that the codes created under this agency were unconstitutional. According to the Constitution, only Congress can make laws. However,

Keynesian economics

Roosevelt's response to the Great Depression was guided by the work of the economist **John Maynard Keynes**. **Keynes** contended that depressions were the result of a vicious cycle in which people see that the economy is bad, so they fear that money will be hard to come by, so they don't spend the money they have, so businesses fail, so the economy worsens, so people fear that money will be hard to come by, and so on. The solution, Keynes argued, was for the government to step in and embark on a program of deliberate **deficit spending**, as the "**multiplier effect**" would ensure that every dollar spent would do several dollars' worth of good in reviving the economy. If the people who needed money the most received a little extra, they would spend it immediately on the things they needed; that money would go to businesses, who could afford to hire more people, who would start receiving paychecks and then spend that money, which would go to businesses, who could afford to hire more people, and so on. The success of Keynesian economics during the Roosevelt administration, especially as embodied in the U.S.'s deficit spending during World War II, led to widespread acceptance of Keynes's theories, which resulted in nearly thirty years of economic expansion, from 1945 to 1973.

the NIRA empowered an agency within the executive branch of government to set wage and price ceilings, maximum work hours, and regulations regarding labor unions. The court ruled that these codes were in effect "executive legislation" and beyond the limits of executive power.

Roosevelt had argued that like war, the Great Depression had created a national crisis that warranted the expansion of the executive branch of government. The following year, the Supreme Court struck down the AAA in *United States v. Butler*. Roosevelt responded by attempting to "pack the court" with justices who supported his policies. The size of the Supreme Court had changed a few times since its creation, but Roosevelt's attempt to increase the size of the court from nine justices to fifteen, giving him the power to pick justices whose views he liked, was too much for most Democrats, let alone Republicans. As a result, this **court-packing scheme** was rejected by Congress.

Roosevelt then continued with a package of legislation called the **Second New Deal**. First, he established the Emergency Relief Appropriation Act, which created the **Works Progress Administration (WPA)**, whose name was later changed to the Works Project Administration. The WPA generated more than 8 million jobs, all paid for by the government. Along with public works projects such as construction, the WPA also employed writers, photographers, and other artists to create travel guides and to record local and personal histories.

The summer of 1935 is often called Roosevelt's **Second Hundred Days** because the amount and importance of legislation passed then is comparable to that of the First Hundred Days. During this period, Congress passed legislation that broadened the powers of the **NLRB**, democratized unions, and punished businesses with anti-union policies. During this time, Congress also created the **Social Security Administration** to provide retirement benefits for many workers, including the disabled and families whose main breadwinner had died. Furthermore, the government increased taxes on wealthy individuals and top-end business profits. The cumulative effect of these programs led to the creation of the **New Deal coalition**, made up of union members, urbanites, the underclass, and blacks (who had previously voted Republican, out of loyalty to the party of Lincoln). This new Democratic coalition swept Roosevelt back into office with a landslide victory in 1936 and held together until the election of Reagan in 1980.

Roosevelt's Troubled Second Term

Several problems marred Franklin Roosevelt's second term. The first major failure of his presidency came as the term began. Angry that the Supreme Court had overturned much of the First New Deal and worried that the same fate awaited the Second New Deal, Roosevelt drafted a **Judicial Reorganization** bill. The bill proposed that Roosevelt be allowed to name a new federal judge for every sitting judge who had reached the age of 70 and had not retired; if passed, it would have allowed Roosevelt to add six new Supreme Court justices and more than forty other federal judges. A not-so-subtle effort at **packing the courts** with judges more sympathetic to Roosevelt's policies, the bill was soundly defeated in the Democratic Congress, and Roosevelt came under intense criticism for trying to seize too much power. Ultimately the court situation worked itself out to Roosevelt's benefit. A number of justices retired not long after the incident, and Roosevelt was able to replace them with more liberal judges.

In 1937 the economy went into a **recession**, a period of continually decreasing output. The cause was twofold: Roosevelt, satisfied that the New Deal was doing its job, cut back government programs in an effort to balance the budget. At the same time, the Federal Reserve Board tightened the credit supply in an effort to slow inflation. Both actions took money out of circulation, resulting in a slower economy. The recession lasted for almost three years and caused a substantial increase in the unemployment rate.

To top off Roosevelt's second term, by 1938, it was becoming evident that Europe might soon be at war again. This situation forced Roosevelt to withdraw some money from New Deal programs in order to fund a military buildup. The administration succeeded in passing a second **AAA** that met the standards set by the Supreme Court's rejection of the first AAA; it also secured the **Fair Labor Standards Act**, which set a minimum wage and established the 40-hour workweek for a number of professions. Not long after, however, the New Deal came to an end.

Did the New Deal work? Historians like to debate this question. Those who argue "yes" point to the many people who escaped life-threatening poverty because of government assistance, and especially to the immediate relief provided by the First New Deal. They also point to the many reforms of banking, finance, and management/union relations. In these areas the New Deal remade America in ways that are still recognizable today. Finally, proponents of the New Deal argue that Roosevelt should be praised for taking bold chances in a conservative political climate; he risked new initiatives when it was clear that old solutions were failing.

On the other hand, those who assert that the New Deal failed can point to the unemployment rate, which remained in double digits throughout the New Deal. Conservative historians argue that the New Deal thus did not solve the unemployment problem. Some on the left agree, contending that the New Deal was too small and too short-lived—look at how unemployment began to spike in 1937 when Roosevelt took his foot off the gas—and that it wasn't until the truly massive deficit spending program put in place in response to World War II that the economy began to recover in earnest. Furthermore, today's social welfare system stems from the New Deal; those who feel that the current American system has failed can point to Roosevelt as the man who started it all. Lastly, the New Deal did not benefit all equally. Minorities, in particular, reaped fewer (and sometimes no) benefits. The AAA actually hurt blacks and tenant farmers by putting them out of work; some of the public works projects underhired blacks, and almost all were segregated.

Foreign Policy Leading up to World War II

In the decade that followed World War I, American foreign policy objectives were aimed primarily at promoting and maintaining peace and have been described as "independent internationalism" rather than "isolationism." The **Washington Conference** (1921–1922) gathered eight of the world's great powers; the resulting treaty set limits on stockpiling armaments and reaffirmed the Open Door Policy toward China. In 1928, 62 nations signed the **Kellogg-Briand Pact**, which condemned war as a means of foreign policy. Although it contained no enforcement clauses, the Kellogg-Briand Pact was widely considered a good first step toward a postwar age.

In Latin America, the United States tried to back away from its previous interventionist policy and replace it with the **Good Neighbor Policy** in 1934. The name, however, is misleading; the United States continued to actively promote its interests in Latin America, often to the detriment of those who lived there. However, the Platt Amendment was repealed at this time. The United States achieved its foreign policy objectives mainly through economic coercion and support of pro-American leaders (some of whom were corrupt and brutal). The United States also figured out how to maintain a strong but less threatening military presence in the area, both by paying for the privilege of maintaining military bases in the countries and by arranging to train the nations' National Guard units.

In Asia, the United States had less influence. Consequently, when Japan invaded Manchuria in 1931 (and in so doing violated the Kellogg-Briand Pact, which Japan had signed), the League of Nations was powerless, and the American government could do little. When Japan went to war against China in 1937, the United States sold arms to the Chinese and called for an embargo on arms sales to Japan. However, fearful of provoking a war with Japan, the government did not order an embargo on commercial shipments to Japan from the United States.

Throughout the Republican administrations of the 1920s, the U.S. government kept tariffs high; this policy is called **protectionism**. Early in Franklin Roosevelt's presidency, the government devised a method of using economic leverage as a foreign policy tool. The **Reciprocal Trade Agreements Act** allowed the president to reduce tariffs if he felt doing so would achieve foreign policy goals. Countries granted **most favored nation** (**MFN**) **trade status** were eligible for the lowest tariff rate set by the United States, if they played their cards right. MFN trade status remains a foreign policy tool today.

Disenchantment with the results of World War I fed isolationist sentiment, a stance amplified by the findings of the **Nye Commission**. Led by Senator Gerald Nye, the commission's report in 1936 revealed unwholesome activities by American arms manufacturers; many had lobbied intensely for entry into World War I, others had bribed foreign officials, and still others were currently supplying fascist governments with weapons. Congress responded by passing a series of **neutrality acts**. The first neutrality act (1935) prohibited the sale of arms to either belligerent in a war. (Roosevelt sidestepped this act in the 1937 sale of arms to China by simply refusing to acknowledge that China and Japan were at war.) The second neutrality act banned loans to belligerents.

All the while, Roosevelt poured money into the military—just in case. As it became more apparent that Europe was headed for war, Roosevelt lobbied for a repeal of the arms embargo stated in the first neutrality act so that America could help arm the Allies (primarily England, France, and, later, the Soviet Union). When war broke out, Congress relented with a third neutrality act, which allowed arms sales and was termed "cash and carry." It required the Allies to (1) pay cash for their weapons, and (2) come to the United States to pick up their purchases and carry them away on their own ships. From the outset of the war until America's entry in 1941, Roosevelt angled the country toward participation, particularly when Poland fell to German troops and other countries followed in rapid succession. In 1940 Hitler invaded France, and a German takeover of both France and England appeared a real possibility. The chance that America might soon enter the war convinced Roosevelt to run for an unprecedented third term. Again, he won convincingly.

Within the limits allowed by the neutrality acts, Roosevelt worked to assist the Allies. He found creative ways to supply them with extra weapons and ships; he appointed pro-Ally Republicans to head the Department of War and the Navy; and he instituted the nation's first peacetime military draft. It becomes increasingly difficult to describe U.S. foreign policy as isolationist by the 1940s. In 1941 Roosevelt forced the **Lend-Lease Act** through Congress, which permitted the United States to "lend" armaments to England, which no longer had money to buy the tools of war. Roosevelt sent American ships into the war zone to protect Lend-Lease shipments, an act which could easily have provoked a German attack. Later in the year, Roosevelt and British Prime Minister Winston Churchill met at the **Atlantic Charter Conference**. The Atlantic Charter declared the Allies' war aims, which included disarmament, self-determination, freedom of the seas, and guarantees of each nation's security.

Given all this activity in the European theater, it seems odd that America's entry to the war came not in Europe but in Asia. Japan entered into an alliance (called the **Tripartite Pact**) with Italy and Germany in 1940. By 1941 France had fallen to Germany, and the British were too busy fighting Hitler to block Japanese expansion, which had continued south into French Indochina (modern-day Vietnam, Cambodia, and Laos). The United States responded to Japanese aggression by cutting off trade to Japan, which was dependent on foreign imports. The embargo included oil, which Japan needed to fuel its war machine. Despite peace talks in November of 1941 between the United States and Japan to avoid war, the United States had broken Japan's secret communication codes and knew that Japan was planning an attack, but did not know the location. Secretary of War Henry Stimson encouraged Roosevelt to wait for the Japanese attack in order to guarantee popular support for the war at home. He did not have to wait long. The Japanese attacked **Pearl Harbor**, Hawaii, on December 7, and U.S. participation in the war began.

World War II

Complicated military strategy and the outcome of key battles played a big part in World War II. Fortunately, you do not have to know much about them for the AP exam; nor do you need to know about the many truly unspeakable horrors the Nazis perpetrated on Europe's Jews, gypsies, homosexuals, and dissidents. You should know about the various wartime conferences, however, when the Allies met to discuss military strategy and the eventual postwar situation. It was no secret that the Grand Alliance between the Soviet Union and the West was tenuous at best, held together by the thread of a common enemy but threatened by Stalin's impatience at the Allies' delay in opening a "second front" while the Soviets bore the brunt of the Nazi onslaught.

The first meeting of the "big three" (Roosevelt, Churchill, and Stalin) took place in the Iranian capital of Tehran in November of 1943. It was here that they planned the Normandy invasion, **D-Day**, and agreed to divide a defeated Germany into occupation zones after the war. Stalin also agreed to enter the war against Japan once Hitler had been defeated. The Allies fought the Germans primarily in the Soviet Union and in the Mediterranean until early 1944, when Allied forces invaded occupied France (on D-Day). The Soviet Union paid a huge price in human and material loss for this strategy and after the war sought to recoup its losses by occupying Eastern Europe. In the Pacific both sides incurred huge numbers of casualties. The Allies eventually won a war of attrition against the Germans, and the Americans accelerated victory in the East by dropping two atomic bombs on Japan.

As it had during the Civil War, World War I, and the New Deal, the government acquired more power than it previously had. The War Production Board allowed the government to oversee the mobilization of industry toward the war effort; in return, businesses were guaranteed generous profits. **Rationing** of almost all consumer goods was imposed. The government sponsored scientific research directed at improving weaponry, developing **radar** and the atomic bomb during this period. The government also exerted greater control over labor. The **Labor Disputes Act** of 1943 (passed in reaction to a disconcerting number of strikes in essential industries) allowed government takeover of businesses deemed necessary to national security, which gave the government authority to settle labor disputes. **Hollywood** was enlisted to create numerous propaganda films, both to encourage support on the home front and to boost morale of the troops overseas. Not surprisingly, the size of the government more than tripled during the war.

FDR signed the **Selective Training and Service Act of 1940**, which created the first peacetime draft in U.S. history and gave birth to the current incarnation of the Selective Service System, which ultimately provided about 10 million soldiers toward the war effort. (Although the draft was discontinued in 1973, after the United States' involvement in Vietnam, the Selective Service System remained in place and currently requires that all male citizens register for the draft within 30 days after turning 18.)

World War II affected almost every aspect of daily life at home and abroad. It created both new opportunities and new tensions within American society. More than a million African-Americans served in the U.S. military during World War

II, but they lived and worked in segregated units. The U.S. army was not desegregated until after the war, during the Truman administration in 1948. A popular image, familiar to most Americans, is that of Rosie the Riveter. Originally featured on a poster of the era, Rosie came to symbolize the millions of women who worked in war-related industrial jobs during World War II. Unfortunately for the cause of feminism, most women were expected to take off the coveralls and put the apron back on when the soldiers returned home.

Again, as during World War I, the government restricted civil liberties. Probably the most tragic instance was the **internment of Japanese Americans** from 1942 to the end of the war. Fearful that the Japanese might serve as enemy agents within U.S. borders, the government imprisoned more than 110,000 Asian Americans, over two-thirds of whom had been born in the United States and thus were U.S. citizens. Some were not even of Japanese descent. None of those interned was ever charged with a crime; imprisonment was based entirely on ethnic background. The government placed these Japanese Americans in desolate prison camps far from the West Coast, where they feared a Japanese invasion would take place. Most lost their homes and possessions as a result of the internment.

The Supreme Court upheld the constitutionality of both the evacuation and internment of Japanese Americans. As in the *Schenck* case of 1919, the Court ruled that a citizen's civil liberties can be curtailed and even violated in time of war. "Citizenship has its responsibilities as well as its privileges, and in time of war the burden is always heavier. Compulsory exclusion of large groups of citizens from their homes, except under circumstances of direst emergency and peril, is inconsistent with our basic governmental institutions. But when under conditions of modern warfare our shores are threatened by hostile forces, the power to protect must be commensurate with the threatened danger..." wrote Justice Hugo Black in *Korematsu v. United States* (1944). It wasn't until 1988 that a government apology was made and reparations of about $1.6 million were disbursed to surviving internees and their heirs.

The End of the War

As the war neared its end in Europe, the apparent victors—the Allies—met to discuss the fate of postwar Europe. In February of 1945, the Allied leaders met at **Yalta** and in effect redrew the world map. By this time the Soviet army occupied parts of Eastern Europe, a result of the campaign to drive the German army out of the USSR.

Stalin wanted to create a "buffer zone" between the Soviet Union and Western Europe; he wanted to surround himself with nations that were "friendly" toward the government in Moscow. Because of the presence of the Red Army, Stalin was given a free hand in Eastern Europe, a decision the other Allies would later regret, with the promise to hold "free and unfettered elections" after the war. Despite this promise, Soviet tanks rolled into Romania three weeks after Yalta, thus beginning the establishment of Soviet **satellites** and the descent of the **Iron Curtain**. (The Iron Curtain was a metaphor coined by Winston Churchill in 1946 to describe the symbolic division of Eastern and Western Europe, and thus the origins of the Cold War following World War II.)

The Allies agreed on a number of issues concerning borders and postwar settlements. They also agreed that once the war in Europe ended, the USSR would declare war on Japan. Toward the end of the war, the Allies agreed to help create the **United Nations** to mediate future international disputes. The Allies met again at **Potsdam** to decide how to implement the agreements of Yalta. This time, **Harry S. Truman** represented the United States, as Roosevelt had died in April. Things did not go as well at Potsdam; with the war's end closer and the Nazis no longer a threat, the differences between the United States and the Soviet Union were growing more pronounced.

Some argue that American-Soviet animosity prompted Truman's decision to use the **atomic bomb** against the Japanese. (By this argument, America feared Soviet entry into the Asian war where the Soviets might then attempt to expand their influence, as they were doing in Eastern Europe. Along the same line of reasoning, one could assert that the United States wanted to put on a massive display of power to intimidate the Soviets.) However, the manner in which the war in the Pacific had been fought to that point also supported Truman's decision. The Japanese had fought tenaciously and remained powerful despite the long war; casualty estimates of an American invasion of Japan ran upward of 500,000. Some military leaders estimated that such an invasion would not subdue Japan for years. In August the United States dropped two atomic bombs, first on **Hiroshima** and then three days later on **Nagasaki**. The Japanese surrendered soon after.

Chapter 11 Drill

See Chapter 13 for answers and explanations.

1. Muckrakers furthered the causes of the Progressive movement by

   (A) organizing grassroots campaigns for political reform at the state level
   (B) suing large companies and donating their court awards to Progressive campaigns
   (C) staging large, violent protests in support of Progressive goals
   (D) warning Americans of the dangers inherent in such radical movements as communism and socialism
   (E) alerting the public to the social ills and corporate corruption targeted by Progressives

2. Prior to the administration of Theodore Roosevelt, the Sherman Antitrust Act had been used primarily to

   (A) dismantle corporate monopolies
   (B) suppress trade unions
   (C) impose import tariffs
   (D) enforce civil rights in the South
   (E) rid the government of corruption

3. Following the Spanish-American War and the acquisition of territory overseas, in a series of cases known as the Insular Cases, the U.S. Supreme Court ruled that

   (A) natives living on American soil abroad were guaranteed the same rights and privileges as U.S. citizens living within the continental United States
   (B) colonial subjects within the American empire were not entitled to the rights guaranteed by the U.S. Constitution
   (C) "the Constitution follows the flag"
   (D) Congress must relinquish control of these overseas possessions and honor their right of self-determination
   (E) the subjugation of people on foreign soil against their consent is unconstitutional

4. Which of the following best summarizes the contents of the Zimmerman telegram, which was intercepted in 1917?

   (A) Germany offered Mexico a chance to regain the land it had lost in the Mexican Cession if Mexico attacked the United States and helped prevent the United States from assisting the Allies.
   (B) A British spy alerted the world to the existence of mass extermination camps in German-held territories.
   (C) The United States assured the British that it would join the war in Europe if the war were to continue for another year.
   (D) The owner of the Boston Red Sox revealed a plan to sell star player Babe Ruth to the New York Yankees for a large amount of cash.
   (E) A U.S. senator promised pro-temperance organizations that a constitutional amendment imposing prohibition would soon pass.

5. Wilson's Fourteen Points plan for peace after World War I included all of the following EXCEPT

   (A) promotion of universal self-determination
   (B) lower tariffs to promote free trade
   (C) repayment of all Allied war expenses by Germany
   (D) across-the-board arms reductions
   (E) the creation of an international peacekeeping organization

6. All of the following can be seen as clashes between traditional and modern culture during the post–World War I era EXCEPT

   (A) the rise of the Ku Klux Klan
   (B) the Teapot Dome Scandal
   (C) the Scopes Monkey Trial
   (D) the Emergency Quota Act of 1924
   (E) Prohibition

7. Buying "on margin" contributed to the stock market crash of 1929 because it

(A) required investors to purchase only high-risk, volatile stocks
(B) imposed high interest rates that discouraged trading
(C) prevented traders from learning the true financial state of the companies in which they invested
(D) allowed traders to pay for stock with projected future profits
(E) mandated that traders sell a stock as soon as it started to lose value

8. Franklin Roosevelt invoked the Good Neighbor Policy in taking which of the following actions?

(A) Providing England with munitions to defend itself against Germany
(B) Creating the Tennessee Valley Authority to provide power in the poor rural South
(C) Banning trade of war-related materials with Japan and freezing Japanese assets in the United States
(D) Establishing the Federal Deposit Insurance Corporation to stabilize savings banks
(E) Recalling U.S. troops from Nicaragua and Haiti

9. The Nye Commission report of 1936 reinforced American isolationism by

(A) revealing unethical profiteering by American munitions companies during World War I
(B) concluding that Germany had no interest in engaging the United States in war
(C) listing the domestic programs that would have to be forfeited if the United States were to increase its overseas commitments
(D) detailing deficiencies in all branches of the U.S. military
(E) blaming the worldwide Depression on corrupt financial practices in Europe

10. In its *Korematsu v. United States* decision, the Supreme Court ruled that

(A) the wartime relocation of West Coast Japanese Americans was not unconstitutional
(B) the Japanese government had no legitimate claim to reparations for the bombings of Hiroshima and Nagasaki
(C) the U.S. government had violated the Constitution by entering the Korean War
(D) immigration quotas based on race were unconstitutional
(E) Japanese Americans are not entitled to protection under government-sponsored Affirmative Action programs

REFLECT ACTIVITY

Respond to the following questions:

- For which content topics discussed in this chapter do you feel you have achieved sufficient mastery to answer multiple-choice questions correctly?

- For which content topics discussed in this chapter do you feel you have achieved sufficient mastery to discuss effectively in an essay?

- For which content topics discussed in this chapter do you feel you need more work before you can answer multiple-choice questions correctly?

- For which content topics discussed in this chapter do you feel you need more work before you can discuss effectively in an essay?

- What parts of this chapter are you going to re-review?

- Will you seek further help, outside of this book (such as a teacher, tutor, or AP Central), on any of the content in this chapter—and, if so, on what content?

Chapter 12
The Postwar Period and into the Twenty-first Century (1945–2001)

TRUMAN AND THE BEGINNING OF THE COLD WAR (1945–1953)

The end of World War II raised two major issues. The first concerned the survival of the combatants; with the exception of the United States, the nations involved in World War II had all seen fighting within their borders, and the destruction had been immense. The second issue involved the shape of the new world and what new political alliances would be formed. This question would become the major source of contention between the world's two leading political-economic systems, capitalism and communism.

The stakes in this power struggle, called the **Cold War** (because there was no actual combat as there is in a "hot war"), were high. Though the major powers (the United States and Soviet Union) didn't enter into combat in the Cold War, the United States did fight hot **"proxy" wars** in Korea and Vietnam during this time. The American economy was growing more dependent on exports; American industry also needed to import metals, a process requiring (1) open trade, and (2) friendly relations with those nations that provided those metals. In addition, with many postwar economies in shambles, competition for the few reasonably healthy economies grew fiercer. Finally, those countries that were strongest before the war—Germany, Japan, and Great Britain—had either been defeated or seen their influence abroad greatly reduced. The United States and the Soviet Union emerged as the two new superpowers. Although they were allies during the second world war, the war's end exposed the countries' many ideological differences, and they soon became enemies.

Truman and Foreign Policy

The differences between Soviet and American goals were apparent even before the war was over, but became even clearer when the Soviets refused to recognize Poland's conservative government-in-exile. (The Polish government had moved to England to escape the Nazis; this government was backed by the United States.) A communist government took over Poland. Within two years pro-Soviet communist coups had also taken place in Hungary and Czechoslovakia. The propaganda in the United States and USSR during this period reached a fever pitch. In each country the other was portrayed as trying to take over the world for its own sinister purposes.

Then, in 1947, communist insurgents threatened to take over both Greece and Turkey, but England could no longer prop up these nations. In a speech before Congress in which he asked for $400 million in aid to the two countries, Truman asserted, "I believe it must be the policy of the United States to support free peoples who are resisting attempted subjugation by armed minorities or outside pressures." This statement, called the **Truman Doctrine**, became the cornerstone of a larger policy, articulated by George Kennan, called "**containment.**" The idea of containment came from what is known as the **Long Telegram**, which Kennan sent to Washington from his duty station in Germany, in 1946. This policy said that the United States would not instigate a war with the Soviet Union, but it would come to the defense of countries in danger of Soviet takeover. The policy aimed to prevent the spread of communism and encourage the Soviets to abandon their aggressive strategies.

Meanwhile, the United States used a tried-and-true method to shore up its alliances—it gave away money. The **Marshall Plan**, named for Secretary of State George Marshall, sent more than $12 billion to Europe to help rebuild its cities and economy. In return for that money, of course, countries were expected to become American allies. Although the Marshall Plan was offered to Eastern Europe and the Soviet Union, no countries in the Soviet sphere participated in the program, as Stalin viewed the initiative as further evidence of U.S. imperialism. The United States also formed a mutual defense alliance with Canada and a number of countries in Western Europe called the **North Atlantic Treaty Organization** (**NATO**) in 1949. Truman did not have an easy time convincing Congress that NATO was necessary; remember, from the time of Washington's Farewell Address, American sentiment has strongly favored avoiding all foreign entanglements.

The crisis in **Berlin** the previous year, however, helped convince Congress to support NATO. The crisis represented a culmination of events after World War II. In 1945 Germany had been divided into four sectors, with England, France, the United States, and the USSR each controlling one. Berlin, though deep in Soviet territory, had been similarly divided. Upon learning that the three Western Allies planned to merge their sectors into one country and to bring that country into the Western economy, the Soviets responded by imposing a **blockade** on Berlin. Truman refused to surrender the city, however, and ordered airlifts to keep that portion under Western control supplied with food and fuel. The blockade continued for close to a year, by which point the blockade became such a political liability that the Soviets gave it up. Don't confuse the **Berlin Blockade** with the **Berlin Wall**. The Berlin Blockade occurred when the Soviets closed off access to the city during the Truman administration in 1948, while the Soviets erected the Berlin Wall in 1961 during the Kennedy administration to divide the city between the East and the West. Constructed of concrete and barbed wire, the wall separated the Soviet sector of Berlin from West Berlin and became a symbol of the Cold War. The wall was finally dismantled in 1989.

Not long after the United States joined NATO, the Soviets detonated their first atomic bomb. Fear of Soviet invasion or subterfuge also led to the creation of the **National Security Council** (a group of foreign affairs advisers who work for the president) and the **Central Intelligence Agency** (the United States' spy network).

As if Truman didn't have enough headaches in Europe, he also had to deal with Asia. Two issues dominated U.S. policy in the region: the **reconstruction of Japan** and the **Chinese Revolution**. After the war the United States occupied Japan, and its colonial possessions were divided up. The United States took control of the Pacific Islands and the southern half of Korea, while the USSR took control of the northern half of Korea. Under the command of General Douglas MacArthur, Japan wrote a democratic constitution, demilitarized, and started a remarkable economic revival. The United States was not as successful in China, where it chose to side with Chiang Kai-shek's Nationalist government against **Mao Zedong**'s Communist insurgents, during China's 20-year civil war. Despite massive American military aid, the Communists overthrew the Nationalists, whose government was exiled to Taiwan. For decades the United States refused to recognize the legitimacy of Mao's regime, creating another international "hot spot" for Americans. Truman also chose to aid the French during the Vietnamese war for independence in Indochina, although most Americans were not aware of this at the time.

McCarthyism

All this conflict with communists resurrected anti-communist paranoia at home, just as anti-communism had swept America during the Red Scare after WWI. In 1947 Truman ordered investigations of 3 million federal employees in a search for "security risks." Those found to have a potential Achilles' heel—either previous association with "known communists" or a "moral" weakness such as alcoholism or homosexuality (which, the government reasoned, made them easy targets for blackmail)—were dismissed without a hearing. In 1949 former State Department official **Alger Hiss** was found guilty of consorting with a communist spy (Richard Nixon was the congressman mostly responsible for Hiss's downfall). Americans began to passionately fear the "enemy within." Even the Screen Actors Guild, then headed by Ronald Reagan, attempted to discover and purge its own communists.

It was this atmosphere that allowed a demagogic senator named **Joseph McCarthy** to rise from near anonymity to national fame. In 1950 McCarthy claimed to have a list of more than 200 known communists working for the State Department. He subsequently changed that number several times, which should have clued people in to the fact that he was not entirely truthful. Unchallenged, McCarthy went on to lead a campaign of innuendo that ruined the lives of thousands of innocent people. Without ever uncovering a single communist, McCarthy held years of hearings with regard to subversion, not just in the government, but in education and the entertainment industry as well. Those subpoenaed were often forced to confess to previous associations with communists and name others with similar associations. Industries created lists of those tainted by these charges, called **blacklists**, which prevented the accused from working, just as blacklists had been used against union organizers at the turn of the last century. McCarthy's downfall came in 1954, during the Eisenhower administration, when he accused the Army of harboring communists. He had finally chosen too powerful a target. The Army fought back hard, and with help from **Edward R. Murrow**'s television show, in the **Army–McCarthy hearings**, McCarthy was made to look foolish. The public turned its back on him, and the era of **McCarthyism** ended, but public distrust and fear of communism remained.

"You've done enough. Have you no sense of decency, sir? At long last, have you left no sense of decency?"
—Army counsel Joseph Welch, speaking back to Joseph McCarthy at the hearings that would effectively end McCarthy's career.

Truman's Domestic Policy and the Election of 1948

The end of the war meant the end of wartime production. With fewer Jeeps, airplanes, guns, bombs, and uniforms to manufacture, American businesses started laying off employees. Returning war veterans further crowded the job market, and unemployment levels rose dramatically. At the same time many people who had built up their savings during the war (since rationing had limited the availability of consumer goods) started to spend more liberally, causing prices to rise. In 1946 the inflation rate was nearly 20 percent. The poor and unemployed felt the effects the most. Truman offered some New Deal–style solutions to America's economic woes, but a new conservatism had taken over American politics. Most of his proposals were rejected, and the few that were implemented had little effect.

The new conservatism brought with it a new round of anti-unionism in the country. Americans were particularly upset when workers in essential industries went on strike, as when the coal miners' strike (by the **United Mine Workers**, or **UMW**) cut off the energy supply to other industries, shutting down steel foundries, auto plants, and more. Layoffs in the affected industries exacerbated tensions. Americans cared little that the miners were fighting for basic rights. Truman followed the national mood, ordering a government **seizure of the mines** when a settlement could not be reached. During a later railroad strike, Truman threatened to draft into the military those strikers who held out for more than he thought they deserved. Consequently, Truman alienated labor, one of the core constituencies of the new Democratic coalition. Labor and consumers, angry at skyrocketing prices, formed an alliance that helped the Republicans take control of the **Eightieth Congress** in the 1946 midterm elections.

Truman also alienated many voters (particularly in the South) by pursuing a civil rights agenda that, for its time, was progressive. He convened the **President's Committee on Civil Rights,** which in 1948 issued a report calling for an end to segregation and poll taxes, and for more aggressive enforcement of anti-lynching laws. Truman also issued an executive order forbidding racial discrimination in the hiring of federal employees and another executive order desegregating the Armed Forces. Blacks began to make other inroads. The NAACP won some initial, important lawsuits against segregated schools and buses; **Jackie Robinson** broke the color barrier in baseball; and black groups started to form coalitions with liberal white organizations, thereby gaining more political clout. These advances provoked an outbreak of flagrant racism in the South, and in 1948 segregationist Democrats, or "**Dixiecrats**," abandoned the party to support Strom Thurmond for president.

With so many core Democratic constituencies—labor, consumers, Southerners—angry with the president, his defeat in 1948 seemed certain. Truman's popularity, however, received an unintentional boost from the Republican-dominated Congress. The staunchly conservative legislature passed several anti-labor acts too strong even for Truman. The **Taft-Hartley Act**, passed over Truman's veto, prohibited "union only" work environments (called **"closed shops"**), restricted labor's right to strike, prohibited the use of union funds for political purposes, and gave

Let's Make A Deal

Both Theodore and Franklin Roosevelt, as well as FDR's successor Harry Truman, offered "deals" to the American public:

	President	**What's the deal with this?**
Square Deal	Theodore Roosevelt	Government promised to regulate business and restore competition
First New Deal	Franklin Roosevelt	Focused on immediate public relief and the recovery of banks
Second New Deal	Franklin Roosevelt	Addressed the shortcomings of the First New Deal and responded to a changing political climate
Fair Deal	Harry Truman	Extension of New Deal vision and provisions for reintegrating WWII veterans into society (e.g., the G.I. Bill)

the government broad power to intervene in strikes. The same Congress then rebuked Truman's efforts to pass health care reform; increase aid to schools, farmers, the elderly, and the disabled; and promote civil rights for blacks. The cumulative effect of all this acrimony made Truman look a lot better to those he had previously offended. Still, as election time neared, Truman trailed his chief opponent, Thomas Dewey. He then made one of the most brilliant political moves in American history: He recalled the Congress, whose majority members had just drafted an extremely conservative Republican platform at the party convention, and challenged them to enact that platform. Congress met for two weeks and did not pass one significant piece of legislation. Truman then went out on a grueling public appearance campaign, everywhere deriding the "do-nothing" Eightieth Congress. To almost everyone's surprise, Truman won re-election, and his coattails carried a Democratic majority into Congress.

The Korean War

The Korean War began when communist North Korea invaded U.S.-backed South Korea. Believing the Soviet Union to have engineered the invasion, the United States took swift countermeasures. Originally intending only to repel the invasion, Truman decided to attempt a reunification of Korea after some early military successes. Under the umbrella of the United Nations, American troops attacked North Korea, provoking China, Korea's northern neighbor. (The Chinese were not too keen on the idea of hostile American troops on their border.) China ultimately entered the war, pushing American and South Korean troops back near the original border dividing North and South Korea. U.S. commander **Douglas MacArthur** recommended an all-out confrontation with China, with the objective of overthrowing the Communists and reinstating Chiang Kai-shek. Truman thought a war with the world's most populous country might be imprudent and so decided against MacArthur. When MacArthur started publicly criticizing the president, who was also the commander-in-chief, Truman fired him for insubordination. MacArthur was very popular at home, however, and firing him hurt Truman politically.

Although peace talks began soon after, the war dragged on another two years, into the Eisenhower administration. When the 1952 presidential election arrived, the Republicans took a page from the Whig playbook and chose **Dwight D. Eisenhower**, a war hero. By this point the presidency had been held by the Democratic party for 20 years. Truman was unpopular; his bluntness is now seen as a sign of his integrity, but during his terms, it offended a lot of potential constituents. In short, America was ready for a change. Eisenhower beat Democratic challenger **Adlai Stevenson** easily.

THE EISENHOWER YEARS (1953–1961)

The '50s are often depicted as a time of **conformity**. Across much of America, a **consensus of values** reigned. Americans believed that their country was the best in the world, that communism was evil and had to be stopped, and that a decent job, a home in the suburbs, and access to all the modern conveniences (aka **consumerism**) did indeed constitute "the good life." Congress had enacted the Serviceman's Readjustment Act, commonly known as the **G.I. Bill of Rights**, in June of 1944. It provided an allowance for educational and living expenses for returning soldiers and veterans who wished to earn their high school diploma or attend college. The G.I. Bill not only helped many Americans achieve the American dream but also helped stimulate postwar economic growth by providing low-cost loans to purchase homes or farms or to start small businesses. The '50s also proved to be an era in which the civil rights movement built on the advances of the 1940s and met some violent resistance; an era plagued by frequent economic recessions; and an era of spiritual unrest that manifested itself in such emerging art forms as **Beat poetry and novels** ("Howl", *On the Road*), teen movies (*Blackboard Jungle*, *The Wild One*, *Rebel Without a Cause*), and **rock 'n' roll** (Elvis Presley, Little Richard, Jerry Lee Lewis, Chuck Berry).

> ## The Kitchen Debate
> Vice President Richard Nixon visited Moscow in 1959 for a cultural fair. While standing in a model American kitchen, Nixon ended up getting into an argument with Soviet leader Nikita Khrushchev that emblematized not only U.S./Soviet relations but also common American attitudes toward gender in the 1950s. An excerpt:
>
> *Nixon*: I want to show you this kitchen. It is like those of our houses in California.
> *Khrushchev*: We have such things.
> *Nixon*: This is our newest model. This is the kind which is built in thousands of units for direct installations in the houses. In America, we like to make life easier for women.
> *Khrushchev*: Your capitalistic attitude toward women does not occur under communism.
> *Nixon*: I think that this attitude toward women is universal.

Domestic Politics in the '50s

Eisenhower arrived at the White House prepared to impose conservative values on the federal government, which had mushroomed in size under Roosevelt and Truman. He sought to balance the budget, cut federal spending, and ease government regulation of business. In these goals he was, at best, only partly successful. The military buildup required by the continuing Cold War prevented Eisenhower from making the cuts to the military budget that he would have liked. He reduced military spending by reducing troops and buying powerful weapons systems (thus shaping the **New Look Army**), but not enough to eliminate deficit spending. The popularity of remaining New Deal programs made it difficult to eliminate them; furthermore, circumstances required Eisenhower to increase the number of Social Security recipients and the size of their benefits. Under Eisenhower the government also began developing the **Interstate Highway System**, partly to make it easier to move soldiers and nuclear missiles around the country. The new roads not only sped up travel, but they also promoted tourism and the development of the suburbs. The initial cost, however, was extremely high. As a result, Eisenhower managed to balance the federal budget only three times in eight years.

Some of the most important domestic issues during the Eisenhower years involved minorities. In 1953 Eisenhower sought to change federal policy toward Native

Americans. His new policy, called **termination**, would liquidate reservations, end federal support to Native Americans, and subject them to state law. However, in devising this policy, Eisenhower did not take Native American priorities into account. He aimed simply to reduce federal responsibilities and bolster the power of the states. Native Americans protested, convinced that termination was simply a means of stealing what little land the tribes had left. The plan failed and was ultimately stopped in the 1960s, but not before causing the depletion and impoverishment of a number of tribes.

The civil rights movement experienced a number of its landmark events during Eisenhower's two terms. In 1954 the Supreme Court heard the case of ***Brown v. Board of Education of Topeka***, a lawsuit brought on behalf of Linda Brown (a black school-age child) by the NAACP. Future Supreme Court Justice Thurgood Marshall argued the case for Brown. In its ruling the Court overturned the "separate but equal" standard as it applied to education; "separate but equal" had been the law of the land since the Court had approved it in *Plessy v. Ferguson* (1896). In a 9 to 0 decision, the Court ruled that "separate educational facilities are inherently unequal" and that schools should desegregate with "all deliberate speed." Although a great victory for civil rights, *Brown v. Board of Education* did not immediately solve the school segregation problem. Some Southern states started to pay the tuition for white children to attend private schools in order to maintain segregation. Some states actually closed their public schools rather than integrate them. Although Eisenhower personally disapproved of segregation, he also opposed rapid change, and so did little. This inactivity encouraged further Southern resistance, and in 1957 the governor of Arkansas called in the state National Guard to prevent a group of black students, the **Little Rock Nine**, from enrolling in a Little Rock high school. Eisenhower did nothing until one month later, when the courts ordered him to enforce the law. Arkansas, in response, closed all public high schools in Little Rock for two years. Eisenhower supported the Civil Rights Acts of 1957 and 1960, which strengthened the voting rights of Southern blacks and the punishments for crimes against blacks, respectively.

Another key civil rights event, the **Montgomery bus boycott**, began in 1955 when **Rosa Parks** was arrested for refusing to give up her seat on a bus to a white man as was required by **Jim Crow** laws. Outrage over the arrest, coupled with long-term resentment over unfair treatment, spurred blacks to stay off Montgomery buses for more than a year. The boycott brought **Martin Luther King Jr.** to national prominence. Barely 27 years old at the time, King was pastor at Rosa Parks's church. Although King was clearly groomed for greatness—his grandfather had led the protests resulting in the creation of Atlanta's first black high school, his father was a minister and community leader, and King had already amassed impressive academic credentials (Morehouse College, Crozer Theological Seminary, University of Pennsylvania, and finally a Ph.D. from Boston University)—the year-long bus boycott gave him his first national podium. In the end a ruling by the Supreme Court resulted in the integration of city buses in Montgomery and elsewhere.

King encouraged others to organize peaceful protests, a plan inspired by his studies of Henry David Thoreau and Mohandas Gandhi. In 1960 black college students in **Greensboro**, **North Carolina**, tried just that approach, organizing a sit-in at a local Woolworth's lunch counter designated "whites only." News reports

of the sit-in, and the resultant harassment the students endured, inspired a sit-in
movement that spread across the nation to combat segregation.

America vs. the Communists

There are a number of terms associated with the Cold War policy of Eisenhower
and Secretary of State **John Foster Dulles** that you need to know. The administration continued to follow the policy of containment, but called it **liberation** to make it sound more intimidating. It carried the threat that the United
States would eventually free Eastern Europe from Soviet control. Dulles coined
the phrase "**massive retaliation**" to describe the nuclear attack that the United
States would launch if the Soviets tried anything too daring. **Deterrence** described
how Soviet fear of massive retaliation would prevent their challenging the United
States and led to an arms race. Deterrence suggested that the mere knowledge
of **mutually assured destruction (MAD)** prevented both nations from deploying
nuclear weapons. Dulles allowed confrontations with the Soviet Union to escalate
toward war, an approach called **brinksmanship**. Finally, the Eisenhower administration argued that the spread of communism had to be checked in Southeast
Asia. If South Vietnam fell to communism, the nations surrounding it would fall
quickly like dominoes; hence, the **domino theory**.

Cold War tensions remained high throughout the decade. Eisenhower had hoped
that the death of **Joseph Stalin** in 1953 might improve American-Soviet relations.
Initially, the new Soviet leader **Nikita Khrushchev** offered hope. Khrushchev
denounced Stalin's totalitarianism and called for "peace-
ful coexistence" among nations with different economic
philosophies. Some Soviet client states took Khrushchev's pronouncements as a sign of weakness; rebellions
occurred in Poland and Hungary.When the Soviets
crushed the uprisings, U.S.–Soviet relations returned to
where they were during the Stalin era. Soviet advances in nuclear arms development (the USSR exploded
its first hydrogen bomb a year after the United States
blew up its first H-bomb) and space flight (the USSR
launched the first satellite, Sputnik, into space, moti-
vating the United States to quickly create and fund the
National Aeronautics and Space Administration, or
NASA) further heightened anxieties.

Meanwhile, the United States narrowly averted war
with the other communists, the Chinese. American-
allied Taiwan occupied two islands close to mainland
China, **Quemoy** and **Matsu**. The Taiwanese used the
islands as bases for commando raids on the commu-

> ## The Arms Race
>
> *Size of bombs*
> - Atomic bomb dropped on Hiroshima, 1945:
>   equal to 12,500 tons of TNT
> - First hydrogen bomb test, 1952:
>   equal to 10,400,000 tons of TNT
> - Soviet Tsar Bomba test, 1961:
>   equal to to 57,000,000 tons of TNT
>
> *Number of warheads*
> - 1945: USA 6; USSR 0
> - 1950: USA 369; USSR 5
> - 1955: USA 3057; USSR 200
> - 1960: USA 20,434; USSR 1605
> - 1970: USA 26,119; USSR 11,643
> - 1980: USA 23,764; USSR 30,062

nists, which eventually irritated the Chinese enough that they bombed the two
islands. In a classic example of brinksmanship, Eisenhower declared that the United States would defend the islands and strongly hinted that he was considering
a nuclear attack on China. Tensions remained high for years, and Eisenhower's
stance forced him to station American troops on the islands. During the 1960

presidential election, Kennedy used the incident as a campaign issue, arguing that the two small islands were not worth the cost of defending them.

Third World Politics

World War II resulted in the breakup of Europe's huge overseas empires. In the decades that followed the war's end, numerous countries in Africa, Asia, and South America broke free of European domination. These countries allied themselves with neither of the two major powers; for this reason they were deemed the **Third World**. Both America and the Soviets sought to bring Third World countries into their spheres of influence, as these nations represented potential markets as well as sources of raw materials. The two superpowers particularly prized strategically located Third World countries that were willing to host military bases.

Neither superpower, it turned out, was able to make major inroads in the Third World at first. **Nationalism** swept through most Third World nations, recently liberated from major world powers. Enjoying their newfound freedom, these countries were reluctant to foster a long-term alliance with a large, powerful nation. Furthermore, most Third World countries regarded both powers with suspicion. America's wealth fostered both distrust and resentment, prompting questions about U.S. motives. America's racist legacy also hurt it in the Third World, where most residents were nonwhite. However, most Third World nations also saw how the Soviets dominated Eastern Europe, and so had little interest in close relations with them. These new nations were not anxious to fall under the control of either superpower.

However, the United States tried to expand its influence in the Third World in other ways. For example, in Egypt the United States tried offering foreign aid, hoping to gain an ally by building the much-needed **Aswan Dam**. Egypt's nationalist leader Gamal Nasser suspected the Western powers of subterfuge; furthermore, he detested Israel, a Western ally. Eventually, he turned to the Soviet Union for that aid. The American government also used **CIA covert operations** to provide a more forceful method of increasing its influence abroad. In various countries, the CIA coerced newspapers to report disinformation and slant the news in a way favorable to the United States, bribed local politicians, and tried by other means to influence local business and politics. The CIA even helped overthrow the governments of Iran and Guatemala in order to replace anti-American governments with pro-American governments. It also tried, unsuccessfully, to assassinate the communist leader of Cuba, **Fidel Castro**.

The 1960 Presidential Election

In 1960 Eisenhower's vice president, **Richard Nixon**, received the Republican nomination. The Democrats nominated Massachusetts senator **John F. Kennedy**. Similar in many ways, particularly in foreign policy, both candidates campaigned against the "communist menace" as well as against each other. Aided by his youthful good looks, Kennedy trounced an awkward Nixon in their first televised debate. Kennedy's choice of Texan **Lyndon Johnson** as a running mate helped shore up the Southern vote for the Northern candidate. Nixon, meanwhile, was hurt by his vice presidency, where he had often served the role of Eisenhower's "attack dog." The fact that Eisenhower did not wholeheartedly endorse Nixon also marred his campaign. Still, it turned out to be one of the closest elections in history, and some believe that voter fraud turned a few states Kennedy's way, without which Nixon would have won.

In his final days in office, Eisenhower warned the nation to beware of a new coalition that had grown up around the Cold War, which he called the military-industrial complex. The combination of military might and the highly profitable arms industries, he cautioned, created a powerful alliance whose interests did not correspond to those of the general public. In retrospect, many would later argue that in his final statement, Eisenhower had identified those who would later be responsible for the escalation of the **Vietnam War**.

THE TURBULENT '60S

At the outset, the '60s seemed the start of a new, hope-filled era. Many felt that Kennedy, his family, and his administration were ushering in an age of "Camelot" (the theatrical play was very popular then). As Arthur had had his famous knights, Kennedy, too, surrounded himself with an entourage of young, ambitious intellectuals who served as his advisers. The press dubbed these men and one woman "the best and the brightest" America had to offer. Kennedy's youth, good looks, and wit earned him the adoration of millions. Even the name of his domestic program, the **New Frontier**, connoted hope. It promised that the fight to conquer poverty, racism, and other contemporary domestic woes would be as rewarding as the efforts of the pioneers who settled the West.

The decade did not end as it had begun. By 1969 America was bitterly divided. Many progressives regarded the government with suspicion and contempt, while many conservatives saw all dissidents as godless anarchists and subversives. Although other issues were important, much of the conflict centered around these two issues: the Vietnam War and blacks' struggle to gain civil rights. As you read through this summary of the decade, pay particular attention to the impact of both issues on domestic harmony.

Kennedy and Foreign Policy

Like Truman and Eisenhower, Kennedy perceived the Soviet Union and communism as the major threats to the security of the United States and its way of life. Every major foreign policy issue and event of his administration related primarily to these Cold War concerns.

Two major events during Kennedy's first year in office heightened American-Soviet tensions. The first involved **Cuba**, where a U.S.-friendly dictatorship had been overthrown by communist insurgents led by **Fidel Castro**. When Castro took control of the country in 1959, American businesses owned more than 3 million acres of prime Cuban farmland and also controlled the country's electricity and telephone service. Because so many Cubans lived in poverty, Cuban resentment of American wealth was strong, so little popular resistance occurred when Castro seized and nationalized some American property. The United States, however, was not pleased. When Castro signed a trade treaty with the Soviet Union later that year, Eisenhower imposed a partial trade embargo on Cuba. In the final days of his presidency, Eisenhower broke diplomatic relations with Cuba, and Cuba turned to the Soviet Union for financial and military aid.

Taking office in 1961, President Kennedy inherited the Cuban issue. Looking to solve the dilemma, the CIA presented the ill-fated plan for the **Bay of Pigs invasion** to the new president. The plan involved sending Cuban exiles, whom the CIA had been training since Castro's takeover, to invade Cuba. According to the strategy, the army of exiles would win a few battles and then the Cuban people would rise up in support, overthrow Castro, and replace his government with one more acceptable to the United States. Kennedy approved the plan but did not provide adequate American military support, and the United States launched the invasion in April 1961. The invasion failed, the Cuban people did not rise up in support, and within two days Kennedy had a full-fledged disaster on his hands. Not only had he failed to achieve his goal, but he had also antagonized the Soviets and their allies in the process. His failure also diminished America's stature with its allies.

Kennedy wasn't a donut

A popular urban legend holds that when President Kennedy went to the Berlin Wall in 1963 and declared, *"Ich bin ein Berliner,"* he made a grammatical error and inadvertently called himself a jelly donut. Sadly for high school history teachers trying to get a laugh out of their classes, this isn't actually true. While the word *"ein"* is omitted when literally declaring one's residence, it is required for figurative statements such as Kennedy's. Kennedy made no error, and the donut legend didn't start circulating until a novelist joked about it twenty years later.

Later in the year Kennedy dealt with a second foreign policy issue when the Soviets took aggressive anti-West action by erecting a wall to divide East and West Berlin. The **Berlin Wall**, built to prevent East Germans from leaving the country, had even greater symbolic significance to the democratic West. It came to represent the repressive nature of communism and was also a physical reminder of the impenetrable divide between the two sides of the Cold War.

In 1962 the United States and the Soviet Union came the closest they had yet to a military (and perhaps nuclear) confrontation. The focus of the conflict was once again Cuba. In October, American spy planes detected missile sites in Cuba. Kennedy immediately decided that those missiles had to be removed at any cost; he further decided on a policy of brinksmanship to confront the **Cuban missile crisis**. He imposed a naval quarantine on Cuba to prevent any further weapons shipments from reaching the island, and then went on national television and demanded that the Soviets withdraw their missiles.

By refusing to negotiate secretly, Kennedy backed the Soviets into a corner; if they removed the missiles, their international stature would be diminished, especially since the quarantine was effectively a blockade, which diplomats defined as an act of war on the part of the United States. Therefore, in return, the Soviets demanded that the United States promise never again to invade Cuba and that the United States remove its missiles from Turkey (which is as close to the USSR as Cuba is to the United States). When Kennedy rejected the second condition, he gambled that the Soviets would not attack in response. Fortunately, behind-the-scenes negotiations defused the crisis, and the Soviets agreed to accept America's promise not to invade Cuba as a pretext for withdrawing the missiles. In return, the United States secretly agreed to remove its missiles from Turkey a few months later, thus making it look like the United States had won. Recent scholarship suggests that it was the Soviet leader Khrushchev who prevented WWIII and a nuclear holocaust.

The policy of containment even motivated such ostensibly philanthropic programs abroad as the **Peace Corps**. The Peace Corps' mission was to provide teachers and specialists in agriculture, health care, transportation, and communications to the Third World, in the hopes of starting these fledgling communities down the road to American-style progress. The government called this process "**nation building**." The Peace Corps had many successes, although the conflict between its humanitarian goals and the government's foreign policy goals often brought about failures as well. Furthermore, many countries did not want American-style progress and resented having it forced upon them.

The greatest theater for American Cold War policy during this era, however, was **Vietnam**, which will be discussed in greater detail shortly.

Kennedy and Domestic Policy

Kennedy began his presidency with the promise that America was about to conquer a **New Frontier**. He pushed through legislation that increased unemployment benefits, expanded Social Security, bumped up the minimum wage, and aided distressed farmers, among other measures.

Kennedy's civil rights agenda produced varied results. Kennedy supported **women's rights**, establishing a presidential commission that in 1963 recommended removing all obstacles to women's participation in all facets of society. Congress enacted the **Equal Pay Act** in 1963, which required that men and women receive equal pay for equal work. Unfortunately, employers continue to get around this federal law by simply changing job titles. However, it was only late in his presidency that Kennedy openly embraced the black civil rights movement. After almost two years of near inaction, in September 1962, Kennedy enforced desegregation at the University of Mississippi. In the summer of 1963, he asked Congress for legislation that would outlaw segregation in all public facilities. After Kennedy's assassination in November, Lyndon Johnson was able to push that legislation—the **Civil Rights Act of 1964**—through Congress on the strength of the late president's popularity and his own skills as a legislator.

Still, Kennedy's presidency proved an active period for the civil rights movement as a number of nongovernmental organizations mobilized to build on the gains of the previous decade. Martin Luther King Jr. led the **Southern Christian Leadership Conference (SCLC)**, which staged sit-ins, boycotts, and other peaceful demonstrations. The Congress of Racial Equality (CORE) organized the **Freedom Riders** movement; the Freedom Riders staged sit-ins on buses, sitting in sections prohibited to them by segregationist laws. They were initially an integrated group, as was the **Student Nonviolent Coordinating Committee (SNCC)**, which did grassroots work in the areas of voter registration and anti-segregationist activism. Such groups met considerable resistance. In 1963 Mississippi's NAACP director, **Medgar Evers**, was shot to death by an anti-integrationist. Not long after, demonstrators in Montgomery, Alabama, were assaulted by the police and fire department who used attack dogs and fire hoses against the crowd. News reports of both events horrified millions of Americans and thus helped bolster the movement. So, too, for reasons mentioned above, did Kennedy's assassination.

Lyndon Johnson's Social Agenda

Like Kennedy, Lyndon Johnson made an early commitment to the civil rights movement, but unlike Kennedy, Johnson took immediate action to demonstrate that commitment. From the time he took office, Johnson started to lobby hard for the **Civil Rights Act of 1964**, which outlawed discrimination based on a person's race, color, religion, or gender. If you can only remember one federal law in U.S. history, this is it! The Civil Rights Act of 1964 is the most comprehensive piece of civil rights legislation enacted in U.S. history and the basis of all discrimination suits to this day. The law prohibited discrimination in employment as well as in public facilities (thus increasing the scope of Kennedy's proposed civil rights act).

Not long after, Johnson oversaw the establishment of the **Equal Employment Opportunity Commission (EEOC)** to enforce the employment clause of the Civil Rights Act. Johnson signed the **Voting Rights Act of 1965** after he was elected in his own right in 1964. This law cracked down on those states that denied blacks the right to vote despite the Fifteenth Amendment. He also signed another civil rights act banning discrimination in housing, and yet another that extended voting rights to Native Americans living under tribal governments.

Johnson had grown up poor and believed that social injustice stemmed from social inequality, and therefore advocated civil rights in employment. Toward the same end he lobbied for and won the **Economic Opportunity Act**, which appropriated nearly $1 billion for poverty relief. After his landslide victory in the 1964 presidential election, Johnson greatly expanded his anti-poverty program. A number of programs combined to form Johnson's **War on Poverty**. **Project Head Start** prepared underprivileged children for early schooling; Upward Bound did the same for high school students. **Job Corps** trained the unskilled so they could get better jobs, while **Volunteers in Service to America (VISTA)** acted as a domestic Peace Corps. In addition, Legal Services for the Poor guaranteed legal counsel to those who could not afford their own lawyer. To further assist the poor, Johnson founded the **Department of Housing and Urban Development (HUD)**, increased federal aid to low-income apartment renters, and built more federal housing projects.

The legislation passed during 1965 and 1966 represented the most sweeping change to U.S. government since the New Deal. Johnson's social agenda was termed the "**Great Society**." Best of all, taxpayers did not feel much pain: Increased tax revenues from a quickly expanding economy funded the whole package. Not everyone liked Johnson's agenda, however; many objected to any increase in government activity, and the extension of civil rights met with bigoted opposition, especially in the South. Thus, ironically, the huge coalition that had given Johnson his victory and his mandate for change started to fall apart because of his successes (and were hastened by a bitter national debate over American involvement in Vietnam).

The Civil Rights Movement

In the early '60s, the civil rights movement made a number of substantial gains. Legislative successes such as those passed under Johnson's Great Society program provided government support. The movement also won a number of victories in the courts, particularly in the Supreme Court. Under Chief Justice **Earl Warren**, the Court, for a brief moment in history, was extremely liberal. The **Warren Court** worked to enforce voting rights for blacks and forced states to redraw congressional districts so that minorities would receive greater representation. The Warren Court expanded civil rights in other areas as well. Among its landmark rulings are those that prohibited school prayer and protected the right to privacy. The Warren Court also made several decisions concerning the rights of the accused. In *Gideon v. Wainwright,* the Court ruled that a defendant in a felony trial must be provided a lawyer for free if he or she cannot afford one. In the ***Miranda v. Arizona***, the Court ruled that, upon arrest, a suspect must be advised of his or her right to remain silent and to consult with a lawyer.

Civil rights victories did not come easily. Resistance to change was strong, as evidenced by the opposition of state governments, police, and white citizens. In Selma, police prevented blacks from registering to vote; in Birmingham, police and firemen attacked civil rights protesters. All over the South the **Ku Klux Klan** and other racists bombed black churches and the homes of civil rights activists with seeming impunity. In Mississippi three civil rights workers were murdered by a group that included members of the local police department.

With news reports of each event, outrage in the black community grew. Some activists abandoned Martin Luther King's strategy of nonviolent protest. Among the leaders who advocated a more aggressive approach was **Malcolm X**, a minister of the **Nation of Islam**. Malcolm X urged blacks to claim their rights "by any means necessary." (His autobiography is an essential document of the history of racism in America.) Later, two groups that previously had preached integration—the **SNCC** and **CORE**—expelled their white members and advocated the more separatist, radical program of **Black Power**. By 1968, when King was assassinated, the civil rights movement had fragmented, with some continuing to advocate integration and peaceful change, while others argued for empowerment through self-imposed segregation and aggression.

The New Left, Feminism, and the Counterculture

Black Americans were not the only ones challenging the status quo in the '60s. Young whites, particularly those in college, also rebelled. For these young adults, the struggle was one against the hypocrisy, complacency, and conformity of middle-class life.

In 1962 the **Students for a Democratic Society** (SDS) formed. Its leftist political agenda, laid out in a platform called the **Port Huron Statement**, set the tone for other progressive groups on college campuses; these groups collectively became known as the **New Left**. New Left ideals included the elimination of poverty and racism and an end to Cold War politics. One particularly active branch of the New Left formed at the University of California at Berkeley. In 1964 students there protested when the university banned civil rights and anti-war demonstrations on campus. These protests grew into the **Free Speech movement**, which in turn fostered a number of leftist and radical political groups on the Berkeley campus.

Most New Left groups, however, were male-dominated and insensitive to the cause of women's rights. Women became frustrated with being treated as second-class citizens and started their own political groups. In 1963 Betty Friedan's book *The Feminine Mystique* openly challenged many people's assumptions about women's place in society. Friedan identified "The problem that has no name" and is credited with restarting the women's movement, a movement that had faded once women's suffrage was achieved with the Nineteenth Amendment in 1920. She was also one of the founders of **NOW**, the **National Organization for Women**, formed in 1966 to fight for legislative changes, including the ill-fated **Equal Rights Amendment** (ERA) to the Constitution. The modern movement for gay rights also began to solidify in the 1960s, with the first Gay Pride parades occurring on the anniversary of the **Stonewall** riots, an event at which gays fought back against the police in New York City.

Feminists fought against discrimination in hiring, pay, college admissions, and financial aid. They also fought for control of reproductive rights, a battle that reached the Supreme Court in the 1973 case *Roe v. Wade*, which enabled women to obtain abortions in all 50 states within the first trimester. Many states argued that they had an obligation to protect "life," as stipulated in the Fourteenth Amendment, and quickly passed state laws prohibiting a woman from having an abortion after the first three months of her pregnancy. Although there is no specific mention of a constitutional right to privacy, the Supreme Court had established this important precedent in 1965 in the case *Griswold v. Connecticut. Roe v. Wade* remains a controversial decision and continues to play a central role in American politics and society.

Rebellion against "the establishment" also took the form of nonconformity, a repudiation of the Eisenhower years. Hippies grew their hair long, wore tie-dyed shirts and ripped jeans, and advocated drug use, communal living, and "free love." Their way of life came to be known as the **counterculture** because of its unconventionality and its total contrast to the staid mainstream culture, which was typified by big band music and banal television variety shows. By the end of the '60s, the counterculture became more widely accepted, and artists such as Andy Warhol, Bob Dylan, Jimi Hendrix, the Beatles, and the Rolling Stones were among the biggest moneymakers in the arts.

The New Left, feminists, the counterculture, and others in the growing left wing of American politics almost uniformly opposed American participation in the Vietnam War. These groups' vocal protests against the war and the fierce opposition they provoked from the government and pro-war Americans created a huge divide in American society by 1968. Before we discuss that fateful year, it is important to understand how and why America became involved in Vietnam.

American Involvement in Vietnam, World War II–1963

From the Truman administration until the fall of Soviet Communism in 1991, U.S. foreign policy leaders asserted an American right to intervene anywhere in the world to stop the spread of communism and to protect American interests. Nowhere did that policy fail more miserably than in Vietnam, where the United States maintained an economic and military presence for almost 25 years. The Vietnam War divided America as no war before had.

"There's a time when the operation of the machine becomes so odious, makes you so sick at heart, that you can't take part! You can't even passively take part! And you've got to put your bodies upon the gears and upon the wheels, upon the levers, upon all the apparatus, and you've got to make it stop! And you've got to indicate to the people who run it, to the people who own it, that unless you're free, the machine will be prevented from working at all!"

—Mario Savio, speaking from the steps of Sproul Hall at the University of California, Berkeley, on December 3, 1964

The origins of America's involvement in Vietnam stretch back to WWII. From the late nineteenth century until World War II, Vietnam was a French colony. France exported the country's resources—rice, rubber, and metals—for French consumption. This foreign exploitation of Vietnam helped foster a nationalist Vietnamese resistance called the **Vietminh**, led by **Ho Chi Minh**. Ho had been schooled in France and had joined the French Communist Party before returning home. In fact, Ho Chi Minh was in Paris during the Versailles Peace Conference in 1919 and approached Woodrow Wilson at the time. Ho asked Wilson to honor his commitment to the right of nations to **self-determination**, as expressed in Wilson's **Fourteen Points**, and to help the Vietnamese expel the French from their country. Wilson ignored Ho Chi Minh's appeal.

Japan invaded Vietnam during World War II and ended French control of the country. Faced with a common enemy, the Vietnamese helped the Allies defeat Japan and probably expected to be granted their independence at the conclusion of the war, as India was in 1947. Shortly after the Japanese surrender in 1945, Ho drafted the Vietnamese Declaration of Independence modeled on the U.S. Declaration of Independence and the French Declaration of Rights of Man and Citizens.

The United States did not recognize Vietnamese independence nor the legitimacy of Ho's government, in part because of America's alliance with France (which wanted its colony back), and in part because Ho was a communist. Instead, the United States recognized the government of Bao Dai, the Vietnamese emperor whom the French had installed in the South, which France still controlled. Subsequently, Vietnam fought a war for independence against the French from 1946 until 1954, when the French were defeated at the Battle of Dien Bien Phu. Although Ho appealed to President Truman for assistance on several occasions, Truman never responded. Ho hoped the United States would honor its commitment to the principle of self-determination and empathize with the Vietnamese rather than support the colonial power. Truman continued to aid the French. The United States financed more than 80 percent of France's war effort in Indochina, a fact few Americans knew then or know now.

In 1954 all of the involved parties met in Geneva, Switzerland, and drew up the **Geneva Accords**, which divided Vietnam at the 17th parallel, with Communist forces controlling North Vietnam and (so-called) democratic forces controlling the South. It was agreed that this division was to be temporary and that elections would be held in two years to reunite the country and determine who would rule a unified Vietnam. The elections never took place, however. The United States, certain that Ho Chi Minh would win an election, sabotaged the peace agreement. First, the United States made an alliance with another South Vietnamese leader named **Ngo Dinh Diem** and helped him oust Bao Dai (whom the United States felt was too weak to control the country). Then, the CIA organized commando raids across the border in North Vietnam to provoke a Communist response (which the South Vietnamese could then denounce). Diem pronounced South Vietnam an autonomous country and refused to participate in the agreed-upon national election. The United States rallied Britain, France, Thailand, Pakistan, the Philippines, New Zealand, and Australia to form the NATO-like **Southeast Asian Treaty Organization** (SEATO) to provide for South Vietnam's defense against Communist takeover.

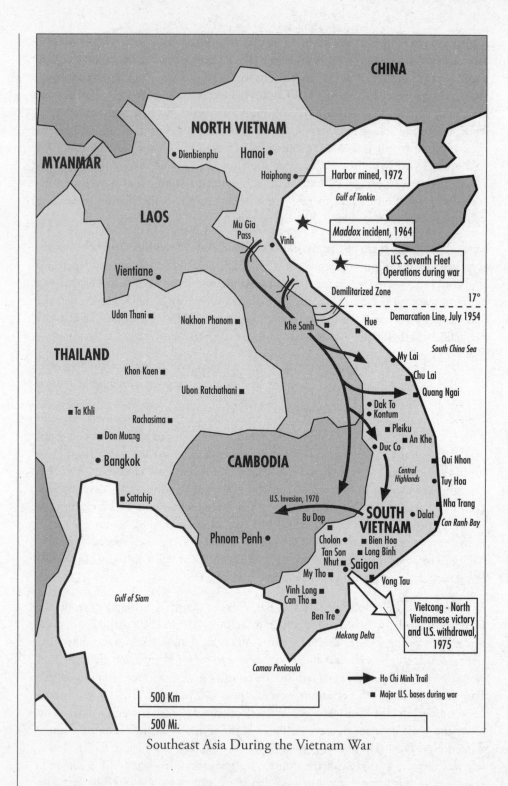

Southeast Asia During the Vietnam War

Unfortunately, the situation continued its downward spiral. Diem, it turned out, was a vicious leader. He took despotic control of South Vietnam, imprisoning political enemies, persecuting Buddhist monks, and closing newspapers that criticized his government. As a result, many South Vietnamese citizens joined the North Vietnamese side. These communist South Vietnamese insurgents were called the **Vietcong**. Rather than cut its losses, the United States continued to support Diem and the South Vietnamese economically. Committed to the policy of containment and intent on nation building, President Kennedy increased America's involvement in Vietnam by sending in military advisors known as the Green Berets. Finally, in 1963, the CIA helped the South Vietnamese military stage a coup to overthrow Diem's government. During the coup, Diem and his brother were killed and Kennedy was appalled by the outcome. A few weeks later, Kennedy was assassinated, and Johnson took control of America's war efforts.

American Involvement in Vietnam, 1964–1968

Upon taking office, Johnson had the opportunity to withdraw American forces in a way that would not have embarrassed his administration. The United Nations, backed by France and the Vietcong, would have intervened and set up a coalition government to rule South Vietnam. Kennedy's advisers, however, convinced Johnson that U.S. forces could overwhelm any opposition in the region. He remained committed to using those forces to achieve "total victory."

In 1964 the United States supported a second coup in South Vietnam; apparently, the United States was not terribly selective as to who ran the country, so long as it was not the Communists. (The United States followed a similar pattern in Latin America.) The U.S. Army also started bombing the neighboring country of Laos, through which the North Vietnamese were shipping weapons to the Vietcong. Then, in August of the same year, reports stated that the North Vietnamese had fired on two American destroyer ships in the **Gulf of Tonkin**. (However, the North Vietnamese attack was never confirmed.) Johnson used the event to get Congress to pass the **Gulf of Tonkin Resolution**, which allowed the president to take any measures he deemed necessary to protect American interests in the region. The Tonkin Gulf resolution gave Johnson carte blanche to escalate U.S. participation in the war. It also is the closest Congress ever came to an official declaration of war in Vietnam. Thus, the first ground troops began to arrive in the early months of 1965.

Soon, Johnson had flooded the region with American troops. He also authorized massive Air Force bombing raids into North Vietnam. Throughout Johnson's administration, the United States essentially took over the war effort from the South Vietnamese; hence, the "**Americanization**" of the Vietnam War. As the war ground on and the draft claimed more young Americans, opposition to the war grew. Protest rallies grew larger and more frequent, and more and more young men either ignored their draft notices or fled to a foreign country (more than 30,000 went to Canada) to avoid military service.

Johnson's advisers continued to assure him that the war was "winnable" until January 1968, when the North Vietnamese launched the **Tet Offensive** (named after the Vietnamese holiday celebrating the New Year). In conjunction with the Vietcong, the North Vietnamese inflicted tremendous damage on American forces and nearly captured the American embassy in the South Vietnamese capital of Saigon. Though the North Vietnamese and Vietcong forces were, in the end, decisively driven back, the severity of the strikes was an ugly shock for the American people, who had been assured by the Johnson administration that the United States was winning the war. This would be a major turning point in the war, as most Americans had been confident their superior technology could easily defeat the underdeveloped Third World nation. The Tet Offensive was a highly calculated series of attacks carried out around the country, demonstrating that American military experts had vastly underestimated the sophistication of Vietnamese strategy. That the North Vietnamese and Vietcong could launch such a large-scale offensive and nearly succeed in taking the American embassy made the American public come to believe it was being lied to and that perhaps this war was not winnable.

The **My Lai Massacre** occurred the same year as the Tet Offensive. American soldiers were becoming more and more frustrated and began to act in unspeakable ways. The most publicized of these horrific events, although not an isolated occurrence, took place in a small village in South Vietnam, where U.S. soldiers abused, tortured, and murdered an estimated 347 to 504 innocent civilians, including women, children, and elderly Vietnamese too infirm to fight. When the story finally broke a year later, the American public was outraged. Public opinion turned and protests against the war grew angrier and more frequent. In response Johnson announced that he would begin peace negotiations with the North Vietnamese government. He also announced, to everyone's surprise, that he would not run for re-election. It was the beginning of the very tumultuous summer of 1968.

The Summer of 1968 and the 1968 Election

Johnson withdrew from the presidential race in large part because his association with the Vietnam War had turned many Americans against him, including many within his own party. Johnson's re-nomination would not have been easy; both **Eugene McCarthy** (no relation to Joseph McCarthy!) and **Robert Kennedy**, John F. Kennedy's brother and former attorney general, were poised to challenge him. Johnson's withdrawal opened the field to a third candidate, Vice President **Hubert Humphrey**.

Early in April 1968 a white assassin killed **Martin Luther King Jr.** The murder ignited black riots in more than 150 towns and cities. Arson, looting, and even murder were committed by the outraged mobs. In Chicago, where the Democratic convention would later be held, the mayor ordered the police to shoot arsonists on sight. To say that King's assassination heightened the already considerable tension surrounding race relations would be a huge understatement. During this time, the Kerner Commission report on race relations came out, stating that "our nation is moving toward two societies, one white and one black—separate and unequal."

Then, in June, frontrunner for the Democratic nomination **Robert Kennedy** was assassinated. Kennedy had come to represent the last bastion of hope for many Americans. Young, handsome, and vital (like his adored older brother), Kennedy was also an aggressive advocate for the poor and a harsh critic of the war in Vietnam. Together, the two assassinations convinced many that peaceful change from within the political system was impossible.

Many disenchanted young Americans came to Chicago in August to demonstrate at the Democratic Convention against government policy. The police were ordered to break up the crowds of protesters, which they did with tear gas, billy clubs, and rifles. Images of American policemen in gas masks clubbing American citizens reached millions of living rooms across the country through television and the newspapers, presenting a picture eerily reminiscent of the police states *against* which America supposedly fought. When the convention chose pro-war Vice President Humphrey over the anti-war McCarthy *and* refused to condemn the war effort, the Democrats alienated many of their core constituency on the left.

Meanwhile, the Republicans handed their nomination to former vice president **Richard Nixon** at a rather peaceful convention. Then, a third candidate entered the national election, Alabama governor **George Wallace**, who ran a segregationist third-party campaign, much like Strom Thurmond had done in 1948 against Harry Truman. Wallace was popular in the South, which had traditionally voted Democratic. Thus, Humphrey was twice cursed: He had alienated his progressive urban base in the North and Wallace was siphoning his potential support in the South. Humphrey denounced the Vietnam War late in the campaign, but it was too little, too late. In one of the closest elections in history, Richard Nixon was elected president.

Nixon, "Vietnamization," and Détente

Nixon entered office promising to end American involvement in Vietnam by turning the war over to the South Vietnamese, a process he called "Vietnamization." He soon began withdrawing troops; however, he also increased the number and intensity of air strikes. Like his predecessors, Nixon was a veteran cold warrior who believed that the United States could, and must, win in Vietnam. He ordered bombing raids and ground troops into Cambodia, in hopes of rooting out Vietcong strongholds and weapons supplies. American involvement in Vietnam dragged on until 1973, when Secretary of State **Henry Kissinger** completed negotiations for a peace treaty with the North Vietnamese.

There are a couple of postscripts to the Vietnam story. First, the negotiated peace crumbled almost as soon as American troops started to vacate the country. In 1975 Saigon fell to the North Vietnamese Army, and Vietnam was united under communist rule. Second, Congress passed the **War Powers Resolution** in 1973 in order to prevent any future president from involving the military in another undeclared war. The War Powers Resolution requires the president to obtain congressional approval for any troop commitment lasting longer than 60 days.

Nixon did have success, however, in his other foreign policy initiatives, especially those concerning the world's two other superpowers, the USSR and China. During Nixon's first term, the United States increased trade with the Soviets, and the administration negotiated the first of a number of arms treaties between the two countries. Results were even more dramatic with China. After a series of secret negotiations, Nixon traveled to communist China, whose government the United States had previously refused to acknowledge. Nixon's trip eased tensions, partly because at the time of the trip, Americans trusted the anti-communist Nixon to improve relations with China, and his trip opened trade relations between the two countries. It also allowed Nixon to use his friendship with the Chinese as leverage against the USSR, and vice versa. (The Chinese and the Soviets, despite both being communist, hated each other.)

The Nixon years added two new terms to the vocabulary of foreign policy. Together, Nixon and Kissinger formulated an approach called **détente**, a policy of "openness" that called for countries to respect each other's differences and cooperate more closely. Détente ushered in a brief period of relaxed tensions between the two superpowers but ended when the Soviet Union invaded Afghanistan in 1979. The **Nixon Doctrine** announced that the United States would withdraw from many of its overseas troop commitments, relying instead on alliances with local governments to check the spread of communism.

Nixon's Domestic Policy

Nixon could not match his successes overseas at home. During Nixon's presidency, the economy worsened, going through a period of combined recession-inflation that economists called stagflation. Nixon attempted to combat the nation's economic woes with a number of interventionist measures, including a price-and-wage freeze and increased federal spending. None of his efforts produced their intended results.

Politically, American society remained divided among the haves and have-nots, the conservatives and the progressives. Much of the political rhetoric on both sides painted the opposition as enemies of the "American way." Several confrontations on college campuses heightened political tensions, most notably when national guardsmen shot and killed four protesters at **Kent State University** in Ohio who were protesting the U.S.'s decision to invade Vietcong camps in neutral Cambodia. This incident became synonymous with the division between the youth and middle America. A similar incident occurred at the historically black Jackson State University in Mississippi, but the media failed to report the incident—further evidence of continued racial conflict in American society. Meanwhile, urban crime levels rose, causing many to flee to the relative tranquility of the suburbs.

Still, in 1972, Nixon won re-election in one of the greatest landslide victories in American political history, defeating liberal Senator George McGovern. Although Nixon won the election easily, both houses of Congress remained under Democratic control, an indication of the mixed feelings many Americans felt toward their political leaders.

Watergate and Nixon's Resignation

In the summer of 1971, two major newspapers published the **Pentagon Papers**, a top-secret government study of the history of U.S. involvement in Vietnam. The study covered the period from World War II to 1968, and it was not complimentary. It documented numerous military miscalculations and flat-out lies the government had told the public. Even though the documents contained nothing about the Nixon administration, Nixon fought aggressively to prevent their publication. The United States was involved in secret diplomatic negotiations with North Vietnam, the USSR, and China at the time, and Nixon and Kissinger both believed that the revelation of secret government dealings in the past might destroy their credibility in the present.

Nixon lost his fight to suppress the Pentagon Papers, a loss that increased Nixon's already considerable paranoia. In an effort to prevent any further leaks of classified documents, Nixon put together a team of investigators called the "**plumbers.**" The plumbers undertook such disgraceful projects as burglarizing a psychiatrist's office in order to gather incriminating information on Daniel Ellsberg, the government official who had turned the Pentagon Papers over to the press. During the 1972 elections, the plumbers sabotaged the campaigns of several Democratic hopefuls and then botched a burglary of Democratic headquarters in the **Watergate** Hotel.

When the plumbers were arrested at the Watergate Hotel, the White House began an all-out effort to cover up the scandal. A Senate hearing into the matter began in early 1973 and dragged on, keeping the story alive in the news for the next year and a half. Information was slowly revealed that incriminated the president's closest advisers. They would resign, then most would be tried and convicted of felonies. (Perjury and destruction of evidence were two popular and successful charges against them.) At last, it was discovered that Nixon had secretly taped all conversations in the White House, including many concerning Watergate. For the next year a legal battle over the tapes raged; the Senate demanded them, and Nixon refused to turn them over, claiming executive privilege. All the while, more damning evidence came to light—much of it in the pages of *The Washington Post,* courtesy of investigative journalists **Bob Woodward** and **Carl Bernstein**—and more former Nixon associates were jailed. When the president lost the battle over the tapes—the Supreme Court ordered Nixon to turn them over to the Senate— he knew his days were numbered, as the tapes revealed a number of unsavory aspects of Nixon's character. Rather than face impeachment proceedings, Nixon resigned in August 1974. His vice president, **Gerald Ford**, took office and almost immediately granted Nixon a presidential **pardon**, thereby preventing a trial.

Gerald Ford

Gerald Ford became president when Nixon resigned. Ford replaced Nixon's first vice president, **Spiro Agnew**, who had resigned in the face of impending criminal charges (relating to corruption during his tenure as governor of Maryland). When Ford selected Nelson Rockefeller as his vice president, it was the first time that neither the president nor the vice president had been elected by the public.

Ford's controversial **pardon** of Nixon brought the Watergate era to a close, but it also cost Ford politically, as it raised suspicions that Nixon and Ford had struck a deal. Ford's political fortunes were further undermined by the weak economy. People were encouraged to wear "WIN" buttons: Whip Inflation Now. An oil embargo organized by Arab nations (under the leadership of **OPEC**) against the United States increased fuel prices, which in turn caused the price of almost everything else to rise. Inflation, coupled with an increasing unemployment rate, and the damage done to his credibility by the media, especially parodies by the actor Chevy Chase on *Saturday Night Live,* sealed Ford's fate. In 1976 he was defeated by Democrat **Jimmy Carter.**

Jimmy Carter

Carter inherited a weakening economy. During his presidency, inflation exceeded 10 percent, and interest rates on loans approached 20 percent. Slow economic growth coupled with inflation to worsen the stagflation that began in Nixon's term. Carter tried to balance the federal budget but failed (as had every president since Eisenhower).

Many of the nation's economic problems resulted from the increased cost of OPEC petroleum. In response, President Carter increased funding for research into alternative sources of power. Carter created a new, cabinet-level government agency, the **Department of Energy**, to oversee these efforts. Many Americans saw nuclear power as a solution to the nation's energy woes. Opponents argued that nuclear power plant failures were potentially catastrophic; their fears were reinforced when a Pennsylvania plant at **Three Mile Island** failed, releasing radioactive materials into the atmosphere.

The high point of the Carter administration came when President Carter personally brokered a **peace agreement between Israel and Egypt**. Israeli-Egyptian conflict dated to the moment of Israel's founding in 1948, when Israel was besieged by hostile Arab neighbors. Tensions between Israel and Egypt were heightened by the 1967 **Six Day War**, during which Israel took control of the Sinai peninsula, a desert region belonging to Egypt. In 1978, however, the leaders of the two countries agreed to meet with each other, in each other's countries. It was a major breakthrough in Israeli-Arab relations; most Arab nations refused even to acknowledge Israel's existence. President Carter hoped to capitalize on this breakthrough. He invited the two leaders to **Camp David** and personally brokered an agreement between the two nations. Ever since, the United States has actively participated in peace negotiations in the region.

Carter enjoyed some foreign policy successes. Along with negotiating the peace treaty between Israel and Egypt, he also concluded an arms agreement with the Soviets. However, Carter also suffered some major setbacks. When the USSR invaded Afghanistan, Carter's efforts proved powerless in forcing a withdrawal. Carter also flip-flopped in Nicaragua, where first he befriended the revolutionary **Sandinista** government and then turned against them as they allied themselves more closely with the USSR and Cuba. Carter's worst crisis involved Iran, when American hostages were taken in retaliation for America's decades-long support of the repressive, deposed Shah. Held for more than a year, the hostages were released only after Ronald Reagan took office.

Reagan, H.W., Clinton, and W. (1980–2001)

Note that, according to the College Board's AP U.S. History web page:

The multiple-choice section may include a few questions on the period since 1980, but neither the DBQ nor the essay questions in Parts B and C deal exclusively with this period.

Translation: If you know nothing about the period after 1980 because your class never got that far, the worst that can happen is that you might miss a few multiple-choice questions. The sections below include a few things you ought to know about U.S. history since 1980. It is useful to know the key events and issues of the last few presidencies. This might even enable you to choose an essay that covers content after 1980.

The Reagan Candidacy

By the late 1970s, many Americans had grown tired of the conflicts of the previous decade. Many were uncomfortable with the growing cynicism toward political leaders. Jimmy Carter hit a raw nerve—and disturbed many Americans—when he complained in a speech that the people were letting themselves be overtaken by a "crisis of confidence." This came to be known as "the malaise speech," though Carter never used the word "malaise" in it.

Ronald Reagan saw that the nation was ready for a major change. In the 1980 presidential campaign, Reagan, a former actor and governor of California, presented himself as Carter's opposite and a Washington "outsider," not tainted by events of the previous two decades, much as Carter had portrayed himself as an outsider in 1976. Where Carter blamed American self-indulgence and consumerism for the country's problems, Reagan stressed the positive aspects of America. Furthermore, many Americans who disagreed with Reagan's conservative politics nonetheless voted for him because they liked him and his "can-do" attitude. Further damaging Carter's chances was the third-party candidacy of liberal Republican John Anderson, who attracted a sizable "protest vote" from those who might otherwise have supported Carter. In the end, Reagan won the 1980 election by a landslide.

Supply-Side Economics

Ronald Reagan tried to revive the economy by applying the theory of **supply-side economics**. Reagan believed that if corporate taxes were reduced, those corporations would earn greater profits. They would then use those profits, he believed, to buy new equipment and hire more employees. As a result, wealth would "**trickle down**" by creating more jobs and reinvigorating the economy. (George H.W. Bush would refer to this policy as "voodoo economics.") Reagan coupled this with large-scale deregulation, particularly in the areas of banking, industry, and the environment. He also successfully lobbied Congress for an across-the-board tax cut for all Americans. This policy increased his popularity with most Americans, although many complained that tax cuts hurt the poor, who pay little in income tax but depend on federal enfranchisement programs (such as welfare, food stamps, and Medicaid) to survive.

At first Reagan's economic policies had little effect. The country continued in a recession for almost two years before the economy revived. Even then, results were mixed. Although inflation subsided, the unemployment rate continued to rise, lending credence to the criticism that, under Reagan, the rich were getting richer while the poor were getting poorer. Rather than reinvesting in the economy, as supply-side economics suggested, the rich used the money saved on taxes to buy luxury items.

Military Spending and Budget Deficits

Ronald Reagan frequently claimed that he sought to decrease the size of the federal government. He called his plan the **New Federalism**, but it was quite the opposite of federalism—its goal was to shift power from the national government to the states. Reagan suggested that the states take complete responsibility for welfare, food stamps, and other social welfare programs currently funded at the national level; in return, the national government would assume the entire cost of Medicaid. Reagan's goal was never accomplished, however. The states feared that the shift would greatly increase the cost of state government, which would require unpopular tax increases at the state level.

At the same time, Reagan convinced Congress to greatly increase military spending. He funded research into a space-based missile shield system called the **Strategic Defense Initiative**, or **SDI** (the program was dubbed "**Star Wars**" by both supporters and detractors). Arguing that America needed to more quickly develop superior arms, Reagan also escalated the arms race with the USSR. Some historians have argued that the arms race bankrupted the Soviet Union and helped bring about an end to the Cold War, while others mainly credit Soviet leader Mikhail Gorbachev for the Cold War's end.

Tax cuts, increased military spending, and the failure of Reagan's New Federalism plan combined to escalate the **federal budget deficit**. Government spending increased while government revenues shrank, forcing the government to borrow money. Congress blamed the deficit on Reagan's tax cuts and called for a tax increase. Reagan, on the other hand, argued that the fault was with Congress, which refused to decrease funding for social welfare programs at the rate the president requested. Neither side budged, and as a result, the federal deficit reached record heights during the Reagan administration.

Foreign Policy Under Reagan

In foreign policy, Reagan sought to end the Cold War by winning it on every front he could in any way he could. He supported repressive regimes and right-wing insurgents in El Salvador, Panama, the Philippines, and Mozambique, all because they opposed communism. During the Reagan administration, the U.S. military led an international invasion of **Grenada** to topple a new Communist government there.

One of Reagan's top foreign policy priorities was support for a group of Nicaraguan insurgents called the "**Contras**." Reports that the Contras were torturing and murdering civilians led Congress to cut off aid to the group, but the Reagan administration was so fully committed to them and opposed to the Sandinistas, who were communists, that it devised a plan to fund them through other channels. The government secretly sold weapons to Iran, then used the income to buy guns for the Contras. The entire process was eventually discovered; it came to be known as the **Iran-Contra affair**. Critics argued that Iran-Contra represented a constitutional crisis, pointing out that the plan had denied Congress the "power of the purse" central to the system of checks and balances. Supporters claimed that the president had broken no laws and that his goals were good ones.

Another foreign policy setback came when the Reagan administration sent marines to **Lebanon** as part of a United Nations peacekeeping force. A suicide bomb killed 240 servicemen and led to an eventual pullout of troops.

Reagan's greatest successes in foreign policy came in U.S.-Soviet relations. At first, Reagan's hard-line anti-communism led to deterioration in relations. The rhetorical war between the two enemies was fierce, Reagan calling the Soviet Union "the evil empire," and hitting an all-time low when he jokingly declared that he had outlawed the USSR, and added "we begin bombing in five minutes." Although not meant to be heard by the public, the joke was picked up by a microphone and later broadcast repeatedly. The escalated arms race further destabilized relations by constantly altering the military balance of power. Ultimately, however, the arms race helped bring the adversaries to the bargaining table, as neither side could afford the high cost.

American-Soviet relations were further helped when reformer **Mikhail Gorbachev** rose to power in the Soviet Union. Gorbachev is best known for his economic policy of *perestroika*, or restructuring, and his social reforms collectively referred to as *glasnost*, or openness. Gorbachev loosened Soviet control of Eastern Europe, increased personal liberties in the Soviet Union, and eventually allowed some forms of free-market commerce in the Communist country. Reagan and Gorbachev met frequently and ultimately negotiated a withdrawal of nuclear warheads from Europe.

George H. W. Bush

The election of 1988 convinced many Americans that progressive liberalism was finally destroyed, as George Bush easily defeated the Democratic candidate, Michael Dukakis, who was then governor of Massachusetts. In accepting his party's nomination, George Bush called for "a kinder, gentler nation," and he is most remembered for declaring, "Read my lips: no new taxes." "Liberalism" had become the "L word" and feminism had become the new "F word." The conventional wisdom held that Americans had settled back into traditional American lifestyles that celebrated values like family and abstinence from sex and drugs (Nancy Reagan had urged kids your age to "Just say NO!"). It appeared as if the **moral majority** had spoken.

The most significant events of the Bush presidency were the ending of the Cold War (symbolized by the dismantling of the Berlin Wall and breakup of the Soviet Union) and the **Persian Gulf War**. If containment had been the guiding policy during the Cold War, but the Soviet Union no longer posed a threat to the world order, it would be left to George Bush to set the course for U.S. foreign policy into the twenty-first century. The test came in August 1990, when Saddam Hussein, the leader of Iraq, invaded Iraq's tiny but oil-rich neighbor Kuwait. When Saddam seized Kuwait's oil fields and threatened the world's access to Middle East oil, Washington reacted immediately. Having learned from Vietnam, Bush built a consensus in Congress and assembled an international coalition against Iraq in the U.N.

Operation Desert Storm consisted mostly of massive air strikes against strategic Iraqi targets, and most Americans watched the war from the safety of their homes on television as if it were a video game. The war ended quickly with few American casualties. Although Iraq was required to submit to U.N. inspectors to insure that there were no **weapons of mass destruction** or chemical warfare production facilities, Saddam Hussein remained in power, a decision many foreign policy experts later came to criticize. It appeared that U.S. foreign policy in the post–Cold War era would focus on political stability in the Middle East and defending human rights.

Post-1980 Society

Though the 1980s were before you were born and may even seem like ancient history to you, historians assert that it can take as many as 50 years or more before enough time has elapsed for people to evaluate the past objectively. Keeping that in mind, let's take a look at some of the major trends and developments that historians have begun to identify in the past 20 or 30 years.

Changing Demographics

As was the case a century ago, when predominantly eastern European immigrants arrived by the millions onto America's shores, immigration in recent decades has significantly affected the shape and tenor of American society. In 1890, 86 percent of immigrants to the United States were from Europe. From the 1970s through today, however, the fastest growing ethnic minorities in the United States have been **Hispanics** and **Asians**, and according to the 2000 census, Hispanics now outnumber African-Americans as the largest minority in the United States. Much of this growth among Asians and Hispanics has been fueled by immigration.

The **Immigration Act of 1965** contributed significantly to the increase in immigration by members of these population groups. This legislation phased out all national quotas by 1968 and set annual limits on immigration from the Western Hemisphere and the rest of the world, essentially relaxing restrictions on non-European immigration. It gave priority to reuniting families and to certain skilled workers (particularly scientists) and **political refugees**. Though the vast majority of immigrants who entered under this legislation did so in order to join family members, searching for employment and escaping from persecution still ranked high among the most common reasons people came to the United States. Several groups admitted under these regulations included Cuban and Southeast Asian refugees created by **Fidel Castro's** revolution and the Vietnam War, respectively.

At the end of the twentieth century, from 1970 to 2000, the number of foreign-born people living in the United States went from 10 million to 31 million, or 11 percent of the total population. Fifty-one percent of those foreign-born were from Latin America, while 27 percent were from Asia, the second-largest group. Not since the turn of the twentieth century has the United States experienced a comparable surge in immigration. In 1915 immigrants made up 15 percent of the total population, the largest percentage in our history so far.

What will all these changes mean for American society? The increasing racial and ethnic diversity of our population has not only sparked heated debate on immigration policy but also on issues such as bilingual education and affirmative action. Discussions of immigration policy have generally centered on illegal immigration, the role and impact that immigrants have on the economy, and the extent to which an influx of new cultures, attitudes, and ideas will reshape society. Tensions created by this new wave of immigration have resulted in various measures to curb **illegal immigration**, abolish bilingual education in some states, and allow both low-skilled and high-skilled workers into the United States on a temporary basis to provide needed labor and services. In 1986, for instance, Congress passed the **Simpson-Mazzoli Act**, which outlawed the deliberate employment of illegal immigrants and granted legal status to some illegal aliens who entered the United States before 1982. However, problems persist.

Whether you believe that immigrants place a burden on social services or support and enrich the development of our economy and society, it is clear that the United States is in the midst of major demographic changes that are visible today. With each new wave of immigration, ethnic enclaves sprout in big cities and neighborhoods, contributing to America's unique mixture of peoples. A century ago, they were communities such as Little Italy in New York City or Chinatown in San Francisco. Today, reflecting more recent population trends, there are places like Little Havana in Miami and Little Saigon in Orange County, California. Americans have also seen an increase in multilingual services and the media catering to Hispanics and Asians in particular. Even political parties openly attempt to attract Hispanics in recognition of their potential political influence. The impact of these changing demographics will be felt for generations to come.

The Clinton Presidency (1993–2001)

William Jefferson Clinton was the first Democrat to be elected president since Jimmy Carter. After more than a decade of Republican control of the White House, Clinton and **Al Gore** took control in January 1993. Although it is doubtful that you would be required to write an essay that went through the 1990s, you could see a few multiple-choice questions about the major events that occurred during Clinton's two terms as president. The following is a brief review of those issues and events.

The first significant event of the Clinton presidency was the establishment of the **North American Free Trade Agreement (NAFTA)**. Although the treaty had been negotiated by the previous Republican administration, Clinton signed it into law in 1993. The agreement did exactly what it sounds like it did—eliminated trade barriers among the United States, Mexico, and Canada. While the treaty was severely criticized by American labor unions, who feared American companies would move their factories elsewhere in order to reduce costs with lower wages and operation costs, corporate interests supported it enthusiastically. Despite often speaking favorably about the concept of free trade, and gradually reducing tariff barriers over time, the United States has historically interfered with trade, usually in the form of high, protective tariffs, when it was beneficial to certain political and economic groups, but always under the guise of protecting the "national interest."

No doubt, the most infamous event of Clinton's presidency was the Clinton-Lewinsky scandal that led to Clinton's impeachment during his second term in office. Some Clinton supporters believe that special prosecutor Kenneth Starr had it in for the Clintons, beginning with his accusations of their dubious real estate dealings in what came to be known as **Whitewater**. Regardless, the U.S. House of Representatives impeached Clinton for perjury, obstruction of justice, and abuse of power. Remember that impeachment is the formal accusation of wrongdoing; it does not mean that the accused is thrown out of office. According to the Constitution, the House of Representatives has the "sole power of impeachment," and any federal official can be impeached for committing treason, bribery, or other "high crimes and misdemeanors." The United States Senate then has the "sole power to try all impeachments." Although Clinton was impeached, he was acquitted by the Senate and remained in office to finish his second term. Several federal judges have been impeached throughout American history, but Clinton was only the second president ever impeached. Lincoln's vice president, Andrew Johnson, was impeached, but he too was acquitted and was not thrown out of office. Students sometimes think that Nixon was impeached for his involvement in Watergate. Not quite. He resigned before the House of Representatives completed the process.

Clinton was really the first president to take office after the end of the Cold War, and he made it clear that one of his major foreign policy goals was the protection of human rights around the world, although some criticized his turning a blind eye to human rights violations in China, defending capitalism over democracy. In 1999, Clinton supported a bombing campaign in the former Yugoslavia under the auspices of NATO. Slobodan Milosevic, president of Serbia, was conducting a brutal policy of "ethnic cleansing" against Balkan Muslims. Milosevic was eventually tried and convicted for committing "crimes against humanity."

Other notable events that took place during the Clinton years include his "Don't ask, don't tell" policy pertaining to gays in the U.S. military and his appointments of Ruth Bader Ginsburg and Stephen Breyer to the Supreme Court. Two significant initiatives that failed were his proposal for a national health care program and campaign finance reform.

THE 2000 ELECTION

While it is incredibly unlikely that you will be asked to know anything specific about the George W. Bush administration, other than the obvious major events like 9/11 and the situation in Iraq (although certainly not in any detail), you may see a question about the 2000 election. According to the Constitution, a candidate must win a majority of electoral votes to win the presidential election. However, because of the "winner-take-all" system regarding the allotment of electoral votes in most states, it is possible for a candidate to win the majority of the popular vote nationwide but lose the presidency. Recall that this happened in 1824, when Jackson won a plurality of the popular vote, but John Quincy Adams became president, and again in 1876, when Samuel J. Tilden lost to Rutherford B. Hayes. On election night in November 2000, it appeared that Al Gore had defeated George W. Bush. However, through a convoluted series of mishaps with the voting procedure in Florida, the results of the Electoral College were questioned. Eventually, the Supreme Court prevented a formal recount of the vote in Florida and George W. Bush, son of former president George H.W. Bush, was elected.

African-Americans in Politics

Following the accomplishments of Freedom Summer in 1964, the **Voting Rights Act of 1965**, and the **Twenty-fourth Amendment** to the Constitution, which prohibited the use of poll taxes, measures such as literacy tests and poll taxes that had been used by many Southern states to deny African-Americans the right to vote were summarily banned. The results in the South were dramatic: In 1960 only 20 percent of eligible African-Americans had been registered to vote, but by 1971, that number had jumped to 62 percent. Cities such as Los Angeles, Chicago, Washington, D.C., Atlanta, and New Orleans elected their first African-American mayors in the 1980s. The nation's first African-American governor was elected in 1990 in Virginia.

In 1968, **Shirley Chisholm** was the first African-American woman elected to Congress; in 1972, she also became the first African-American to run for president. **Reverend Jesse Jackson** also ran for the Democratic presidential nomination in 1984 and 1988, winning many of the primary elections. According to the U.S. Census Bureau in 2000, there were 1,540 African-American legislators, representing 10 percent of the total number of legislators nationwide. **Colin Powell** and **Condoleezza Rice**, both secretaries of state under **President George W. Bush**, occupied the most powerful political office that African-Americans had held since Thurgood Marshall was appointed to the Supreme Court by Lyndon Johnson in the 1960s. Of course, those records were surpassed with the historic 2008 election of Barack Obama as president of the United States.

Urban Problems

As in the past, people in the 1950s and 1960s flocked to the cities for employment and cheaper housing. African-Americans continued to move to Northern and Western cities as they had done during World Wars I and II, while other minorities, including immigrants from Latin America, were drawn to cities for similar reasons. By the 1970s and 1980s, however, mounting urban problems—overcrowding, increasing unemployment and crime rates, and decaying and inadequate housing and commercial areas—initiated a trend of mostly white, middle-class Americans leaving the cities for the suburbs (a phenomenon nicknamed "white flight"); the open spaces, shopping malls, and better-funded schools of the suburbs also enticed people to move. When middle-class families moved to the suburbs, businesses and industries that once provided vital jobs and tax revenue for cities followed. The result was that poor people and racial minorities remained in cities where there were insufficient funds for housing, sanitation, infrastructure, and schools.

Meanwhile, televised **urban riots** in the 1960s, such as those in Los Angeles, Chicago, and New York after the assassination of Martin Luther King Jr., only served to widen the gap between cities and suburbs and to heighten racial tensions. One of the worst urban riots occurred much later in 1992 in South Central Los Angeles, where many African-Americans expressed outrage at the acquittal of four white police officers who were videotaped beating a black man, **Rodney King**.

Tensions between urban and suburban areas surfaced in ways that highlighted both racial and class animosity. In 1974–1975 the **forced busing** of students resulted in violence in South Boston when black students from a poorer section were bused into a predominantly white, working-class neighborhood school by court order. Buses were vandalized and attacked while riot police tried to quell the mob. White families moved from South Boston or sent their children to private schools, while even some black families opposed the forced busing, arguing instead that the schools in their black neighborhoods should receive better funding. Busing continued in many major cities through the late 1990s, and although many schools did achieve greater racial integration, the strategy was not without its critics. Indeed, the Supreme Court decision in *Milliken v. Bradley* (1974) held that an interdistrict remedy for unconstitutional segregation found in one district exceeded the scope of the violation.

But while the image of the scary inner city still has a hold on some imaginations, it is no longer supported by statistics. Both violent crime and property crime have plunged since the early 1990s, and crime in 2010 reached its lowest level in forty years. In large urban areas the drop in crime has been even more pronounced. Affluent young professionals have flocked back to city centers. There is an active debate over what has caused this encouraging trend—one theory credits falling levels of lead in the environment due to legislation in the early 1970s, as lead poisoning is linked to criminal activity. Whatever the reasons, the dramatic drop in crime has led to a revitalization of American cities over the course of the past twenty years.

The Conservative Resurgence

Dismayed with what they perceived to be the excesses of the civil rights movement, the counterculture movement, and feminism, some Americans were eager to bring the country back to traditional values based on religious principles. Other Americans were alarmed by the rising cost of social welfare programs created by the New Deal and Johnson's Great Society. The conservative resurgence began in the 1970s at the grassroots level with a variety of groups that focused on single issues such as ending abortion, criticizing affirmative action, emphasizing traditional gender roles and the nuclear family, and opposing the **Equal Rights**

Amendment for women and gay rights, particularly concerning the question of same-sex marriage.

Instrumental in energizing conservatives throughout the 1970s and 1980s were right-wing evangelical Christians, members of a branch of Protestantism that emphasized a "born-again" religious experience and adherence to strict standards of moral behavior taken from the Bible. **Evangelicalism**, particularly fundamentalist sects, became increasingly prominent in political life from the 1970s through the 1990s. Fundamentalists denounced the moral relativism of liberals and believed in a literal interpretation of the Bible. Evangelical groups also became increasingly political. Conservative evangelicals and fundamentalists such as **Billy Graham, Jerry Falwell,** and **Pat Robertson** helped to mobilize other like-minded citizens to support the Republican Party and bring together various conservative groups to form a movement known as the **New Right**. The growing strength of the New Right was evident in the key role it played in helping to elect **Ronald Reagan** in 1980, and in 1994 when the Republican Party under **Newt Gingrich** recaptured control of both houses of Congress under Democratic President **Bill Clinton**. Evangelical Christians continued to support Republicans with the election and re-election of George W. Bush. However, the election of Barack Obama in 2008 and his re-election in 2012 have led many political observers to conclude that the conservative resurgence has ebbed and that American history has entered a new phase.

Chapter 12 Drill

See Chapter 13 for answers and explanations.

1. All of the following threatened Harry Truman's chances for re-election in 1948 EXCEPT

   (A) Truman's positions on civil rights
   (B) rampant inflation
   (C) the Dixiecrat candidacy of Strom Thurmond
   (D) public dissatisfaction with the Korean War
   (E) Truman's anti-union policies

2. Loyalty oaths, blacklists, and Alger Hiss are all associated with the

   (A) civil rights movement
   (B) New Deal
   (C) Red Scare
   (D) Great Society
   (E) Jazz Age

3. John Foster Dulles, secretary of state under Eisenhower, intensified Cold War rhetoric with Washington's New Look defense program that emphasized

   (A) threatening Moscow with "massive retaliation"
   (B) containment
   (C) collective security
   (D) summit diplomacy
   (E) shuttle diplomacy

4. During the 1950s and early 1960s, the Warren Court was often criticized for

   (A) backing down from the Brown decision in its other civil rights rulings
   (B) exercising judicial restraint
   (C) protecting civil rights for African-Americans while denying rights for political activists and communists
   (D) in effect, enacting "judicial legislation" through its rulings on individual rights
   (E) overturning the ruling in *Plessy v. Ferguson* but maintaining the Court's decision in *Korematsu v. United States*

5. John F. Kennedy was unable to accomplish much of his stated civil rights agenda during his lifetime primarily because

   (A) the war in Vietnam demanded his full attention
   (B) African-American leaders refused to work with him
   (C) his vice president, Lyndon Johnson, opposed any changes to civil rights law
   (D) the violent tactics of the civil rights movement made any association with it politically untenable
   (E) his slim coalition included Southern segregationists

6. Which of the following does NOT accurately describe the presidential election of 1968?

   (A) The Democratic Party was fractured due to dissent over the Vietnam War.
   (B) A frontrunner for one of the major parties was assassinated during the primary season.
   (C) Both major-party candidates campaigned as Washington outsiders.
   (D) A third-party candidacy split the traditionally Democratic Southern vote.
   (E) The Republican nominee faced little opposition in the primaries.

7. Inflation throughout the 1970s was driven in large part by

   (A) the cost of funding the Vietnam War
   (B) rapidly increasing gasoline and oil prices
   (C) government investment in the space program
   (D) a dramatic reduction of income tax rates
   (E) a scandal within the savings and loan industry

8. The incident that began a chain of events that became one of the most infamous presidential scandals in American history and eventually led to the resignation of Richard Nixon was the

(A) burglary of Daniel Ellsberg's psychiatrist's office
(B) political sabotage of Nixon's opponent, George McGovern
(C) illegal use of the CIA to hush up the FBI's investigation of the events surrounding the publication of the Pentagon Papers
(D) use of the IRS to play dirty tricks on leading Democrats
(E) break-in and attempted bugging of the Democratic party's national headquarters

9. The top goals of the Reagan presidency included

(A) eliminating all social programs and balancing the federal budget
(B) reducing the size of the federal government and increasing defense spending
(C) using the federal government to enforce civil rights and reducing U.S. influence in Central America
(D) increasing income tax rates and strengthening environmental regulations
(E) promoting nuclear energy and overthrowing Iraqi dictator Saddam Hussein

10. Since the end of the Cold War, the continuing American impulse to intervene in the economic and political affairs of other nations around the world is motivated by all of the following EXCEPT

(A) fears of renewed Soviet expansion
(B) the protection of human rights
(C) American economic interests
(D) the desire to promote and develop democratic institutions in former communist and Third World nations
(E) lingering fears of the threat of nuclear and biological warfare

REFLECT ACTIVITY

Respond to the following questions:

- For which content topics discussed in this chapter do you feel you have achieved sufficient mastery to answer multiple-choice questions correctly?

- For which content topics discussed in this chapter do you feel you have achieved sufficient mastery to discuss effectively in an essay?

- For which content topics discussed in this chapter do you feel you need more work before you can answer multiple-choice questions correctly?

- For which content topics discussed in this chapter do you feel you need more work before you can discuss effectively in an essay?

- What parts of this chapter are you going to re-review?

- Will you seek further help, outside of this book (such as a teacher, tutor, or AP Central), on any of the content in this chapter—and, if so, on what content?

Chapter 13
Chapter Drills:
Answers and
Explanations

CHAPTER 5 DRILL

1. **C** Indentured servitude promised freedom and a parcel of land to those who survived its seven-year term of service. Fewer than half did; most indentured servants worked in the fields performing grueling labor, and many died as a result. Indentured servitude was available only to the English, and nearly 100,000 took advantage of it.

2. **A** The Mayflower Compact states that government derives its power from the consent of the governed, not from divine mandate. This distinguishes government under the Mayflower Compact from the monarchial government the Pilgrims left behind in England. You should have been able to eliminate (E) based on the fact that the U.S. Constitution did not originally grant equal rights to all U.S. residents regardless of race or gender.

3. **D** Virginia, one of the earliest colonies, developed around the tobacco trade; tobacco was the colonies' first important cash crop. You should have eliminated (E) by using common sense; fresh fruit would hardly have remained fresh during the long sea journey from the colonies back to England. Cotton (A) did not become a major export until the early nineteenth century, when the invention of the cotton gin made large-scale cotton farming practical.

4. **B** During the colonial era, the British subscribed to the economic theory of mercantilism, which held that a favorable balance of trade and control of hard currency were the keys to economic power. Ultimately, the theory of capitalism, famously championed by Adam Smith, supplanted mercantilism as the predominant economic theory of the West.

5. **E** The French and Indian War gave the British unchecked control over North America and a huge war debt. Searching for ways to repay the debt, the British sought greater contributions from, and subsequently greater control over, its American colonies. The Age of Salutary Neglect, an era during which the British basically allowed the colonies to govern themselves, was over.

6. **C** During the Age of Salutary Neglect, Britain regarded the colonies primarily as a market for exports and a resource of raw materials. England imposed numerous import and export restrictions on the colonies in an effort to maintain its monopoly on colonial markets. The colonists, naturally, tried to smuggle cheaper goods into the country and smuggled products out of the country in order to sell them. The British established their own military-style courts—called vice-admiralty courts—to enforce trade laws because they knew the colonists themselves would not.

7. **C** The Stono Uprising was an early slave rebellion (1739) in which African slaves rose against their oppressors. The Stono Uprising is sometimes referred to as the Cato Rebellion.

8. **E** The vast majority of colonists lived in rural areas. By 1750 roughly 5 percent of the colonial population resided in cities. Philadelphia, Boston, Williamsburg, Baltimore, and Boston were the most important cities of the era; all were built around ports.

9. **D** The purpose of America's first colleges was to train homegrown clergy so that the colonies would no longer have to import its clergy from England. The four oldest extant colonial universities—Harvard, William & Mary, Yale, and Princeton—were all originally affiliated with specific Protestant faiths.

10. **A** Provided the colonies continued to buy British goods and to supply the British with raw materials, England did not care how the colonies governed themselves. England did impose its will (through the vice-admiralty courts) when the colonies attempted to shirk their economic responsibilities, but otherwise took a laissez-faire approach. As a result, the colonies developed a tradition of independence that contributed to their eventual rebellion against the Crown.

CHAPTER 6 DRILL

1. **D** Benjamin Franklin developed the Albany Plan, a first stab at a united colonial government empowered to collect taxes and raise a military. Although the delegations to Albany signed off on the plan, none of the colonial legislatures would have anything to do with it; they were uninterested in ceding any powers, even in the interest of strengthening the colonies as a whole. Franklin responded with his famous "Join or Die" cartoon, which showed the colonies as a snake cut into segments, each representing a colony.

2. **D** 1763, the year the Treaty of Paris ended the French and Indian War, is often considered to be a major turning point in British-colonial relations, as it marks the end of Britain's policy of salutary neglect. Beginning with the Proclamation of 1763, the colonists began to feel England "tightening the screws." The passage of the Sugar and Stamp Acts set off a chain of new restrictions that set the colonists on the road to revolution. Although you no doubt know the phrase "No taxation without representation!" the colonists did not actually want to send colonial representatives to sit in the British Parliament in London. Rather, as the resolutions of the Stamp Act Congress make clear, they believed that only their own colonial legislatures had the power to tax them. They initially understood that they were British subjects and that Parliament had the right to enact mercantilist restrictions to regulate trade. However, they soon voiced their concern that there was a significant difference between taxation and legislation.

3. **A** In the run-up to the Revolutionary War, colonists complained that Parliament had no business taxing them because the colonists lacked representation in the legislature. Their slogan, "No taxation without representation!" neatly summed up their argument (and it was catchy, too!). The British responded with the theory of virtual representation, which stated that the colonists were represented in Parliament because members of Parliament represent all British citizens, not just the voters who elected them. Like most political debates, this one reeked of disingenuousness on both sides. The colonists knew that any delegation they sent to Parliament would be essentially power-

less; what they really wanted was the right to set their own taxes, not a representative in the legislature. The British knew full well that their MPs did not give a tinker's damn about the colonists or their interests; what they wanted was for the colonists to shut up and pay their taxes.

4. **A** A recent DBQ on the AP exam asked to what extent the colonists had developed a sense of unity by the eve of the Revolution. One could certainly argue that most colonists considered themselves to be loyal British subjects even after fighting had begun in Lexington and Concord in April 1775. Many historians view the Declaration of Independence, written in July 1776, as propaganda to convince those still loyal to England to fight for their independence. At the start of the French and Indian War, Benjamin Franklin had proposed the Albany Plan of Union, which was rejected by the colonists in favor of maintaining individual colonial sovereignty. The Stamp Act Congress of 1765 is historically significant because it marks the beginning of colonial unity and resistance against the British.

5. **B** Much of the American Declaration of Independence is derived from the writings of John Locke, particularly his Two Treatises of Government, published in 1690, in which he challenged the theory of divine right of kings and put forth what is known as social contract theory. Both Locke and Rousseau believed that man was born free, but it was Rousseau who argued that "Man must be forced to be free" and submit to the "General Will."

6. **C** During the Age of Salutary Neglect, Britain regarded the colonies primarily as a market for exports and a resource of raw materials. England imposed numerous import and export restrictions on the colonies in an effort to maintain its monopoly on colonial markets. The colonists, naturally, tried to smuggle cheaper goods into the country and smuggled products out of the country in order to sell them. The British established their own military-style courts—called vice-admiralty courts—to enforce trade laws because they knew the colonists themselves would not.

CHAPTER 7 DRILL

1. D   The Articles of Confederation had intentionally created a weak central government, granting Congress few regulatory powers so as to avoid recreating an American Parliament. Shays's Rebellion threatened the survival of the newly-established republic, because the farmers in western Massachusetts were rebelling against their state government for the very same reason the colonists had rebelled against England—taxes. Under the Articles of Confederation, Congress could neither raise nor support a federal militia, so when Massachusetts requested federal assistance in squelching Daniel Shays and his farmer friends, no help was available. Had this question been about the Whiskey Rebellion during George Washington's administration, (A) would have been the correct answer. (A) also demonstrates the difference between the limited power of the federal government under the Articles of Confederation and the stronger federal government established by the Constitution. (E) refers to Bacon's Rebellion. (C) is not correct, although excessive taxation was certainly one of the major causes of the American Revolution and subsequent rebellions. It is interesting to note that we did not have a federal income tax until the Sixteenth Amendment was ratified in the early twentieth century.

2. E   Remember that the Articles of Confederation created a weak central government. Remember also that the AP U.S. History Exam loves to test this fact, so there's no way the answer to this question can be (E), because (E) suggests that the central government under the Articles was strong. That would turn this into a trivia question, and the AP doesn't ask trivia questions; it asks questions that address important themes and major trends in American history. Under the Articles, the central government relied on the states to collect taxes. It could not overrule state law. Its ability to negotiate treaties was one of the few effective powers it was granted. No wonder the nation floundered under its first constitution; its second stab at a constitution would prove much more successful.

3. C   Washington's presidency was all about establishing precedents. He was extremely conscious of this fact and proceeded cautiously throughout his two terms, aware that future presidents would follow his example. Thus, he rarely used his presidential veto, hoping to encourage future executives to accommodate the legislature on most matters. He didn't want the Congress to have complete control over the executive branch, though; he believed in the system of checks and balances. Thus, when the House of Representatives demanded all of Washington's papers regarding negotiations for the unpopular Jay Treaty, Washington refused. He reasoned that the papers were none of the House's business because only the Senate—with whom Washington did share the papers—is required to ratify treaties. His action established the precedent of executive privilege, a nebulous executive right to protect sensitive information and executive privacy. The right is occasionally invoked by the executive and almost as frequently challenged by the legislature, with the two typically working out a solution of compromise before the matter can reach the courts.

4. E   The strict constructionist interpretation of the Constitution is that Congress may use only those powers specifically enumerated in the Constitution. Other powers, regardless of how necessary they may be to national interests, are prohibited. The broad constructionist interpretation, in contrast,

holds that Congress has numerous implied powers. For example, Congress has the power to print money, borrow money, and collect taxes; thus, the Constitution implies that Congress has the power to create a bank, the proper instrument for exercising these powers.

5. **D** John Marshall was not the first Chief Justice of the Supreme Court, but he certainly was the man most responsible for giving the Court its teeth and much of the power it wields today. *Marbury v. Madison* was Marshall's first significant decision and established the principle of judicial review, which enables the Court to declare a federal or state law unconstitutional. *McCulloch v. Maryland* (C) was another landmark decision of the Marshall Court; this case dealt with the Second Bank of the United States and established the principle of federal supremacy. And it is important to note that while Marshall was an important federalist, he did not establish the principle.

6. **B** The Louisiana Purchase grew out of the government's efforts to purchase New Orleans from the French; President Jefferson wanted control of the city because it sits at the mouth of the Mississippi River, an essential trade route. Jefferson sent James Monroe to France to negotiate the sale. The French, desperate for cash and nearly as desperate to divest themselves of New World holdings, offered to sell the entire massive Louisiana Territory, giving the United States control of both banks of the Mississippi River (as well as a tremendous amount of western land). As a result, American traders could travel the length of the river unimpeded, and trade subsequently boomed. Many of the incorrect answers to this question are anachronistic; the date of the purchase was too early for there to be "numerous French factories" in the territory, (C), or to allow for "the immediate completion of the transcontinental railroad," (D). The Louisiana Territory does not extend to the Pacific coast, so (E) cannot be correct.

7. **A** The War of 1812 was very unpopular with New England Federalists who called the war "Mr. Madison's War." The economic policies of Jefferson and Madison disrupted trade, and as a result, were detrimental to New England merchants and shippers. Consequently, a group of New England Federalists met in Hartford, Connecticut in 1814 to articulate a list of grievances against the Democratic-Republicans and their policies. While some men suggested secession, others suggested amending the Constitution to protect New England's commercial interests against what they perceived to be a dangerous, growing threat from the agrarian, Republican South. Because we "defeated" the British in what is often termed the Second War for Independence, the Federalists were seen as big babies and ultimately discredited. With the election of James Monroe in 1816, the United States had entered the Era of Good Feelings, a relatively brief period when there was only one political party—the Republicans. Although the War of 1812 damaged New England commerce initially, in the long run, the Embargo Act of 1807 and the War of 1812 forced Americans to be less dependent on British goods and indirectly stimulated the growth of industry in antebellum New England.

CHAPTER 8 DRILL

1. **A** The election of 1824 is one of the more infamous elections in American political history and exposes one of the unanticipated flaws in the Electoral College system. Because of the winner-take-all system of awarding electoral votes in most states, it is possible for a candidate to actually win the popular vote nationwide but lose the election. According to the Constitution, a candidate must win a majority, not a plurality, of electoral votes to win the presidential election. If no one candidate receives the requisite majority, the election is "thrown into the House," and the Houses of Representatives chooses the president from among the top three candidates. In the event this occurs, each state casts only one vote. Because there were five candidates running for president in 1824, it was almost impossible for anyone to receive a majority. Realizing that he did not have enough support to win the presidency, Henry Clay threw his support to John Quincy Adams in exchange for Adams's promise to make Clay his secretary of state. Jackson believed he lost the election because of this "corrupt bargain."

2. **D** The tariff in question here is the infamous Tariff of Abominations, so named by the Southern states that protested that this protective tariff benefited the New England manufacturers at the expense of cotton exporters in the South. The enactment of the Tariff of 1828 led to the nullification crisis a few years later when South Carolina declared the tariff null and void. (A similar situation had occurred in 1798 when Jefferson and Madison penned the Virginia and Kentucky resolutions in protest against the Alien and Sedition Acts.) In the case of *Marbury v. Madison*, Marshall had argued that only the Supreme Court could rule a law to be unconstitutional, not individual states. Eventually, a compromise tariff was brokered and the crisis was resolved. Nevertheless, the nullification crisis during Andrew Jackson's administration exposed the increasing tension of economic sectionalism that would propel the nation to civil war 30 years later.

3. **A** Andrew Jackson generally sided with the states on the issue of states' rights, preferring to limit the powers of the federal government to only those he perceived to be essential. He also favored his Western constituency to the power elite of the Northeast, whom he regarded with suspicion. Thus, Jackson scuttled the Second National Bank, a large federal program championed by Northeastern bankers, and the American System, a large public works program.

4. **B** The Cherokee were considered part of the "Five Civilized Tribes" living in the South, having established a republic in the state of Georgia. Unfortunately the discovery of gold within the Cherokee nation's borders was the catalyst for the tribe's forced relocation. Georgian citizens wanted to enforce the Indian Removal Act in order to have access to the territory. Although the Supreme Court ruled in favor of the Cherokees, President Andrew Jackson did not comply with the decision. States' rights were an important issue during Jackson's presidency, and he did not want to intervene on behalf of the Cherokee nation.

5. **E** Brook Farm, the Oneida Community, and New Harmony were all utopian communities that arose during the antebellum period in response to what some people perceived to be the ill effects of a growing commercial society.

CHAPTER 9 DRILL

1. **D** A trick question; Texas was annexed by the United States in 1845, prior to the start of the Mexican-American War. All the other territories mentioned in the answer choices came to the United States as a result of the Treaty of Guadalupe Hidalgo, which ended the war.

2. **E** The term "Bleeding Kansas" refers to the battle in Kansas between pro-slavery and abolitionist forces. The doctrine of popular sovereignty had created the circumstances that led to the gruesome conflict; it left the slave status of each territory up to its residents, to be decided at the time when the territory was ready to write a constitution and apply for statehood. Both sides wanted Kansas badly, and both sent representatives into the territory to form governments. President Pierce recognized the pro-slavery government, but abolitionist forces cried "foul" and continued their fight to establish Kansas as a free state. More than 200 people died in the resulting skirmishes.

3. **B** The Emancipation Proclamation did not free all the slaves. Instead, it freed only those slaves in rebel territories not controlled by the Union. In other words, it was completely unenforceable; it immediately took effect only in those places where Union forces had no power to act, but ultimately had a significant impact as Union troops took over Confederate territory. The Emancipation Proclamation had a huge symbolic effect, though, as it clearly cast the Civil War as a war against slavery. Free blacks and escaped slaves rushed to join the cause; nearly 200,000 joined the Union army as a consequence of the Emancipation Proclamation.

4. **D** Many historians argue that Andrew Johnson was neither the man nor the politician that Lincoln was. Johnson locked horns with the Radical Republicans in Congress over several issues pertaining to Reconstruction. Johnson had vetoed the Tenure of Office Act, which required a president to obtain Senate approval before firing an appointed official. The Senate argued that if it had the power to confirm nominations, it should also be allowed to have a say in the event a president wanted to fire someone. Congress overrode Johnson's veto; Johnson fired his secretary of state, the Radical Republican Henry Stanton; and the House of Representatives impeached the President of the United States for the first time in American history. Johnson was acquitted, however, by one vote in the Senate and thus remained in office to finish his term.

5. **B** The election of 1876 is another one of the disputed elections in American political history. Although Samuel J. Tilden, then Governor of New York, won the popular vote nationwide, there were several states that contested the results of the election. Consequently, a special bipartisan commission was set up to determine the outcome of the election. In what became known as the "Compromise of 1877," Rutherford B. Hayes won the presidential election by a margin of one single electoral vote. Hayes had promised to remove federal troops still stationed in the South after the Civil War, thus ending military reconstruction.

CHAPTER 10 DRILL

1. **E** The scalawags were white Southerners who supported Republican policies during Reconstruction. Carpetbaggers were Northerners who traveled south to exploit the turmoil following the Civil War for their own political gain. The Redeemers were white Democrats who were determined to get revenge on the Republicans for imposing their radical policies of Reconstruction on Southern states and thus hoped to "redeem" the South.

2. **A** If you remember that the Supreme Court of the late nineteenth century was extremely conservative and extremely pro-business—and you should remember that, because it's important—you should have been able to eliminate answers (B) and (D) immediately. If you remember the profound impact of such decisions as *Plessy v. Ferguson*—and you should also remember that—you could have eliminated answers (C) and (E).

3. **D** "Vertical integration" is another name for monopoly. Monopolies ran rampant in the late 1800s; the government did little to prevent them, and the courts actively encouraged them. Of the incorrect answers, (C) refers to assembly line production, and (E) refers to the Gospel of Wealth. (A) and (B) are just made up.

4. **C** James A. Garfield's presidency is remembered for one thing: Garfield's assassination at the hands of a disgruntled office seeker. His assassin, Charles Guiteau, was actually a mentally disturbed individual who imagined himself an important player in Garfield's electoral success. Guiteau convinced himself that he deserved a big fat government job as a reward for his efforts, and when he received none he retaliated by shooting Garfield. Garfield's successor, Chester Arthur, signed the Pendleton Act, which replaced the spoils system Guiteau had hoped to exploit with a merit-based system for selecting civil servants.

5. **C** Although one might certainly make a valid claim that labor unions were necessary during the late nineteenth century when working conditions were dangerous, unsanitary, and exploitative, unions were very unpopular because they were associated with political radicalism and violence. The Haymarket incident began as a mass meeting organized by anarchists, held in Haymarket Square in Chicago in 1886 in sympathy and protest of events related to striking workers at the McCormick Harvester Company plant nearby. When police tried to break up the meeting, someone threw a bomb into the crowd, leaving seven policemen dead and several wounded. This incident convinced the American public that unions were dangerous and ultimately led to the decline of the Knights of Labor.

6. **E** If you can't immediately identify the correct answer to this one, use common sense to eliminate incorrect answers. Japan is a huge nation relative to Hawaii; its economy couldn't realistically depend on trade with the island, (A). (B) contradicts one of the main themes of the period—the Age of Imperialism, when every Western power, including the United States, was gathering colonies in the East. Would the United States have ceded Hawaii to Japan during that period? Unlikely, and much less likely still that the AP exam would ask about an anomalous agreement. (C) suggests Japan was a bastion of democracy in the late nineteenth century; in fact, it was ruled by an emperor. (D) incorrectly locates Hawaii in the Eastern Hemisphere.

CHAPTER 11 DRILL

1. **E**   "Muckrakers" is a term Theodore Roosevelt coined to describe the investigative journalists of his day. They included Ida Tarbell, whose book on Standard Oil revealed corruption in the oil industry and big business in general; Upton Sinclair, whose stomach-turning account of the meatpacking industry drove public outcry for government regulation of food production (the Food and Drug Administration was created as a result of Sinclair's book The Jungle); and Lincoln Steffens, whose The Shame of the Cities exposed many Americans to the extent of urban poverty and corruption in urban government. Muckrakers helped fuel the public outcry for government reform, the main goal of the Progressive movement.

2. **B**   Conservative courts and pro-business administrations allowed the Sherman Antitrust Act to be used to restrain labor but rarely to restrain business. Theodore Roosevelt changed all that. With public support Roosevelt transformed the Sherman Antitrust Act into a tool with which to break up monopolies. He focused his attention on corrupt monopolies whose activities countered the public interest, leaving alone trusts that operated more or less honestly. His approach garnered broad public acclaim, earning him the nickname "the Trustbuster."

3. **B**   As a result of winning the Spanish-American War in 1898, the United States acquired Guam, Puerto Rico, the Philippines, and for all intents and purposes, Cuba. (Although we had claimed we had no interest in acquiring Cuba and could empathize with its colonial status, having once been a colony ourselves, the Platt Amendment rendered the island a virtual colony of the United States.) The situation in the Philippines created intense debate between business interests that saw the enormous economic benefits to acquiring "stepping stones" to profitable Chinese trade and those Americans who believed having colonies contradicted our fundamental democratic principles. Once we acquired overseas possessions, a question arose as to the rights and privileges of the native peoples living within the American Empire. In a series of Supreme Court cases known as the Insular Cases, the Court ruled that the "Constitution did not follow the flag," and thus, colonial subjects were not entitled to the same rights as U.S. citizens living at home or abroad.

4. **A**   This is a straight recall question. You either know what the Zimmerman telegram is or you don't. If you know it, you're going to get this question right. If you don't, use process of elimination to get rid of anachronistic answers, (B), or answers that seem un-AP-like because they don't reinforce important themes of U.S. history, (D) and (E). You should know, however, that the Zimmerman telegram was one of the reasons the United States entered World War I.

5. **C**   In the aftermath of World War I, President Wilson favored a peace that would promote openness in international affairs, free trade, and diplomacy. He also sought universal arms reductions and a mechanism for enforcing world peace, which was to be achieved through the League of Nations. He did not seek a punitive treaty that forced Germany to pay heavy reparations; the European allies, however, insisted. Wilson was able to negotiate very little of his Fourteen Points plan, but he remained optimistic that the League of Nations would eventually broker a more fair postwar peace. Unfortunately, Wilson's hopes were never realized.

6. **B**   The Ku Klux Klan evoked the execrable Southern traditions of racism and physical intimidation against the modern drive for expanded civil rights. The Scopes Monkey Trial pitted religion against the modern notion of evolution. The Emergency Quota Act of 1924 was passed to check immigration from non-western European countries; its champions felt the nation's western European traditions were threatened by immigrants from southern Europe, eastern Europe, South America, and Asia. Prohibition pitted religion against modern licentiousness. The Teapot Dome Scandal, on the other hand, was just an example of good old-fashioned political corruption.

7. **D**   Buying "on margin" allowed investors to buy stock with only a small amount of cash; the rest was borrowed from stockbrokers and banks against the presumed profits from subsequent stock sales. The system worked only as long as stock prices kept rising; once they started to fall, all hell broke loose. In response to market weakness in the fall of 1929, investors who had long believed the market was overvalued started to sell off their stocks, causing prices to drop. Noting the market downturn, stockbrokers demanded that clients repay margin loans and, when their clients couldn't repay, dumped the stocks on the market in order to recoup some of their losses. The law of supply and demand sent stock prices spiraling uncontrollably downward. Over a period of two months, the market lost nearly half its value and many, many investors—including some of the nation's biggest banks—were ruined.

8. **E**   Roosevelt coined the phrase "Good Neighbor Policy" to reflect a shift in American attitudes toward Latin America. In the past, American intervention in the region had incited great resentment of the United States. Roosevelt announced a new U.S. commitment to autonomy throughout the hemisphere and showed his intentions by withdrawing U.S. troops from Nicaragua and Haiti. He later resisted sending troops to Cuba to quell a revolution.

9. **A**   Americans were already predisposed to isolationism by nature before they heard the results of the Nye Commission's investigations. They had been promised that World War I was "the war to end all wars." Less than 20 years later, Europe was apparently on the verge of another big confrontation. The sentiment in the United States was, "Let them sort this out themselves." Those feelings were strengthened when the Nye Commission revealed that many American munitions companies had violated an arms embargo in order to arm the nation's enemies. It further revealed that U.S. banks had lobbied for U.S. entry into the war in order to protect more than $2 billion in loans to Britain and its allies. The report left Americans more cynical about the motives of its leaders and less susceptible to calls for intervention overseas.

10. **A**   Fred Korematsu was among the more than 110,000 Japanese Americans ordered to relocate from the West Coast to internment camps during World War II. Korematsu refused, was arrested, and took his case all the way to the Supreme Court. The Court ruled that the government had not exceeded its power, noting that extraordinary times sometimes call for extraordinary measures; three of the nine justices dissented. History has not judged Roosevelt's internment policy kindly. In 1998 Fred Korematsu was awarded the Presidential Medal of Honor.

CHAPTER 12 DRILL

1. **D** The Korean War didn't begin until 1950.

2. **C** Fear of communist infiltration and subversion reached hysterical proportions in the post–World War II era, making all sorts of excessive responses to the communist threat not only possible but likely. Loyalty oaths were instituted by private companies, state governments, and even the federal government, based on the apparent belief that communist spies are capable of espionage but not of lying under oath. Blacklists banned suspected subversives from work in many industries, destroying the lives of many innocent people. Alger Hiss was accused of passing government secrets to the Soviet Union. He professed his innocence to his dying day, although Soviet files released in the post-Soviet era suggest his guilt. The Hiss case was front-page news. Richard Nixon played a prominent role in Hiss's prosecution, thereby earning Nixon the national spotlight for the first time.

3. **A** The key to this question is the phrase "intensified Cold War rhetoric." Words like "massive retaliation" didn't exactly improve relations with the Soviet Union. While containment was the guiding principle of U.S. foreign policy throughout the Cold War, this question is asking something more specific. And although Dulles did forge many alliances with smaller nations (collective security), (A) is a better answer. Summit diplomacy was practiced by Reagan and Gorbachev, while the term "shuttle diplomacy" was applied to Henry Kissinger under Nixon.

4. **D** You should be familiar with the important decisions of the Marshall Court (1801–1835) and the Warren Court (1953–1969). Marshall is remembered as a Federalist who strengthened the new federal government and encouraged economic development of the new nation. The Warren Court was an activist court, best remembered for increasing the rights of individuals, specifically the rights of the accused. (For example, the Gideon and Miranda cases were decided by the Warren Court.) According to the Constitution, only Congress can make laws, but in effect, many of the Warren decisions established social policy, which many conservative critics saw as "judicial legislation."

5. **E** Kennedy's victory in 1960 was by the tiniest of margins. He could not have won, or governed, without the support of Democrats in the South, many of whom opposed any federal strengthening of civil rights law. As a result, Kennedy had to tread carefully on the issue of African-American civil rights, a cause he had supported forcefully during his campaign. He used the attorney general's office to bring suits to force desegregation of Southern universities and appointed African-Americans to prominent positions in his administration but made no effort at civil rights legislation until his final year in office. After Kennedy's assassination, new President Lyndon Johnson invoked Kennedy's memory and commitment to civil rights to force the Civil Rights Act of 1964 through Congress.

6. **C** The Republican candidate, Richard Nixon, was a former vice president. The Democratic candidate, Hubert Humphrey, was the current vice president and, before that, a longtime senator. Neither could have campaigned as a Washington outsider, and neither did. The Democrats were fractured

over the war; the party was home to both aggressive cold warriors and the anti-war movement. Robert Kennedy was assassinated in June; many believe he would have won the nomination had he not been killed. George Wallace formed a third party and campaigned on states' rights and segregation, siphoning off key votes in the South, where the Democrats had traditionally done well. Nixon's only opposition in the Republican primaries came from Nelson D. Rockefeller, who campaigned halfheartedly, and Ronald Reagan, who, at the time, was seen as too extreme to ever win the presidency. Reagan never changed, but the country did.

7. **B** Gasoline and oil prices shot through the roof in the 1970s, affecting a wide range of industries that relied on the fuels to run. The result was widespread inflation throughout the decade.

8. **E** This is the event that started it all—the break-in to the Watergate complex in Washington, D.C., where the Democratic party had its national headquarters. All of the other choices became part of the cover-up and are known collectively as "Watergate," which ultimately forced the resignation of Richard Nixon, the only President to resign in American history. Nixon resigned before he was impeached and was subsequently pardoned by Gerald Ford.

9. **B** Reagan believed in limited federal government. Part of his goal in lowering tax rates was to reduce the federal budget (thus federal programs). But Reagan was also a stalwart cold warrior who believed that military strength was the best check against the Soviet Union and communism in general. He campaigned vigorously for new weapons systems, including the Strategic Defense Initiative, a space-based, anti-missile system dubbed "Star Wars."

10. **A** Though American relations with Russia remain uneasy, fears of Soviet expansion are a thing of the past; the Soviet Union ceased to exist in 1992, ending the Cold War.

Chapter 14
Key Terms and Concepts

A NOTE ON THE KEY TERMS

The list of key terms that follows provides a comprehensive review of U.S. history. We've divided the terms into three major time periods and then separated the terms into categories: concepts, events, people, and policies (which includes major Supreme Court decisions and important federal legislation.) Write a brief explanation or identification of each term in the space provided. Some students even find making flash cards helpful.

Keep the following suggestions in mind as you go through these terms. If it is a concept, do not simply write a definition; try to think of a historical example that illustrates the concept. For example, you might define *brinksmanship* and then cite the Cuban Missile Crisis as an example. Be certain you can explain the causes and effects of each major event. This will help you with the essay questions where you are required to showcase an analytical understanding of issues. The Supreme Court cases and major laws should be placed within their historical context. It is always useful to ask yourself the question "Why at this time?" Again, you should not merely state what the Court decided or law required but also understand the case's or law's impact on American society at the time.

Most of these terms are printed in **bold**, *italic*, or ***bold italic*** type throughout the history review of the book (Chapters 5 through 12). If you cannot find a particular term, use your textbook or the Internet.

CHAPTER 5: THE SEVENTEENTH AND EARLY EIGHTEENTH CENTURIES

Concepts

Black codes _____

City upon a hill _____

Encomiendas _____

Evangelicalism _____

Headright system _____

Indentured servitude _____

Joint-stock company _____

Mercantilism _____

Middle Passage _____

Proprietary colony _____

Puritanism _____

Royal colony _____

Salutary neglect _____

Slavery _____

Tariffs _____

Events

Bacon's Rebellion _____

Glorious Revolution in England _____

The Great Awakening _____

King Philip's War _____

King William's War _____

Pequot War _____

Salem witchcraft trials _____

The "starving time" _____

Stono Uprising _____

People (Individuals and Groups)

Anne Hutchinson _____

Benjamin Franklin _____

Calvinists _____

Congregationalists _____

George Whitefield _____

Huguenots _____

John Rolfe _____

John Smith _____

Jonathan Edwards _____

Pilgrims _____

Pocahontas _____

Powhatan Confederacy _____

Puritans _____

Roger Williams _____

Separatists _____

Sir Walter Raleigh _____

Places

Cahokia _____

The Chesapeake _____

Jamestown _____

The lower South _____

Massachusetts Bay colony _____

Middle colonies _____

New England _____

Policies, Agreements, Court Rulings, Etc.

Act of Toleration _____

Dominion of New England _____

Edict of Nantes _____

Fundamental Orders of Connecticut _____

Halfway Covenant _____

Maryland Toleration Act _____

Mayflower Compact _____

Navigation Acts _____

CHAPTERS 6–10: THE LATE EIGHTEENTH AND NINETEENTH CENTURIES

Concepts

Adams's "midnight appointments" _____

Assembly line _____

Beard Thesis (of the Constitution) _____

First Bank of the United States (BUS) _____

Freeport Doctrine _____

The Frontier Thesis _____

Gospel of Wealth _____

Horizontal integration _____

Interchangeable parts _____

Jeffersonian republicanism _____

Jingoism _____

Judicial Review _____

"Kitchen cabinet"_____

Loose construction _____

Lowell System _____

Manifest Destiny _____

Nativism _____

Non-consumption and non-importation _____

"Pet" banks _____

Popular sovereignty _____

President's cabinet _____

Second Bank of the United States (BUS) _____

Second Party system _____

Social Darwinism _____

Spoils system _____

Standard Oil Co. _____

States' rights _____

Strict construction _____

Trust _____

Turner Thesis _____

U.S. Steel Corporation _____

Utopian communities _____

Vertical integration _____

War profiteering _____

Washington's Farewell Address _____

"White man's burden" _____

Yellow journalism _____

Events

Annapolis Convention _____

Antietam _____

Atlanta Exposition/Compromise _____

Battle of New Orleans _____

"Bleeding Kansas" _____

Boston Massacre _____

Boston Tea Party _____

Boxer Rebellion _____

Chesapeake Affair _____

Compromise of 1877 _____

Constitutional Convention of 1787 _____

Credit Mobilier scandal _____

"Cross of Gold" speech _____

Era of Good Feelings _____

Federalist Papers _____

Filipino insurrection _____

French and Indian War _____

German and Irish immigration _____

Gold Rush in California _____

Great Migration _____

Hartford Convention _____

Haymarket Square riot _____

Homestead strike _____

Indian Removal Act (1830) _____

King George's War _____

Lincoln-Douglas debates _____

Maysville Road Veto _____

Mexican-American War _____

Pullman strike _____

Reform movements _____

Second Great Awakening _____

Seneca Falls Convention _____

Seward Purchase of Alaska _____

Shays's Rebellion _____

Sherman's march through Georgia _____

Sioux Wars _____

South Carolina Exposition and Protest _____

South Carolina Ordinance of Nullification _____

Spanish-American War _____

Stamp Act Crisis _____

Swing Around the Circle _____

Trail of Tears _____

Tripoli War _____

U.S.S. Maine _____

Uncle Tom's Cabin published _____

Undeclared naval war with France _____

Union Pacific and Central Pacific joined/transcontinental line _____

Whiskey Rebellion _____

Whiskey Ring Scandal _____

XYZ Affair _____

People (Individuals and Groups)

Abraham Lincoln _____

Alfred Thayer Mahan (author of *The Influence of Sea Power Upon History*)

_____

American Anti-Slavery Society _____

American Federation of Labor _____

American Protective Association _____

Andrew Carnegie _____

Andrew Jackson _____

Andrew Johnson _____

Anti-Federalists _____

Anti-Masonic Party _____

Benjamin Harrison _____

Booker T. Washington _____

Border Ruffians _____

"Boss" Tweed _____

Chief Joseph and the Nez Perce _____

Citizen Edmond Genêt _____

Civil Service Commission _____

Committees of Correspondence _____

Coxey's Army _____

Daniel Webster _____

Dorothea Dix _____

Elizabeth Blackwell _____

Elizabeth Cady Stanton _____

Emerson and Thoreau _____

Eugene V. Debs _____

Federalists _____

First Continental Congress _____

Forty-niners _____

Franklin Pierce _____

Frederick Douglass _____

Frederick Jackson Turner (author of *The Significance of the Frontier in American History*)

_____

Free Soil Party _____

George Washington _____

George III _____

The Grange Movement _____

Greenback Party _____

Henry Clay _____

Horace Mann _____

James Buchanan _____

James Garfield _____

James Monroe _____

James Polk _____

Jane Addams _____

John Adams _____

John Brown _____

John C. Calhoun _____

John D. Rockefeller _____

John Marshall _____

John Quincy Adams _____

Joseph Pulitzer _____

Knights of Labor _____

Know-Nothing (American) Party _____

Ku Klux Klan _____

Liberty Party _____

Martin Van Buren _____

Mormon Church _____

Nat Turner _____

National Labor Union _____

Populist Party / platform _____

Queen Liliuokalani / Hawaii _____

Radical Republicans _____

Robber barons _____

Robert Fulton _____

Rough Riders _____

Rutherford B. Hayes _____

Samuel Gompers _____

Second Continental Congress _____

Seventh Day Adventist Church _____

Shakers _____

Sons of Liberty _____

Stephen Douglas _____

Susan B. Anthony _____

Temperance societies _____

Terrence Powderly _____

Thomas A. Edison _____

Thomas Jefferson _____

Thomas Paine _____

Ulysses S. Grant _____

Whig Party _____

William Henry Harrison _____

William Jennings Bryan _____

William McKinley _____

William Randolph Hearst _____

Women's Christian Temperance Union (WCTU) _____

Workingmen's Party _____

Yeomen _____

Zachary Taylor _____

Places

Brook Farm _____

Brooklyn Bridge _____

Burned-over district _____

Confederate States of America (the Confederacy) _____

Cuba _____

Erie Canal _____

Hawaii _____

Mississippi River _____

New Orleans _____

Oklahoma Territory _____

The Philippines _____

Puerto Rico, Samoa, Guam _____

Tenements _____

Policies, Agreements, Court Rulings, Etc.

Adams-Onis Treaty _____

Albany Plan of Union _____

Alien and Sedition Acts _____

Amendments to the Constitution:

Thirteenth Amendment _____

Fourteenth Amendment _____

Fifteenth Amendment _____

American System (Henry Clay's) _____

Amnesty Act _____

Articles of Confederation _____

Bill of Rights _____

Black codes _____

Bland-Allison Act _____

Bradwell v. Illinois _____

(British) Proclamation of 1763 _____

Charles River Bridge v. Warren Bridge _____

Cherokee Nation v. Georgia _____

Chinese Exclusion Act _____

Chisholm v. Georgia _____

Command of the Army Act _____

Compromise of 1850 _____

Compromise of 1877 _____

Compromise Tariff _____

Confiscation Act _____

Continental Association _____

Cumberland (National) Road _____

Dawes Severalty Act _____

Declaration of Independence _____

Declaratory Act _____

Dred Scott v. Sandford _____

Emancipation Proclamation _____

Embargo Act _____

Force Bill _____

Franco-American Alliance _____

Freedmen's Bureau _____

Fugitive Slave Act _____

Gibbons v. Ogden _____

Great Compromise (Connecticut Compromise) _____

Homestead Act _____

Independent Treasury Act _____

Indian Removal Act _____

Insular Cases _____

Interstate Commerce Act _____

Intolerable (Coercive) Acts _____

Jay Treaty _____

Judiciary Act of 1789 _____

Kansas-Nebraska Act _____

Land Ordinance of 1785 _____

Lecompton Constitution _____

Lincoln's Proclamation of Amnesty and Reconstruction _____

Lincoln's Ten-Percent Plan _____

Marbury v. Madison _____

Massachusetts Circular Letter _____

McCulloch v. Maryland _____

McKinley Tariff _____

Military Reconstruction Act _____

Missouri Compromise _____

Monroe Doctrine _____

Morrill Land Grant Act _____

Munn v. Illinois _____

Nonintercourse Act, Force Act, Macon's Bill #2 _____

Northwest Ordinance of 1787 _____

Olive Branch Petition _____

Open door policy _____

Oregon Treaty _____

Ostend Manifesto _____

Pendleton Civil Service Reform Act _____

Pinckney's Treaty _____

Plessy v. Ferguson _____

Protective Tariff _____

Quartering Acts _____

Rush-Bagot Agreement _____

Sherman Antitrust Act _____

Sherman Silver Purchase Act _____

Special Field Order No. 15 _____

Stamp Act and Stamp Act Congress _____

Sugar and Currency Acts _____

Tallmadge Amendment _____

Tariff of Abominations _____

Tea Act _____

Teller Amendment _____

Tenure of Office Act _____

Townshend Acts _____

Treaty of Ghent _____

Treaty of Guadalupe Hidalgo _____

Treaty of Paris _____

Trent Affair _____

United States v. E. C. Knight Co. _____

Virginia and Kentucky Resolutions _____

Wabash case _____

Wade-Davis Bill _____

Webster-Ashburton Treaty _____

Wilmot Proviso _____

Wilson-Gorman Tariff _____

Worcester v. Georgia _____

CHAPTERS 11 AND 12: THE TWENTIETH CENTURY

Concepts

Atomic bomb _____

Axis Alliance _____

Civil rights movement _____

Court packing _____

Domino theory _____

Fourteen Points _____

Freedom Rides _____

Gospel of Wealth _____

Harlem Renaissance _____

Interstate Highway System _____

Iron Curtain _____

Loyalty Boards _____

Manhattan Project _____

Military-industrial complex _____

Mutually assured destruction (MAD) _____

New Deal _____

New Freedom _____

New Nationalism _____

Nixon's "Enemies List" _____

"Peace Without Victory" _____

"Problem that has no name" _____

Prohibition _____

"Proxy" wars _____

Radio _____

Reaganomics _____

Satellites _____

Self-determination _____

Sit-ins _____

Submarine warfare _____

Supply-side economics _____

Trickle-down theory _____

Triple Alliance _____

Triple Entente _____

U-Boats _____

Urban riots _____

"Vietnamization" _____

Zimmerman telegram _____

Events

Army-McCarthy hearings _____

Berlin Blockade and Airlift _____

Bonus Expeditionary Force _____

Cold War _____

Court packing _____

Cuban Missile Crisis _____

D-Day _____

Democratic National Convention, Chicago _____

Fall of Saigon _____

Geneva Conference (1954) _____

Great Migration _____

Iran hostage crisis _____

Iran-Contra affair _____

Japanese American internment _____

The Jazz Singer _____

Korean War _____

Lusitania _____

March on Washington _____

Montgomery bus boycott _____

My Lai Massacre _____

Nixon resigns _____

Operation Desert Storm _____

Paris peace talks _____

Pentagon Papers _____

Persian Gulf War _____

Russo-Japanese War _____

Saturday Night Massacre _____

Scopes Monkey Trial _____

Six Day War _____

Sputnik _____

Stock market crash _____

Stonewall Riots _____

Tet Offensive _____

Triangle Shirtwaist Factory fire _____

Watts Riots _____

World War I _____

World War II _____

People (Individuals and Groups)

Adolf Hitler _____

Al Gore _____

Alger Hiss _____

Alliance for Progress _____

Archduke Ferdinand _____

Ashcan School _____

Barack Obama _____

Benito Mussolini _____

Betty Friedan _____

Bill Clinton _____

Black Panthers _____

Bolsheviks _____

Bull Moose Party _____

Calvin Coolidge _____

Charles Lindbergh _____

Chicago Seven _____

Committee to Re-elect the President (CREEP) _____

Congress of Industrial Organizations (CIO) _____

Congress of Racial Equality (CORE) _____

Dixiecrats _____

Dwight D. Eisenhower _____

Earl Warren _____

Ernest Hemingway _____

Ethel and Julius Rosenberg _____

Eugene McCarthy _____

F. Scott Fitzgerald _____

Fidel Castro _____

Flappers _____

Franklin Delano Roosevelt _____

Free Speech Movement, Berkeley _____

General Douglas MacArthur _____

George H. W. Bush _____

George W. Bush _____

Gerald Ford _____

Harry S. Truman _____

Henry Cabot Lodge _____

Henry Ford _____

Henry Kissinger _____

Herbert Hoover _____

Hideki Tojo _____

Ho Chi Minh _____

House Un-American Activities Committee (HUAC) _____

International Workers of the World _____

Jacob Riis _____

James Meredith _____

Jimmy Carter _____

John F. Kennedy _____

John Maynard Keynes _____

Joseph McCarthy _____

Little Rock Nine _____

Lyndon Johnson _____

Malcolm X _____

Marcus Garvey _____

Margaret Sanger _____

Martin Luther King Jr. _____

Monica Lewinsky _____

Muckrakers _____

NAACP _____

NASA _____

National Municipal League _____

National Organization for Women (NOW) _____

National Woman Suffrage Association _____

New Left _____

New Right _____

Nikita Khruschev _____

North Atlantic Treaty Organization (NATO) _____

Organization of American States _____

Organization of Petroleum Exporting Countries (OPEC) _____

Progressive Party/Movement _____

Richard Nixon _____

Robert Kennedy _____

Ronald Reagan _____

Sacco and Vanzetti _____

Saddam Hussein _____

Sandra Day O'Connor _____

Sinclair Lewis _____

Slobodan Milosevic _____

Southeast Asia Treaty Organization (SEATO) _____

Southern Christian Leadership Conference _____

Student Nonviolent Coordinating Committee _____

Students for a Democratic Society (SDS) _____

Theodore Roosevelt _____

Thurgood Marshall _____

United Nations _____

Upton Sinclair _____

The Urban League _____

Warren Burger _____

Warren G. Harding _____

William Howard Taft _____

William Rehnquist _____

Women's Trade Union League _____

Woodrow Wilson _____

The Wright brothers _____

Places

Bay of Pigs _____

Berlin Wall _____

Bosnia _____

Camp David _____

Gulf of Tonkin, Vietnam _____

Hiroshima _____

Kosovo _____

Kuwait _____

Little Rock, Arkansas _____

Los Alamos _____

Nagasaki _____

Pearl Harbor _____

Persian Gulf _____

Potsdam _____

Three Mile Island _____

Tin Pan Alley _____

Watergate _____

Yalta _____

Policies, Agreements, Supreme Court Decisions, Major Legislation, Government Agencies, Etc.

Abrams v. United States _____

Agricultural Adjustment Act _____

Atlantic Charter _____

Amendments to the Constitution:

Sixteenth Amendment _____

Seventeenth Amendment _____

Eighteenth Amendment _____

Nineteenth Amendment _____

Twenty-first Amendment _____

Baghdad Pact _____

Baker v. Carr _____

Brown v. Board of Education of Topeka _____

Camp David Accords _____

Central Intelligence Agency _____

Civil Rights Act of 1964 _____

Civilian Conservation Corps _____

Clayton Antitrust Act _____

Containment _____

Department of Housing and Urban Development _____

Eisenhower Doctrine _____

Elementary and Secondary Education Act and Higher Education Act

_____

Emergency Banking Relief Bill _____

Emergency Quota Act _____

Engel v. Vitale _____

Environmental Protection Agency (EPA) _____

Equal Rights Amendment _____

Escobedo v. Illinois _____

Espionage Act _____

Fair Deal _____

Fair Labor Standards Act _____

Federal Deposit Insurance Corporation _____

Federal Emergency Relief Act _____

Federal Highway Act _____

Federal Reserve Act _____

Federal Trade Commission Act _____

Fordney McCumber Act _____

Full Employment Act _____

Furman v. Georgia _____

Geneva Conference _____

Gideon v. Wainwright _____

Glass-Steagall Banking Act _____

Good Neighbor Policy _____

Great Society _____

Griswold v. Connecticut _____

Hawley-Smoot Tariff _____

Helsinki Accord _____

Kellogg-Briand Pact _____

Korematsu v. United States _____

Lend-Lease Act _____

Marshall Plan _____

McCarran Internal Security Act _____

McCarran-Walter Immigration and Nationality Act _____

Meat Inspection Act _____

Medicare and Medicaid _____

Miranda v. Arizona _____

Munich Agreement _____

NAFTA _____

National Defense Act _____

National Industrial Recovery Act _____

National Origins Act _____

National Security Council _____

National War Labor Board _____

NATO _____

Nazi-Soviet Pact _____

Neutrality Act _____

New York Times v. United States _____

Nixon Doctrine _____

Nixon v. United States _____

Northern Securities Co. v. United States _____

Office of Economic Opportunity _____

Panama Canal treaties _____

Peace Corps _____

Platt Amendment _____

Port Huron Statement _____

Project Apollo _____

Pure Food and Drug Act _____

Reconstruction Finance Corporation _____

Regents of University of California v. Bakke _____

Roe v. Wade _____

Roosevelt Corollary _____

SALT-II _____

Schecter Poultry Co. v. United States _____

Schenck v. United States _____

Securities and Exchange Commission _____

Sedition Act _____

Selective Service Act of 1917 _____

Selective Training and Service Act of 1940 _____

Servicemen's Readjustment Act (G.I. Bill) _____

Social Security Administration _____

Standard Oil Co. v. United States _____

Star Wars _____

Strategic Arms Limitation Treaty (SALT) _____

Taft-Hartley Act _____

Tennessee Valley Authority _____

Treaty of Versailles _____

Tripartite Pact _____

Truman Doctrine _____

United States v. Butler _____

Voice of America _____

Volstead Act _____

Voting Rights Act _____

Wagner Act/National Labor Relations Act _____

War Powers Resolution _____

Warsaw Pact _____

Washington Naval Conference _____

Works Progress Administration _____

Part V
Practice Tests

Chapter 15
Practice Test 1

AP® United States History Exam

SECTION I: Multiple-Choice Questions

DO NOT OPEN THIS BOOKLET UNTIL YOU ARE TOLD TO DO SO.

At a Glance

Total Time
55 minutes
Number of Questions
80
Percent of Total Grade
50%
Writing Instrument
Pencil required

Instructions

Section I of this exam contains 80 multiple-choice questions. Fill in only the ovals for numbers 1 through 80 on your answer sheet.

Indicate all of your answers to the multiple-choice questions on the answer sheet. No credit will be given for anything written in this exam booklet, but you may use the booklet for notes or scratch work. After you have decided which of the suggested answers is best, completely fill in the corresponding oval on the answer sheet. Give only one answer to each question. If you change an answer, be sure that the previous mark is erased completely. Here is a sample question and answer.

Sample Question   Sample Answer

The first president of the United States was   Ⓐ ● Ⓒ Ⓓ Ⓔ
(A) Millard Fillmore
(B) George Washington
(C) Benjamin Franklin
(D) Andrew Jackson
(E) Harry Truman

Use your time effectively, working as rapidly as you can without losing accuracy. Do not spend too much time on any one question. Go on to other questions and come back to the ones you have not answered if you have time. It is not expected that everyone will know the answers to all of the multiple-choice questions.

About Guessing

Many candidates wonder whether or not to guess the answers to questions about which they are not certain. Multiple-choice scores are based on the number of questions answered correctly. Points are not deducted for incorrect answers, and no points are awarded for unanswered questions. Because points are not deducted for incorrect answers, you are encouraged to answer all multiple-choice questions. On any questions you do not know the answer to, you should eliminate as many choices as you can, and then select the best answer among the remaining choices.

GO ON TO THE NEXT PAGE.

UNITED STATES HISTORY
SECTION I
Time—55 minutes

Directions: Each of the questions or incomplete statements below is followed by five suggested answers or completions. Select the one that is best in each case and then blacken the corresponding space on the answer sheet.

1. A major weakness of the Articles of Confederation was that they

   (A) created a too-powerful chief executive
   (B) did not include a mechanism for their own amendment
   (C) made it too difficult for the government to raise money through taxes and duties
   (D) denied the federal government the power to mediate disputes between states
   (E) required the ratification of only a simple majority of states

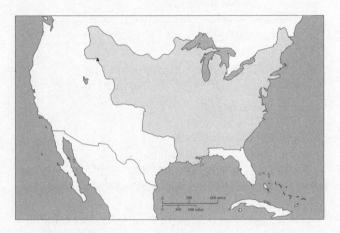

2. The shaded region on the map above shows the land held by the United States immediately following the

   (A) American Revolution
   (B) passage of the Northwest Ordinance
   (C) negotiation of the Treaty of Greenville
   (D) Louisiana Purchase
   (E) War of 1812

3. Manifest Destiny is the belief that

   (A) the colonists were destined to leave the British empire because of the distance between the New World and England
   (B) women are biologically predestined to lives of child rearing and domestic labor
   (C) America's expansion to the West Coast was inevitable and divinely sanctioned
   (D) the abolition of slavery in the United States was certain to come about, because slavery was immoral
   (E) American entry into World War I was unavoidable and was in America's long-term interests

4. In his opinion on the case *Dred Scott v. Sandford*, Chief Justice Roger Taney ruled that

   (A) the Supreme Court had the right to rule on the constitutionality of any federal law
   (B) "separate but equal" facilities for people of different races were constitutional
   (C) corporations were entitled to the same protections guaranteed individuals under the Fourteenth Amendment
   (D) school prayer violated the principle of "separation of church and state"
   (E) Congress had no right to regulate slavery in United States territories

GO ON TO THE NEXT PAGE.

5. Following the Civil War, most freed slaves

   (A) stayed in the South and worked as sharecroppers
   (B) joined the pioneering movement as it headed West
   (C) moved to the North to work in factories
   (D) took work building the nation's growing railroad system
   (E) moved to Liberia with the aid of the American Colonization Society

6. All of the following policies pursued by President Theodore Roosevelt were main objectives of the American Progressives EXCEPT

   (A) passage of the Pure Food and Drug Act
   (B) creation of national forests and protected wildlife reserves
   (C) initiation of antitrust lawsuits against various corporate monopolies
   (D) intervention in the affairs of Central American governments
   (E) expansion of the power of the Interstate Commerce Commission

7. Which of the following statements about the Treaty of Versailles is true?

   (A) The United States Senate rejected it because it treated Germany too leniently.
   (B) The United States Senate rejected it because it required increased American involvement in European affairs.
   (C) The United States Senate approved it, with reservations concerning the division of Eastern Europe.
   (D) The United States Senate approved it without reservations.
   (E) It was never voted on by the United States Senate.

8. The 1956 boycott of the Montgomery bus system

   (A) was led by Malcolm X
   (B) started because the city doubled bus fares
   (C) was instigated by the arrest of Rosa Parks
   (D) lasted for three weeks and failed to achieve its goal
   (E) resulted from the assassination of Martin Luther King Jr.

9. Senator Joseph McCarthy gained national prominence with his accusation that

   (A) American meat packers disregarded fundamental rules of sanitation
   (B) the Federal Bureau of Investigation was violating many innocent citizens' right to privacy
   (C) some congressmen were taking bribes in return for pro-business votes
   (D) massive voter fraud was common throughout the Southwest
   (E) the State Department had been infiltrated by communist spies

10. The Puritans believed that the freedom to practice religion should be extended to

    (A) Puritans only
    (B) all Protestants only
    (C) all Christians only
    (D) all Jews and Christians only
    (E) all inhabitants of the New World, including Africans and Native Americans

11. The Sugar Act of 1764 represented a major shift in British policy toward the colonies in that, for the first time, the British

    (A) allowed all proceeds from a tax to stay in the colonial economy
    (B) attempted to control colonial exports
    (C) offered the colonists the opportunity to address Parliament with grievances
    (D) required the colonies to import English goods exclusively
    (E) levied taxes aimed at raising revenue rather than regulating trade

GO ON TO THE NEXT PAGE.

12. In response to several unfavorable Supreme Court rulings concerning New Deal programs, Franklin Roosevelt

    (A) urged the voting public to write letters of protest to Supreme Court justices
    (B) submitted four separate Constitutional amendments broadening the powers of the presidency
    (C) abandoned the New Deal and replaced it with a laissez-faire policy
    (D) instructed both the legislative and executive branches to ignore the rulings
    (E) proposed legislation that would allow him to appoint new federal and Supreme Court judges

13. The Know-Nothing Party focused its efforts almost exclusively on the issue of

    (A) religious freedom
    (B) the right to bear arms
    (C) the prohibition of alcohol
    (D) women's rights
    (E) immigration

14. The "new immigrants" who arrived in the United States after the Civil War were different from the "old immigrants" in that they

    (A) came mostly from Latin American countries
    (B) settled in rural areas in the Midwest where land was plentiful
    (C) were better prepared than previous immigrants had been to face the challenges of urban life
    (D) spoke different languages and had different customs than most Americans and thus were not easily assimilated
    (E) came from Asia rather than Europe

15. The "Ghost Dance" movement among Western Native Americans stressed all of the following EXCEPT

    (A) the belief that the world would soon come to an end
    (B) rejection of alcohol and other trappings of white society
    (C) unity among Native Americans of different tribes
    (D) nonviolence
    (E) the use of magic to neutralize the effectiveness of whites' weaponry

16. The Industrial Revolution had which of the following effects on slavery in the South?

    (A) The creation of numerous labor-saving machines vastly reduced the need for slave labor.
    (B) Rapid growth in the textile industry encouraged Southern planters to grow cotton, thereby making slavery more important to the economy.
    (C) The government bought and freed Southern slaves, then transported them to the North, where factories were experiencing a major labor shortage.
    (D) The Industrial Revolution began as the Civil War was ending and it provided work for many former slaves.
    (E) New farm machinery required slaves and masters to work more closely together, with a resulting reduction of mutual hostility.

GO ON TO THE NEXT PAGE.

STRIKE-BREAKING

UNION-BUSTING

FACT-FINDING

Strike-Breaking

17. The 1933 political cartoon shown above makes the point that

(A) infighting within and among unions prevented their rise to economic power
(B) government inspectors turned their backs to illegal repression of labor unions
(C) attacks on unions were so well concealed that the government did not know where to begin its investigations
(D) from their beginnings, labor unions were controlled by organized crime
(E) the government moved too hastily in investigating misbehavior in labor unions

18. In which decision did the Supreme Court invalidate the practice of "separate but equal" facilities for blacks and whites?

(A) *Marbury v. Madison*
(B) *Bradwell v. Illinois*
(C) *Plessy v. Ferguson*
(D) *Brown v. Board of Education of Topeka, Kansas*
(E) *Holden v. Hardy*

19. The Bay of Pigs invasion of Cuba, in 1961, was carried out by

(A) Caribbean mercenaries hired by the United States
(B) American soldiers
(C) the Soviet navy
(D) Cuban exiles trained by the Central Intelligence Agency
(E) Cuban Communist rebels led by Fidel Castro

20. Roger Williams was banished from Massachusetts Bay in 1636 for advocating

(A) the separation of church and state
(B) women's suffrage
(C) bigamy
(D) the export of tobacco
(E) independence from England

21. All of the following influenced the United States' decision to declare war against Great Britain in 1812 EXCEPT

(A) the impressment of American sailors
(B) British control of the Atlantic and resulting interference in United States trade with Europe
(C) the American government's certainty that its navy was more powerful than Great Britain's
(D) Great Britain's alliances with American Indian tribes, which curtailed United States westward expansion
(E) the failure of the Embargo Act

22. The Missouri Compromise can be described by all of the following EXCEPT

(A) It provided a method for counting slaves among state populations when determining the size of the states' congressional delegations.
(B) It allowed Missouri to be admitted to the Union as a slave state.
(C) It created the free state of Maine from territory that belonged to Massachusetts.
(D) One of its purposes was to maintain the equal representation of free states and slave states in the Senate.
(E) It included a northern border in the Louisiana Territory above which slavery was thereafter prohibited.

GO ON TO THE NEXT PAGE.

23. Between 1820 and 1854, the greatest number of immigrants to the United States came from

   (A) France
   (B) Russia
   (C) Spain
   (D) England
   (E) Ireland

24. Congress brought impeachment proceedings against Andrew Johnson primarily because

   (A) Johnson sought to block the punitive aspects of Congressional Reconstruction
   (B) Johnson's Republican policies had fallen out of favor with the Democratic majority
   (C) the Johnson administration was riddled with corruption
   (D) Johnson's pro-North bias was delaying the readmission of Southern states to the Union
   (E) many congressmen personally disliked Johnson, although they agreed with his policies

25. The Open Door Policy in 1899 primarily concerned

   (A) independence movements in Africa
   (B) Mexican immigration to the United States
   (C) the removal of trade tariffs from United States–European trade
   (D) trade with China
   (E) the United States' colonies in Central America

26. Which of the following was NOT a major contributing factor to the onset of the Great Depression?

   (A) Technological advances had allowed farmers and manufacturers to overproduce, creating large inventories.
   (B) The federal government interfered too frequently with the economy, causing investors to lose confidence.
   (C) The average wage earner was not earning enough money to afford the many consumer goods new technology had made available.
   (D) Stock investors had been allowed to speculate wildly, creating an unstable and volatile stock market.
   (E) Major businesses were controlled by so few producers that the failure of any one had a considerable effect on the national economy.

27. The Truman Doctrine declared the government's commitment to assist

   (A) Japanese families affected by the atomic bomb blasts in Hiroshima and Nagasaki
   (B) any nation facing widespread poverty as a result of World War II
   (C) free nations in danger of takeover by repressive governments, especially Soviet-style communism
   (D) American farmers, who suffered through major price drops after World War II ended
   (E) American families who could not afford to build homes without government aid

28. The United States' primary reason for participating in the war in Vietnam was

   (A) to fight under the terms of its military alliance with Japan
   (B) to provide military aid and assistance to Vietnamese leader Ho Chi Minh
   (C) to promote Asian autonomy and anticolonialism
   (D) because American foreign policy experts believed that, without intervention, communism would spread from Vietnam throughout Southeast Asia
   (E) because the government felt obliged to protect the Unites States' considerable business interests in Vietnam

29. The First Great Awakening was a direct response to

   (A) Puritanism
   (B) The Enlightenment
   (C) Transcendentalism
   (D) Existentialism
   (E) Postmodernism

GO ON TO THE NEXT PAGE.

"Society everywhere is in conspiracy against the manhood of every one of its members…. The virtue in most request is conformity. Self-reliance is its aversion."

30. The passage above was written by

(A) Ralph Waldo Emerson
(B) Jonathan Edwards
(C) Harriet Beecher Stowe
(D) Charles G. Finney
(E) Andrew Carnegie

31. The Free-Soil party advocated which of the following?

(A) The freedom of settlers within the territories to determine the slave status of their new state
(B) Passage of the Homestead Act to give free land to all Western settlers
(C) The exclusion of slavery from any of the new territories
(D) The policy of giving newly-freed slaves "40 acres and a mule" following the Civil War
(E) The destruction of the sharecropping system

32. Which of the following states the principle of "virtual representation," as it was argued during the eighteenth century?

(A) Paper money has value even though it is inherently worth very little.
(B) Slave populations must be counted when figuring congressional apportionment, even though slaves may not vote.
(C) American property-holding colonists may, if they so desire, join their state legislatures.
(D) All English subjects, including those who are not allowed to vote, are represented in Parliament.
(E) All English subjects are entitled to a trial before a jury of their peers.

33. By the first decade of the nineteenth century, American manufacturing had been revolutionized by the advent of

(A) interchangeable machine parts
(B) the electric engine
(C) transcontinental railroads
(D) labor unions
(E) mail-order catalogues

34. The principle of popular sovereignty stated that

(A) whenever a new area was settled, all United States citizens were required to vote on the slave status of that area
(B) slavery would not be permitted in any area after 1848
(C) the president, after meeting with public interest groups, was to decide on whether slaves would be allowed in a given territory
(D) settlers in the Western territories, not Congress, would decide whether to allow slavery in their territory
(E) any settlers disagreeing with federal laws governing slavery were free to ignore those laws

35. Which of the following is NOT a requirement set by the Reconstruction Act of 1867 for Southern states' readmission to the Union?

(A) Blacks had to be allowed to participate in state conventions and state elections.
(B) The state had to ratify the Fourteenth Amendment to the Constitution.
(C) The state had to pay reparations and provide land grants to all former slaves.
(D) The state had to rewrite its constitution and ratify it.
(E) Congress had to approve the new state constitution.

36. Which of the following is true of the American rail system in the nineteenth century?

(A) Government subsidies and land grants played a major role in its expansion.
(B) The entire national system was planned before the first railway was constructed.
(C) Transcontinental rail travel was not possible at any time during the century.
(D) The development of the rails had little effect on the development of American industry.
(E) A more highly developed rail system gave the Confederacy a decided advantage in the Civil War.

GO ON TO THE NEXT PAGE.

**Percent of U.S. immigration
total per decade, by nationality**

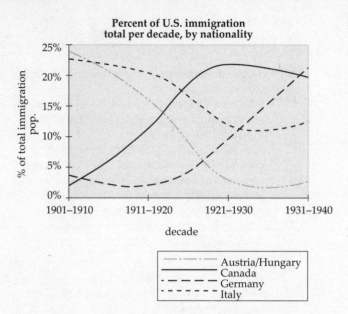

Austria/Hungary
Canada
Germany
Italy

37. Which of the following best explains the changes in immigration patterns reflected in the chart above?

(A) The Depression resulted in a massive wave of Canadian emigration.

(B) After World War I ended, the Austrian and Hungarian economies improved.

(C) Between 1920 and 1930, Congress passed immigration restrictions that discriminated against southern and eastern Europeans.

(D) During the years represented on the chart, relations between the United States and Germany improved greatly.

(E) Between the years 1900 and 1910, the Italian government instituted a number of measures restricting emigration.

38. All of the following contributed to the spirit of isolationism in the United States during the 1930s EXCEPT

(A) disclosures that munitions manufacturers had lobbied for American involvement in World War I, then profited heavily from the war

(B) a foreign policy tradition that could be traced to Washington's Farewell Address

(C) a universal lack of awareness of the goals of the Third Reich

(D) memories of the cost, both in financial terms and in human life, of participation in World War I

(E) the desire to focus resources on recovery from the Depression rather than on strengthening the military

39. Jack Kerouac's *On the Road* and *The Dharma Bums* articulated the ideals of

(A) the silent majority

(B) the "lost generation"

(C) Middle America

(D) the Beat generation

(E) conservative academics

40. Legislation and executive orders associated with the Great Society created all of the following EXCEPT

(A) the Works Progress Administration

(B) the Equal Employment Opportunity Commission

(C) Medicare

(D) the Department of Housing and Urban Development

(E) Project Head Start

41. Which of the following most accurately describes the system of indentured service in the Chesapeake settlement during the seventeenth century?

(A) Indentured servants were slaves for life; however, their children were born free and could own property.

(B) Most indentured servants were lured by the promise of freedom and property upon completion of their service.

(C) Most indentured servants were convicted criminals sentenced to servitude in the New World.

(D) The vast majority of indentured servants died within two years of arriving in the New World.

(E) Indentured servants were not protected under colonial law.

GO ON TO THE NEXT PAGE.

42. The Northwest Ordinance of 1787 was a significant achievement because it

    (A) laid claim to all of North America east of the Mississippi River
    (B) represented one of the rare successes of diplomacy between the United States government and American Indians
    (C) defined the process by which territories could become states
    (D) opened all territories west of the states to slavery
    (E) was the only piece of legislation to pass through Congress under the Articles of Confederation

43. The rapid growth of American towns in the 1920s and 1930s was made possible primarily by the

    (A) invention of the steam locomotive
    (B) greater access to information provided by radio and television
    (C) mass production of automobiles
    (D) end of open-range cattle ranching
    (E) advent of electric lighting

44. Reform movements during the first half of the nineteenth century attempted to accomplish all of the following EXCEPT

    (A) convince people not to drink alcohol
    (B) widen the division between church and state
    (C) rehabilitate criminals
    (D) induce humane treatment for the insane
    (E) bring about an end to slavery

"The price which society pays for the law of competition…is great; but the advantages of this law are also greater…. [W]hether the law be benign or not, we must say of it: It is here; we cannot evade it;…it is best for the race, because it ensures the survival of the fittest in every department."

45. The above passage is characteristic of

    (A) Calvinism
    (B) Social Darwinism
    (C) Progressivism
    (D) cultural pluralism
    (E) egalitarianism

46. The United States army supported Panama's 1903 war of independence against Colombia primarily because

    (A) the United States was sympathetic to the rebels' democratic ideals
    (B) the Monroe Doctrine required the United States to support all wars of independence in the Western Hemisphere
    (C) Colombia was asking too high a price for control of the projected Atlantic-Pacific canal
    (D) the success of Panama's rebellion would have lowered sugar prices in the United States considerably
    (E) the Colombian government was guilty of numerous human rights violations in Panama

47. All of the following were elements of Henry Clay's American System EXCEPT

    (A) protective tariffs on imports
    (B) the establishment of the Second Bank of the United States
    (C) the construction of the National Road and other roadways
    (D) the creation of large numbers of federal jobs in areas with unemployment problems
    (E) incentives to develop manufacturing and interstate trade

48. Which of the following is true about the internment of those Japanese living in the United States during World War II?

    (A) The majority of those confined were native-born Americans.
    (B) Many of those relocated were known dissidents.
    (C) Only 2,000 Japanese Americans were relocated.
    (D) Congress passed a law requiring the relocation of all aliens during the war.
    (E) Those who were relocated eventually recovered their homes and possessions.

GO ON TO THE NEXT PAGE.

49. Anglo-American women in colonial times

    (A) could own property or execute legal documents only if they were widowed or unmarried
    (B) enjoyed more liberties and rights than did Native American women
    (C) attended church less frequently than did Anglo-American men
    (D) were more likely than men to do agricultural work
    (E) were required by law to learn to read and write, in order to teach their children

50. In the seventeenth century the Chesapeake Bay settlement expanded its territorial holdings more quickly than did the Massachusetts Bay settlement primarily because

    (A) Massachusetts settlers were entirely uninterested in expansion
    (B) a high birthrate and healthy environment resulted in a population boom in the Chesapeake region
    (C) no Native Americans lived in the Chesapeake Bay area, and the colonists were free to expand their settlements at will
    (D) farmland in the Chesapeake area was less fertile, and so more of it was needed to support sustenance farming
    (E) farming of the chief Chesapeake export, tobacco, required a great deal of land

51. The debate over the First Bank of the United States was significant because it raised the issue of

    (A) whether the new government should issue paper currency
    (B) how strictly the Constitution should be interpreted
    (C) whether the United States should pay back its war debt to France
    (D) how to finance the construction of the railroads
    (E) whether the president had the power to act unilaterally on important economic issues

52. The Lowell System of early nineteenth-century textile manufacturing was noteworthy for its

    (A) practice of hiring only adult males at a time when textiles was considered "women's work"
    (B) commitment, in the face of the Industrial Revolution, to maintaining the old, "by-hand" method of manufacture
    (C) efforts to minimize the dehumanizing effects of industrial labor
    (D) pioneering advocacy of such issues as parental leave, vacation time, and health insurance for employees
    (E) particularly harsh treatment of employees

53. The election of 1824 marked a turning point in presidential politics because, for the first time,

    (A) the presidency was won by someone who was not a member of the Federalist Party
    (B) a presidential and vice-presidential candidate ran together on one ticket
    (C) all the candidates campaigned widely throughout the states
    (D) political parties officially participated in the election
    (E) the system of choosing nominees by congressional caucus failed

54. In the late nineteenth century, political machines such as Tammany Hall were successful primarily because

    (A) federal legislation sanctioned their activities
    (B) they operated primarily in rural areas, where the government could not monitor their activities
    (C) they focused on accomplishing only a narrow set of human rights objectives
    (D) they championed the suffragettes and received their support in return
    (E) machine politicians provided needed jobs and services to naturalized citizens in return for their votes

GO ON TO THE NEXT PAGE.

55. The disagreement between W. E. B. Du Bois and Booker T. Washington regarding the status of African-Americans in the early twentieth century is best summed up as a debate over

    (A) what social injustices federal legislation should correct first
    (B) whether African-Americans should emigrate to Africa
    (C) whether state governments or the federal government should be the primary vehicle of social change
    (D) how prominent a role African-American churches should play in the struggle for civil rights
    (E) whether African-Americans should first seek legal or economic equality with white Americans

56. One of the unintended effects of Prohibition was that it

    (A) caused a national epidemic of alcohol withdrawal
    (B) brought about a decrease in alcoholism and an increase in worker productivity
    (C) resulted in a substantial increase in the abuse of hard drugs, particularly heroin
    (D) lowered the cost of law enforcement by decreasing the incidence of drunkenness
    (E) provided organized crime syndicates with a means to gain both wealth and power

57. The 1927 motion picture *The Jazz Singer* was the first major commercial film to feature

    (A) color images
    (B) the illusion of three dimensions
    (C) synchronous sound
    (D) special effects
    (E) a dramatic plot

58. Which of the following was LEAST likely a factor in the decision to drop atomic bombs on Hiroshima and Nagasaki?

    (A) Hope that a quick victory in the Pacific would hasten an Allied victory in Europe
    (B) Fear that the Soviet Union would soon enter the war with Japan
    (C) Concern that a land war in Japan would result in massive American casualties
    (D) Awareness that Japanese forces were numerous and spread throughout Asia
    (E) Desire to demonstrate to other world powers the potency of America's new weapon

59. The failed Equal Rights Amendment to the Constitution was intended to prevent discrimination against

    (A) African-Americans
    (B) Native Americans
    (C) children and adolescents
    (D) legal immigrants
    (E) women

60. Which of the following statements about the Stamp Act is NOT true?

    (A) Because it most affected lawyers and writers, the Stamp Act fostered a particularly eloquent opposition to the Crown.
    (B) Colonial legislatures sent letters of protest to Parliament threatening secession from England if the Stamp Act was not repealed.
    (C) Opposition to the Stamp Act built upon colonial resentment of the Sugar and Currency Acts.
    (D) Among the colonists' reactions to the Stamp Act was an effective boycott of British goods.
    (E) According to the Stamp Act, those who violated the law were not entitled to a jury trial.

61. The doctrine of nullification stated that

    (A) legal immigrants may be deported when they fall into a state of destitution
    (B) Congress may override an executive order with a two-thirds majority vote
    (C) the government may take control of a bank if its cash reserves fall below a certain percentage of its total deposits
    (D) municipal and county governments may rescind licenses granted by the state
    (E) a state may repeal any federal law that it deems unconstitutional

GO ON TO THE NEXT PAGE.

62. Alexis de Tocqueville attributed American social mobility to

    (A) the continuation of European traditions in the New World
    (B) Americans' rights to speak freely and to bear arms
    (C) the government's tolerance of labor unions and progressive organizations
    (D) the lack of an aristocracy and the availability of frontier land
    (E) mandatory public education

63. Which of the following changes in westward migration occurred in 1848?

    (A) The number of pioneers headed for the Oregon territory decreased while the number headed for California greatly increased.
    (B) The first great wave of migration ended, and the number of migrants remained extremely low until after the Civil War.
    (C) For the first time, pioneers began to settle areas west of the Mississippi River.
    (D) Large numbers of free blacks, unwelcome in the East, began to resettle in the West.
    (E) The government began to enforce quotas limiting the number of people who could migrate each year.

64. The free silver campaign of 1896 received its greatest popular support from

    (A) New England businessmen, who were discriminated against under the existing banking system
    (B) Southern women, who incorporated it into a larger campaign for economic equality
    (C) bankers, who had run out of paper currency to invest
    (D) gold miners, who stood to profit from the movement's success
    (E) farmers, who hoped that a more generous money supply would ease their debt burdens

65. The United States took control of the Philippines in 1898

    (A) by purchasing it from China
    (B) as a result of the Spanish-American War
    (C) after conquering the autonomous Philippine government
    (D) when Japan exchanged it for a promise of non-aggression
    (E) as the leader of a multinational coalition called in to suppress a revolution there

"Free speech would not protect a man falsely shouting fire in a theater and causing panic."

66. The excerpt above is from a 1919 Supreme Court ruling prohibiting speech that represented a "clear and present danger." The defendant in the case had

    (A) given a speech urging black residents of Chicago to demand equal rights
    (B) written a magazine article in support of the Russian revolution
    (C) sent letters to military draftees arguing that conscription was illegal
    (D) given a speech suggesting that Texas should be returned to Mexico
    (E) posted fliers denouncing a department store in St. Louis

GO ON TO THE NEXT PAGE.

Percent of U.S. population completing high school and college

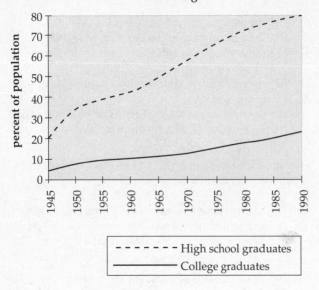

67. Which of the following best accounts for the trend illustrated in the chart above?

    (A) Increased affluence beginning in the postwar era allowed people the opportunity to stay in school longer.
    (B) The Supreme Court decision *Brown v. the Board of Education* led to increased enrollment in colleges and universities.
    (C) During the 1960s, increasing numbers of high school graduates rejected the notion that a college education was desirable.
    (D) The first state passed a compulsory education law in 1946, and others quickly followed.
    (E) Jobs in advanced technical and medical industries generally require postgraduate degrees.

68. The 1968 George Wallace presidential campaign on the American Independence ticket probably helped Richard Nixon win the election because

    (A) Wallace's racism directed voters' attention away from the Watergate scandal
    (B) Wallace won several traditionally Democratic Southern states
    (C) Wallace's participation sent the election to the House of Representatives, where Nixon was more popular
    (D) in the final week, Wallace withdrew from the race and threw his support to Nixon
    (E) Wallace and Humphrey, the Democratic candidate, held similar views on all the major issues

69. The English colonists who settled Virginia and the neighboring Indian tribes had widely different attitudes about all of the following subjects EXCEPT

    (A) whether property could be privately owned
    (B) what type of work was appropriate for men and women
    (C) the superiority of English society over Indian culture
    (D) the centrality of religion in daily life
    (E) the means by which leaders should receive and exercise power

70. Puritan emigration from England came to a near-halt between the years 1649 and 1660 because, during that period,

    (A) most English Puritans were imprisoned for heresy
    (B) most Puritans converted to Catholicism
    (C) the New England settlement had become too overcrowded, and colonial legislatures strongly discouraged immigration
    (D) the Puritans controlled the English government
    (E) Parliament outlawed travel to the New World

71. The Monroe Doctrine stated that the United States had legitimate reason to fear European intervention in the Western Hemisphere because

    (A) Europe's militaries were considerably more powerful than those of the United States
    (B) the overpopulation of Europe made future incursions in the New World a real possibility
    (C) Europe's forms of government were fundamentally different from those of the United States and newly liberated South American countries
    (D) the United States anticipated reprisals for its frequent interference in European affairs
    (E) the United States ultimately intended to annex all of the Western Hemisphere

GO ON TO THE NEXT PAGE.

72. Supreme Court decisions concerning Native Americans in 1831 and 1832

    (A) reinforced the rights of states to remove Native Americans from disputed lands
    (B) denied them the right to sue in federal court but affirmed their rights to land that was traditionally theirs
    (C) voided previous treaties between Native Americans and the United States on the grounds that the treaties were unfair
    (D) granted tribes official status as foreign nations
    (E) ruled that the federal government had a unilateral right to relocate Native Americans to lands west of the Mississippi

73. In the 1830s, Southern states passed a number of laws regarding the behavior of free blacks. These laws were intended to

    (A) encourage free blacks to migrate to the North
    (B) impose a uniform procedure regarding the retrieval of fugitive slaves
    (C) increase the pool of available black skilled laborers in the growing Southern economy
    (D) guarantee the rights of free blacks traveling through slave states
    (E) create an official set of guidelines concerning "acceptable" treatment of slaves

74. By what means did the United States take possession of the Oregon Territory?

    (A) The United States was granted the territory in a postwar treaty with France.
    (B) The United States bought it from the Native Americans who lived there.
    (C) U.S. settlers were the first to arrive in the region; they claimed it for their country.
    (D) Great Britain ceded it to the United States as part of a negotiated treaty.
    (E) The French sold it to the United States as part of the Louisiana Purchase.

75. Which of the following was the intended result of the Dawes Severalty Act of 1887?

    (A) Railroad companies would be persuaded to stop unfair pricing through a number of government incentives.
    (B) Recently arrived European immigrants would be enticed into settling in the less populated West.
    (C) Legislators would be less likely to accept bribes because of the severity of the penalty.
    (D) Southern state legislatures would be motivated to strike racist laws from their books in return for greater federal aid.
    (E) Native Americans would be coaxed off reservations by land grants and would thus assimilate into Western culture.

76. During the decade following passage of the Sherman Antitrust Act, most courts applied the rule to break up

    (A) railroad monopolies
    (B) utility companies
    (C) telegraph cartels
    (D) labor unions
    (E) political machines

77. The term "welfare capitalism" refers to the corporate practice of

    (A) providing social services for the unemployed poor who live near a factory
    (B) offering workers incentives, such as pensions and profit sharing, to dissuade them from joining unions
    (C) marketing only to those potential customers who earn considerably below the national average wage
    (D) raising prices in stores whenever AFDC checks are sent
    (E) selling inventories to the government at highly inflated prices

GO ON TO THE NEXT PAGE.

78. The Underwood-Simmons Tariff of 1913 was endorsed by

    (A) opponents of Teddy Roosevelt's Square Deal
    (B) most Democrats who advocated lower duties
    (C) supporters of Teddy Roosevelt's New Nationalism
    (D) opponents of Woodrow Wilson
    (E) conservative Democrats who advocated high protective tariffs

79. The Agricultural Adjustment Act of 1933 sought to lessen the effects of the Depression by

    (A) paying farmers to cut production and, in some cases, destroy crops
    (B) purchasing farms and turning them into government collectives
    (C) instituting an early retirement program for farmers over the age of 50
    (D) encouraging farmers to increase production
    (E) subsidizing food processing plants in order to lower food prices

80. During the 1960s, the Student Nonviolent Coordinating Committee (SNCC) shifted its political agenda in which of the following ways?

    (A) Although it started as an anti-war organization, by the mid-1960s the SNCC was solely pursuing a civil rights agenda.
    (B) The SNCC, initially a Christian organization, officially allied itself with the Nation of Islam in 1963.
    (C) Although initially integrationist, by 1966 the SNCC advocated black separatism.
    (D) The SNCC originally concerned itself exclusively with political issues on college campuses; over the years, the organization broadened its agenda.
    (E) The SNCC initially sought to achieve its goals through litigation; later, it pursued its agenda through peaceful demonstrations.

END OF SECTION I

UNITED STATES HISTORY
SECTION II
Total time—130 minutes

Part A: Document-Based Essay Question

(Suggested writing time— 45 minutes. This question counts for 45 percent of the total essay section score.)

Directions: The following question requires you to construct a coherent essay that integrates your interpretation of Documents A–I and your knowledge of the period referred to in the question. High scores will be earned only by essays that both cite key pieces of evidence from the documents and draw on outside knowledge of the period.

1. When World War I broke out, the United States declared its policy of neutrality. To what extent did the United States follow a policy of neutrality between 1914 and 1917?

    Use the documents and your knowledge of the era to construct your response.

Document A

Source: President Woodrow Wilson, message to Congress (August 19, 1914)

The effect of the war upon the United States will depend upon what American citizens say and do. Every man who really loves America will act and speak in the true spirit of neutrality, which is the spirit of impartiality and fairness and friendliness to all concerned.

The people of the United States are drawn from many nations, and chiefly from the nations now at war. It is natural and inevitable that there should be the utmost variety of sympathy and desire among them with regard to the issues and circumstances of the conflict.

Such divisions amongst us would be fatal to our peace of mind and might seriously stand in the way of the proper performance of our duty as the one great nation at peace, the one people holding itself ready to play a part of impartial mediation and speak the counsels of peace and accommodation, not as a partisan, but as a friend.

GO ON TO THE NEXT PAGE.

Document B

Source: Hugo Munsterberg, Harvard University professor, letter to Woodrow Wilson (November 19, 1914)

Dear Mr. President:

[I] ask your permission to enter into some detail with regard to the neutrality question. But let me assure you beforehand that I interpret your inquiry as referring exclusively to the views which are expressed to me by American citizens who sympathize with the German cause or who are disturbed by the vehement hostility to Germany on the part of the American press. My remarks refer in no way to the views of official Germany…

First, all cables sent by and received by wire pass uncensored, while all wireless news is censored. This reacts against Germany, because England sends all her news by cable, whereas Germany alone uses the wireless…

Second, the policy of the administration with regard to the holding up, detaining and searching of Germans and Austrians from neutral and American vessels is a reversal of the American policy established in 1812. It has excited no end of bitterness.

Third, the United States permitted the violation by England of the Hague Convention and international law in connection with conditional and unconditional contraband.… [O]n former occasions the United States has taken a spirited stand against one-sided interpretations of international agreements. The United States, moreover, [previously] insisted that conditional contraband can be sent in neutral or in American [ships] even to belligerent nations, provided it was not consigned to the government, the military or naval authorities… By permitting this new interpretation the United States practically supports the starving out policy of the Allies [and seriously handicapping] Germany and Austria in their fight for existence…

Many of the complaints refer more to the unfriendly spirit than to the actual violation of the law. Here above all belongs the unlimited sale of ammunition to the belligerents…

Document C

Source: Robert Lansing, *War Memoirs* (1935)

The author was acting secretary of state during the period described below.

The British authorities…proceeded with their policy [of blockading American ships headed for mainland Europe] regardless of protests and complaints. Neutral ships were intercepted and, without being boarded or examined at sea, sent to a British port, where their cargoes were examined after delays, which not infrequently lasted for weeks. Even a vessel which was finally permitted to proceed on her voyage was often detained so long a time that the profits to the owners or charterers were eaten up by the additional expenses of lying in port and by the loss of the use of the vessels during the period of detention.

GO ON TO THE NEXT PAGE.

Document D

Source: Secretary of State William Jennings Bryan, letter to the Chairman of the Senate Committee on Foreign Relations (January 20, 1915)

Dear Mr. Stone:

I have received your letter…referring to frequent complaints or charges made…that this Government has shown partiality to Great Britain, France, and Russia against Germany and Austria during the present war… I will take them up…

(1) Freedom of communication by submarine cables versus censored communication by wireless.

The reason that wireless messages and cable messages require different treatment by a neutral government is as follows: Communications by wireless can not be interrupted by a belligerent. With a submarine cable it is otherwise. The possibility of cutting the cable exists… Since a cable is subject to hostile attack, the responsibility falls upon the belligerent and not upon the neutral to prevent cable communication.

A more important reason, however, at least from the point of view of a neutral government is that messages sent out from a wireless station in neutral territory may be received by belligerent warships on the high seas. If these messages…direct the movements of warships…the neutral territory becomes a base of naval operations, to permit which would be essentially unneutral.

(4) Submission without protest to British violations of the rules regarding absolute and conditional contraband as laid down in the Hague conventions, the Declaration of London, and international law.

There is no Hague convention which deals with absolute or conditional contraband, and, as the Declaration of London is not in force, the rules of international law only apply. As to the articles to be regarded as contraband, there is no general agreement between nations…

The United States has made earnest representations to Great Britain in regard to the seizure and detention by the British authorities of all American ships… It will be recalled, however, that American courts have established various rules bearing on these matters.

(9) The United States has not interfered with the sale to Great Britain and her allies of arms, ammunition, horses, uniforms, and other munitions of war, although such sales prolong the conflict.

There is no power in the Executive to prevent the sale of ammunition to the belligerents.

The duty of a neutral to restrict trade in munitions of war has never been imposed by international law…

(20) General unfriendly attitude of Government toward Germany and Austria. If any American citizens, partisans of Germany and Austria-Hungary, feel that this administration is acting in a way injurious to the cause of those countries, this feeling results from the fact that on the high seas the German and Austro-Hungarian naval power is thus far inferior to the British. It is the business of a belligerent operating on the high seas, not the duty of a neutral, to prevent contraband from reaching an enemy…

I am [etc.]

W.J. Bryan

GO ON TO THE NEXT PAGE.

Document E

Source: *New York Times*, notice (May 1, 1915)

NOTICE!

TRAVELLERS intending to embark on the Atlantic voyage are reminded that a state of war exists between Germany and her allies; that the zone of her waters includes the waters adjacent to the British Isles; that, in accordance with formal notice given by the Imperial German Government, vessels flying the flag of Great Britain, or of any of her allies, are liable to destruction in those waters and that travellers sailing in the war zone on ships of Great Britain or her allies do so at their own risk.

IMPERIAL GERMAN EMBASSY

Document F

Source: Report from the American Customs Inspector in New York (1915)

Q: Did the *Lusitania* have on board on said trip 5400 cases of ammunition? If so, to whom were they consigned?

A: The *Lusitania* had on board, on said trip, 5468 cases of ammunition. The Remington Arms-Union Metallic Cartridge Co. shipped 4200 cases of metallic cartridges, consigned to the Remington Arms Co., London, of which the ultimate consignee was the British Government. G. W. Sheldon & Co. shipped three lots of fuses of 6 cases each, and 1250 cases of shrapnel, consigned to the Deputy Director of Ammunition Stores, Woolwich, England.

GO ON TO THE NEXT PAGE.

Document G

Source: Woodrow Wilson, speech to Congress (March 24, 1916)

…I have deemed it my duty, therefore, to say to the Imperial German Government, that if it is still its purpose to prosecute relentless and indiscriminate warfare against vessels of commerce by the use of submarines, notwithstanding the now demonstrated impossibility of conducting that warfare in accordance with what the Government of the United States must consider the sacred and indisputable rules of international law and the universally recognized dictates of humanity, the Government of the United States is at last forced to the conclusion that there is but one course it can pursue; and that unless the Imperial German Government should now immediately declare and effect an abandonment of its present methods of warfare against passenger and freight carrying vessels, this Government can have no choice but to sever diplomatic relations with the Government of the German Empire altogether.

This decision I have arrived at with the keenest regret; the possibility of the action contemplated I am sure all thoughtful Americans will look forward to with unaffected reluctance. But we cannot forget that we are in some sort and by the force of circumstances the responsible spokesmen of the rights of humanity, and that we cannot remain silent while those rights seem in process of being swept utterly away in the maelstrom of this terrible war. We owe it to a due regard to our own rights as a nation, to our sense of duty as a representative of the rights of neutrals the world over, and to a just conception of the rights of mankind to take this stand now with the utmost solemnity and firmness…

Document H

Source: Arthur Zimmerman, confidential telegram to German Ambassador Johann von Bernstoff (January 1917)

On the first of February we intend to begin unrestricted submarine warfare. In spite of this, it is our intention to endeavor to keep the United States of America neutral.

If this attempt is not successful, we propose an alliance with Mexico, on the following terms: that we shall make war together and together make peace. We shall give general financial support, and it is understood that Mexico is to reconquer the lost territory in New Mexico, Texas, and Arizona. The details are left to you regarding settlement.

You are instructed to inform the President of Mexico of the above in the greatest confidence as soon as the outbreak of war with the United States is certain. You will also suggest that Japan be requested to take part at once and that he also mediate between ourselves and Japan.

Please call to the attention of the President of Mexico that the employment of ruthless submarine warfare now promises to compel England to make peace in a few months.

Foreign Minister Zimmerman

GO ON TO THE NEXT PAGE.

Document I

Source: *Des Moines Register*, 1917

The Python

GO ON TO THE NEXT PAGE.

UNITED STATES HISTORY
SECTION II

Parts B and C: Standard Essay Questions

(Suggested writing time—70 minutes. These questions count for 55 percent of the total essay section score.)

Part B

Directions: Choose ONE question from this part. You are advised to spend five minutes planning and 30 minutes writing your response. Cite relevant evidence in support of your generalizations and present your arguments clearly and logically.

2. Discuss any TWO of the following as they pertain to self-government in the New England settlements prior to 1650:

    Constitutionalism
    Democracy
    Freedom of religion

3. For the period between 1844 and the Civil War, evaluate the impact of slavery as a political issue on any THREE of the following parties:

    Democratic Party
    Free-Soil Party
    Know-Nothings (American Party)
    Republican Party
    Whig Party

Part C

Directions: Choose ONE question from this part. You are advised to spend five minutes planning and 30 minutes writing your response. Cite relevant evidence in support of your generalizations and present your arguments clearly and logically.

4. Analyze the reasons for the popularity of the Progressive movement during the first two decades of the twentieth century.

5. Discuss the role of collective security in determining U.S. foreign policy in the late twentieth century. To what extent was this a continuation of or departure from U.S. foreign policy earlier in the century? Discuss two of the following alliances in your response:

    The UN
    NATO
    SEATO

STOP

END OF EXAM

Chapter 16
Practice Test 1:
Answers and
Explanations

ANSWER KEY

1. C	21. C	41. B	61. E
2. D	22. A	42. C	62. D
3. C	23. E	43. C	63. A
4. E	24. A	44. B	64. E
5. A	25. D	45. B	65. B
6. D	26. B	46. C	66. C
7. B	27. C	47. D	67. A
8. C	28. D	48. A	68. B
9. E	29. B	49. A	69. D
10. A	30. A	50. E	70. D
11. E	31. C	51. B	71. C
12. E	32. D	52. C	72. B
13. E	33. A	53. E	73. A
14. D	34. D	54. E	74. D
15. D	35. C	55. E	75. E
16. B	36. A	56. E	76. D
17. B	37. C	57. C	77. B
18. D	38. C	58. A	78. B
19. D	39. D	59. E	79. A
20. A	40. A	60. B	80. C

Once you have checked your answers, remember to return to page 4 and respond to the Reflect questions.

MULTIPLE-CHOICE SECTION EXPLAINED

1. **C**   After fighting a war of liberation against the English monarchy, the colonists were leery of estab-
    lishing a too-powerful national government. They erred too much on the side of caution, however;
    by severely limiting the government's ability to levy taxes and duties, the framers of the Articles
    essentially hobbled the fledgling government. The Articles also curtailed the government's ability
    to regulate international trade, enforce treaties, and perform other tasks necessary to international
    relations. Havoc ensued. The British refused to abandon military posts in the states, and the gov-
    ernment was powerless to expel them. Furthermore, the British, French, and Spanish began to
    restrict U.S. trade with their colonies. That, coupled with the government's reluctance and inability
    to tax its citizens, nearly destroyed the country's economy.

    Answer choice (A) is incorrect because the Articles did not create an executive, just a unicameral
    legislature. (B) is incorrect because the Articles could be amended, but only by unanimous ap-
    proval of the states. (D) is incorrect; the Articles gave the government the power to mediate such
    disputes, on appeal raised by the states. The Articles required unanimous approval by the 13 states,
    not a simple majority, as (E) states.

2. **D**   In 1802 Spain ceded New Orleans to the French. This caused considerable unease in the Jefferson
    administration; while Spain had never taken advantage of New Orleans' strategic location (it con-
    trols access to the Mississippi River from the Gulf of Mexico, and vice versa), France seemed much
    more likely to exploit the advantage. Jefferson sent James Monroe to France to offer to buy New
    Orleans for $2 million. What the Americans did not know, however, was that Napoleon had de-
    cided to withdraw from the New World entirely in order to deploy his troops in Europe, which he
    hoped to conquer. Thus, Monroe received a pleasant surprise when he arrived in Paris: The French
    offered to sell the entire territory for $15 million.

3. **C**   The idea of Manifest Destiny was originally advanced by a newspaper editor in the 1840s, and it
    quickly became a part of the public's and government's vocabulary. Part and parcel with the doc-
    trine of Manifest Destiny was the notion that Europeans, especially English-speaking Europeans,
    were culturally and morally superior to those whom they supplanted, and so were entitled to the
    land even if others were already living on it. Manifest Destiny was later invoked as a justification
    for the Spanish-American War.

4. **E**   Dred Scott was a slave whose owner had traveled with him into the free state of Illinois and also
    into the Wisconsin Territory, where slavery was prohibited. Scott declared himself a free man, and
    a series of court cases ruled variously for and against his claim. The case finally reached the Su-
    preme Court in 1857. Taney's ruling was remarkable in that it far exceeded the scope of the case.
    Taney could simply have ruled on the merits of the case; instead, he decided to establish a wide-
    ranging precedent. Slaves, he said, were property, and as such could be transported anywhere. Be-
    cause slaves were not citizens, Taney further reasoned, they could not sue in federal court (thereby
    eliminating the possibility of the court reviewing any such cases in the future). Taney topped off
    his decision by stating that Congress could neither prevent settlers from transporting their slaves

to western territories nor could it legislate slavery in those areas, thus nullifying the Missouri Compromise and rendering the concept of popular sovereignty unconstitutional. Taney's decision is infamous for its lack of compassion for Scott and slavery, and is significant in that it hastened the inevitable Civil War.

Answer choice (A) describes *Marbury v. Madison*; (B) describes *Plessy v. Ferguson*; (C) describes many Supreme Court cases of the 1890s; and (D) describes *Engel v. Vitale*. You should know the *Marbury*, *Plessy*, and Dred Scott decisions, but not *Engel*, by name.

5. **A** Remember that most slaves had no job skills and could neither read nor write. They had no money and nowhere to go when slavery was abolished. Some slaves took off in search of their scattered families, but most stayed exactly where they were and worked as tenant farmers or sharecroppers. Under the new wage-labor system, plantations were subdivided into smaller farms of 30 to 50 acres, which were then leased to freedmen under a one-year contract. Tenants would work a piece of land and turn over 50 percent of their crops to the landlord. Often, other expenses, such as rent for a run-down shack or over-priced groceries, available only through the landowner, would be deducted from whatever was produced. One of the services initially provided by the Freedmen's Bureau was to help freed slaves who could neither read nor write understand the contracts they were about to sign. The system of sharecropping persisted well into the twentieth century, keeping many blacks in positions of poverty and degradation.

Answer choice (C) is incorrect for reasons stated above. The Great Migration of Southern blacks into Northern cities did not take place until World War I, long after Reconstruction. Choice (D) is incorrect because Chinese immigrants were used to construct our nation's railroad system, much of which had been completed by the end of the Civil War.

6. **D** Progressives were primarily concerned with domestic reform; their agenda was the greater empowerment of labor, women, and the poor. The successes of the Progressive Era include those mentioned in the answer choices, the beginning of direct elections for the U.S. Senate, and the establishment of three popular political tools: the ballot initiative, the referendum, and the recall. The Progressives pursued no coherent foreign policy per se.

7. **B** Many Americans supported the U.S. war effort only grudgingly, and then only after German (and, to a lesser extent, British) interference with American shipping had provoked the United States to action. Many argued that America should stick to the foreign policy suggested in both George Washington's farewell address and the Monroe Doctrine, and therefore (1) avoid political alliances with other countries, and (2) remain neutral regarding European conflicts. Wilson negotiated the Treaty of Versailles (the peace treaty following World War I) for the United States. He was unable to get a treaty that reflected his conciliatory Fourteen Points, as the Allies demanded a treaty that punished Germany harshly. Nonetheless, Wilson did the best he could and returned with a document he was ready to present to the Senate. The treaty included provisions for the League of Nations (which Wilson had fought hard for) and contained a clause that could have been interpreted as committing the American military to the defense of European borders. Wilson, a Democrat,

tried to sell this treaty to the Republican Senate, but could not muster the two-thirds majority required for ratification, and so the treaty was never approved by the United States.

8. **C** Rosa Parks was arrested after she refused to give up her seat on a bus to a white man; a Montgomery ordinance required blacks to sit in the back of the bus and to surrender their seats to whites if asked to do so. Outrage over the arrest, coupled with long-term resentment over Jim Crow laws, provided the impetus for the year-long boycott.

The boycott also brought Martin Luther King Jr. (1929–1968) to national prominence. Twenty-seven years old at the time, King was pastor at Rosa Parks's church. Although clearly groomed for greatness—his grandfather had led the protests resulting in Atlanta's first black high school, his father was a minister and community leader, and King had already amassed impressive academic credentials (Morehouse College, Crozer Theological Seminary, University of Pennsylvania, and finally a Ph.D. from Boston University)—the yearlong bus boycott gave him his first national podium. King organized peaceful protests based on the principles of Thoreau and Mohandas Gandhi, and in these he saw the springboard to the national civil rights movement he would spearhead for the next decade (until his assassination).

9. **E** Senator McCarthy leapt onto the national scene when he stated that he knew of 205 known Communists in the State Department. McCarthy soon changed the number, first to 57 and then to 81. That should have called his credibility into question, but somehow it didn't. The charges gained immediate national attention, and McCarthy had discovered a potent political issue: America's widespread fear of communism, heightened by the Chinese Revolution and the USSR's successful detonation of an atomic bomb. In the years to come he would preside over numerous investigative hearings, but he would never uncover any communist spies. He brought about his own downfall when he accused the Army of harboring communists. During televised hearings, McCarthy came across as foolish, bullying, and occasionally drunk, and subsequently lost his credibility, even among his many devoted followers.

10. **A** The Puritans came to the New World to escape religious and political persecution in England. Believing that theirs was the one true church, the Puritans saw no contradiction in denying others the same rights they had sought in England. In their communities freedom of worship was solely a Puritan right. Non-Puritans were limited politically as well: only property-owning male Puritans were allowed to vote in the colonial assemblies (which, oddly, were quite democratic, within the extremely limited parameters of their membership). Those who questioned the church too aggressively—as did Roger Williams and Anne Hutchinson—were banished from the community. Williams went on to found the colony of Rhode Island, which for decades was the only place in New England where religious liberty was granted.

11. **E** Throughout the colonial period the English subscribed to the economic theory of mercantilism, which held, among other things, that a nation's wealth rested on colonial holdings, a favorable balance of trade, and a large store of precious metals. Mercantilists held that governments must regulate trade through taxes so as to preserve their self-interest. Accordingly, English taxes and

levies on the colonists (prior to the Sugar Act) were proposed and accepted as acts of a mercantilist protectionism. The Sugar Act was something different. England accrued a large war debt during the French and Indian War. Since, it was argued, the war was fought to protect the colonists, the colonists should share in its expense. Revenues from the Sugar Act were earmarked toward repaying that debt. The colonists saw things differently, however. Many argued that Englishmen could not be taxed without their consent, and that since the colonists had no representatives in Parliament, they simply could not be taxed. The Sugar Act is often regarded as a major catalyst in the chain of events that led to the Revolutionary War.

12.   E   The question refers to Roosevelt's notorious "court packing" plan. Unhappy with the Supreme Court and the federal judiciary, whose conservatism several times resulted in the nullification of New Deal programs, Roosevelt proposed that he be allowed to name a new federal judge for every sitting judge who had reached the age of 70 and not retired. The plan would have allowed Roosevelt to add six new Supreme Court justices and more than 40 other federal judges. The proposal was not at all popular and was roundly defeated in the Senate. It also helped fuel the arguments of those who contended that FDR had grown too powerful. Not long after the court packing incident, several conservative justices retired and FDR replaced them with liberals, so he achieved his goal despite the failure of his plan.

13.   E   The Know-Nothings were a nativist group formed in response to the growing concentration of immigrants—particularly Italian and Irish Catholics—in Eastern cities. The party grew out of a number of secret societies whose members were instructed to tell outsiders nothing, hence the party's name: When asked anything about their groups, Know-Nothings would respond, "I know nothing." Their program included a 25-year residency requirement for citizenship; they also wanted to restrict all public offices to only those who were native-born Americans. By 1855 they had changed their name to the American Party, and in 1856, they fielded a presidential candidate (former president Millard Fillmore). Within a few years the party had disbanded, destroyed by their disagreements over slavery. Most Northern Know-Nothings joined the Republican party.

14.   D   Historians describe the immigrants who came to the United States before the Civil War as "old immigrants." These men and women came predominantly from countries in northwestern Europe. For the most part, they were Protestants and spoke English and easily became part of the melting pot we call America. Following the Civil War, however, the "new immigrants" came predominantly from nations in southeastern Europe, including Russians, Italians, and Poles. Many of these people were Catholics and Jews and were culturally very different from most Americans by that point. These new immigrants were not easily assimilated. They tended to settle amongst themselves in ethnic neighborhoods in major cities like New York and Chicago where there was a demand for unskilled labor in the numerous factories of these big cities.

15.   D   The Ghost Dancers arose in the late 1800s when the sad fate awaiting the great Native American tribes of the era was becoming all too apparent. Wovoka, a Paiute Indian, started the Ghost Dance movement, which resembled a religious revival. It centered on a dance ritual that enabled participants

to envision a brighter future, one in which whites no longer dominated North America. Wovoka preached unity among Native Americans and the rejection of white culture and its trappings, especially alcohol. He also preached the imminent end of the world, at which point the Indian dead would rise to reclaim the land that was rightfully theirs. Sioux Ghost Dancers believed in the power of "ghost shirts," garments blessed by medicine men that were capable of stopping bullets. This belief led to a rise in Sioux militancy and ultimately contributed to their massacre at Wounded Knee in 1890.

16.　**B**　The Industrial Revolution began in earnest in the United States after the War of 1812, and the first fast-growing industry was textiles (most textile mills, by the way, were in New England). England also had a booming textile industry and, at war's end, began buying all the American cotton it could. Farmers started expanding to the west, buying land and planting cotton wherever possible. All these new plantations required lots of labor; hence, an increase in demand for slaves. It's worth noting that other major Southern crops—tobacco, for instance—were not wildly profitable under the slave system. The growth of the textile industry and its voracious need for cotton, however, solidified the role of slavery in antebellum Southern agriculture.

17.　**B**　Although it's hard to imagine today, labor unions had a very rough go of it for many decades. At first, government policy and law were directed only at the protection of corporations and their property. Eventually, legislature passed bills protecting the rights of workers to organize and to bargain collectively. Enforcement of those protections, however, was lax to nonexistent; as a result, many union workers were subject to all sorts of harassment. The use of scabs and strike-breaking thugs was common; workers who dared to organize could lose their jobs and even their lives. The cartoon depicts the government conducting a misdirected fact-finding mission at a time when abuses against labor unions are obvious.

18.　**D**　In 1954 the Supreme Court ruled invalid the "separate but equal" standard approved by the court in *Plessy v. Ferguson* (1896). In a 9 to 0 decision, the court ruled that "separate educational facilities are inherently unequal." The suit was brought on behalf of Linda Brown, a black school-age child, by the NAACP. Then-future Supreme Court Justice Thurgood Marshall argued the case. About the other cases mentioned here: *Marbury v. Madison* is the case that established the principle of judicial review. *Bradwell v. Illinois* is an 1873 decision in which the court upheld the state of Illinois' right to deny a female attorney the right to practice law simply on the basis of gender. That case represented a setback for both women's rights and the Fourteenth Amendment. In *Holden v. Hardy*, the Court ruled that states could pass laws regulating safety conditions in privately owned workplaces.

19.　**D**　The Cuban Revolution, led by Fidel Castro, ousted the government of Fulgencio Batista in 1959. Not long after, Castro began nationalizing American-owned property (United States companies owned 40 percent of Cuba's sugar industry and practically all of its telephone and electricity services). Eisenhower broke off diplomatic relations with Cuba as he was leaving office and suggested an invasion of Cuba to incoming President Kennedy. The CIA presented Kennedy with its plan: Cuban exiles, trained by the CIA, would land at the Bay of Pigs and fight the Communists. According to the CIA scenario, the Cuban people would then rise up in support of the American-backed rebels, resulting in a new revolution and the ouster of Castro. To say the plan didn't work is an understatement. The invasion was poorly planned, poorly executed, and did not receive any support from the Cuban people. After two days it was over, and the new administration had suffered a major embarrassment.

20. **A** Williams was quite a radical thinker for his time and place. After accepting a position as teacher in the Salem Bay settlement, Williams both taught and published a number of controversial principles. He believed, for example, that the king of England had no power to give away land that clearly belonged to the Native Americans. He also felt that the state was an imperfect vehicle for the imposition of God's will on Earth, and therefore advocated religious tolerance and the separation of church and state. Such ideas were anathema to the Puritans, who had settled Massachusetts Bay to establish precisely the type of state that Williams preached against. Neither easygoing nor good sports, the Puritans eventually banished Williams. Williams moved to what is now Rhode Island, received a charter, and founded a new colony. Rhode Island's charter allowed for the free exercise of religion; it did not require voters in its legislature to be church members.

21. **C** Nobody in the U.S. government was so foolish as to believe that America's navy was superior to England's, then the greatest in the world. In fact, had the American navy been so powerful, the war would never have been necessary, because American naval vessels could have accompanied merchant ships and ensured their safe passage across the Atlantic. England had the dominant navy and exploited its advantage throughout the beginning of the nineteenth century. Strapped for soldiers—England was at war with Napoleon, among others—the British confiscated American ships and forced their crews (some of whom, incidentally, were British deserters) to join the British navy. England also interfered with U.S.–European trade in an effort to gain the upper hand over France (by denying the French American goods and commerce). The United States retaliated by passing the Embargo Act in 1807, which basically ended all foreign imports and domestic exports. The act, intended to protect American merchants, provoked Great Britain to exploit even further its advantage on the seas. It failed miserably, causing a near-collapse of New England's economy. Meanwhile, Southern and Western settlers were anxious for expansion; their desires were thwarted by powerful alliances between the British and American Indians. Southerners, rallying behind Henry Clay, a "war hawk," called for war.

22. **A** The provision for counting slaves when determining apportionment in the House of Representatives is part of the body of the Constitution, known as the Three-Fifths Compromise. All of the other answer choices describe aspects of the Missouri Compromise, negotiated by Speaker of the House Henry Clay. The compromise forestalled the Civil War until after the Mexican War and Mexican Cession when compromise was no longer possible. The slavery issue would continue to be the cause of regional division in the United States until after the Civil War.

23. **E** Overpopulation and poor harvests in Ireland fueled a steady stream of immigration to the United States. Between the years 1820 and 1854 the Irish made up the single largest immigrant group

for all but two of the years. The peak immigration period was between 1847 and 1854, when the potato famine struck Ireland; during those years, well over 1 million Irish left for America. In 1854 German immigrants began to outnumber the Irish, although Irish immigration remained at such a level that, by 1900, there were more Irish in the United States than in Ireland.

24.   A   Johnson, a Southern Democrat whom Lincoln had chosen as a vice-presidential candidate to balance the ticket in 1864, became president upon Lincoln's assassination. Although a vocal opponent to secession, Johnson nonetheless was sympathetic to the South and hoped to effect a quick reconciliation after the war. His Reconstruction plan was implemented during a recess of Congress; its intent was to gently shift the Southern power base from the aristocracy to the region's many small farmers and craftsmen. When Congress reconvened, Northern legislators were shocked to find that Johnson had allowed Southern states to elect former Confederate soldiers and government officials as their representatives. Led by Radical Republicans, Congress first refused to seat the Southern delegations, then proceeded to draft a more far-reaching Reconstruction, which included punitive measures. From then on, Johnson and Congress waged open war. Twice the House Judiciary Committee considered impeachment proceedings. The third time was the charm; the official reason was that Johnson had violated the Tenure of Office Act (through which Congress had usurped Johnson's power to fire Cabinet members), but the real reason was their constant disagreements over the course of Reconstruction. Impeachment failed by one vote, after which Johnson served the last few months of his term and retired.

25.   D   The United States formed its Open Door Policy in response to Europe's aggressive colonization of China. Fearful that the stronger European imperial forces would partition China, the United States called for guaranteed free trade in the region and the preservation of China's traditional borders. Europe might have disregarded the policy had not Chinese insurrections (e.g., the Boxer Rebellion in 1900) made it extremely difficult for Europe to control China. European imperialists had to band together, and accept help from the U.S. military, in order to avoid expulsion. The United States pursued the Open Door Policy because policy makers had come to believe in the necessity of trading in as many regions as possible, maintaining a favorable trade balance, and expanding the U.S. economy on a continual basis.

26.   B   In fact, the federal government did almost nothing to regulate the economy even though many within the government foresaw the potential for economic disaster. Many possible remedies—an income tax to redistribute wealth, a tighter money supply to discourage speculation, aggressive enforcement of antitrust regulations—were rejected. Meanwhile, manufacturers were overproducing, causing them to stockpile large inventories and lay off workers; consumers weren't making enough money to buy what, in some cases, they built at work; and the wealth of the nation was concentrated in a very few, often irresponsible, hands. The system was too fragile, and when it started to tumble, it fell entirely to pieces very quickly.

27.   C   In 1947 the United States received word from London that the British could no longer afford to support Greece, at the time a client state. Both Greece and Turkey were in danger of falling to communist insur-

gents, a result Truman was intent on preventing. In a speech before Congress, in which he asked for almost $500 million in aid to allies in the two countries, Truman declared what came to be known as the Truman Doctrine: "I believe it must be the policy of the United States to support free peoples who are resisting attempted subjugation by armed minorities or outside pressures." Truman got the aid, Greece and Turkey remained allied with the West, and the Cold War intensified.

28. **D** Answer choice (D) sums up the "domino theory," first articulated by President Eisenhower. In a speech explaining America's interest in Vietnam, Eisenhower said, "You have a row of dominoes set up; you knock over the first one, and what will happen to the last one is that it will go over very quickly."

Some of the incorrect answers are noteworthy. Ho Chi Minh was leader of the North Vietnamese, who were Communists; Ho had been a U.S. ally during World War II and had even received CIA assistance, but ultimately the United States opposed him for political reasons. The United States first came to assist France, the colonial power in Vietnam, so U.S. policy was hardly anti-colonial. Finally, the United States had few business interests in the area at the time, although the government was interested in the Vietnamese rice market, which fed America's strongest ally in the region, Japan.

29. **B** The term "First Great Awakening" refers to a period of resurgence of religious activity that took place between the 1730s and the 1760s. Its most prominent spokesmen were the Congregationalist preacher Jonathan Edwards and the Methodist preacher George Whitefield. From 1739 until his death in 1770, Whitefield toured the colonies preaching what has since come to be known as revivalism. The period was marked by the creation of a number of evangelical churches and emphasis on the emotional power of religion. Whitefield was a native of England, where the Enlightenment was in full swing; its effects were also beginning to be felt in the colonies.

The Enlightenment was a natural outgrowth of the Renaissance, during which Europe rediscovered the great works of the ancient world and began to assimilate some of its ideals. While European thinkers of the time did not turn their backs on religion, they also entertained ideas about the value of empirical thought and scientific inquiry that were not entirely consonant with contemporary religious beliefs. Further, they began to view humanity as a more important—and God as a less important—force in shaping human history. The First Great Awakening is usually characterized as a response to the threats posed by the intellectual trends of the Enlightenment.

30. **A** The term "self-reliance" should have been your tip-off here; it's the title of one of Emerson's most famous essays (in which this quote appears). Emerson was a leader of the influential Transcendentalist movement, which preached nonconformity, individualism, and the belief that God was tangible and merciful, unlike the Calvinists, who described God as a distant, unforgiving judge of humanity. Transcendentalism is often seen as a rebellion against Calvinism and other forms of religious orthodoxy.

31. **C** The Free-Soil Party was created in the mid-1840s and was more like a faction or interest group than a political party. However, unlike a faction, it developed a political platform and nominated a

candidate (Martin Van Buren) for the presidential election of 1844. The Free-Soil party attracted anti-slavery "Conscience" Whigs, former members of the Liberty party, and pro-Wilmot Proviso Democrats. The Wilmot Proviso was rejected by Congress but suggested that there be no slavery in any territory acquired from Mexico. Free Soilers were opposed to the extension of slavery into the new territories. Remember: The Constitution protected slavery where it already existed, but many people believed Congress could prevent the further spread of slavery as the U.S. acquired new land. Although the Free-Soil party did not exist for long, its major principles were adopted by the new Republican party, which was formed in 1854 and was opposed to the extension of slavery into the new territories. (The United States had acquired the Mexican Cession as a result of the Treaty of Guadalupe Hildalgo, which ended the Mexican War in 1848. Unlike the Louisiana Purchase, which had doubled the size of the United States in 1803, adding many valuable natural resources that would contribute to the economic development of the new nation, the Mexican War propelled the nation to civil war.)

32.   D   The debate over virtual representation arose during the 1760s in the wake of English tax hikes imposed on the colonies, especially the Stamp Act, which led to the Stamp Act Congress. Anti-tax colonists argued that, because the colonists were not represented in Parliament, they could not justly be taxed; this argument was based on the widely held belief that the government could not tax a citizen without his consent. The English responded with the concept of virtual representation, which, as answer choice (D) correctly states, holds that all English subjects are "virtually" represented in Parliament, even if they have not voted for a specific representative or, indeed, have not voted at all.

33.   A   In 1798 Eli Whitney patented a process for manufacturing interchangeable parts. Several years later, at a demonstration before John Adams and Thomas Jefferson, Whitney took apart a number of guns he had built, scrambled the parts, and then reassembled the guns. Whitney's audience was astonished; previously, manufacturers had custom-fitted parts, and so guns, machines, etc., could only be assembled from their own, specifically fitted parts. The idea took national manufacturing by storm. Whitney's innovation brought about the end of cottage industries and gave rise to an American Industrial Revolution so successful that, by 1850, Europe was sending delegations to the United States to study its manufacturing systems. As a side note: The innovation also made Whitney rich, something his cotton gin had failed to do because that invention was so widely pirated.

34.   D   In the election of 1848, the Democrats realized that their party was crumbling because its members could not agree on whether to allow slavery in the Western territories. They sought a policy to appease both abolitionists and slaveholders; the result of that search was the concept of popular sovereignty. By allowing the settlers to decide the slave status of an area, popular sovereignty took some pressure off Congress, which was growing increasingly divided over the issue. It also took pressure off the political parties, which were coming apart due to the irreconcilable regional differences of their members. Henry Clay invoked the notion of popular sovereignty in the Compromise of 1850, but the compromise contained a purposefully ambiguous interpretation of what popular sovereignty meant. While the ambiguous wording was necessary to make the Compromise of 1850 possible, it also made future disagreements over the issue inevitable.

35. **C** The Reconstruction Act of 1867, Congress's plan for the rehabilitation of the South, was much harsher than President Johnson's plan. Johnson, like Lincoln (who began planning the method for readmitting Southern states before his assassination), wanted a reconciliatory plan that punished only the most prominent leaders of the secession. Radical Republicans in Congress wanted something much tougher, and Johnson's plan was so lenient (in the first postwar Congress, Johnson's plan would have allowed the former president of the Confederacy to take a seat in Senate) that it drove many moderates into the radicals' camp. The result was the Reconstruction Act, a punitive measure that imposed a number of strict requirements on Southern states as preconditions for their readmission to the Union. Answer choices (A), (B), (D), and (E) list all of those preconditions; the fact that Congress did not impose any requirements such as the one described in answer choice (C) pretty much doomed postwar Southern blacks to poverty.

36. **A** During the century, the federal government gave over 180 million acres to railroad companies; state and local governments gave away another 50 million. For the federal government the goal was the completion of a national rail system in order to promote trade. Local governments often wanted the railroad to come to a specific town, since a rail station was a great boon to growth.

   The incorrect answers are all entirely false. The nation's railroads grew haphazardly, and frequently different lines could not be joined because the tracks were of different gauges, (B). The transcontinental railroad was completed in 1869, (C), and was the single greatest factor in the growth of the American steel industry, (D). The North had a much more sophisticated rail system than the South, which gave the Union a great advantage in the Civil War, (E).

37. **C** The "Second Wave" of immigration starting in 1890 brought fewer northern and western Europeans and more southern and eastern Europeans. The result was increased ethnic tensions in the United States and, eventually, calls to limit immigration. Congress's first measure, the Emergency Quota Act of 1921, limited annual immigration levels to 3 percent of the number of people from that country living in the United States in 1910. In 1924 Congress tightened restrictions further, lowering the quota to 2 percent and changing the reference date to 1890, thereby dramatically lowering quotas for southern and eastern Europeans. A third law, in 1927, loosened restrictions a little (but not much). As a result, Canadians and others from the Americas soon became, proportionally, the greater share of U.S. immigrants.

38. **C** Hitler made little secret of either his totalitarian inclinations or his expansionist goals. He had written about both in his autobiography, *Mein Kampf*, while in prison in 1925; the book was widely circulated in the 1930s. Furthermore, news reporters, government officials, and many others witnessed firsthand the transformation of Germany under Hitler. While Americans may not have known the full extent of the Nazis' plans, they certainly had a good general idea.

   However, Senate hearings conducted between 1934 and 1936 by Senator Gerald Nye revealed unwholesome activities by American arms manufacturers; many had lobbied intensely for entry into World War I, others had bribed foreign officials, and others still were supplying Fascist governments. This, coupled with the great losses the country had suffered in World War I, created a strong anti-war sentiment in the United States. Liberal pacifists argued further that intervention in Europe would require a costly military build-up at a time when money might be better spent pulling the nation out of the Depression. Finally, there was America's traditional neutrality, which dated back to Washington's admonition to avoid permanent alliances with other nations.

39. **D** The Beat generation rose in reaction to the growing complacency and materialism of 1950s America, particularly as it was manifested in the suburbs. Kerouac's characters are the antithesis of the typical suburbanite: They hop freight trains, drink and take drugs, engage in extramarital sex, write poetry, and study Eastern mysticism. Other Beat writers include Allen Ginsberg, Lawrence Ferlinghetti, William Burroughs, and Gary Snyder. "Silent majority" is the term Richard Nixon used to describe those who supported his policy in Vietnam (as opposed to the vocal critics who protested it). The "lost generation" is the group of 1920s writers such as Ernest Hemingway who spent much of their creative lives in Europe. Middle America is, according to the *American Heritage Dictionary*, "That part of the U.S. middle class thought of as being average in income and education and moderately conservative in values and attitudes." Although many academics teach Kerouac's works, those works do not express the ideals of conservatives among anybody's ranks.

40. **A** The WPA was created in 1935 as part of the New Deal. Its purpose was twofold; to improve the United States through large-scale building and arts projects, and to provide work for the unemployed. The EEOC was created to police discriminatory hiring practices. Medicare ensures that the elderly do not go without health care. HUD develops government projects to revitalize inner-city residential areas and polices discriminatory housing practices. Project Head Start helps ensure that low-income preschoolers receive adequate food, health care, and other preparation for schooling.

41. **B** A population boom, political unrest, and hard economic times are the main factors that motivated many Englishmen and women—nearly 100,000—to go to the New World as indentured servants. Most were young farmers (not criminals), between the ages of 15 and 24, who were attracted by the promise of ultimate liberty and, until, 1670, a parcel of land upon completion of their period of service (usually between four and seven years). Compared with conditions at home, indenture represented real opportunity. Disease and hard work conspired to kill over one-third of those who came, but the rest survived to make up the majority of the European populations of Maryland and Virginia. Colonial law offered indentured servants some protections: Masters were required to feed, clothe, and house servants, and were prohibited from beating them excessively.

42. **C** The Northwest Ordinance of 1787, along with ordinances of 1784 and 1785, created a process for distributing land to settlers. The Northwest Ordinance was the most important of them, because it also provided settlers with a number of civil rights (trial by jury, freedom of religion, freedom from excessive punishment), abolished slavery in the territories, and set specific regulations concerning the conditions under which a territory could apply for statehood. The ordinance covered the territories northwest of the Ohio River and east of the Mississippi River, up to the Canadian border. This area was inhabited by a number of American Indian tribes, none of whom were consulted before the government started giving their homes to settlers. Violence ensued, and peace did not

come until 1795, when the United States gained a military advantage over the Miami Confederacy, its chief opponent in the area. The Northwest Ordinance remained important long after the northwest territory was settled, because of its pertinence to the statehood process and to the issue of slavery.

43. **C** In order for working people to move away from urban centers (where most of the jobs were), they needed a means of getting to and from work. By the early 1920s, the automobile provided just that. Mass production had lowered production costs and thus transformed the auto from a luxury item to an affordable convenience. Automobiles remained status symbols and were thus doubly sought after.

About the incorrect answers: The steam locomotive was invented at the turn of the nineteenth century. Televisions were not widely owned until the mid-1950s. Open-range cattle ranching took place on the open stretches of the Great Plains, far away from any cities (close to which suburbs must, by definition, be). The availability of electricity certainly made life more convenient for those who could afford it, but electric lighting, by itself, had little impact on the growth rate of suburbia.

44. **B** The many reform movements of the early nineteenth century were the result of a combination of factors. Religious fervor grew during the Second Great Awakening, which began in the post–Revolutionary War period. With that fervor came the desire of many to do good works. Also contributing was the industrial boom that occurred after the War of 1812. Rapid industrialization had several unwholesome effects. One was the growth of cities, which was accompanied by urban poverty and despair. Another was the widening gulf between the commercial and moral realms: As businesses became larger and competition more keen, the ethical treatment of employees became less of a concern for many businessmen.

The memberships of many reform societies were made up almost exclusively of Christian middle-class women. They formed benevolent groups, ministered to the sick, visited shut-ins, and preached the gospel. Through their contact with the less fortunate, these women saw the ill effects of industrialization and looked for ways to remedy them. In time their goals broadened to include emancipation of the slaves. Given the religious background of these reform movements, separation of church and state was not often part of their agenda.

45. **B** Social Darwinism took its cue from Darwin's theory of evolution, which states that natural selection determines the survival and demise of living beings. Many of the wealthy in the late nineteenth century used Darwin's theories as a justification for their phenomenal wealth in the face of widespread poverty (much of which they had helped create through low wages and poor working conditions). The quote above is taken from Andrew Carnegie's book *The Gospel of Wealth*. The applicability of Darwin's theory, which treats phenomena that occur over millennia, to the effects of the Industrial Revolution in the late nineteenth century is certainly questionable.

About the incorrect answers: Calvinism is the theological doctrine of John Calvin; it stresses the predetermination of the soul's status in the afterlife. Progressivism was a political movement in the early twentieth century; it championed labor unions, women's suffrage, and the direct election of senators.

Cultural pluralism is a fancy way of expressing the idea that America is a melting pot. Egalitarianism is the belief that all individuals should have equal political, social, and economic rights.

46. **C** The United States desperately wanted a canal somewhere on the Latin American isthmus so that American ships could travel from coast to coast without circumnavigating South America. Nicaragua was Washington's first choice, but powerful American businessmen with investments in Panama convinced (or bribed, in many cases) Congress to adopt the Panama Canal plan. At the time, Panama was part of Colombia. Unable to cut a favorable deal with the Colombian government, the United States saw an opportunity in Panama's political instability. Roosevelt encouraged Panamanian rebels, sent military aid when they revolted, and then cut a much sweeter deal with the new Panamanian government for control of the canal. The creation of the Panama Canal raised the stakes in Central America considerably. American interest in the smooth operation of the canal was such that, in the first two decades of the twentieth century, U.S. troops intervened in the region six times. The idea that any threat to regional stability was a threat to U.S. interests was known as the Roosevelt Corollary to the Monroe Doctrine.

47. **D** Clay's American System was initiated during the Madison administration. A Republican, Madison believed in a limited role for the federal government; in fact, he sanctioned only those road and waterway projects that were truly interstate, arguing that intrastate travel should be the responsibility of the states. At the time the government's suggestion to the unemployed was "Move where there's work!"; the feasibility of a federal jobs program was still over a century away. However, in the period following the War of 1812, the country and its leaders experienced increased feelings of nationalism, and Republicans felt that some federal action, if it served the national interest, could be beneficial. Poor roadways had hurt the United States during the war, and everyone agreed that the routes of long-distance travel needed improvement. A shortage of capital during the war convinced everyone that a National Bank was necessary (even though many still continued to distrust banks and blame them for the nation's financial woes). Finally, the American System sought to develop U.S. commercial capacities through protective tariffs and incentives for American merchants and manufacturers.

48. **A** More than 110,000 Japanese Americans were relocated during World War II. Most lost their homes and possessions, to the tune of an estimated $40 million. The relocation was mandated by presidential order; Congress was compliant in that it never acted to stop it, but that was the extent of congressional participation. There were not 100,000 Japanese American dissidents in the United States before the war, nor even half that many, making answer choice (B) incorrect. A question about this shameful episode in U.S. history appears on almost every AP U.S. History Exam.

49. **A** Those few women who reached the age of maturity and remained unmarried had the same legal standing as men, except that they were denied the right to vote in colonial legislatures. Widows had the same legal rights as unmarried women; however, married women forfeited nearly all rights to their husbands. Married women could neither sue nor be sued; sign contracts, deeds, or a will; or buy, sell, or own property. Anything a woman owned prior to marriage became her husband's property.

Answer choice (B) is incorrect: Although the role of women in Native American societies varied greatly from tribe to tribe, many women played a much more active role than Anglo-American women were permitted. (C), too, is wrong: Church attendance was essentially mandatory in New England, although when attendance slacked off toward the end of the seventeenth century, it was mostly men, not women, who were skipping church. Indoors was considered women's domain; they were expected to keep house while the men did agricultural work (thus, (D) is incorrect). Answer choice (E) is wrong: There was no law such as the one it describes.

50. **E** Area Native Americans introduced the Chesapeake settlers to tobacco, and its export to England proved an immediate success. Tobacco farming requires abundant acreage, because the crop drains nutrients from the soil and therefore cannot be grown repeatedly in the same fields. Accordingly, Chesapeake area settlers sought and received large land grants from the Virginia Company (prior to 1624) or the Crown (from 1624, when Virginia became a royal colony) until there was no more land to acquire.

The other answers to this question are flat-out wrong. (A): Massachusetts settlers certainly were interested in expansion, but at a slower rate. Unlike Chesapeake settlers, Massachusetts colonists built permanent, sturdy houses and settled in towns. (B): The birthrate and life expectancy were higher in the Massachusetts Bay colony; the Chesapeake region was more conducive to epidemic, and the English settlers, used to more temperate weather, found its climate inhospitable. Furthermore, whereas many Massachusetts settlers arrived with their entire families intact, most Chesapeake settlers arrived alone. Men greatly outnumbered women in the Chesapeake region, and so marriage and family life were less common there than in Massachusetts. (C): Both areas were populated by Indians when the colonists arrived; indeed each group would have starved to death had it not been for the Native Americans' assistance. (D): Land in the Chesapeake region was more fertile, not less, than land in the Massachusetts Bay region.

51. **B** As the United States' first secretary of the treasury, Alexander Hamilton had to handle the nation's considerable war debt. His solution included the formation of a national bank, modeled on the Bank of England. Through the bank, Hamilton hoped to consolidate and manage the nation's debt and provide an agency through which a national currency could be circulated. He also wished to broaden the powers of the federal government (Hamilton, a Federalist, favored a strong central government). Both houses of Congress approved Hamilton's plan, but Washington (then president) was reluctant to sign the bill because he was uncertain of its constitutionality. (Note: Washington performed very conservatively as president, aware that any action he took would set a precedent for his followers. Accordingly, he used his veto only when he was certain that a bill was unconstitutional.)

The debate that followed defined the two main schools of thought on constitutional law. On one side were the strict constructionists, led by Jefferson and Madison. Both were wary of a strong central government and interpreted the Constitution accordingly. The strict constructionists argued that the Constitution allowed Congress only those powers specifically granted it or those "necessary and proper" to the execution of its enumerated powers. While a bank might be convenient and perhaps beneficial, they argued, it was not necessary, and thus its creation was beyond the powers of the national government. Hamilton, not surprisingly, disagreed. In his "Defense of the Constitutionality of the Bank," he proposed what has come to be known as the broad-constructionist view. He argued that the creation of a bank was an implied power of the government, because it already had explicit power to coin money, borrow money, and collect taxes. Hamilton argued that the government could do anything in the execution of those enumerated powers—including creating a bank—that was not explicitly forbidden it by the Constitution. Washington agreed with Hamilton and signed the bill.

52. C The Lowell System is named after the town of Lowell, Massachusetts, where it originated. In their effort to recruit workers from outlying farmlands, Lowell manufacturers offered a number of incentives that, together, constituted one of the most humanitarian packages available to factory workers at the time. The workers—practically all of whom were women—were offered cash bonuses up front, housing in company boarding houses, and access to a wide range of cultural events. Owners' motivations were economic—they were suffering from a shortage of labor and so were trying to entice workers—but they were also partly humanitarian; horror stories of the effects of the Industrial Revolution in England were reaching, and frightening, Americans. Massive immigration in the following decades, and, with it, the arrival of a large source of cheap labor, brought the Lowell System to its end.

53. E Between 1800 and 1820, party nominees to the presidency were chosen by congressional caucus, then approved by state electors (delegates to a state nominating convention). Before 1824, electors were chosen by a variety of methods. Many electors were chosen by state legislatures, which chose electors who agreed with the choices of the caucus (often they were the same men who had participated in the caucus). By 1824, however, a majority of states allowed voters to choose their presidential electors directly. When the Republican caucus chose William H. Crawford in 1824, others, among them John Quincy Adams, Henry Clay, and Andrew Jackson, decided to challenge the nomination. Their opposition, along with their accusations that the caucuses were undemocratic, brought about the demise of the caucus system.

A couple of the incorrect answers are noteworthy. Answer choice (B) refers to an early constitutional problem remedied by the Twelfth Amendment. Prior to 1804 the person with the most votes in the electoral college became president; the one who received the second-most votes became vice president. In 1796 this created an administration in which the two highest office holders, Adams and Jefferson, were of different parties. In 1800 it caused confusion when Jefferson and his running mate, Burr, received an equal number of votes in the electoral college. The election was thrown to the House of Representatives, who chose Jefferson on the 35th (!) ballot. Answer choice (C) refers to the election of 1840, sometimes referred to as "the first modern election" because candidates wooed the electorate directly during the campaign.

54. E Waves of European immigration throughout the nineteenth century swelled cities' populations. Governments of the time were nowhere near as activist as they are today, and only a very few

provided even minimal services to immigrants as they accommodated themselves to their new homeland; ethnic communities and churches were expected to provide such services. A number of enterprising, unscrupulous men recognized in these immigrants the opportunity for great political power. Such men, known as political bosses, helped immigrants find homes and jobs and acquire citizenship and voting rights. In essence, these bosses created entire communities, then provided them with all sorts of services: food and loans for the poor, parks and protection for the community. In return, the communities were expected to provide loyal political support, which they did, originally out of loyalty, and later, as the machines became extremely powerful, out of both loyalty and fear. The bosses could then hand an election to a politician of their choice, in return for favors. Political machines filled a need, albeit in an expensive and unethical way. They fell from power when governments started to provide many of the services machines had provided.

55. E Booker T. Washington was a famous agricultural scientist and the founder of the Tuskegee Institute in Alabama; W. E. B. Du Bois was a noted sociologist and the founder of the National Negro Committee, which later became the NAACP. Washington is often characterized as an assimilationist; indeed, he stressed that the best method for blacks to achieve equality in the United States was to gain economic power and integrate (or assimilate) into white society. In his most famous speech, delivered at the Atlanta Cotton Exposition of 1895, Washington stressed these views and also suggested that blacks would withdraw from Southern politics in return for guarantees of educational opportunity. Du Bois strongly disagreed; he viewed Washington's plan as one in which blacks would be required to earn the equality that should already rightfully be theirs. Du Bois argued instead for full equality for blacks before the law. Many historians explain the differences between these two men by pointing to their backgrounds: Washington, the son of slaves and a thoroughly self-made man, valued self-reliance. He lived his life in the South and had few illusions about how receptive Southern whites would be to black equality. Du Bois was a Northerner who studied at Harvard and in Germany, which may explain why he was more receptive to idealistic goals.

56. E The Eighteenth Amendment to the Constitution (1919) prohibited the manufacture or sale of alcoholic beverages in the United States. At first it worked fairly well; World War I had given Americans a sense of purpose and self-sacrifice, and the concept of abstinence was popular with Northern religious conservatives and fundamentalists elsewhere. The law did lower the incidence of public drunkenness and increase productivity (the law's intended effect, which is why answer choice (B) is incorrect). Eventually, however, such a large contingent wanted to drink that it couldn't be contained. Especially in the cities, a massive underground industry arose to serve drinkers. That industry was controlled by organized crime, which became much more powerful as a result. Crime enforcement costs rose dramatically with the level of illegal activity, and soon it was clear that Prohibition had failed. In 1933 the Twenty-first Amendment, repealing Prohibition, was passed.

57. C Prior to *The Jazz Singer*, movies were silent. Dialogue appeared on title cards on the film, and music was provided by a live accompanist or ensemble. Much of *The Jazz Singer* is silent, but it

contains a number of scenes with synchronous dialogue and singing. It was a huge hit, and within a few years the majority of Hollywood movies were "talkies."

58.   **A**   The Axis powers surrendered months before the bombing of Hiroshima and Nagasaki, so speeding the end of war in Europe could not have been a consideration. The United States was primarily concerned with the difficulty of defeating the Japanese forces; they were both powerful and tenacious. Earlier land battles with the Japanese had resulted in heavy casualties for both sides. But the United States was also concerned about the Soviet Union; with the war in Europe over, the Cold War was beginning. Harry Truman was anxious to finish the war in Japan before the USSR could enter the fray and establish a greater presence in the region. He also hoped that, by demonstrating the power of the atomic bomb, he could intimidate the Soviets and other potential enemies.

59.   **E**   The first Equal Rights Amendment was introduced in Congress in 1923. It failed a floor vote every year thereafter until 1948, at which point it stopped clearing the Judiciary Committee in order to get a floor vote. It finally emerged from Judiciary in 1970, passed both houses with overwhelming majorities, and seemed on its way to ratification. At that point, a considerable coalition of fundamentalists and other social conservatives (including many women) rose up against it. It failed to win ratification in the necessary three-quarters of state legislatures, despite Congress granting its supporters a three-year extension on the ratification deadline. The amendment proscribed, in general terms, discrimination on the basis of gender.

60.   **B**   The colonists objected strongly to the Stamp Acts (1765–1766) but still considered themselves loyal English subjects. The language and tone of the Resolutions of the Stamp Act Congress are respectful and humble.

The Stamp Act required that all printed matter—including all legal documents, licenses, pamphlets, and newspapers—bear a government stamp, on which a duty was to be paid (in hard currency, which, because of the Currency Act and an unfavorable trade balance, was very rare). Violators were tried in vice-admiralty courts (basically military courts, so that the accused was denied the right of a trial before sympathetic peers). The law particularly affected lawyers, writers, and other elites and intellectuals, who in turn immediately began to eloquently publicize their opposition. The Sugar and Currency Acts had raised the hackles of the New England colonists, but most colonists saw themselves as loyal British subjects. Opposition to these new restrictions and regulations was weak and poorly organized; however, those protests laid the groundwork for more effective opposition to the Stamp Act. Ultimately, the colonists settled upon a three-tiered attack on the Stamp Act: raise public consciousness on the issue (through meetings, held by the Sons of Liberty), petition Parliament (none of these petitions included threats of rebellion), and boycott British imports. The last strategy effectively brought British merchants into the political mix; they lobbied Parliament for a repeal because many depended on colonial commerce. Parliament did repeal the Stamp Act but passed the Declaratory Act to remind the colonists who was boss.

61.   **E**   The doctrine is a central tenet of the radical wing of the states' rights movement. It grows out of the principle that the main purpose of the Constitution is to protect the states against the potential

tyranny of the national government; thus, the states have the right to nullify any federal law. The doctrine first appears in the Kentucky Resolutions, in which Jefferson argued (as he also would in the debate over the First Bank of the United States) that the Tenth Amendment prohibits the federal government from exercising powers not explicitly given it by the Constitution.

The doctrine played a central role in a dispute between President Andrew Jackson and the state of South Carolina. The state declared its right to nullification in response to the Tariff of 1828, popularly known as the Tariff of Abominations. The state did not actually nullify any federal laws until 1832, when it nullified a different tariff. A potentially violent confrontation was averted when Henry Clay negotiated the compromise Tariff of 1833, in response to which South Carolina repealed its nullification law. The concept of nullification remained a powerful one up through the Civil War, when it was invoked by secessionists, and is, in fact, argued today by many so-called "patriot" militias and groups.

62. **D** Tocqueville arrived in the United States in the 1830s; his assignment from the French government was to study U.S. prisons. He was immediately impressed by the level of interest the general public took in politics, and later came to admire the relative impermanence of the social hierarchy, especially compared with Europe's rigid social order. In his popular and influential *Democracy in America*, he argues that the absence of an aristocracy, along with the seemingly limitless amount of land available to the west, allowed Americans tremendous opportunities for self-advancement.

Some of the incorrect answers are noteworthy. (C) is quite wrong: There were few unions to speak of at this early stage in American economic development, and when the government took sides in labor-management disputes, it was invariably to side with management. (E) also is chronologically inaccurate: Mandatory education and public schools were not widespread phenomena in the United States until after the Civil War.

63. **A** In January 1848 a carpenter discovered gold at Sutter's Mill, California. Word spread quickly, and soon the Gold Rush was on. Western migrants continued to travel west on the Oregon Trail until they reached Fort Hall (in modern Idaho), but then they turned south on the California Trail and headed for where the gold was supposed to be. Most wound up disappointed, as only a very few found much gold. In seven years California's population grew from 15,000 to 300,000. One observer noted that, by 1849, the western section of the Oregon Trail (which led into the Oregon Territory) "bore no evidence of having been much traveled."

64. **E** The free silver campaign aimed to increase the money supply through the free coinage of silver. It was the great cause of the Populist party, which argued that the existing monetary practices favored the wealthy and elite, particularly in the Northeast. Free coinage of silver, the party argued, would cause inflation but would also put more money in circulation, making it easier for farmers to pay off their debts. Furthermore, Populists felt that a larger money supply was appropriate to the United States' tremendous growth rate at that time. The policy was naturally quite popular with farmers, but not with bankers, who would have had their loans repaid with devalued currency. Free silver was a central issue in the 1896 election, during which the Populists and the Democratic party joined forces.

65. **B** The Spanish took control of the Philippines early in the sixteenth century (the country is named after Philip II, a Spanish King). The United States recognized the nation's value as a port for Pacific trade, and during the Spanish-American War attacked and destroyed the Spanish fleet, effectively ending Spanish control there. Spain granted ownership of the nation to the United States in the treaty that followed the war. You should know that the Filipinos had been waging a war of independence against the Spanish and continued to fight the United States for years. In the 1930s the United States allowed the Philippines to govern its internal affairs and was preparing to grant it full independence when World War II broke out. The Japanese captured the Philippines, forestalling Filipino independence until the island was liberated by the United States.

66. **C** The case was *Schenck v. United States*, and it tested the validity of the Espionage Act of 1917, which forbade "false" statements intended to obstruct the draft or foment rebellion in the military; it also forbade the use of the mail to send any treasonous material. Schenck and his co-defendants had sent fliers arguing against the draft to conscripts, for which they were tried and convicted in a lower court. The Supreme Court upheld the conviction. Oliver Wendell Holmes wrote the majority opinion, which included the passages in the question as well as this: "When a nation is at war many things that might be said in times of peace are such a hindrance to its effort that their utterance will not be endured so long as men fight."

67. **A** America's economic recovery during World War II continued through the postwar years. When the war ended, the Depression-era generation found that it finally had money for luxuries and the leisure time in which to enjoy them. This new level of comfort meant that, in growing numbers of American families, children no longer had to drop out of school to get jobs as a matter of survival. Furthermore, many of those who lived through the Depression believed that education was a hedge against bad economic periods, and they strongly encouraged their children to study further. The result was steadily increasing graduation rates.

About the wrong answers: (B) *Brown v. the Board of Education* concerned school segregation. The chart clearly indicates that college enrollments increased during the 1960s, so (C) is incorrect. Massachusetts passed a compulsory education law in 1852; by World War II, most states had some form of compulsory education. And while (E) is true, it addresses postgraduate study, which is not represented in the chart, and it discusses career choices that relatively few people pursue.

68. **B** George Wallace was governor of Alabama and a staunch segregationist. Unhappy with the direction his national party, the Democrats, was taking, Wallace mounted a third-party candidacy in 1968. Wallace knew he could never win a national election, but he hoped to win enough states in the South to throw the election to the House of Representatives, where his chances would be better. Wallace garnered 10,000,000 votes and took 46 electoral votes. In some states where he didn't win, he gathered enough potential Democratic votes to throw the state to Nixon. In the end Nixon was able to win enough states to take the electoral college.

69. **D** The English settlers who arrived in Virginia in 1607 would almost certainly have starved to death had it not been for assistance they received from the Powhatan Confederacy, a group of six nearby

Algonkian tribes. The Algonkians traded with the colonists, providing food in return for weapons and tools, in hopes that an alliance with the Europeans would provide them with an advantage against enemy tribes. The alliance was an uneasy one at best; despite their sometimes pathetic reliance on the Algonkians, the English settlers refused to consider seriously the legitimacy of Algonkian culture. Some of these areas of difference are enumerated in the answer choices. (A): The English not only claimed the right to private property—an alien notion to the Algonkians—but they also refused to acknowledge the Algonkians' right to their hunting grounds, on the basis that the land was not cultivated. (B): In Algonkian society, women worked the fields and men hunted; the English found this barbaric, as they considered farming to be work and hunting a leisure activity, both falling strictly in the domain of a man's work. (C): The English certainly considered their society superior, and the Algonkians certainly did not agree. (E): The English came from a monarchical society, in which leadership positions were inherited and power was nearly absolute; in Algonkian society, authority was conferred by fellow tribe members and could be revoked. The two groups were both deeply religious, making (D) the correct answer.

70. **D** The period between 1649 and 1660 is often referred to as the "Interregnum," Latin for "between kings," because during that brief period England had no king. Rather, it was governed as a republican commonwealth, with its leader, Oliver Cromwell, named "lord protector."

The English Civil Wars, between 1642 and 1648, are often called the Puritan Revolution, because they pitted the Puritans against the Crown. Royalists fought for the divine right of the king to rule and the maintenance of the Church of England (the Episcopal church) as the official church of state. The Puritans fought for a republican Commonwealth and a greater level of state tolerance for freedom of religion. The Puritans won and, for a little over a decade, ruled England. The death of Cromwell (1658) robbed the Puritans of their best-known and most respected leader, and by 1660 the Stuarts were restored to the throne. During the Interregnum, Puritans had little motive to move to the New World. Everything they wanted—freedom to practice their religion, representation in the government—was available to them in England. With the restoration of the Stuarts, many Puritans sought the opportunities and freedoms of the New World, bringing with them the republican ideals of the revolution.

71. **C** The Monroe Doctrine basically declares the United States' prerogative over the Western Hemisphere, with an accompanying promise by the United States not to interfere in matters in the Eastern Hemisphere. Monroe's declaration followed a period in which a number of Latin American colonies fought and won wars of independence. After carefully considering the pros and cons, the United States decided to recognize the new governments (Europe had not yet done so). Fear that Spain, France, or even England might try to conquer these new countries led Monroe and his secretary of state, John Quincy Adams, to devise a policy of mutual noninterference. That policy was completed and announced at a time when France was occupying Spain, further validating American fears that European governments did not respect others' autonomy. Monroe declared the United States' willingness to recognize and respect sovereign governments, and pointed out that difference between the United States and Europe in justifying his doctrine. He further declared

the United States' right to intercede in the Americas when U.S. interests were threatened. Europe basically ignored the Monroe Doctrine, because the U.S. military lacked the power to enforce it. However, no one intervened in the Western Hemisphere because England wouldn't let them, which made the Monroe Doctrine look like a big success. It was invoked with greater success by later administrations, most notably Teddy Roosevelt's.

72. **B** In the 1831 case *Cherokee Nation v. Georgia*, Chief Justice John Marshall ruled that American Indian tribes were neither foreign nations nor states, and as such had no standing in federal court: In short, he ruled they had no right to sue. He argued further, however, that the tribes had a right to their lands and could not be forced to give them up by anyone, including the federal government. The 1832 case *Worcester v. Georgia* reaffirmed that position. When the state of Georgia tried to relocate the Cherokees, Marshall ruled that only the federal government, not the states, had authority over Native Americans within the boundaries of the United States. President Jackson didn't like Marshall's rulings and simply ignored them, pursuing an aggressive policy aimed at pushing tribes farther and farther west. The result was the Trail of Tears, the involuntary westward migration of the Cherokees. Over one-quarter died of disease and exhaustion during the three- to four-month forced march (supervised by the U.S. Army).

73. **A** These laws or "black codes" pertained to those few free blacks in the South. (Do not confuse them with the more widespread, better-known black codes imposed by Southern legislatures in the period between the end of the Civil War and the beginning of military Reconstruction.) As slavery became a more divisive issue both nationally and locally, Southern slave owners began to fear the presence of free blacks. They saw such blacks as potential instigators of rebellion. Furthermore, many viewed blacks as inferior and resented their freedom. Finally, freed slaves made up the majority of skilled laborers in the South, meaning that they were competing with whites for better-paying work.

Accordingly, the Southern states sought ways to encourage free blacks to leave the South; barring that, the states sought to severely restrict their freedoms. To that end, they enacted black codes. In various states black codes required black skilled laborers to be licensed, banned blacks from specific jobs, such as river captains and pilots, forbade blacks to assemble in public, and prohibited teaching blacks to read and write. Not surprisingly, many free Southern blacks moved north. Interestingly, many Northern states tried to discourage their migration.

Southern whites (particularly large property holders) feared free blacks so much that as time passed, they placed greater and greater restrictions on the ability of slaveholders to free their slaves. By the end of the 1830s, most Southern states required court and/or legislative approval of a manumission (a fancy word for "freeing slaves"). By the 1850s some states had entirely outlawed manumission.

74. **D** The United States almost fought a war over the Oregon Territory, which consisted of present-day Oregon, Washington, and parts of Montana and Idaho. Originally, American expansionists and settlers demanded all the territory up to the 54°40' boundary, and were willing to fight the British (who held it as part of their Canadian territories) to get it. Contemporaneous conflicts near Mexico caused President Polk to reconsider war with Great Britain; he feared that two wars would spread

forces dangerously thin, as well as damage his popularity with voters. Therefore, Polk decided to negotiate a settlement with the British—the United States accepted a boundary at the 49th parallel—and directed his military activities southward. The United States subsequently entered a war with Mexico, which netted it much of the territory that makes up the Southwestern states.

75. **E** In the 1860s the government initiated its reservation policy by which Native Americans were granted (usually less desirable) portions of the lands they inhabited. The policy failed on many fronts, and by the 1880s the government was searching for a different tack. Congress struck on the Dawes Severalty Act, which offered individual Native Americans 160-acre plots in return for leaving their reservations; through this program Congress hoped to hasten the assimilation of Native Americans, whose cultures most congressmen held in contempt. The results were not good: Most American Indians preferred to remain among their tribes and did not accept the offer. Those who did accept usually ended up selling their land to whites, who often placed considerable pressure on them to do so.

76. **D** Although supporters of antitrust legislation had hoped to create a law that would break up corporate monopolies, the only law they could get through Congress was the vaguely worded Sherman Antitrust Act (1890). It clearly forbade "every contract, combination in the form of trust or otherwise, or conspiracy in the restraint of trade"; however, it did not define these terms, leaving their interpretation up to the business-friendly courts. In a number of cases, judges made ludicrous rulings in favor of business (in 1895, eight of nine Supreme Court justices ruled that a sugar company controlling 98 percent of the refining process did not violate the law). Many courts were quick to determine that labor unions represented "a conspiracy in the restraint of trade," and until the beginning of the twentieth century the law was most often used to harass and break unions. All that changed in 1901, when Teddy Roosevelt gained the presidency and pursued a number of successful antitrust suits against business monopolies.

77. **B** "Welfare" usually refers to help for the less fortunate, so eliminate (D) and (E), which say nothing about services for the underprivileged. You should also cross out (C), because while this refers to doing something for the poor, it isn't about helping them. Now, focusing on "capitalism," the parts about "incentives," "profit sharing," and "dissuade them from joining unions" should make this a logical choice.It should also point you in the direction of (B), because the period in question was one in which businesses actively and aggressively fought unionization. This is actually similar to the previous question.

78. **B** The Underwood-Simmons Tariff was passed under Woodrow Wilson. (Hint: "Under," then "w" for Wilson.) Although Wilson was one of the three Progressive presidents (Roosevelt and Taft being the other two), he was the only Democrat. The Republican party has supported big business since the end of the nineteenth century, and therefore, high protective tariffs are usually enacted when Republicans are in office.

While it is true that there were some conservative Democrats who advocated high protective tariffs, letter (E) is incorrect because the Underwood-Simmons Tariff *lowered* duties on imported goods, and therefore conservative Democrats did not endorse this legislation.

79. **A** As he began his first term, Roosevelt was faced with an agricultural market in which the bottom had dropped out; farmers had so overproduced that their crops were worth virtually nothing. Roosevelt's solution, the AAA, provided payments to farmers in return for their agreement to cut production by up to one-half. The money to cover this program came from increased taxes on meat packers, millers, and other food processors. The program stabilized agricultural prices and increased American income from imports, but it came to an end when the Supreme Court declared it unconstitutional in 1936. A second AAA in 1938 served much the same purpose while avoiding those aspects that voided the first AAA.

80. **C** The SNCC originated in 1960 to promote anti-segregationism and black voting rights in the South. Although it was primarily a black organization, whites also participated in the SNCC, and in its early years the committee pursued an integrationist agenda. However, years of Southern opposition, often entailing jailings and beatings, radicalized the organization. In 1966 Stokely Carmichael took over the SNCC and expelled its white members. Proclaiming that blacks could never receive justice in the white-dominated mainstream, Carmichael advocated black power through separatism and violence against those who would continue to suppress blacks.

THE DBQ EXPLAINED

The document-based question begins with a mandatory 15-minute reading period. During these 15 minutes, you'll want to (1) come up with some information not included in the given documents (your outside knowledge) to include in your essay; (2) get an overview of what each document means; (3) decide what opinion you are going to argue; and (4) write an outline of your essay.

This DBQ concerns U.S. neutrality prior to World War I. You will have to explore to what extent the United States followed a policy of neutrality between 1914 and 1917. On the following pages, we will talk about how you might successfully explore this topic.

The first thing you want to do, BEFORE YOU LOOK AT THE DOCUMENTS, is brainstorm for a minute or two. Try to list everything you remember about the period leading up to the United States' entry into World War I. This list will serve as your reference to the outside information you must provide in order to earn a top grade.

Next, read over the documents. As you read them, take notes in the margins and underline those passages that you are certain you are going to use in your essay. If a document helps you remember a piece of outside information, add that information to your brainstorming list. If you cannot make sense of a document or it argues strongly against your position, relax! You do not need to mention every document to score well on the DBQ.

Here is what you need to look for in each document to get the most out of it:

- The author
- The date
- The audience (for whom was the document intended?)
- The significance

Remember: You are being asked to write 50 percent document interpretation and 50 percent outside information. Don't get so lost in the documents that you forget to bring in outside information. Readers will not be able to give you a high score unless you have both! What readers really don't like is a laundry list of documents: That is, a paper in which the student merely goes through the documents, explaining each one. Those students are often the ones who forget to bring in outside information, because they are so focused on going through the documents.

Here is what you might see in the time you have to look over the documents:

The Documents

Document A

This is an excerpt from Wilson's declaration of neutrality. It makes several important points you can use.

Neutrality is defined as "impartiality and fairness and friendliness to all concerned." This standard will enable you to argue that the United States was, or was not, neutral.

The American people come from the different nations at war. The political implication is that even if the U.S. government wanted to enter World War I, the varied national backgrounds of the electorate would make it difficult to rally the nation to one side or the other. Even before Vietnam, American politicians knew the risks of entering an unpopular war.

Wilson envisions a prominent role for the United States resulting from neutrality. He sees the United States as "the one people holding itself ready to play a part of impartial mediation and speak the counsels of peace and accommodation, not as a partisan, but as a friend." This point argues that the United States entered the war as a neutral force, or, at the very least, intended to.

Document B

This excerpt is from a letter a respected German-American intellectual wrote to Wilson early in the war. It describes German-American perceptions of U.S. favoritism toward the Allies.

This document persuasively argues that U.S. policies at the time favored the Allies. The details are important, but less important than the overall point; the document illustrates that an intelligent critique of U.S. policy, held up to its own definition of neutrality, is possible. In fact, when Wilson received this letter, he sent it to his secretary of state with a note essentially saying, "This letter makes a pretty strong case."

Munsterberg's second point, regarding the detention and searching of Germans and Austrians, is not often mentioned in discussions of the events leading up to World War I, and you are not expected to have heard of this policy. However, it does provide ammunition for those arguing that the United States was never neutral; searching civilians is, at the very least, an act of aggressive mistrust. If Allied travelers were not being treated the same way—and the letter implies they were not—then it indicates favoritism.

The issue of contraband could lead you to discuss the British blockade. (Document C provides more evidence of the effect of the British blockade.) Contraband is illegal merchandise. During war, contraband always includes weapons and other supplies necessary to the successful execution of war. The notion that contraband is illegal does not preclude the United States from selling arms to Europe; this same document demonstrates that the United States did just that. It does mean, however, that a country executing a successful blockade has the right to confiscate contraband. Munsterberg is saying that England defined contraband very broadly, including on its list of contraband items supplies that the German civilian population needed to survive. He complains that the United States was not aggressive enough in protesting this practice.

The last paragraph talks about the U.S. sale of arms to belligerents. This information can be interpreted in many ways. You could argue that to sell arms is essentially non-neutral, even if you sell to both sides. To make this argument, you would have to equate neutrality with pacifism (something Wilson does in Document A) and then assert that arms sales prolong the war, and so are counterproductive to the goals of neutrality. On the other hand, you could argue that because of the successful British blockade, arms sales were predominantly to the Allies; arms shipments to Germany never made it through the blockade. Again, Document C will help bolster this position.

Document C

This quotation often comes from the memoirs of Robert Lansing, acting secretary of state and, later, secretary of state under Wilson.

Lansing describes the effects of the British blockade. Note, merchants are losing profits and Americans are being terribly inconvenienced.

You might use this to argue favoritism toward the British. Since the British were interfering with U.S. trade, why didn't we go to war against them? To the contrary, you could point out that as it became clear that U.S. commercial interests were at stake, U.S. involvement in the war became more likely. In other words, the United States started out neutral, but the British blockade and German submarine warfare slowly forced America into the war. (See Documents E, F, G, and H.) You can also use this document to further discuss the effects of the British blockade on (1) the Allies and (2) the Central Powers. As you do, ask yourself whether the United States' response to the blockade was consistent with its policy of neutrality.

Document D

This is a report from then-Secretary of State William Jennings Bryan (he would soon resign in protest) to the Senate. It is still early in the war.

Do not be intimidated by the length of this passage! The main point is simple. The government felt that its actions were neutral. This letter can be seen as a response to the complaints voiced in Munsterberg's letter.

Bryan discusses communication, the blockade, arms sales, and perceived hostility toward the governments of the Central Powers. In almost every case, he argues that England's advantages in geographic location and naval power are causing America's perceived breaches of neutrality.

If you are arguing that the United States was neutral, you might mention (if you remember) that Bryan, a pacifist, was committed to neutrality. His feeling that U.S. actions were neutral could be presented as strong evidence for your case.

If you are arguing that the United States was not neutral, you might contend that because Bryan is reporting to the Senate, he paints the rosiest picture he can. You might also mention (if you remember) that Bryan resigned not long after because of his disagreements with U.S. policy.

Document E

This advertisement ran in 50 American newspapers just before the *Lusitania* sailed.

This document gives you the opportunity to discuss German submarine warfare. The British blockade was too effective for the Germans to fight it conventionally. The Germans therefore turned to the U-boat, or submarine. Submarines gave the Germans the advantage of surprise, as the British had no means of detecting them. You could argue that because submarine attacks resulted in the deaths of U.S. citizens, the use of submarines constituted a hostile act that ultimately forced the neutral United States into war. You might mention that Wilson regarded submarines as a violation of international law (see page 191) and, as such, repeatedly asked the Germans to curtail their usage.

On the contrary, you might claim that the British blockade forced Germany to use submarines, and that by not opposing the blockade more aggressively, the United States was essentially siding with the Allies.

This document, along with Document F, also gives you the opportunity to discuss the sinking of the *Lusitania* and its effects, both on U.S. policy and on anti-German sentiments in the general population. The shift in American public opinion away from neutrality is a factor you might mention in your discussion of U.S. entry into the war. Document I provides more evidence of this shift in public opinion.

Document F

This customs report provides evidence that the *Lusitania* carried weapons.

This document can be paired with Munsterberg's complaint about arms sales (Document B) to support the argument that the United States was not neutral. Note that the shipment is headed for England. Your outside knowledge that the sinking of the *Lusitania* led to William Jennings Bryan's resignation as secretary of state would also be helpful here. Remember, the United States protested the sinking vigorously and demanded reparations. Bryan pointed out that the ship carried arms and quietly assured the Germans that the United States understood why the ship was sunk. In short, Bryan was at odds with official government policy, and he resigned when he realized that his advice to the president was going unheeded. His replacement, Robert Lansing, more active in defending American interests than Bryan, was willing to trade a reduction in American commerce for peace.

If you are arguing for neutrality, it is best to mention this document only in passing. Note that in Document D, Bryan explains how the United States reconciles arms sales and neutrality. His justification, in short, is that international law does not outlaw such sales.

Document G

Wilson gave this speech after the Germans sunk the *Sussex*, an unarmed French channel steamer. The document is from 1916, almost a year after the sinking of the *Lusitania*.

Wilson threatens to break off diplomatic relations with Germany—a first step toward war.

Wilson invokes international law. Because Wilson interpreted international law as severely restricting submarine warfare, submarine attacks by Germany particularly angered him. Wilson considered himself and the United States the defenders of international law.

Wilson continues to declare America's international role as a mediator and peacemaker, as he did in his neutrality speech (Document A). This insistence indicates that Wilson still considers the United States a neutral force.

You might point out that a year after the sinking of the *Lusitania* and that of several other ships, the United States is still not at war. This fact strongly argues for neutrality through early 1916.

Document H

German Foreign Minister Arthur Zimmerman sent this telegram to German Ambassador Johann von Bernstoff.

Zimmerman instructs Bernstoff to "cut a deal" with the Mexicans. The telegram states that if the Mexicans start a border war with the United States, the Germans will help them. As a result, Mexico will regain much of the Southwest.

The telegram also notes that the Germans are about to resume unrestricted submarine warfare, which they had renounced in a treaty with the United States following the sinking of the Sussex.

The telegram mentions involving Japan in the war, thus widening the conflict.

Many Americans saw this telegram, which was made public in late February 1917, as the final straw. Because it showed Germany's willingness to intervene in American affairs and to draw other parts of the world into the conflict, the telegram convinced many Americans that Germany was power-mad. The cartoon (Document I) reinforces that perception.

Document I

This is an editorial cartoon that appeared in 1917, just prior to U.S. entry into the war.

If you find the inclusion of this document confusing, just skip it. You have plenty to write about without it. Remember, you will do better on the DBQ writing about what you know than by taking a wild—and perhaps incorrect—guess at what the test writers were thinking when they included a certain document. Again, you do not need to refer to all the documents to get a high score on the DBQ.

This document illustrates the shift in America's perception of Germany and America's readiness to go to war. Here, Germany is clearly depicted as an evil force that must be stopped, hardly a view consistent with a policy of neutrality.

Outside Information

We have already discussed much more than you could possibly include in a 45-minute essay. Do not worry. You will not be expected to mention everything or even most of what we have covered in the section above. You will, however, be expected to include some outside information; that is, information not mentioned directly in the documents.

Here is some outside information you might have used in your essay. The information is divided into two groups: general concepts and specific events.

General Concepts

- Even before the war the United States relied more on trade with the British than with Germany. After the war began, this dependence became even heavier as the British blockade decreased American trade with Germany. The war effort also resulted in an increase in British orders for American goods. This increase occurred because the war had decreased British productivity. The British had taken men out of factories and put them in the army, and they also had converted some commercial manufacturing to munitions manufacturing.

- When the war started, official U.S. policy stated that American banks should not lend money to any nation at war. However, bankers pressured the administration to change this policy because Europe did not have the money to pay for the American goods it was ordering. Also, the loans were profitable, and American banks feared losing a lucrative opportunity to banks in other neutral nations. The majority of these loans went to the Allies.

- Wilson hoped the war would end in a draw. He thought a victorious Germany "would change the course of our civilization and make the United States a military nation." He also felt that an Allied victory would shift the balance of power too favorably toward England and France. Many of Wilson's advisors, however, were both pro-British and anti-German.

- "Wilsonianism," Wilson's idealized vision of the future, included universal, non-exploitative, free market capitalism; universal political constitutionalism, which would lead to the disappearance of empires; and universal cooperation and peace through the offices of the League of Nations. Wilson was also anxious to create a world leadership role for the United States. Many of his actions can be explained as the pursuit of these goals.

- Wilson held very strong views concerning international law, and those views favored the British. According to international law, an attacker had to warn a passenger or merchant ship before attacking. Submarines did not do this, for the obvious reason that it would cancel the greatest advantage submarines had; namely, the element of surprise. Germany argued that submarines provided their only means of breaking British control of shipping channels, but this assertion did not persuade Wilson.

Specific Events

- The British blockade—From the beginning of the war, the British used their advantage at sea. They blocked shipping channels and confiscated any contraband headed for a Central Power country. Furthermore, England defined contraband very broadly, including some food and commercial products on its contraband list. The United States lodged numerous complaints against the practice, but the British government always paid for what it confiscated. The payment satisfied merchants and took enough pressure off Washington that the U.S. government never forced the issue.

- The sinking of the *Lusitania*, May 7, 1915—You will lose big points if you say that this event caused the United States to enter the war; the United States waited another two years before it started to fight. The *Lusitania* was a luxury liner that sailed from New York to England. When it sank, it took with it 1,198 passengers, among them 128 Americans. As Document F illustrates, the *Lusitania* was carrying a considerable amount of contraband, including over 4 million rounds of rifle ammunition. Still, Wilson and most of his advisors considered Germany's attack on the ship barbaric. As a result of the attack, anti-German sentiments among voters grew stronger and more widespread.

- William Jennings Bryan's resignation—Bryan resigned in the aftermath of the Lusitania incident. An ardent pacifist, Bryan wanted the United States to respond to the incident with a strongly worded letter of protest to both the English and the Germans. Bryan also suggested that the United States ban American passengers from any ship flying the flag of a belligerent country. Wilson rejected both recommendations. He sent a letter of protest only to the Germans, and he refused to restrict American travel abroad. Bryan resigned in protest. In response to Wilson's letter, the Germans temporarily halted U-boat attacks on passenger ships.

- The sinking of the *Arabic*—In mid-August 1915, the Germans sank another passenger liner. This time only two Americans died, but the government was furious about the breach of etiquette. The Germans pledged again never to attack a passenger liner without advance warning, a promise they did not keep.

- Gore-McLemore resolution—After the sinking of the *Arabic*, Congress began to seriously consider a resolution prohibiting Americans from traveling on armed merchant ships or on ships carting contraband. Wilson fought this Gore-McLemore resolution. Wilson remained adamant that neutral nations should have free access to international waters. The resolution was defeated.

- The sinking of the *Sussex* and the Sussex Agreement—In February 1917, the Germans sank a French channel steamer called the Sussex. No Americans died, although four were injured. However, the incident had a big impact because the *Sussex* was neither armed nor was it carrying contraband. In short, its sinking convinced many people that either (1) German submarines could not tell what they were shooting at, or (2) the Germans did not care that they were killing civilians. Either way, it supported the widespread sentiment that submarine warfare was barbaric. Germany again agreed not to attack passenger ships without warning. Wilson was still resolutely determined to stay out of the war, so he accepted the agreement.

- The presidential election of 1916—Despite the many quarrels with England and Germany, most Americans still wanted no part of the European hostilities. All the major candidates campaigned against entry into the war. The Republican, Hughes, courted German-American votes and depicted Wilson as partial to the Allies. Wilson campaigned on the slogan "He kept us out of war." As the campaign wore on, however, he also began to stress "preparedness" for the possibility of war. Wilson won by a narrow margin.

- More details about the Zimmerman note—By the time this telegram was leaked to the press, Germany had already warned the United States of its plans to resume unrestricted submarine warfare. The reason for the shift in policy is that the Germans realized that without the submarines they would soon lose the war. The resumption of submarine warfare greatly angered Wilson. When the British intercepted the telegram, Wilson had already severed diplomatic ties with Germany and was considering his future options. Wilson received the telegram on February 24, 1917, and the newspapers received it four days later.

  The telegram represents a last-ditch effort on Germany's part to keep the United States out of the war. Germany knew that its resumption of submarine warfare would draw the United States into the war. Planning to distract the United States with a border skirmish, Germany hoped to buy enough time to win the war in Europe before U.S. reinforcements could arrive. Because the Mexican Revolution had just replaced a government friendly to the United States with one much more hostile, the U.S. government took the threat of a German-backed Mexican attack in the Southwest very seriously.

  It particularly galled the United States that Zimmerman sent the telegram through U.S. State Department channels. The United States had opened those channels to him in hopes of bringing the Germans back to the negotiating table. When he used those same channels to plot war against the United States, it was regarded as an act of extreme hostility and bad manners.

  The United States did not immediately declare war. In the weeks that followed, Wilson asked Congress for a policy of "armed neutrality," which would allow American merchant ships to mount offensive weapons. Debate was fierce, showing how strong anti-war sentiment was even at the time. The United States did not officially declare war until the following month, on April 2, 1917.

- The Nye Commission investigations of 1933—The Nye Commission, investigating American business practices in the years leading up to World War I, revealed that American arms merchants had lobbied intensely for entry into the war. The commission also discovered that these merchants had reaped enormous profit from arms sales, first from whomever they could get them to in Europe, then from the U.S. government.

Choosing a Side

We have just covered an intimidating amount of material. Do not worry; your essay only has to cover some of the points mentioned above. This review mentions nearly everything you might include in a successful essay, not everything that must be in a successful essay.

Your next task is to choose a position to argue and then construct a strong justification from your notes on the documents and outside information. Document-based questions are written so that there is no one right answer, and there are many different defensible positions to this question. There are also many different ways to argue the same point; that is, there is no one right way to write an essay for any given argument.

Here are some positions you might argue:

- The United States was neutral at the beginning of the war, but a combination of factors—such as economic interests, German transgressions of international law, and America's predisposition toward England—ultimately drew America into the war.

- The United States was neutral at the beginning of the war, but was provoked to fight by German aggression.

- The United States claimed neutrality, and maybe its leaders even convinced themselves that their actions were neutral, but in reality U.S. actions helped the Allies. Consequently, the United States was never really neutral.

- The United States was correct in claiming neutrality because its policies adhered to its standards of neutrality. However, the Central Powers legitimately accused the United States of acting in a way that assisted the Allies and so were justified in regarding the United States as non-neutral. The question is semantic; whether the United States was neutral depends on how you define neutrality.

The only position you should certainly avoid is the claim that the United States had always sided fully with the Allies and lied about neutrality in order to help them. There is simply too much evidence of Wilson's commitment to neutrality to support that argument.

Planning Your Essay

Unless you read extremely quickly, you probably will not have time to write a detailed outline for your essay during the 15-minute reading period. However, it is worth taking several minutes to jot down a loose structure of your essay, because it will actually save you time when you write. First, decide on your thesis and write it down in the test booklet. (There is usually some blank space below the documents.) Then take a minute or two to brainstorm all the points you might put in your essay. Choose the strongest points and number them in the order you plan to present them. Lastly, note which documents and outside information you plan to use in conjunction with each point. If you organize your essay before you write, the actual writing process will go much more smoothly. More important, you will not write yourself into a corner, and suddenly find yourself making a point you cannot support or heading toward a weak conclusion (or worse still, no conclusion at all).

For example, if you are going to argue that the United States was neutral at the start of the war, but a combination of factors eventually forced America's entry, you might write down an abbreviated version of that thesis, such as:

Started neutral, forced into war

Then you would brainstorm a list of ideas and events you wanted to mention in your essay, such as:

Started neutral
British blockade
Business losing money from blockade
Wilson didn't want Germany to win war
U-boats violate international law
U-boats kill U.S. civilians
Zimmerman telegram
Lusitania
Sussex
American people were against war
Americans a little more favorable to war by 1917

Next, you would want to figure out which of your brainstorm ideas could be the main idea of a paragraph, which could be used as evidence to support a point, and which should be eliminated. You would probably want to begin your first paragraph by stating your thesis and then discussing how the United States was neutral at the start of the war. Your first point, "Started neutral," could be the main idea of that paragraph. That the "American people were against the war" would help explain why the United States was neutral, so you could use that as evidence. At this point, your list might look this way:

Started neutral   1
British blockade
Business losing money from blockade
Wilson didn't want Germany to win war
U-boats violate international law
U-boats kill U.S. civilians
Zimmerman telegram
Lusitania
Sussex
American people were against war   evidence for point 1
Americans a little more favorable to war by 1917

What else would you want to mention in this paragraph? Certainly refer to Document A, Wilson's statement of American neutrality and his definition of neutrality. Use that definition to explain how each of America's ensuing actions was either neutral or favorable to the Allies. You might also mention Wilson's desire to turn the United States into a world power, and how he viewed neutrality as a means toward that end. Mentioning this point helps you fulfill the requirement to include outside information.

Next you might want to discuss the British blockade and America's response to it. That would make "British blockade" the subject of paragraph 2; "business losing money from blockade" is something you might want to mention in this paragraph. Now your list might look this way:

Started neutral	1
British blockade	2
Business losing money from blockade	evidence for point 2
Wilson didn't want Germany to win war	
U-boats violate international law	
U-boats kill U.S. civilians	
Zimmerman telegram	
Lusitania	
Sussex	
American people were against war	evidence for point 1
Americans a little more favorable to war by 1917	

In this paragraph you probably also want to mention Documents B, C, and D. Document D, Bryan's letter to the Senate, gives the strongest evidence of U.S. neutrality. You might want to use Documents B and C (Munsterberg's complaint to Wilson and Lansing's description of the effects of the blockade) to explain how the United States found itself more involved in Europe's war than it perhaps had expected to be.

Proceed in this way until you have finished planning your strategy. Try to fit as many of the documents into your argument as you can, but do not stretch too far to fit one in. An obvious, desperate stretch will only hurt your grade.

As you write remember that you do not have to fall entirely on one side or another of this issue. History is complex, and simple explanations are rarely accurate ones. If your essay argues that the United States intended to remain neutral and then discusses the events referred to by the documents in the context of neutrality, you will get a 9 on your DBQ essay, even if it does not characterize each U.S. action as neutral or non-neutral.

Arguing Against Neutrality

If you choose to argue that the United States was not neutral, you should concentrate on Documents A, B, and C. Use Document A, Wilson's congressional address, for the definition of neutrality, then use the other documents and outside knowledge to argue that the United States did not meet its own definition. Document B, Munsterberg's letter, really helps your position as it points out how U.S. actions appeared non-neutral at the time these events were taking place. Use Document C, Lansing's criticism of the British blockade, to argue that the United States put up with abuses from the British at the same time they were denouncing Germany for similar abuses. Focus also on Document F, which describes the substantial arms shipment aboard the *Lusitania*. You might then incorporate the other documents by claiming that Germany responded reasonably to its situation and that the United States, as a neutral nation, should have understood its actions. That position, by the way, is how William Jennings Bryan felt; if you knew that and included it in your essay, you would have gotten major bonus points for outside knowledge.

What You Should Have Discussed

Regardless of what side of the issue you argued, your essay should have discussed all of the following:

- Wilson's declaration of neutrality and his definition of neutrality
- Munsterberg's letter
- Bryan's response to Munsterberg
- the British blockade
- German submarine warfare
- the sinking of the *Lusitania*
- Zimmerman telegram

Give yourself very high marks for outside knowledge if you mentioned any three of the following:

- Wilsonianism
- U.S. balance of trade with the Allies and the Central Powers
- U.S. loans to England and France
- Wilson's cabinet and its predisposition toward England
- Wilson's interpretation of international law regarding submarine warfare
- Bryan's resignation
- the sinking of the *Sussex*
- the Gore-McLemore resolution
- the sinking of the *Arabic*
- "armed neutrality"
- the Nye Commission

THE FREE-RESPONSE QUESTIONS EXPLAINED

For all of your essays, you will want to take a stand, and then back it up with specific examples. Your first paragraph should contain your thesis, and the next two or three should support that thesis with historical data. Don't forget to include a paragraph addressing the other side. (Veteran history teacher Eric Rothschild calls this "the Idiot Paragraph," as in: "Of course there are those idiots who believe that....") Finally, save time for a strong conclusion in which you restate your thesis, tying together your opening statement and your supporting data. Your conclusion needn't be long, but you do need one.

Question 2—New England Before 1650

2. Discuss any TWO of the following as they pertain to self-government in the New England settlements prior to 1650:

    Constitutionalism
    Democracy
    Freedom of religion

This question is probably the more difficult of the two from which you have to choose, primarily because by the time you take the test, it will have been almost a year since you studied the colonial period. It helps to remember that the Puritans settled New England, provided you remember anything specific about the Puritans.

Below are lists of concepts and events you might include in your essay. There is a list for each of the three subjects—constitutional government, democracy, and freedom of religion—and each list is broken into two sub-lists. The first sub-list contains that which you practically have to mention to get a decent grade, and the second sub-list consists of items whose mention would definitely raise your score. Of course, just citing facts is not enough to get a high grade; your essay also has to make sense.

Also, to get those extra points, your essay has to show that you understand the significance of those facts and events. In other words, it does not suffice to simply mention Roger Williams; you also have to state why he was banished from Massachusetts Bay and what his exile reveals about religious tolerance in New England. So, to get a really good grade, you have to mention that he founded Rhode Island and established freedom of religion there. For maximum points you have to note that Rhode Island was the only New England settlement prior to 1650 that acknowledged the rights of all faiths.

Basic Facts

- By 1650 New England had five major English settlements. They were Massachusetts Bay, Plymouth, Connecticut, New Haven, and Rhode Island.

- Separatists settled Plymouth in 1620. The Massachusetts Bay Company settled near Cape Cod in 1630. Connecticut, New Haven, and Rhode Island were settled in the 1630s.

- The New England colonies were self-governing, meaning that they had the right to choose their own governor. By 1700 most of the self-governing colonies had been changed to royal colonies.

Constitutionalism (This choice is the toughest of the three and probably the best one to skip.)

If you chose constitutionalism, your essay pretty much had to mention the following:

- The Mayflower Compact—This document is not a constitution in the strictest sense because it does not provide for an actual government. Still, it was an important forerunner to constitutional government in the New World. Those who signed it agreed to self-government and to abide by the laws they passed.

- The Fundamental Orders of Connecticut—While you may not know it by name, the Fundamental Orders of Connecticut is the formal constitution written by Connecticut settlers and enacted in 1639. (If you know its name and date, give yourself bonus points.) You do have to know that this document was the first formal constitution in the New World and that it stated that the power of government rests in the consent of those being governed. In this assertion, the Connecticut settlers distinguished themselves from the royalists, who often argued that the king, and therefore the government, ruled by divine right (that is, that the king's power came from God, who chose the king).

Give yourself extra credit for mentioning the following:

- The Massachusetts Bay Charter—Acting as a constitution of sorts, it provided the mechanism for self-government. As mentioned above, Massachusetts Bay was technically ruled by the king, but actually it was governed by the company's general court, established in the company charter. All property holders—thus, nearly all the white males in the settlement—voted for deputies (representatives) to the general court. The charter also required the company's proprietors to seek the advice and consent of all freemen before making laws.

- English traditions—(1) The Magna Carta (1215) established a few fundamental, inalienable rights for property holders. (2) The concept of limited government—the idea that the king ruled by the people's consent, and not by divine right—was gaining wider acceptance in England at the time. (3) The existence of a bicameral legislature—the House of Lords and the House of Commons—gave the colonists a tradition in both representative government and constitutional government.

- The English Civil War—In the early seventeenth century, Parliament, backed by reform forces that included the Puritans, began to demand changes to make government more responsive to and representative of the people. King Charles responded by dissolving Parliament in 1629. When he finally recalled Parliament in 1640 (because his government was failing), Puritans demanded major constitutional reforms. Charles refused and a long, bloody war followed. When Puritan forces won in 1649, Charles lost his head and England, briefly, had a constitution. The whole episode demonstrates that the Puritans were strongly committed to constitutionalism.

- The New England Confederation—Founded in 1643, the confederation of New England colonies was mostly powerless because it had no executive power. However, it did settle some border disputes, and it represented the people's willingness to create governmental agencies and to (sort of) abide by their decisions.

Democracy

Your essay pretty much has to mention the following:

- All the New England colonies had elected legislatures by 1650.

- Most had bicameral legislatures, with a lower house elected by all freemen and an upper house usually made up of appointees. Freemen also usually elected the governor.

- New England had a tradition of town meetings at which many of the decisions concerning local government were made.

- Women, indentured servants, and slaves could not vote.

- Except in Rhode Island, only Puritans had the right to vote.

- Otherwise, voting rights were extended to all property holders. Because most settlers were enticed to the New World by the prospect of owning land and because in the early years land was plentiful, nearly all the white male colonists could vote.

Give yourself extra credit for mentioning the following:

- The Massachusetts Bay Company, while technically controlled by the king, had little contact with England. It was empowered to make almost all important decisions. It set an early precedent for self-government in the New World.

- Although initially governed by the owners of the company, Massachusetts Bay's governors soon extended democratic rights to all Puritan property-owning settlers. The colony was ruled by a general court to which all towns were allowed to elect delegates.

- The Plymouth settlement formed a legislature as soon as the settlement expanded beyond a couple of towns.

- The Puritans valued the ideal of the covenant. They believed they had a covenant with God, and they used the covenant as a model for their secular behavior. Accordingly, the Puritans expected everyone to work for the communal good and that everyone would have a voice in how the community was run.

- When settlers moved into the Connecticut Valley, they had their first run-in with Native Americans. The settlers essentially tried to bully the natives out of their land. In the resulting Pequot War, settlers torched villages and killed women and children. You might mention this as evidence of the settlers' rather limited sense of fair play and justice, which are usually considered democratic ideals.

- English traditions—See *Constitutionalism*, above.

- The English Civil War—See *Constitutionalism*, above.

Freedom of Religion

You have to mention the following:

- Even though the Puritans had fled England because of religious persecution, they did not allow freedom of religion in their colonies.

- Roger Williams—Williams came to the New World to minister in the Salem Bay settlement (part of the Massachusetts Bay colony). His writings and teachings advocated separation of church and state and the free practice of all religions in the New World. He also had some other radical ideas, such as suggesting that the English had no right to take land away from Native American tribes. The Puritans banished Williams from the colony in 1636. He moved to modern-day Providence and in 1642 received a charter for the colony of Rhode Island. The charter specified that Rhode Island would protect the freedom of religion. By 1650 Rhode Island was still the only New England colony that allowed individuals to follow their religious faiths in freedom.

- Anne Hutchinson—Hutchinson fell from favor with the Puritans because of her ideas. She believed in the power of grace and also that God spoke directly to certain, chosen people. Those people, she argued, did not need Puritan ministers or the Church because God assured those He spoke to that they would be saved. Her position was known as "antinomianism." Hutchinson's message appealed to many Puritans because of its assurances of salvation. She was considered dangerous, doubly so because she was becoming a powerful woman in a society in which women were definitely second-class citizens. The General Court of Massachusetts brought her up on charges of defaming the ministry, found her guilty, and banished her. She started a settlement in Portsmouth, Rhode Island.

- There was no separation of church and state, as evidenced by the charges against Anne Hutchinson.

About the Structure of Your Essay

For this essay, you want a thesis statement that allows you to discuss the basic characteristics of early American democracy. One way to achieve this is to discuss these developments in the context of their contribution to later developments in American self-governance. For example, you might phrase your thesis in the following manner: "While Rhode Island was atypical in providing true freedom of religion, even allowing those who were not Puritans to vote, New England in general was surprisingly democratic and self-governing from the time of its settlement to 1650." This type of general statement allows you to write a "laundry list" essay in which you discuss as many pertinent facts and concepts as time allows with regard to your two chosen subthemes (constitutionalism, democracy, or freedom of religion). A simple conclusion, perhaps mentioning the similarities and differences between Puritan society and the more pluralistic democratic societies that followed it, would also be helpful.

Question 3—Slavery and Political Parties

3. For the period between 1844 and the Civil War, evaluate the impact of slavery as a political issue on any THREE of the following parties:

> Democratic Party
> Free-Soil Party
> Know-Nothings (American Party)
> Republican Party
> Whig Party

To do well on this essay, you must keep in mind that slavery was a regional issue. Parties that crossed regions were torn apart by the issue; parties that were isolated to a particular region stayed together, but lacked a national mandate with which to lead the entire nation. Of course, you also have to remember at least one (and up to three) political parties that have not existed for 130 years.

There is a lot you can write about on this question. The reader will know that you will not have time to get to everything you could write about, and that is to your advantage. Make sure you get to the most important information, particularly the major historical events and issues that determined these parties' ultimate success or failure.

Here are the lists of what you might have mentioned in your essay:

Basic Facts and Events

You pretty much have to mention the following:

- Major land acquisitions during Polk's presidency—Slavery would eventually have torn the nation apart anyway, but U.S. expansion accounted for its becoming such a big political issue when it did. The acquisition of the Oregon territory and the annexation of territories in the Southwest led both Southerners and Northerners to fear that the balance of power in Congress would shift to one side or the other.

- Kansas-Nebraska Act (1854)—This legislation nullified the Missouri Compromise by allowing Kansas and Nebraska to determine the status of slavery in their territories, through popular sovereignty.

- *Dred Scott* decision (1857)—This Supreme Court ruling rewrote the terms of the argument over slavery. It declared slaves to be property, consequently denying them the ability to sue in federal court, and the ruling also denied Congress the right to legislate the status of slavery in the territories.

Give yourself extra points if you figure out a way to mention the following:

- The Compromise of 1850—This legislation left the fate of slavery in the territories ambiguous, thus enforcing the notion of popular sovereignty. The compromise also created a stricter fugitive slave law.

- "Bleeding Kansas"—After the Kansas-Nebraska Act of 1854 allowed the possibility of slavery in the Kansas territory, abolitionists and pro-slavery forces rushed into the area in order to dominate the political scene. Each side claimed victory, then attacked the other. Widespread violence ensued.

Democratic Party

You pretty much have to mention the following:

- The Democrats held the presidency during Polk's administration from 1844 to 1848, and then again during Pierce's and Buchanan's administrations from 1852 to 1860. As a national party the Democrats tried their hardest to straddle both sides of the slavery issue. Polk's acquisition of new territory, however, heightened tensions on the slavery issue (see "Major land acquisitions during Polk's presidency," above).

- The Democrats considered Pierce a safe nominee for president in 1852 because nobody knew who he was. Also, the Democrats hoped that the Compromise of 1850 had laid the slavery issue to rest for a while. In 1856 they chose Buchanan because he had been out of the country on diplomatic service and therefore had not been muddied by the slavery debate.

- By 1860 the party had split. It held two conventions and nominated two candidates, one a Southerner (John C. Breckinridge), the other a Midwesterner (Stephen Douglas). Slavery had torn the party apart into regional divisions.

Give yourself extra points for mentioning:

- The Wilmot Proviso, authored by Democrat David Wilmot, would have banned slavery in the southwestern territories annexed from Mexico. John C. Calhoun, also a Democrat, fought the Wilmot Proviso strenuously. He argued that the federal government had no right to regulate slavery in the territories; most other Southern politicians soon picked up his argument.

- Anti-slavery Democrats called pro-slavery Democrats "hunkers," implying that they were so hungry for political power that they would court slave owners. Pro-slavery Democrats called anti-slavery Democrats "barn burners" because, they said, such folks would burn down the barn in order to kill the rats.

Free-Soil Party

You pretty much have to mention the following:

- The party formed around a single issue—preventing slavery in the territories annexed from Mexico.

- The Compromise of 1850, and particularly its stricter fugitive slave law, helped the party gain support in the North. It attracted antislavery Democrats and Conscience Whigs.

- The Republican Party eventually absorbed much of the Free-Soil Party. The two parties had virtually identical policies on slavery. Because the Republicans appealed to a wider range of voters, many Free-Soilers felt they could better accomplish their objectives in the larger Republican Party.

Give yourself extra points if you mention the following:

- The Free-Soil Party elected nine congressmen in 1848.

- The *Dred Scott* decision killed the Free-Soil Party once and for all by taking away its one issue. Free-Soilers wanted the federal government to regulate slavery; *Dred Scott* ruled that it could not.

Know-Nothings (American Party)

You pretty much have to mention the following:

- The Know-Nothings formed around a single issue—anti-immigration. They hated Catholics, particularly the Irish and Roman Catholics.

- The movement started out in secret societies. Members would plan election strategies at private meetings and then vote en masse on election day, often swinging elections. Because they were so secretive about their agenda, they became known as the "Know-Nothings."

- Events conspired to make slavery a more important issue than immigration during the 1850s. In the North the Republicans eventually attracted most of the Know-Nothings.

Give yourself extra points if you mention the following:

- In 1854 the party did very well in state and congressional elections.

- The party ran Millard Fillmore for president in 1856. He received over 20 percent of the vote. Fillmore, a former Whig president, attracted many Whigs to the party.

- Know-Nothings argued that Catholics were dangerous because they served the Pope, not the American government.

- The Republican Party had a nativist streak, which also attracted the Know-Nothings to the Republican Party. Nativism is defined as the favoring of citizens over immigrants, accompanied by general fear of those perceived as outsiders.

Republican Party

You pretty much have to mention the following:

- Formed in 1854, the Republican Party organized around the effort to defeat the Kansas-Nebraska Act. The passage of Kansas-Nebraska and the ensuing turmoil (see "Bleeding Kansas," above) helped build the party's popular base.

- The Republican Party originated as the Whig Party, then the second-most popular party, which splintered over the issue of slavery. At the same time Free-Soilers, looking for a more powerful, broader anti-slavery program, found it in the Republican Party.

- The schism in the Democratic Party in 1860 practically guaranteed the election of the Republican candidate, Abraham Lincoln. The Republicans were considered a third party in that election; it is the only time a third-party candidate has ever won a United States presidential election.

- The Republican party was truly regional. Lincoln's name did not even appear on the ballot in any Southern states. He won with just under 40 percent of the popular vote.

Give yourself extra points if you mention the following:

- In 1856 the Republican presidential candidate was John C. Frémont. His campaign slogan, "Free Soil, Free Labor, Free Speech, Free Men, Fremont," indicated the party's platform and its open courtship of Free-Soilers.

- The disappearance of the Whigs and Know-Nothings by 1860, and the conversion of those parties' members to the Republican Party, provided the voters Lincoln needed to win.

Whig Party

You pretty much have to mention the following:

- The Whig Party was made up of disparate groups. However, the members of its coalition often had opposing political goals. Whigs drew their support from states' rights Southerners, former Federalists, anti-Masons, Eastern financial conservatives, and merchants. Consequently, their presidential candidates were usually military heroes who had loose political platforms. It was a party destined to fall apart; the only question was when, and over what issue.

- Slavery and the death of the party's great leaders, Henry Clay (from Kentucky) and Daniel Webster (from Massachusetts), caused its demise. (Note the cross-regionalism of the party leadership.) Clay and Webster worked out the Compromise of 1850, which became the Whig position on slavery. Both men died within two years of the compromise's enactment, leaving a leadership void in the party. Meanwhile, Southern Whigs sought more aggressive pro-slavery representation; anti-slavery Northern Whigs, often called Conscience Whigs, drifted first into the Free-Soil Party, then into the Republican Party.

Give yourself extra points if you mention the following:

- By 1856 so little endured of the Whig Party (just four years earlier one of the nation's two major parties) that the remaining members did not even bother to nominate a presidential candidate. At their convention they simply endorsed the American Party's nomination of Millard Fillmore.

About the Structure of Your Essay

How easy this essay is to write probably depends a lot on how you decide to structure your discussion of the subject. One effective way is to discuss the key events leading up to the Civil War in your first paragraph, then discuss how those events affected the three parties you choose to write about in your next three paragraphs. A concluding paragraph mentioning sectionalism would be a nice touch.

A much less efficient method is to devote a paragraph to each major event and describe how that event affected each of the three parties you choose. If you try to write your essay this way, you probably will experience a lot of stress. Because the main point of your essay should be the history of these political parties, it will be easier to focus all your attention on one party at a time.

Question 4—Progressivism

4.   Analyze the reasons for the popularity of the Progressive movement during the first two decades of the twentieth century.

This essay gives you an opportunity to discuss the causes of the Progressive movement and its achievements. The following is a list of facts and concepts you might include in your essay.

You pretty much have to mention the following:

- Public disenchantment with business practices—By 1900 many major businesses were controlled by virtual monopolies. Those who controlled the businesses were fabulously wealthy; those who worked for them were impoverished. Businesses had little regard for the welfare of their workers or their customers. The government and judiciary proved to be shamelessly pro-business in their policies and rulings.

- Public horror at city conditions—Business's abuses adversely influenced the state of the cities. Urban dwellers lived under cramped, unsanitary conditions. Often entire families, including children, worked in factories for sub-living wages. City governments were controlled by political machines, who helped their impoverished patrons survive but did nothing for their long-term welfare.

- Growth of the middle class—During this time, the U.S. middle class was growing. With their newfound comfort and respectability, many middle-class Americans wanted to increase their political power. They formed associations such as lawyers' American Bar Association and women's National Woman Suffrage Association. The groups served as interest groups that lobbied for progressive reform. Many in the middle class, outraged by the excesses of business and the corruption of government, fought to correct them.

- Progressivism built on the foundation laid by the Populist movement of the 1890s—Populism had fought for moral causes, sought to counter the trend toward monopoly, and worked to widen access to the democratic process. Progressivism picked up these traditions, and so inherited the farmers and clergy who had made up the Populist coalition.

- Journalists helped the spread of Progressivism—With magazine articles and books like Upton Sinclair's *The Jungle*, American "muckrakers" broadened public awareness of corporate excesses.

- Teddy Roosevelt's presidency—Roosevelt used the office of the presidency as a bully pulpit to popularize Progressive ideals. During his tenure, he filed numerous antitrust suits against large corporations, tightened food and drug regulations, created national parks, and broadened the government's power to protect land from overdevelopment. Roosevelt took many of the cues from the book *The Promise of American Life* by Herbert Croly. The book argues forcefully for using the power of the central government to effect progressive reform.

Give yourself extra points if you mention the following:

- Other Progressive successes broadened the movement's appeal. On the state and local level, many new regulations were enacted, including child labor laws, limits on the lengths of the work day, minimum wage requirements, corrupt-practices acts, and housing codes. Many states adopted the initiative, referendum, and recall, thus empowering voters. Cities improved public transportation, adopted stricter health codes, and converted to a city-manager system. States introduced income taxes to redistribute wealth and provide public services.

- Wisconsin governor Robert La Follette led the way for many Progressive state leaders. He initiated such reforms as direct primaries, equitable tax structures, and the regulation of railways, all later adopted by many other states.

- Taft and Wilson continued the Progressive tradition in the White House. Taft strengthened antitrust law and expanded conservation efforts. During his term, two Progressive amendments, the national income tax and the direct election of senators, were added to the Constitution. Wilson created the Federal Trade Commission, lobbied for and enforced the Clayton Antitrust Act, and helped create the Federal Reserve, which gave the government greater control over the nation's finances. During his term, the Nineteenth Amendment gave women the right to vote.

- The many successes of Progressivism actually helped bring about its downfall. Each success satisfied a portion of the Progressive coalition, and, once satisfied, these people tended not to work as hard for Progressive goals. World War I also split the Progressive coalition. Some supported the war while others opposed it, but the feelings on both sides of the issue were strong. When the war ended, Americans were tired of crusading for justice, and the Progressive movement petered out.

About the Structure of Your Essay

You really should start this essay with a description of the social causes of Progressivism—then you can go on to enumerate its achievements. Add bonus points if you get around to discussing why the Progressive movement came to an end.

Question 5—Late Twentieth-Century Foreign Policy

5. Discuss the role of collective security in determining U.S. foreign policy in the late twentieth century. To what extent was this a continuation of or departure from U.S. foreign policy earlier in the century? Discuss two of the following alliances in your response:

> The UN
> NATO
> SEATO

This essay requires you to demonstrate an understanding of the concept of collective security and then provide historical examples that illustrate the role of collective security in the formation of U.S. foreign policy in the postwar period. That's the easy part, however. Remember that if you're aiming to get a 4 or 5 on this exam, you need to write analytical, not merely descriptive, essays. The College Board often utilizes this continuation/departure format in a social or foreign policy question, asking you to determine if the U.S. government is doing the same thing it always has or if this is a new policy. A really strong thesis and subsequent essay will not only answer the last part of this question but also discuss why the United States chose to alter its course at this time in history.

To earn a high score on this essay, your introduction should do the following:

*   Provide a historical context for the entire essay—You might begin this essay by reminding your reader that in his Farewell Address, George Washington had urged the new nation to avoid permanent entangling alliances. Subsequent administrations followed Washington's advice throughout the entire nineteenth and early twentieth centuries. We did not enter a major military alliance until World War I, and even then, we attempted to retreat to our traditional policy of isolationism when the war was over.

*   You could then discuss the Senate's defeat of the Treaty of Versailles and the failure of the United States to join the League of Nations. This will enable you to argue that U.S. foreign policy following World War II was a *departure* from previous policy.

*   Regardless of whether or not you choose the UN as one of the two alliances about which to write in your essay, you should mention the wartime conferences that established the UN at the conclusion of World War II.

*   If you plan to write about NATO, then you should mention the uneasy alliance between the Soviet Union and the United States during World War II. You should also discuss the decisions reached at Yalta and the subsequent Soviet takeover of Eastern Europe. Be careful not to go into too much detail here. This is only your introduction, but it is important to include enough information to set the stage for the rest of your essay. This information also answers the "Why at this time?" question and will strengthen your thesis.

*   It is not necessary to provide the historical background to SEATO in your introduction; you can do that in the body paragraph if you choose to write about this alliance. A brief discussion of NATO, however, might provide the rationale as to why the United States formed SEATO in 1954.

- Be sure to include a definition of collective security somewhere in your introduction. It is usually a good idea to define the terms you will use in whatever essay you are writing. For example, it never hurts to define terms like democracy, nationalism, or imperialism.

- Your introduction MUST contain your thesis. It should be one concise statement that responds to the question and makes it clear to the reader where you stand. A strong thesis should answer a "why" question; so in this case, you should not only state that these international alliances were a clear departure from previous U.S. foreign policy, but you might also blame them on Stalin, for example. Your thesis should not be a factual statement. Try to say something controversial, as long as you have historical evidence to support what you are writing. Don't just say "We created the UN because we didn't join the League of Nations after World War I." This is a weak and boring argument.

The Body Paragraphs and How to Structure this Essay

As is often the case, the question itself sets up a very straightforward structure for your essay. The essays on the AP exam are not creative writing assignments! Find a formula that works for you and stick to it. If the question instructs you to choose two or three events or items from a short list, then write a solid paragraph about each issue. Your essay will be better organized if you arrange your paragraphs in chronological order. In this particular question, the author has done that for you.

The UN

Many historians believe that the Treaty of Versailles was one of the major causes of World War II. Others see the failure of collective security to prevent another world war and blame the impotence of the League of Nations for its failure to stop German, Italian, and Japanese aggression throughout the 1930s. Some critics argue the League would have been stronger had the United States been a member. You should remember that the League of Nations was proposed by Woodrow Wilson in his Fourteen Points as a means of maintaining world peace. The United Nations was formed after World War II in part to replace the League of Nations and in response to the horrors committed during World War II.

The most obvious choice here is the Korean War. You should begin this paragraph with a brief discussion of the Truman Doctrine and the articulation of the policy of containment by George Kennan. The Korean conflict is often considered the first test case of containment. Mao's forces won a victory in China in 1949, and when Soviet-supported North Korean troops invaded South Korea the following year, the UN Security Council declared North Korea an aggressor and voted to send in troops. Although the United States provided the majority of manpower, we went into Korea in 1950 under the protective umbrella of the United Nations. The Soviets had successfully tested an atomic bomb in 1949. Given the threat of atomic warfare, the United States felt more secure as part of an international peacekeeping organization.

NATO

In 1949 the United States, Canada, Great Britain, France, Italy, Belgium, the Netherlands, Luxembourg, Portugal, Denmark, Norway, and Iceland signed the North Atlantic Treaty. Each nation agreed that it would view an attack on any one nation as an attack on them all. Greece and Turkey were admitted to the organization three years later. Unlike the UN, which is an international peacekeeping organization, NATO is an international defensive military alliance. The United States' entrance into NATO was a significant departure from traditional U.S. foreign policy and marked the first peacetime military alliance in U.S. history. If the Truman Doctrine was an ideological response to the establishment of Soviet satellites following World War II, and the Marshall Plan "put our money where our mouth is," then NATO may be seen as the military component of this equation.

You might choose either the war in Bosnia or the Persian Gulf War to illustrate NATO in action.

SEATO

In 1954 eight nations—including the United States and its major western allies, Great Britain and France, signed a collective defense treaty with the Philippines, Thailand, and Pakistan to form what became known as the Southeast Asia Treaty Organization. In essence it was basically a Southeast Asian version of NATO. Each member nation pledged to come to the defense of another member nation in the event it was attacked. However, unlike NATO, an attack on one nation would not necessarily be viewed as an attack on them all. The United States agreed to the provisions of the treaty on the condition that the aggressor be a member of the communist bloc. Although the organization was intended to provide an "anti-communist shield" to the nations of Southeast Asia, SEATO was not invoked to protect Cambodia, Laos, or Vietnam during the Vietnam War, as one would have suspected. In fact, the Geneva Accords specifically precluded South Vietnam, Cambodia, and Laos from joining the organization. France lost interest almost immediately and did not feel bound to the other member nations after Vietnam gained its independence following the French defeat in the battle of Dien Bien Phu. The United States tried to make the situation in Vietnam a collective security issue, as evidenced by the rhetoric of the domino theory, but was unsuccessful. In effect SEATO never had the teeth nor muscle that NATO had, and it was dissolved in 1977.

The Conclusion

A strong conclusion does more than merely summarize what you have already written. It also moves forward in time to literally bring your essay to a conclusion. For example, in this essay, you would discuss the role of the United States in the UN today, perhaps noting President Bush's disregard for the UN in taking unilateral action in going to war against Iraq. You might also discuss the expansion of NATO in recent years to include former Soviet satellites. Chances are, by this point in the exam, you will have run out of steam, and the people reading your last essay know this. This conclusion can be brief, but say something significant. Don't waste your last ounce of energy by merely being repetitive.

HOW TO SCORE PRACTICE TEST 1

Section I: Multiple-Choice

$$\underline{\hspace{4cm}} \times 1.1250 = \underline{\hspace{4cm}}$$

Number of Correct   Weighted
(out of 80)   Section I Score
                              (Do not round)

Section II: Free Response

(See if you can find a teacher to score your essays.)

Question 1 $\underline{\hspace{3cm}} \times 4.5000 = \underline{\hspace{3cm}}$
              (out of 9)   (Do not round)

Question 2 $\underline{\hspace{3cm}} \times 2.7500 = \underline{\hspace{3cm}}$
              (out of 9)   (Do not round)

Question 3 $\underline{\hspace{3cm}} \times 2.7500 = \underline{\hspace{3cm}}$
              (out of 9)   (Do not round)

AP Score Conversion Chart U.S. History	
Composite Score Range	AP Score
111–180	5
91–110	4
76–90	3
57–75	2
0–56	1

Sum   = $\underline{\hspace{4cm}}$
                 Weighted Section II
                 Score (Do not round)

Composite Score

$$\underline{\hspace{4cm}} + \underline{\hspace{4cm}} = \underline{\hspace{4cm}}$$

Weighted   Weighted   Composite Score
Section I Score   Section II Score   (Round to nearest
                                                   whole number)

Chapter 17
Practice Test 2

AP® United States History Exam

DO NOT OPEN THIS BOOKLET UNTIL YOU ARE TOLD TO DO SO.

At a Glance

Total Time
55 minutes
Number of Questions
80
Percent of Total Grade
50%
Writing Instrument
Pencil required

Instructions

Section I of this exam contains 80 multiple-choice questions. Fill in only the ovals for numbers 1 through 80 on your answer sheet.

Indicate all of your answers to the multiple-choice questions on the answer sheet. No credit will be given for anything written in this exam booklet, but you may use the booklet for notes or scratch work. After you have decided which of the suggested answers is best, completely fill in the corresponding oval on the answer sheet. Give only one answer to each question. If you change an answer, be sure that the previous mark is erased completely. Here is a sample question and answer.

Sample Question   Sample Answer

The first president of the United States was   Ⓐ ● Ⓒ Ⓓ Ⓔ
(A) Millard Fillmore
(B) George Washington
(C) Benjamin Franklin
(D) Andrew Jackson
(E) Harry Truman

Use your time effectively, working as rapidly as you can without losing accuracy. Do not spend too much time on any one question. Go on to other questions and come back to the ones you have not answered if you have time. It is not expected that everyone will know the answers to all of the multiple-choice questions.

About Guessing

Many candidates wonder whether or not to guess the answers to questions about which they are not certain. Multiple-choice scores are based on the number of questions answered correctly. Points are not deducted for incorrect answers, and no points are awarded for unanswered questions. Because points are not deducted for incorrect answers, you are encouraged to answer all multiple-choice questions. On any questions you do not know the answer to, you should eliminate as many choices as you can, and then select the best answer among the remaining choices.

GO ON TO THE NEXT PAGE.

UNITED STATES HISTORY
SECTION I
Time—55 minutes

Directions: Each of the questions or incomplete statements below is followed by five suggested answers or completions. Select the one that is best in each case and then blacken the corresponding space on the answer sheet.

1. During the seventeenth century, colonists' daily life was influenced the most by

   (A) the Baptists in the Carolinas
   (B) the Puritans in Massachusetts
   (C) the Baptists in Rhode Island
   (D) the Anglicans in Virginia
   (E) the Catholics in Maryland

2. The "war hawks" in the period leading up to the War of 1812 garnered most of their support from

   (A) New England
   (B) urban areas
   (C) the South and West
   (D) the Northwest Territories
   (E) the Middle Atlantic states

3. Which of the following reformers fought for the rights of the mentally ill?

   (A) Ralph Waldo Emerson
   (B) Horace Mann
   (C) Dorothea Dix
   (D) Lucretia Mott
   (E) Helen Hunt Jackson

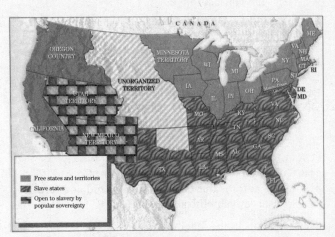

4. The map above illustrates

   (A) the Missouri Compromise
   (B) the Military Reconstruction Acts
   (C) the Wade-Davis Bill
   (D) the Compromise of 1850
   (E) the Mexican Cession

5. Jacob A. Riis was a famous "muckraker" who wrote about

   (A) government corruption
   (B) the powerful unions of the nineteenth century
   (C) the misery of tenement life
   (D) the civil rights movement
   (E) global warming

GO ON TO THE NEXT PAGE.

6. All of the following occurred during the 1920s, EXCEPT

(A) a bull market on Wall Street
(B) the passage of the Interstate Highway Act
(C) a rise in consumerism
(D) Prohibition
(E) the Harlem Renaissance

7. Which book was a major impetus in the growth of the women's movement in the 1960s?

(A) Betty Friedan's *The Feminine Mystique*
(B) Rachel Carson's *Silent Spring*
(C) Pearl S. Buck's *The Good Earth*
(D) Lorraine Hansbury's *A Raisin in the Sun*
(E) Harriet Beecher Stowe's *Uncle Tom's Cabin*

8. All of the following acts of President Ronald Reagan's administration are characterized as a return to conservative political values EXCEPT

(A) cuts in the federal budget
(B) the appointment of Sandra Day O'Connor to the Supreme Court
(C) tax cuts for corporations
(D) the loosening of government regulation
(E) supply-side economics

9. One way that the leaders of the Massachusetts Bay Colony encouraged the younger generation to join the church was by writing

(A) The Mayflower Compact
(B) The Fundamental Orders
(C) The Halfway Covenant
(D) The Cambridge Agreement
(E) The Fundamental Constitution

10. In his Farewell Address George Washington warned against

(A) deficit spending by the government
(B) foreign entanglements and the formation of political parties
(C) excessive use of executive power
(D) protests by Western farmers over excise taxes
(E) government reliance on excise taxes

"If I could save the Union by freeing all the slaves, I would do it…. What I do about slavery, and the colored race, I do because I believe it helps to save the Union."

11. The above statement was made by which of the following people?

(A) Horace Greeley
(B) Abraham Lincoln
(C) Stephen Douglas
(D) James Buchanan
(E) Ulysses S. Grant

12. When Abraham Lincoln issued the Emancipation Proclamation,

(A) it added a moral dimension to the Civil War, which became a war to end slavery rather than a war to preserve the Union
(B) he became known as the "Great Emancipator"
(C) the South was demoralized because it had lost a significant portion of its manpower
(D) British liberals persuaded Parliament to enter the war on the side of the South because England was dependent on Southern cotton
(E) slavery was abolished in all states within the Confederacy

GO ON TO THE NEXT PAGE.

13. What best accounts for the sharp increase of immigrants during the period 1880–1910?

 (A) Many southern and eastern Europeans turned to America for financial gain and political freedom.
 (B) Irish farmers were forced to leave their homes due to agricultural disasters.
 (C) Germans were seeking ways to avoid military conscription.
 (D) The United States welcomed immigrants by providing housing and employment.
 (E) Missionary societies encouraged immigration from all over the world.

14. The Wagner Act dealt with the rights of

 (A) farmers
 (B) veterans
 (C) labor unions
 (D) the homeless
 (E) bankers

15. All of the following occurred in 1968 EXCEPT

 (A) The Tet Offensive
 (B) the assassination of Martin Luther King
 (C) the assassination of Robert F. Kennedy
 (D) The Gulf of Tonkin Resolution
 (E) riots at the Democratic National Convention in Chicago

16. The two political issues that most concerned the Counterculture Movement of the 1960s were

 (A) U.S. involvement in Vietnam and flag burning
 (B) the civil rights movement and censorship
 (C) U.S. involvement in Vietnam and the civil rights movement
 (D) Separation of church and state and honesty in government
 (E) censorship and the draft

17. Which of the following was a result of the Albany Congress?

 (A) The colonies began to unite and take action against the British.
 (B) The Iroquois Nation signed a peace agreement with the colonies.
 (C) Benjamin Franklin convinced the Huron and Iroquois tribes to settle their differences.
 (D) The Iroquois remained neutral and the colonists rejected Franklin's plan for unity.
 (E) Benjamin Franklin was able to convince the colonists and the British of his plan for a united defense against France.

18. All of the following are associated with loose constructionism during the early years of the United States of America EXCEPT

 (A) the Federalists
 (B) Hamilton's Bank
 (C) the "Elastic Clause"
 (D) restrictions on federal legislative powers
 (E) federal government assumption of state debts

19. All of the following were prominent anti-slavery leaders, EXCEPT

 (A) Nat Turner
 (B) John Brown
 (C) William Lloyd Garrison
 (D) Sojourner Truth
 (E) Preston Brooks

20. When Lincoln was elected president in 1860, the immediate effect was the

 (A) secession of South Carolina
 (B) celebration of anti-abolitionists in Northern cities
 (C) congressional censure of several Northern senators
 (D) issuance of the Emancipation Proclamation
 (E) demand for a national draft policy

GO ON TO THE NEXT PAGE.

21. Upton Sinclair's *The Jungle* influenced the country and ultimately led to the passage of

    (A) The Clayton Antitrust Act
    (B) The Hepburn Act
    (C) The Sherman Antitrust Act
    (D) The Pure Food and Drug Act
    (E) The Forest Reserve Act

22. John Steinbeck's *The Grapes of Wrath* portrays the dismal plight of

    (A) poor immigrants
    (B) escaped slaves
    (C) factory workers during the Great Depression
    (D) farmers during the Dust Bowl
    (E) Civil War soldiers

23. The G.I. Bill provided World War II veterans with

    (A) free housing and medical care
    (B) student loans for education
    (C) free education and loans to buy homes, farms, and small businesses
    (D) a guaranteed job within the U.S. government
    (E) low-cost education in return for two more years of service in the armed forces

24. Which of the following statements about Watergate is true?

    (A) It was the first time a president had been involved in a scandal while in office.
    (B) It was of little interest to the American people.
    (C) It led to the resignation of President Nixon.
    (D) It led to the impeachment of President Nixon.
    (E) It bolstered the popularity of the Republican Party.

JOIN, or DIE.

25. The cartoon above served as

    (A) Ben Franklin's exhortation to the colonies to unite against British authority
    (B) Ben Franklin's exhortation to the colonies to unite against the French
    (C) the Committee of Correspondence's warning of impending attack against the colonies
    (D) the slogan of the Sons of Liberty after the Boston Tea Party
    (E) Thomas Paine's warning against political repression

26. The Battle of Saratoga proved to be a significant turning point in the Revolutionary War because it

    (A) was a major defeat for the rebel forces and motivated Benjamin Franklin to go to England to negotiate with the British
    (B) demonstrated to France that the Americans might win the war and subsequently led to the Franco-American Alliance of 1778
    (C) demonstrated the superiority of British naval power, thus convincing the Americans to alter their strategy
    (D) exposed the weakness of American military leadership and paved the way for General George Washington to assume command of the Continental Army
    (E) meant that England would renounce all future claims to French territory in North America

GO ON TO THE NEXT PAGE.

27. President James K. Polk is most closely associated with

    (A) Manifest Destiny
    (B) the abolitionist movement
    (C) economic development
    (D) the Whig Party
    (E) women's suffrage

28. Which of the following was NOT a result of Reconstruction?

    (A) An increase in membership in the Ku Klux Klan
    (B) The passage of three Constitutional Amendments
    (C) The election of black senators and representatives
    (D) The emergence of two distinct factions within the Republican Party
    (E) Government grants of 40 acres and a mule to each freedman

29. W. E. B. Du Bois was an important leader of

    (A) the National Association for the Advancement of Colored People (NAACP)
    (B) the feminist movement
    (C) the Department of Commerce and Labor
    (D) the Ku Klux Klan
    (E) the Student Nonviolence Coordinating Committee

30. All of the following increased government power during World War I EXCEPT the

    (A) War Industries Board
    (B) Creel Committee
    (C) Food Administration
    (D) Espionage Act
    (E) Dawes Plan

31. Each of the following actively sought to expose communist sympathizers within the United States after World War II, EXCEPT

    (A) Richard Nixon
    (B) Alger Hiss
    (C) Whittaker Chambers
    (D) Joseph McCarthy
    (E) Roy Cohn

32. In his 1985 State of the Union Address, Ronald Reagan articulated his foreign policy goals in what has come to be known as the Reagan Doctrine. Like Truman, Reagan pledged to

    (A) support anti-communist resistance movements, particularly in the Third World
    (B) sponsor covert military operations to overthrow communist regimes in Eastern Europe
    (C) ease tensions between the Soviet Union and the United States
    (D) broker a peace agreement between the Palestinians and the Israelis
    (E) defend human rights in the Western Hemisphere

33. Which of the following did NOT contribute to the emergence of the New Right of the 1970s and 1980s?

    (A) The moral majority movement
    (B) The popularity of Ronald Reagan
    (C) The "stagflation" economic condition of the 1970s
    (D) Religious revivalism
    (E) The drop in the stock market

GO ON TO THE NEXT PAGE.

34. The most notable achievement of the United States under the Articles of Confederation was

    (A) the creation of a strong executive office to lead the national government
    (B) the empowerment of Congress to regulate commerce
    (C) the empowerment of Congress to collect taxes
    (D) the provision for land sales in the Northwest that would benefit the entire nation
    (E) the establishment of simple majority rule in the legislature to establish national policy

35. All of the following sparked support for the abolitionist movement EXCEPT

    (A) John Brown's raid
    (B) *The Liberator*
    (C) the Fugitive Slave Act
    (D) the Wilmot Proviso
    (E) the Conscription Act

36. Which of the following American architects is considered by many to be the father of the modern skyscraper, thus changing the face of cities like Chicago in the late nineteenth and early twentieth centuries?

    (A) Henry Hobson Richardson
    (B) Stanford White
    (C) Louis H. Sullivan
    (D) Louis Kahn
    (E) Frank Lloyd Wright

37. Which of the following acts was the most beneficial to labor?

    (A) The Clayton Antitrust Act
    (B) The Sherman Antitrust Act
    (C) The Elkins Act
    (D) The Hepburn Act
    (E) The Mann-Elkins Act

38. All of the following occurred during Franklin Roosevelt's First Hundred Days EXCEPT

    (A) the National Bank Holiday
    (B) passage of the Glass-Steagall Act
    (C) passage of the National Industrial Recovery Act
    (D) passage of the Agricultural Adjustment Act
    (E) passage of the Social Security Act

39. Which of the following accurately describes the Taft-Hartley Act of 1947?

    (A) It encouraged the use of union strikes as long as they remained peaceful.
    (B) It outlawed the use of injunctions.
    (C) President Truman vetoed it.
    (D) It banned the use of "yellow dog contracts."
    (E) It required political contributions from labor unions to be subject to federal taxes.

40. All of the following were an outgrowth of the Cold War EXCEPT

    (A) our entry into the space race
    (B) an upgrade of the American public educational system, including the introduction of the AP program
    (C) the building of bomb shelters
    (D) the establishment of the Peace Corps
    (E) the establishment of the Office of Economic Opportunity

GO ON TO THE NEXT PAGE.

41. During the Revolutionary War, the Loyalists

    (A) were few in number and had little, if any, significance
    (B) made up approximately 20-30 percent of the population
    (C) were mostly former indentured servants who felt obligated to the Crown
    (D) were mostly from the royal colony of Virginia and felt loyal to the Crown
    (E) had their largest following in New England, where the benefits of the mercantilist system were most visible

42. The success of the Constitutional Convention of 1787 hinged on compromises over

    (A) slavery and representation in Congress
    (B) taxation and term limits
    (C) the number of branches of government to be formed
    (D) voting rights for women
    (E) universal manhood suffrage

43. Which of the following was LEAST influential in bringing about Andrew Jackson's victory in the presidential election of 1828?

    (A) Support for Jackson among less prosperous voters
    (B) Jackson's promise to bring new people into the government
    (C) Jackson's defense of Native American property rights
    (D) Jackson's promise to reform the electoral system
    (E) The reputation Jackson earned as a war hero as a result of the Battle of New Orleans

44. All of the following statements concerning the Wade-Davis Bill are true EXCEPT

    (A) Lincoln used his pocket veto to defeat it
    (B) the bill required a majority of the population of the former Confederate states to take an oath of allegiance
    (C) the bill stipulated that Congress would administer the Reconstruction program
    (D) the bill abolished slavery
    (E) the bill provided for financial compensation to former slaves

45. Theodore Roosevelt's Square Deal can best be described as

    (A) conservation, trust-busting, consumer protection
    (B) protective tariffs, centralized banking, conservation
    (C) equal opportunity, women's suffrage, laissez-faire economics
    (D) laissez-faire economics, support of labor unions, conservation
    (E) government ownership of business, conservation, naval preparedness

46. All of the following were causes of the Great Depression EXCEPT

    (A) a weak foreign trade
    (B) an overextension of credit
    (C) agricultural overproduction
    (D) the establishment of public works projects
    (E) an unequal distribution of wealth

47. The 1947 grant of $400 million dollars in aid to Greece and Turkey was in accordance with which of the following U.S. policies?

    (A) Eisenhower Doctrine
    (B) Monroe Doctrine
    (C) Truman Doctrine
    (D) Roosevelt Corollary
    (E) Good Neighbor Policy

GO ON TO THE NEXT PAGE.

48. Which civil rights organization was led by Martin Luther King Jr. and practiced civil disobedience to achieve its goals?

    (A) The Student Nonviolent Coordinating Committee
    (B) The Black Panthers
    (C) The Congress of Racial Equality
    (D) The National Association for the Advancement of Colored People
    (E) The Southern Christian Leadership Conference

49. During the period preceding the Revolutionary War, the British act provoking the most outrage among the colonists was

    (A) parliament's defense of "virtual representation"
    (B) the monopoly given to the British East India Company
    (C) the passage of the Boston Port Act
    (D) the passage of the Molasses Act
    (E) the passage of the Quebec Act

50. In 1775 the Second Continental Congress

    (A) decided to cut all ties with Britain
    (B) voted to work out a plan for self-rule
    (C) adopted the Olive Branch Petition, declaring colonial loyalty to the Crown
    (D) began to draft the Articles of Confederation
    (E) revised the colonial plan for military preparedness

51. All of the following Supreme Court decisions during John Marshall's tenure as Supreme Court Justice strengthened the federal government EXCEPT

    (A) *Fletcher v. Peck*
    (B) *Gibbons v. Ogden*
    (C) *Marbury v. Madison*
    (D) *McCulloch v. Maryland*
    (E) *Dred Scott v. Sandford*

52. Which of the following was NOT a result of the Compromise of 1877?

    (A) Rutherford B. Hayes became president.
    (B) The remaining Confederate states were readmitted to the Union.
    (C) Military Reconstruction ended.
    (D) The Democrats took back the House and the Senate.
    (E) Federal provisions for a Southern transcontinental railroad were made.

53. Roosevelt's Big Stick Policy in Latin America was best characterized by his

    (A) repudiation of the Monroe Doctrine
    (B) belief that European nations had the right to protect their economic interests in any remaining colonies throughout the region
    (C) recognition of the sovereignty of newly-independent nations in the Western Hemisphere
    (D) belief that the United States had an obligation to protect security and stability by assuming the role of an international police force throughout the Western Hemisphere
    (E) support of high protective tariffs to promote American economic interests throughout the region

54. In the *Schecter Poultry Corp. v. U.S.* case of 1935, which of Franklin Roosevelt's New Deal measures came under attack?

    (A) The National Labor Relations Board
    (B) The Judicial Reorganization bill
    (C) The National Recovery Act
    (D) The Agricultural Adjustment Act
    (E) The Federal Farm Loan Act

GO ON TO THE NEXT PAGE.

55. During the 1950s, many black and white activists fought against the persistence of Jim Crow laws throughout the South by all of the following methods EXCEPT

(A) bringing lawsuits in federal courts
(B) using violence to intimidate local politicians
(C) boycotting local businesses that supported segregation
(D) staging sit-ins in segregated public places and facilities
(E) forging a coalition between Southern black churches and civil rights advocates

56. During the 1980s, President Ronald Reagan

(A) signed the welfare reform bill
(B) persuaded Anwar Sadat and Menachem Begin to sign the Camp David Accords
(C) sent troops to fight in the Persian Gulf War
(D) cut taxes and social services
(E) increased taxes

57. Which of the following events represented the most significant action on the part of the colonists against British authority?

(A) Bacon's Rebellion
(B) The Whiskey Rebellion
(C) The Albany Congress
(D) Pontiac's Rebellion
(E) The Stamp Act Congress

58. Which of the following statements concerning the Federalist Papers is true?

(A) Jefferson, Madison, and Hamilton drafted them.
(B) They contained essays that both defended and criticized the Constitution.
(C) They were written as propaganda to support the ratification of the Constitution.
(D) They were banned in the New York newspapers.
(E) They outlined the dangers of Republicanism in a new nation.

59. The Force Act of 1832 was passed in response to

(A) the Indian Removal Act
(B) the Tariff/Nullification crisis
(C) the election of President Martin Van Buren
(D) Clay's American System
(E) the Bank Recharter Bill

60. The Niagara Movement resulted in

(A) the formation of the NAACP
(B) the emergence of the National Urban League
(C) the development of agricultural colleges, such as the Tuskegee Institute
(D) the repeal of the black codes
(E) the establishment of the Freedmen's Bureau

61. All of the following are true concerning the women's suffrage movement EXCEPT

(A) it benefited from the support of the Progressives of the early 1900s
(B) it remained racially segregated during the latter part of the nineteenth century
(C) it was viewed as radical during much of its existence
(D) some of its early leaders were first active in the Abolitionist movement
(E) it first met success in the New England states

62. During the time of Woodrow Wilson's presidency, the Irreconcilables and the Reservationists had strong feelings concerning

(A) the Treaty of Versailles
(B) Wilson's Fourteen Points
(C) Article 231
(D) the Sedition Act of 1918
(E) the Mandate System

GO ON TO THE NEXT PAGE.

63. Which of the following Cold War measures met with the most resistance in Congress?

    (A) U.S. entry into the Korean War
    (B) U.S. entry into NATO
    (C) The Berlin Airlift
    (D) The Truman Doctrine
    (E) The McCarran Internal Security Bill

64. The most important factor in the defeat of Democratic presidential candidates in the elections of 1952 and 1968 was

    (A) the Democrats' plan to reorganize the Supreme Court
    (B) the American public's desire to avoid conflict and return to a more conservative political and social life
    (C) the Democratic Party platform pledge to increase taxes in order to pay off the national debt
    (D) the Democratic candidates' controversial positions on civil rights legislation
    (E) the Democratic Party's unequivocal support of the Equal Rights Amendment

65. All of the following were manifestations of mercantilist theory EXCEPT

    (A) the triangular trade
    (B) the Navigation Acts
    (C) Admiralty Courts
    (D) virtual representation
    (E) the plantation economy

66. The chief goal of the Alien and Sedition Acts was to

    (A) suppress immigration
    (B) limit the power of the press
    (C) check the power of the Democratic-Republicans
    (D) uphold the rights guaranteed by the First Amendment
    (E) introduce the theory of nullification and states' rights

67. Which of the following statements related to the Lowell System is NOT true?

    (A) In Lowell, farm girls were hired to work in the factories.
    (B) Lowell was a company town developed to provide supervision of, and education for, its factory workers.
    (C) The Lowell System included some of the first fully integrated factories—they transformed raw materials into a finished product.
    (D) The Lowell System provided an easy way for women to become financially independent.
    (E) The Lowell System developed as a result of the United States' burgeoning textile industry.

68. Which of the following is most closely associated with the Populist movement?

    (A) Support of labor unions
    (B) The "front porch" campaign of William McKinley
    (C) Free coinage of silver
    (D) Private ownership of railroads and utilities
    (E) Protective tariffs

GO ON TO THE NEXT PAGE.

69. Which of the following statements regarding the American Federation of Labor is true?

    (A) It excluded unskilled workers.
    (B) Its beliefs were based on the utopian ideas of earlier reformers.
    (C) It did not believe striking was a useful tactic.
    (D) Its greatest appeal was to new immigrants, many of whom were unskilled.
    (E) It published anti-capitalism pamphlets.

70. The supply-side economic theory of Treasury Secretary Andrew Mellon most probably inspired the

    (A) trickle-down economic theory supported by Ronald Reagan
    (B) deficit-spending economic theory of John M. Keynes
    (C) Glass-Steagall Banking Reform Act
    (D) Keating-Owen Act
    (E) Federal Trade Commission Act

71. All of the following were part of Johnson's Great Society program EXCEPT

    (A) the Civil Rights Act of 1964
    (B) Medicare and Medicaid
    (C) the establishment of the Department of Housing and Urban Development
    (D) the balanced budget mandate
    (E) the Economic Opportunity Act

72. Which of the following was NOT a provision of the Land Ordinance of 1785 or the Northwest Ordinance of 1787?

    (A) Each territory could apply for statehood once it had 60,000 inhabitants.
    (B) Slavery was outlawed in the Northwest Territory.
    (C) Once a new state was admitted to the Union, it was granted all the privileges of existing states.
    (D) The national government would make provisions for public education for all new states.
    (E) Land sales in admitted territories would be protected from speculators.

73. Which of the following does NOT represent the views of Prime Minister Grenville after the Seven Years' War?

    (A) He felt that the Crown needed to control trade and raise revenue.
    (B) He felt that the colonists should help pay the debt incurred by the war.
    (C) He felt that Parliament had the right to increase taxes on the colonies.
    (D) He felt that the British had to exert tighter control over the colonies.
    (E) He wanted to reward the colonies through his extension of salutary neglect.

74. The election of 1800 is historically and politically significant because it

    (A) marked the death of the Federalist party
    (B) demonstrated that our Founding Fathers were correct in their suspicions about factions
    (C) demonstrated the significance of the Electoral College
    (D) ushered in the Era of Good Feelings
    (E) demonstrated that political parties could, in fact, bring about a peaceful revolution in a republican form of government

75. In 1798 President John Adams delivered the following message to Congress:

    "I will never send another minister to France without assurances that he will be received, respected, and honored as the representative of a great, free, powerful, and independent nation."

    What event inspired this comment?

    (A) The Citizen Genêt Affair
    (B) The XYZ Affair
    (C) Jay's Treaty
    (D) The Hartford Convention
    (E) The Pinckney (Transcontinental) Treaty

GO ON TO THE NEXT PAGE.

76. Which of the following best describes the situation in Kansas during the 1850s?

    (A) As a result of the policy of popular sovereignty, Kansas became the site of much violence and bloodshed.
    (B) Kansas was clearly on the side of the pro-slavery forces.
    (C) The people of Kansas were overwhelmingly abolitionist, as evidenced by the Lecompton Constitution.
    (D) Kansas was permitted to enter the Union as a slave state in order to keep the balance of power even in the Senate.
    (E) Kansas was one of the few states that refused to participate in the slave trade.

77. Which of the following is true of the Dawes Severalty Act of 1887?

    (A) In honoring communal land holdings, it reflected an appreciation of Indian culture.
    (B) It was an attempt to assimilate the Indians into American society through individual land grants.
    (C) It outlawed the Ghost Dance Movement.
    (D) It compensated Indians for the land they had lost at the Battle of Wounded Knee.
    (E) It did away with individual land ownership by Indian leaders.

78. All of the following contributed to the rise of big business EXCEPT

    (A) horizontal and vertical integration
    (B) formation of monopolies
    (C) interlocking directorates
    (D) laissez-faire economic policy
    (E) the Northern Securities decision of 1904

79. Franklin Roosevelt's New Deal programs came under attack from both ends of the political spectrum. Two of the most vocal opponents, one left-wing and the other conservative, were

    (A) Huey Long and Charles Coughlin
    (B) Frances Perkins and Charles Townshend
    (C) Wendell Wilkie and Harold Ickes
    (D) Thomas Dewey and Huey Long
    (E) Charles Evans Hughes and Alf Landon

80. The federally mandated desegregation of the civil service was first implemented in the

    (A) Peace Corps
    (B) armed forces
    (C) Department of Justice
    (D) National Park Service
    (E) Supreme Court

END OF SECTION I

UNITED STATES HISTORY
SECTION II
Total time—130 minutes

Part A

(Suggested writing time—45 minutes. This question counts for 45 percent of the total essay section score.)

Directions: The following question requires you to construct a coherent essay that integrates your interpretation of Documents A–I <u>and</u> your knowledge of the period referred to in the question. High scores will be earned only by essays that both cite key pieces of evidence from the documents and draw on outside knowledge of the period.

1. To what extent was the breakup of the Union in 1861 a result of the conflict over slavery and to what extent was it due to other factors? Using your knowledge of the antebellum period, construct an essay that explains the reasons the nation went to war and what circumstances led to this point of national crisis.

    Use the documents and your knowledge of the time period 1844–1861 to construct your answer.

Document A

Source: "Annexation," by John L. O'Sullivan, *United States Magazine and Democratic Review*, July 1845

Why, were other reasoning wanting, in favor of now elevating this question of the reception of Texas into the Union, out of the lower region of our past party dissension, up to its proper level of a high and broad nationality, it surely is to be found, found abundantly, in the manner in which other nations have undertaken to intrude themselves into it, between us and the proper parties to the case, in a spirit of hostile interference against us, for the avowed object of thwarting our policy and hampering our power, limiting our greatness and checking the fulfillment of our manifest destiny to overspread the continent allotted by Providence for the free development of our yearly multiplying millions.

Document B

Source: President James K. Polk's War Message to Congress, May 11, 1846

As war exists, and notwithstanding all our efforts to avoid it, exists by the act of Mexico herself, we are called upon by every consideration of duty and patriotism to vindicate with decision the honor, rights and dignity of this country.

GO ON TO THE NEXT PAGE.

Document C

Source: Ralph Waldo Emerson, 1846

"The United States will conquer Mexico, but it will be as the man swallows the arsenic."

Document D

Source: Representative David Wilmot, from the Congressional Globe, 29th Congress, 2nd session, Appendix, February 8, 1847

But, sir, the issue now presented is not whether slavery shall exist unmolested where it now is, but whether it shall be carried to new and distant regions, now free, where the footprint of a slave cannot be found. This, sir, is the issue. Upon it I take my stand, and from it I cannot be frightened or driven by idle charges of abolitionism.

I ask not that slavery be abolished, I demand that this government preserve the integrity of free territory against the aggressions of slavery—against its wrongful usurpations.

Sir, I was in favor of the annexation of Texas… Yes, sir, here was an empire larger than France given up to slavery. Shall further concessions be made by the North? Shall we give up free territory, the inheritance of free labor? Must we yield this also?

…But, sir, we are told that the joint blood and treasure of the whole country being expended in this acquisition, therefore it should be divided, and slavery should be allowed to take its share. Sir, the South has her share already.

…Now, sir, we are told that California is ours, that New Mexico is ours—won by the valor of our arms. They are free. Shall they remain free? Shall these fair provinces be the inheritance and homes of the white labor of freemen or the black labor of slaves? This, sir, is the issue.

GO ON TO THE NEXT PAGE.

Document E

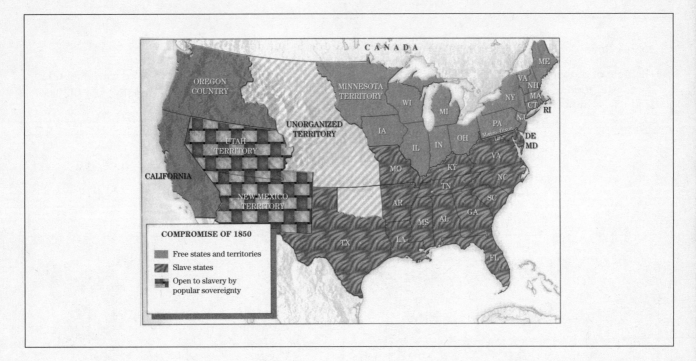

COMPROMISE OF 1850
- Free states and territories
- Slave states
- Open to slavery by popular sovereignty

Document F

THE KANSAS-NEBRASKA ACT, 1854
- Free states and territories
- Slave states
- Open to slavery by popular sovereignty, Compromise of 1850
- Open to slavery by popular sovereignty, Kansas-Nebraska Act, 1854

GO ON TO THE NEXT PAGE.

Document G

Source: Roger Taney, in the Supreme Court opinion in *Dred Scott v. Sandford*, 1857

The right of property in a slave is distinctly and expressly affirmed in the Constitution…. No word can be found in the Constitution which gives Congress a greater power over the slave property or which entitles property of that kind to less protection than property of any other description.

Document H

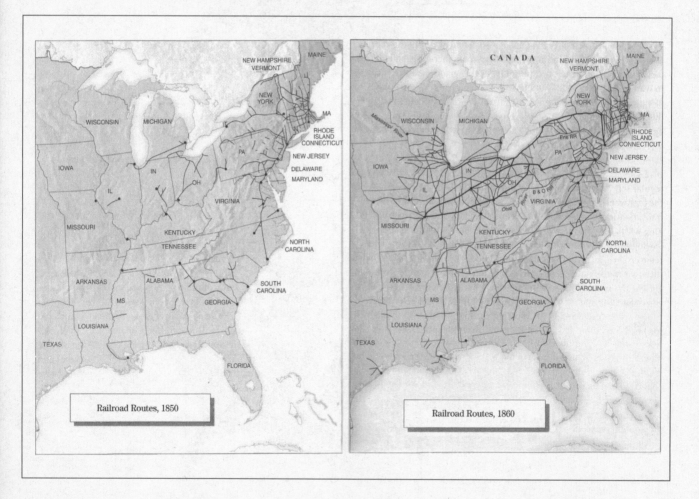

Railroad Routes, 1850

Railroad Routes, 1860

GO ON TO THE NEXT PAGE.

Document I

PROGRESSIVE DEMOCRACY—PROSPECT OF A SMASH UP.

GO ON TO THE NEXT PAGE.

UNITED STATES HISTORY
SECTION II

Parts B and C: Standard Essay Questions

(Suggested writing time—70 minutes. These questions count for 55 percent of the total essay section score.)

Part B

Directions: Choose ONE question from this part. You are advised to spend five minutes planning and 30 minutes writing your response. Cite relevant evidence in support of your generalizations and present your arguments clearly and logically.

2. To what extent was the American Revolution a radical break with the past and to what extent was it a conservative attempt to protect the status quo?

3. Analyze the ways in which TWO of the following represented a shift in the ideals of Jeffersonian republicanism during the period 1800–1824:

   The Louisiana Purchase
   Marbury v. Madison
   The War of 1812
   The Monroe Doctrine

Part C

Directions: Choose ONE question from this part. You are advised to spend five minutes planning and 30 minutes writing your response. Cite relevant evidence in support of your generalizations and present your arguments clearly and logically.

4. Explain how TWO of the following influenced U.S. foreign policy during the 1920s:

   Social and economic issues within the United States
   War debts and reparations
   Political ideology

5. Discuss the ways in which TWO of the following changed both the social fabric and political structure of America during the 1960s:

   Social and economic issues within the United States
   The civil rights movement
   The Vietnam War
   The Women's Movement

STOP

END OF EXAM

Chapter 18
Practice Test 2:
Answers and
Explanations

ANSWER KEY

1. B	21. D	41. B	61. E
2. C	22. D	42. A	62. A
3. C	23. C	43. C	63. B
4. D	24. C	44. E	64. B
5. C	25. B	45. A	65. D
6. B	26. B	46. D	66. C
7. A	27. A	47. C	67. D
8. B	28. E	48. E	68. C
9. C	29. A	49. C	69. A
10. B	30. E	50. C	70. A
11. B	31. B	51. E	71. D
12. A	32. A	52. D	72. E
13. A	33. E	53. D	73. E
14. C	34. D	54. C	74. E
15. D	35. E	55. B	75. B
16. C	36. C	56. D	76. A
17. D	37. A	57. E	77. B
18. D	38. E	58. C	78. E
19. E	39. C	59. B	79. A
20. A	40. E	60. A	80. B

MULTIPLE-CHOICE SECTION EXPLAINED

1. **B**   The Puritans influenced every aspect of the lives of the inhabitants of Massachusetts. John Winthrop, governor of the colony, also served as its religious leader after he brought over 1,000 Puritans in 1630. People like Anne Hutchinson and Roger Williams were banished from the colony for challenging the dogma of the church or interpreting the Bible on their own.

2. **C**   Most of the support came from the West (led by Henry Clay) and the South (led by John Calhoun). The pro-British maritime centers of the East in New England were actually against the war with Britain.

3. **C**   Dorothea Dix fought for the rights of the mentally ill by calling for the establishment of insane asylums and reform in prisons.

4. **D**   The Compromise of 1850, Henry Clay's last compromise, postponed the war for 11 years. It admitted California into the Union as a free state, allowed new territories to use popular sovereignty with regard to the slavery issue, passed a tougher Fugitive Slave Law, and stopped the slave trade in Washington, D.C.

5. **C**   Photojournalist Jacob Riis exposed the misery of tenement life in his book *How the Other Half Lives*, published in 1890.

6. **B**   The Interstate Highway Act was passed in 1955 during Eisenhower's presidency. It authorized the construction of 41,000 miles of expressway. All of the others occurred during the 1920s.

7. **A**   Betty Friedan's 1963 book, *The Feminine Mystique*, helped spark the feminist movement. Friedan, a Smith graduate, chronicled the lives of affluent wives and mothers living out the American Dream, yet finding themselves unfulfilled and unhappy.

8. **B**   In 1981 Ronald Reagan, in a move supported by various groups across the political spectrum, made Sandra Day O'Connor the first woman to serve on the Supreme Court. All the other choices represent typically conservative policy decisions by Reagan.

9. **C**   The Halfway Covenant extended the privilege of baptism to all children of baptized people, not just those who had the personal experience of conversion. The Covenant was an attempt to bring more people into the church and do away with some of the distinctions between the "elect" and all others.

10. **B**   In his farewell address, Washington warned against "permanent alliances" with foreign nations and the dangers of a party system.

11. **B**   Abraham Lincoln wrote this in an 1862 letter to anti-slavery editor Horace Greeley, identifying the preservation of the Union rather than the emancipation of the slaves as his primary reason for going to war.

12. **A** The Emancipation Proclamation freed the slaves in the Confederacy but not in the border states (which were still part of the Union), so it didn't immediately free any slaves at all. It did, however, give hope to slaves who saw the document as a clarion call for their freedom, and it also made it unlikely that Great Britain would enter the war on the side of the Confederacy, now even more isolated in its support for slavery. Similar to how the Declaration of Independence shifted the purpose of the American Revolution, the Emancipation Proclamation turned the Civil War into a moral crusade to end slavery.

13. **A** The largest wave of immigration to this country occurred during this period and was a result of political and economic upheaval. This so-called "new immigration" brought immigrants from southern and eastern Europe as well as Asia. Between 1880 and 1910, approximately 12 million people came to the United States, many to escape poverty or political persecution.

14. **C** The Wagner Act, also known as the National Labor Relations Act, recognized the rights of labor to organize and bargain collectively.

15. **D** All of the events occurred during the pivotal year of 1968, except the Gulf of Tonkin Resolution, which was passed in 1964 in response to reports of an armed attack on U.S. ships in the Gulf of Tonkin in Southeast Asia.

16. **C** The two largest issues that concerned the Counterculture Movement were the civil rights of minorities and the war in Vietnam. The many demonstrations that took place during this period (such as the civil rights march on Washington in 1963 and the anti-war "moratoriums" in Washington during 1968 and 1969) had these two issues as their primary focus.

17. **D** Franklin was unable either to enlist the allegiance of the Iroquois or to convince the colonists to unite during the French and Indian War.

18. **D** Loose constructionism extends, rather than restricts, the powers of the federal government and was supported by Hamilton and the Federalists.

19. **E** Preston Brooks was the South Carolinian Representative who beat Massachusetts Senator Charles Sumner with a cane after Sumner blamed the South for the "Bleeding Kansas" incident.

20. **A** After the election of Lincoln was announced, South Carolina seceded from the Union, and was soon joined by Alabama, Mississippi, Florida, Georgia, Louisiana, and Texas. Several months later the other four states—Virginia, North Carolina, Arkansas, and Tennessee—joined the secession, and the Confederacy was formed.

21. **D** The Pure Food and Drug Act was passed after Sinclair wrote *The Jungle*, which exposed the filth and disease that was rampant throughout the slaughterhouses of Chicago.

22. **D** John Steinbeck's 1939 best-selling novel, *The Grapes of Wrath*, depicts the lives of farmers forced to flee the drought-ridden Midwest during the Depression years. About 350,000 Oklahomans and Arkansans trekked to southern California in search of work.

23. **C** The 1944 Servicemen's Readjustment Act, otherwise known as the G.I. Bill, made provisions for sending 8 million veterans to school, and enabled the Veteran's Administration to guarantee about $16 million in loans for homes, farms, and small businesses.

24. **C** President Nixon resigned in 1974 to avoid impeachment proceedings over accusations of obstruction of justice regarding the Watergate affair.

25. **B** Ben Franklin drew this cartoon in 1754, to try to convince the colonies to unite against the French during the French and Indian War.

26. **B** While the College Board maintains that there is little military history on the AP exam (because they believe it favors male students), you should know the diplomatic or political significance of the major battles of both the American Revolution and Civil War. This is a very easy question if you remember that the Battle of Saratoga convinced France to enter the war against its traditional enemy, Great Britain. The other important battle you should know is the surrender at Yorktown in 1781.

   (A) is incorrect because Benjamin Franklin actually went to France (wearing a fur cap like a frontiersman!) in an attempt to gain France's sympathy for the American cause. (D) is also incorrect because George Washington was appointed leader of the Continental Army before the start of the war, long before the Battle of Saratoga.

27. **A** James K. Polk is known as the Manifest Destiny president, because it was during his term that the country extended so many of its borders.

28. **E** All of the answer choices were results of Reconstruction except (E), which was suggested but never implemented. (Note of interest: Spike Lee's film production company is called 40 Acres and a Mule, a reference to broken promises made to African-Americans.)

29. **A** W. E. B. Du Bois is best remembered for being the founding head of the National Association for the Advancement of Colored People, an organization created to secure equal rights for all people regardless of race.

30. **E** The Dawes Plan (1924) attempted to facilitate German reparation payments. By loaning $200 million in gold bullion to Germany, the United States hoped to stabilize the German economy and enable Germany to pay off its debts.

31. **B** Alger Hiss was the target of the House Un-American Activities Committee (HUAC). He was convicted of perjury in 1950. All of the other choices were "commie hunters."

32. **A** There are several presidential doctrines you should know for this exam; for example, the Monroe Doctrine and the Truman Doctrine. In most cases these "doctrines" were delivered as speeches to Congress but became statements of U.S. foreign policy. Alarmed by the establishment of Soviet satellites in Eastern Europe and the potential Soviet threat to Greece and Turkey following WWII, Truman pledged his support to prevent the spread of communism in Europe (although he did not

use those exact words). As a cold warrior, Ronald Reagan was committed to providing covert and overt assistance to anti-communist resistance movements, particularly in nations like Afghanistan and Nicaragua.

33.   E   The drop in the stock market, which occurred in 1987, was not a contributing factor to the emergence of the New Right. All of the other factors did lead to this renewal of conservatism.

34.   D   The land sales in the Northwest were structured so that they would benefit the entire nation and gave newly created states equal status with the older states. None of the other choices were actually accomplished under the Articles of Confederation, which did not provide for a strong central government.

35.   E   The Conscription Act actually hurt the abolitionist movement, because it led to the conscription of many Northern immigrants who had no desire to fight the war.

36.   C   Although Louis H. Sullivan was not actually the first architect to build tall buildings, he is credited with developing the steel frame that enabled buildings to be constructed higher and higher. He is also credited with coining the phrase "form follows function" and is considered by many to be the father of modern architecture.

Although you cannot know everything for this exam, you probably should know who Louis Sullivan (C) and Frank Lloyd Wright (E) were. Frank Lloyd Wright is considered by most historians and critics to be the greatest American architect. Wright began his career working under Sullivan and eventually developed his own unique "Prairie Style." One of Wright's most famous works is Fallingwater, a private residence constructed in western Pennsylvania for the owner of a leading department store in Pittsburgh at the time. Henry Hobson Richardson (A) is another famous American architect, but it's OK if you don't know who he was. His style is very different from Sullivan's and Wright's and is often described as Richardsonian Romanesque. Stanford White (B) is probably more notorious for having been involved in a scandalous affair that led to his murder, although New Yorkers know him as the architect of the second Madison Square Garden (which was torn down in the 1920s) and the arch in Washington Square Park near NYU.

37.   A   Samuel Gompers once referred to the Clayton Antitrust Act as "The Magna Carta of labor," because in addition to strengthening the Sherman Antitrust Act, it also exempted labor unions from antitrust prosecution and legalized strikes and picketing.

38.   E   The Social Security Act was part of FDR's Second New Deal—it was passed in 1935. All the other choices were part of the first wave of New Deal legislation, passed between March and June 1933.

39.   C   President Truman vetoed this anti-labor law, and labor leaders condemned it as a "slave labor law." It outlawed the closed shop, made unions liable for damages that resulted from disputes, and required union leaders to take a non-communist oath.

40.   E   The Office of Economic Opportunity was established under Johnson as part of his Great Society Program. The other four were all enacted during, or because of, the Cold War (including the AP program!).

41. B   The Loyalists made up a significant portion of the colonial population. They were spread through-out the colonies, but were least numerous in New England, where the independence movement had most of its support and mercantilism was the weakest.

42. A   The two most important agreements made at the convention were the Great Compromise, which dealt with the issue of proportionate versus equal representation for the states in the legislative branch, and the Three-Fifths Compromise, which defined the issue of how slaves would be count-ed for the purposes of congressional representation and taxation.

43. C   Jackson did not believe in property rights for Native Americans, many of whom he had helped displace from their homes in the American Southeast.

44. E   All are true except (E). Ex-slaves were not to be given financial compensation (or any other kind of compensation) under the Wade-Davis Bill, and in fact they never received any significant financial compensation at all. Many former slaves had hopes of receiving "40 acres and a mule" from the Freedman's Bureau, which had settled nearly 10,000 black families on land taken from abandoned plantations along the sea islands of South Carolina and Georgia and areas of Mississippi. However, these efforts stopped as Reconstruction collapsed and sharecropping took hold throughout the for-mer Confederacy.

45. A   Theodore Roosevelt's Square Deal program was intended to conserve the Earth's resources, control corporations through government regulation, and protect the consumer.

46. D   All of the other factors contributed to the Depression. President Hoover established the first feder-ally-funded public works projects in an attempt to halt the economic decline.

47. C   The Truman Doctrine of 1947, also known as the Containment Policy, espoused a strategy of mili-tary and political preparedness against the Soviets and support for foreign governments thought to be threatened by communists. Truman's grant of $400 million of aid to Greece and Turkey was meant to help them stand up to a communist threat.

48. E   The Southern Christian Leadership Conference, an interracial group founded shortly after the Montgomery Bus Boycott, practiced the doctrine of nonviolence and passive resistance. They mo-bilized largely through the black churches, which were widespread and powerful throughout the segregated South.

49. C   The Boston Port Act was one of the so-called Intolerable or Coercive Acts passed in 1774 as pun-ishment for the Boston Tea Party. This act permitted the British navy to take control of the port of Boston.

50. C   At that time the Continental Congress, which was still relatively conservative, offered King George III the Olive Branch Petition, which professed loyalty to the Crown and asked the king to stop the hostilities.

51. **E** The decision in the *Dred Scott* case actually limited the power of the federal government by stating that Congress had no authority to determine where slavery could and could not go. Furthermore, this was not a Marshall decision.

52. **D** The Democrats allowed Hayes, the Republican candidate, to assume the presidency in return for the end of Reconstruction and the other measures listed, but they did not take back the House and Senate.

53. **D** The Big Stick Policy is the nickname given to The Roosevelt Corollary to the Monroe Doctrine and should be studied along with Taft's Dollar Diplomacy and Wilson's Moral Diplomacy. The United States often intervened in Latin America at the turn of the nineteenth and early twentieth century to protect and promote U.S. economic interests but often did so under the guise of protecting the political stability and security of whatever nation was being policed.

54. **C** The *Schecter* case, also known as the "sick chicken case," ruled that the NRA (National Recovery Act) violated the Constitution. The Court held that Congress did not have the right to delegate legislative powers to the executive branch and that congressional control of interstate commerce could not apply to a local fowl business.

55. **B** Many students think the civil rights movement began in the 1960s, but in fact, the NAACP had been trying to overturn the Supreme Court's decision in *Plessy v. Ferguson* since its founding in 1909. World War II provided further impetus for change as many Americans saw the hypocrisy of fighting against totalitarian dictatorships abroad while we practiced discrimination and violation of civil liberties within our own country. Groups like the Southern Christian Leadership Conference (SCLC) under the leadership of the Reverend Dr. Martin Luther King Jr. along with the Student Nonviolent Coordinating Committee (SNCC) advocated nonviolent tactics such as boycotts, sit-ins, and civil disobedience.

56. **D** Keeping his promise to cut taxes and slow the growth of government spending, Reagan repealed many of the social programs that had begun during Johnson's presidency. He did, however, sharply increase funding for the military, which, combined with his tax reductions, led to the addition of nearly $2 trillion to the national debt.

57. **E** The Stamp Act was one of the first united actions of the colonists against King George III.

58. **C** The Federalist Papers were written by Alexander Hamilton, John Jay, and James Madison, in an effort to drum up support for the ratification of the Constitution and the cause of Republicanism.

59. **B** In 1832 Andrew Jackson managed to push the Force Act through Congress. The bill threatened South Carolina with the use of military force should it refuse to abide by (or "nullify") tariff laws.

60. **A** The NAACP was founded in 1909 as a result of the Niagara Movement, which was led by W. E. B. Du Bois and others who met in Niagara, New York, in 1905. The movement took a more militant approach to solving the problems of racism than the gradualist policies of Booker T. Washington's Afro-American Council.

61. **E** Women were first granted the right to vote in Wyoming in 1869, half a century before the Nineteenth Amendment was passed, making women's suffrage the law of the land.

62. **A** Some members of Congress supported the Treaty of Versailles wholeheartedly; some supported parts of it (Reservationists); and some supported none of it (Irreconcilables).

63. **B** Isolationists in Congress were afraid that if the United States joined NATO, the nation would be pulled into war. Similar concerns had been raised about the League of Nations after World War I.

64. **B** The election of Eisenhower in 1952 reflected the desire of many Americans to disentangle the country from the Korean War and to return to a more conservative economic policy, which they hoped would lead to an economic boom that could keep pace with the baby boom. The election of Nixon in 1968 also reflected a desire for a return to a more conservative social and political approach. George Wallace, running as a third-party candidate, received almost 10 million votes in this election by appealing to those who believed in segregation, states' rights, and "law and order." Democratic candidate Hubert Humphrey suffered from his close ties to President Lyndon Johnson, who had escalated the Vietnam War. It also didn't help that the Democratic National Convention of 1968 was the scene of bitter riots and violence in the streets of Chicago, whereas the Republican convention that year ran without a hitch. In both the elections of 1952 and 1968, Americans were tired of conflict and wanted to return to good times. The more conservative Republican Party was the answer to their wishes.

65. **D** Virtual representation, which is unrelated to mercantilist theory, was the theory by which the British justified their practice of taxing the colonies and passing laws to govern them without giving them the benefit of representation in Parliament.

66. **C** The Federalist-sponsored Alien and Sedition Acts aimed to limit the power of the Democratic-Republicans. To accomplish this, the act both restricted immigration (most new immigrants joined the Democratic-Republican Party) and provided for censorship of newspaper articles.

67. **D** Even though women under the Lowell System were earning wages, they did not become financially independent as a result.

68. **C** The Populists fought for the rights of the farmers and supported the free coinage of silver instead of the traditional reliance on the gold standard (which was seen as favoring bankers and lenders). Their leader, William Jennings Bryan, gave his most memorable speech in which he stated that the poor were being "crucified on a Cross of Gold." The Populists also believed in government ownership of railroads and utilities and opposed the tariff policies of William McKinley.

69. **A** The American Federation of Labor was composed of skilled craft unions and did not include unskilled workers. The AFL believed that the strike was their most powerful weapon against injustice. It fought for economic goals and remained mostly nonpolitical, believing that labor could thrive within a capitalist system as long as it got its share.

70. **A** The supply-side economic theory, like Reagan's trickle-down theory, states that a reduction of taxes will stimulate business, increase personal savings, and expand economic activity.

71. **D** All of the other choices were indeed part of the Great Society program. Rather than balancing the budget, the Great Society reforms meant a significant increase in federal spending, which grew faster than government revenues through taxes.

72. **E** Land sales were not protected from speculators under the ordinances. All the other answers are true.

73. **E** Grenville's policies put an end to salutary neglect, rather than extending it.

74. **E** The election of 1800 is often referred to as the "Revolution of 1800" because there was a peaceful transfer of power from one political party to another. Washington and Adams had both been Federalists, while Jefferson, the newly elected President, was a Democratic-Republican. Men still had their doubts whether a republican form of government was feasible given the size and diversity of the new United States. Republics were desirable but fragile forms of government, and factions were believed to be detrimental to political stability.

     The demise of the Federalist party (A) was brought about by the Hartford Convention in 1814. The Era of Good Feelings (D) is associated with the two administrations of James Monroe, who was elected in 1816 and reelected in 1820 when there was only one political party—the Republicans. The Electoral College (C) did not take into account the existence of political parties because they did not exist when the Constitution was written. In fact, the results of the early elections were hampered by this factor. For example, John Adams was a Federalist elected in 1796, but his vice president was Thomas Jefferson, a Democratic-Republican.

75. **B** These words were in reference to the XYZ affair, in which a French official demanded a bribe from a U.S. envoy simply for the privilege of doing diplomatic business.

76. **A** The violent conflict in Kansas between abolitionist and pro-slavery forces unleashed by the Kansas-Nebraska Act came to be known as "Bleeding Kansas."

77. **B** The Dawes Act sought to do away with tribal ownership of land by granting private property rights to Indians, in the hope that they would be assimilated into white culture.

78. **E** The Northern Securities Company, a railroad holding company that formed a monopoly in the Northwest, was dismantled by the Supreme Court after Theodore Roosevelt attacked it as part of his trust-busting program.

79. **A** Huey Long, the onetime governor and senator of Louisiana, made promises of wealth to all through his "soak the rich" programs and claimed that Roosevelt hadn't gone far enough in aiding the poor. Charles Coughlin, known as "The Radio Priest," broadcast his criticisms to millions of listeners in weekly radio sermons.

80. **B** During the Korean War, President Truman desegregated the army, but his other efforts at desegregation met with little success. Due to Southern filibustering, he was unable to form a new Fair Employment Practices Commission to curb discrimination in hiring.

THE DBQ EXPLAINED

The document-based question begins with a mandatory 15-minute reading period. During these 15 minutes, you'll want to (1) come up with some information not included in the given documents (your outside knowledge) to include in your essay; (2) get an overview of what each document means; (3) decide what opinion you are going to argue; and (4) write an outline of your essay.

The first thing you will be inclined to do, after reading the question, is to look at the documents. Resist temptation. Instead, the first thing you should do is brainstorm for several minutes about what the question is asking of you. Try to list everything you remember about the causes of the Civil War. This list will serve as your reference to the outside information you must provide in order to earn a top grade.

Then, and only then, read over the documents. As you read them, take notes in the margins and underline those passages that you are certain you are going to refer to in your essay. If a document helps you remember a piece of outside information, add that information to your brainstorming list. If you cannot make sense of a document, don't worry. You do not need to mention every document to score well on the DBQ.

Here is what you need to look for in each document to get the most out of it:

- The author
- The date
- The audience (for whom was the document intended?)
- The significance

Remember: You are being asked to write 50 percent document interpretation and 50 percent outside information. Don't get so lost in the documents that you forget to bring in outside information. Readers will not be able to give you a high score unless you have both! What readers really don't like is a laundry list of documents: that is, a paper in which the student merely goes through the documents, explaining each one. Those students are often the ones who forget to bring in outside information, because they are so focused on going through the documents.

So, what is this DBQ all about?

This DBQ asks you two things: (1) to what extent was the Civil War caused by the slavery issue and to what extent was it caused by other factors, and (2) what circumstances led to the breakup of the Union. In the first part you are actually being asked to identify factors *other than slavery* that caused the breakup of the Union, although you aren't being asked to rule out slavery as a cause. Your job is to decide how much of the Civil War was caused by slavery and how much was caused by other factors. In those other factors, you might find ideas that will help you answer the second part.

Note that the question asks, "to what extent." That means you are being asked to rank the causes of the Civil War. You might state that slavery was the leading cause, but there were other causes. You might state that slavery was only one of several equally important causes leading up to the war. You might state that all the other causes had slavery at the root, or you might state that too much weight has been given to slavery as the single cause of the war. There is no right answer. That is the fun of it. You could earn a top score by writing about how slavery was only a fraction of the issue, and the gal sitting across the room from you could also earn a top score by stating that slavery was the only issue!

The Documents

Document A

This is the article from which the famous phrase "Manifest Destiny" was taken. O'Sullivan states that it is the American destiny, ordained by God, to populate the country from coast to coast, in order to provide "for the free development of our yearly multiplying millions." The use of the word "free" should not be overlooked, and the idea that we should challenge any foreign power who attempts to "thwart our policy," "hamper our power," or "limit our greatness" also needs to be addressed. As stated earlier, the Mexican War and cession, which rested upon Manifest Destiny, should not be overlooked in any discussion about the Civil War.

Document B

This declaration of war against Mexico links that war with the war that followed (like we saw in Document A). Note the use of the words "honor, rights and dignity of this country." Clearly, in Polk's opinion, it was our right and responsibility to thwart Mexico in territorial expansion, but these words also sound like abolitionist words, so the issue of slavery also fits in well here. An astute student might also relate this document to the "spot" resolutions, in which Congressman Abraham Lincoln asked President James K. Polk to identify the exact "spot" where "American blood had been shed on American soil."

Document C

This quotation by transcendentalist Ralph Waldo Emerson illustrates the connection between the Mexican War and the Civil War. An astute student might also refer to the fact that fellow transcendentalist Henry David Thoreau compared John Brown to Jesus in his martyrdom for the cause of abolition, and that Thoreau spent a night in jail rather than pay his tax that would support slavery.

Document D

This document is taken from Pennsylvania Representative David Wilmot's proposal before Congress. The Wilmot Proviso proposed that Congress award President Polk the $2 million he asked for while the United States was fighting the Mexican War, and in return that any land we wrested from Mexico remain free from slavery. If you were going to argue that U.S. territorial expansion, or the Mexican War, was a major factor in the breakup of the Union, you would certainly want to use this document to support your thesis. The Wilmot Proviso passed the House twice but was defeated in the Senate. Clearly, the argument over the acquisition of vast western lands added to the sectional debate over the extension of slavery. If you were going to argue that slavery was the most significant reason for the breakup of the Union, you could still use this document in that context. If it weren't for the issue of slavery, the issue of what to do with the Mexican cession wouldn't have been so heated.

Document E

This document, which shows the territorial changes of the Compromise of 1850, can be used in a multitude of ways. First, it speaks to the issue of what efforts were made to keep the Union together. Second, it displays the precarious state of the Union, with free and slave states vying for power. Third, it covers the issue of popular sovereignty in the Utah and New Mexico territories. Lastly, it shows California entering the Union as a free state. An astute student would also want to point out the aspects of the compromise that the map does not show: namely, that it was crafted by Mr. Compromise himself, Henry Clay, and that, in addition to territorial matters, it endorsed a tougher Fugitive Slave Law to pacify the South. It should be pointed out that the compromise bought time for the nation, and that while it was far from perfect, it held up the Union for another 11 shaky years. Another way this document could be used would be if your thesis includes the failure of the era's compromises, and/or ineffectual or misguided politicians.

Document F

The Kansas-Nebraska Act of 1854, largely the work of Senator Stephen Douglas of Illinois, put an end to the North-South truce by introducing the notion of popular sovereignty—in other words, the act allowed the people of a territory to decide whether or not they wanted slavery. The consequences were disastrous for the Union. The act not only led to bloodshed, when groups on both sides of the slavery debate (an anti-slavery group was led by John Brown) took up arms in "Bleeding Kansas," but it also repealed the Missouri Compromise, which had stated that there would be no slavery north of the 36°30′ line. The Northern abolitionists felt that the act permitted "squatters" to decide the fate of slavery in a territory and that it was a concession to Southern slaveowners.

The act was a result of Douglas's plan to build a transcontinental railroad through the central United States, with a major hub in Chicago, in his state of Illinois. In order to get Southern support, he proposed that the former Nebraska Territory be divided into the Kansas Territory and the Nebraska Territory and that the settlers there be free to decide whether or not to allow slavery. After much debate in Congress, the act was passed by both houses and signed by President Pierce into law. Another result of the act was that Northerners and Westerners banded together to form a political party devoted to the prohibition of slavery in the territories. They called themselves the Republican Party, and they pulled members from both the Democratic Party and the Whigs.

This document can be used in many ways: It is an example of a failed compromise; it underlines the issue of slavery; it points to the breakdown of political institutions over the issue of slavery; and it explores what attempts were being made to keep the Union together. Don't leave this document out! It is too important, for all of the reasons just stated, to omit. It should also serve to remind you of two key players in this struggle: Stephen Douglas and John Brown.

Document G

This well-known, unfortunate Supreme Court case turned a man into property. Dred Scott, a slave in Missouri, was taken to the free state of Illinois and then to the free territory of Wisconsin, where he lived for several years before returning to Missouri. Once he returned to Missouri, he sued for his freedom, arguing that his period of residence on free soil made him a free citizen. After he lost in the Missouri Court, he appealed to the Supreme Court, where Southern Democrat Chief Justice Roger Taney ruled against Scott. Abolitionists felt that he should be free under the Missouri Compromise, because Scott had lived in free land, above the 36°30′ line. If he lost his freedom once he returned, then didn't that nullify the Missouri Compromise? This document is filled with goodies: The slavery issue is front and center, as is the issue of political endeavor, whether successful or not. If you are arguing that slavery was at the center of our disunion, clearly the Supreme Court decision illustrates that fact. If you are arguing that the political climate, leaders, laws, court cases, and resolutions were behind the breakup of the union, this document serves you well, too.

Document H

This document illustrates the differences between the North and South in terms of industrial development. In the 1850s there was an explosion of new railroad construction, most of which was concentrated in the North. The many miles of track that existed in the North highlight the economic struggle that took place between the agricultural South and the industrial North. In Charles and Mary Beard's interpretation of what caused the Civil War, they argue that the war was not fought over slavery per se, but that it represented a deeply rooted economic struggle, akin to the American Revolution, that brought about major changes in class relations and power. The North wielded its industrial might over the less-advanced agrarian South, with the effect of destroying the cotton economy and plantation system.

Document I

This cartoon shows the Democratic Party headed for disaster in the election of 1860. The party is not only split internally, represented by the politicians in the cart headed in different directions, but also about to be rammed by the oncoming train of the Republican Party (note that a train is a much more modern form of transportation!). The Democrats, splintered into two, offered the presidential candidacies of both Stephen Douglas, who had the support of the North, and John Breckinridge (President James Buchanan's vice president) of Kentucky, who had the support of the South. The Republicans ran Abraham Lincoln, and the Constitutional Union Party ran John Bell of Tennessee. The election of Lincoln sealed the fate of the Union. Because he would not compromise on the issue of slavery in the territories, and perhaps because he underestimated the secession movement of the South, the Union fell apart. This document can be used to illustrate the political breakdown leading to the war, and it could also be used to demonstrate the power of the slavery issue.

Choosing a Side

The first thing you want to do is to decide what kind of a statement you are going to make. You have already brainstormed all your outside information, made some notes or a quick outline, and decided where to plug in the documents. Because there is no right way to answer this, and many ways to make your argument, here are some positions you might want to argue.

- Slavery was an issue in the breakup of the Union, but it wasn't the only one. There were other equally important factors, such as

    1) the differences in regional lifestyles, with the North being more industrial and the South being more agricultural
    2) the erosion of the traditional party system, including the splintering of the Democratic and Whig parties, which paved the way for the Republican Party
    3) a generation of blundering political leaders, from Polk to Buchanan
    4) the passions of a few zealous reformers
    5) the effect of the Mexican War and the popular sovereignty crisis that ensued over the territories

- Slavery was the underlying issue from which all other issues flowed. If it hadn't been for slavery, the issue of territorial expansion, political alignments, and differences in economies wouldn't have been enough to rip the Union apart.

- Politics tore the country apart. The laws and compromises made by a well-intentioned government backfired on the nation. If it hadn't been for the Missouri Compromise, the Compromise of 1850, and the Kansas-Nebraska Act, the North and South may have stayed united, accepting their differences.

- The Civil War was caused by the idea of Manifest Destiny, the belief that it was the nation's God-given right to expand across the continent, gobbling up all available land. If Americans hadn't held these beliefs, the issue of slavery may not have extended to such a widespread area.

Planning Your Essay

Unless you read extremely quickly, you probably won't have time to write a detailed outline for your essay during the 15-minute reading period. However, it is worth taking several minutes to jot down a loose structure of your essay, because it will actually save you time when you write. First, decide on your thesis and write it down in the test booklet. Then take a few minutes to brainstorm all the points you might put in your essay. Choose the strongest points and number them in the order you plan to present them. Lastly, note which documents and outside information you plan to use in conjunction with each point. If you organize before you write, the actual writing process will go much more smoothly. More important, you will not write yourself into a corner, and suddenly find yourself making a point you cannot support or heading toward a weak conclusion (or worse still, no conclusion at all).

What You Should Have Discussed

Regardless of which thesis you choose, your essay should discuss all of the following:

- The issue of slavery
- The Mexican War and cession
- The *Dred Scott* decision
- The Northern industrial economy v. the Southern agricultural one
- The issue of popular sovereignty in the territories
- The Compromises of 1820 and 1850
- Abolitionists
- The Kansas-Nebraska Act

Give yourself very high marks for outside knowledge if you mention any five of the following:

- The Lincoln-Douglas debates
- The Freeport Doctrine
- John Brown
- "Bleeding Kansas"
- The Fugitive Slave Act
- Personal liberty laws
- Harriet Beecher Stowe's *Uncle Tom's Cabin*
- The Republican Party
- Whigs
- Free-Soilers
- Spot resolution
- The Tallmadge Amendment
- William Lloyd Garrison's *The Liberator*
- The Brooks-Sumner affair
- The Gadsden Purchase

Give yourself a pat on the back if you mention any of the following:

- The Ostend Manifesto
- Hinton Helper's *Impending Crisis of the South*
- The Know-Nothing Party
- The Lecompton Constitution
- The Crittenden Compromise
- Conscience Whigs
- Cotton Whigs
- "Barnburners"
- Henry Clay
- Franklin Pierce
- James K. Polk
- James Buchanan
- Millard Fillmore
- Lewis Cass
- Roger Taney
- John C. Calhoun

THE FREE-RESPONSE QUESTIONS EXPLAINED

Question 2—The Revolution

2. To what extent was the American Revolution a radical break with the past and to what extent was it a conservative attempt to protect the status quo?

If you choose this question, keep in mind the three major theories concerning the issue. One holds that the Revolution was truly radical in its ideological quest for liberty and in the social and economic changes it brought about. A second theory holds that, on the contrary, simple economic and material interests, led by the colonists' desire to control their own economy, propelled the Revolution. A third holds that both ideology and material interests inspired our Revolution and that only by understanding the relationship between the two can we fully comprehend it.

If you decide to write about how the American Revolution was a radical break with the past, your essay pretty much has to mention the following:

- The establishment of representative government in the new United States and the expansion of voting rights
- The political changes that resulted from our new republican form of government, including the concept of Federalism, a written constitution, and the delicate balance between the rights of the state and those of the individual
- The notion that the colonists were spurred to revolution by their study of the ideas of the Enlightenment and their dislike of British rule

Give yourself extra points if you mention any of the following:

- Thomas Paine's *Common Sense* and how it swayed public opinion in favor of independence by stating that it was against common sense for people to pledge loyalty to a corrupt and distant king whose laws were unreasonable
- The social changes brought about by the Revolution, such as the abolition of aristocratic titles and the separation of church and state
- The economic opportunities that resulted from our no longer being a British colony and the rise our independence gave to free enterprise and capitalism
- Any of the relevant Revolutionary theorists or historians, such as Bailyn, Beard, Nash, or Boorstin

If you decide to write about how the American Revolution was a conservative attempt to maintain the status quo, then your essay pretty much has to mention the following:

- That some of the colonists' most important motives for seeking independence were based on economic self-interest, such as their desire to escape British taxes and British control of trade
- That the colonists sought to maintain the same social structure that existed under British rule, which included patronage and a devotion to patriarchal authority
- That the status of women and blacks remained pretty much unchanged after the Revolution

Give yourself bonus points if you mention any of the following:

- The class aspect of the Revolution, including the idea that the Revolution wasn't only about "home rule" but about "who should rule at home" (in other words, the Revolutionaries thought that American aristocrats should rule instead of British aristocrats)
- The issue of slavery and how this war "for freedom" did nothing to abolish it, and, in fact, gave rise to a nation that enshrined slavery in its Constitution, with the notorious "Three-Fifths Clause" in Article I
- That the Revolution did not make great strides in the status of women. Extra bonus points for including Abigail Adams's letter to her husband, John, in which she writes: "Remember the ladies and be more generous and favorable to them than your ancestors"
- That American distribution of wealth was not radically changed by the Revolution, which meant that those at the top of the social ladder were able to hold on to what they had

About the Structure of Your Essay

Remember that the best essays make the reader aware that you know both sides of the argument, even though you support one side more than the other. Try to take one side, and support it with as many details as you can (names, dates, documents, publications). Before your conclusion, you will want to include a paragraph in which you explain why the other side is wrong. For instance, if you were to write a glowing essay about how revolutionary the American Revolution was, one of your paragraphs would include the fact that, yes, certain lives, like those of women and blacks, were not radically altered by the Revolution, but that nonetheless this doesn't undermine the Revolution's many other radical achievements, because…. You are showing here that you understand the question well enough to have taken either side, but have chosen one over the other because you are an AP student who has learned to think for yourself! Don't forget to end with a strong conclusion that reinforces your original thesis.

Question 3—Jeffersonian Republicanism

3.   Analyze the ways in which TWO of the following represented a shift in the ideals of Jeffersonian republicanism during the period 1800–1824:

> The Louisiana Purchase
> *Marbury v. Madison*
> The War of 1812
> The Monroe Doctrine

If you choose to do this essay, you must be sure to begin by defining the ideals of Jeffersonian republicanism before going on to give examples! Then you need to explain how the ideals shifted or changed. The four choices should help you come up with your thesis statement by serving as clues to get you started. You are asked to delve into two of the choices—you earn no bonus points for doing three or all four. It is better to answer the question and develop your analysis of the two topics that you choose. If you think some of the categories overlap, which they often do, then you can weave in some information from one of the others, but only if it is framed within one of the two you choose.

Note the dates. The years given are 1800–1824. You know that Jefferson served two terms as president, from 1800–1808, and that he was succeeded by James Madison (1809–1816) and then James Monroe (1817–1824.) These three were known as the Virginia Dynasty, and it was only with the 1824 election of former Federalist John Quincy Adams of Massachusetts that the dynasty ended. So remember that you are not limiting yourself to Jefferson in this essay. You are being asked to address *all three presidencies.*

Basic Facts

Your essay pretty much has to mention the following basic facts:

- Jeffersonian republicanism stood for a limited central government, states' rights rather than federal rights, strict construction of the Constitution, a devotion to agricultural interests, a restricted military, and support of the Bill of Rights.
- Jefferson was followed by Madison and then Monroe, and they were all Virginian Republicans who shared the same basic ideals.
- During this period, Republicans started to act like Federalists.

Give yourself extra credit for mentioning the following:

- It was common practice for the secretary of state to become president after serving in the previous cabinet. Madison was Jefferson's secretary of state before assuming the presidency, and Monroe was Madison's secretary of state before he became president.
- The election of 1800 was viewed as "The Revolution of 1800" because (1) the Republicans replaced the Federalists in the executive branch, and (2) no blood was shed in this transfer of power from one political party to the other.
- Jefferson stated in his inaugural address: "We are all Republicans, we are all Federalists."

The Louisiana Purchase

If you choose this category, your essay pretty much has to mention the following:

- There was no provision in the Constitution for the purchase of the Louisiana Territory, and Jefferson was acting like a loose constructionist when he purchased it.
- The Louisiana Purchase doubled the size of this country and was sold to us by the French for $15 million.
- Although Jefferson had doubts about whether the United States had the authority to accept the offer, he agreed to it by reasoning that it would benefit the entire country and it had the support of Congress.
- The Louisiana Purchase provided the country with national unity and boosted the popularity of the Republicans.

Give yourself extra credit for mentioning the following:

- The decline of the Federalists as a result of the Louisiana Purchase

Marbury v. Madison

Your essay pretty much has to mention the following:

- The court case of 1803 established the power of judicial review.
- John Marshall was the Supreme Court Justice who ruled on this case.
- This case, like the Louisiana Purchase, extended the power of the judiciary, and thus the federal government.

Give yourself extra credit for mentioning the following:

- While the case itself was over a minor issue (the power of the court to force the delivery of a commission), it actually gave the Supreme Court the enormous power of being able to nullify an act of Congress.
- This case was over the "midnight appointments" of John Adams, which the newly elected Jefferson was trying to block.
- Jefferson also tried to block other Federalist judicial measures by supporting the impeachment of Federalist Justice Samuel Chase.

The War of 1812

You pretty much have to mention the following:

- The Jeffersonians were acting like Federalists in the expansionist and militaristic venture known as the War of 1812.
- The war called into question the classic Republican commitments to limited federal power and to peace.
- The war was conducted during the presidency of James Madison.

Give yourself extra credit for mentioning the following:

- The United States started the fight because it felt the British were violating American neutrality rights at sea and also stirring up trouble on the western frontier.
- The "war hawks" in Congress were led by Henry Clay of Kentucky and John C. Calhoun of South Carolina, representing the support of the West and South.
- The country was divided on this war, both by region and by political alliances.
- Jefferson's Embargo Act of 1807, which prohibited our trade with foreign nations, harmed the nation's economy and plunged us into a depression.
- The Embargo Act was followed by the Nonintercourse Act of 1809 and then Macon's Bill #2 in 1810. All three acts aimed at settling the violation of neutral shipping rights peacefully.
- Madison, like Jefferson, attempted a combination of economic pressure and diplomacy to deal with Britain, but ultimately brought us into war.
- The New England Federalists were so opposed to "Mr. Madison's War" that they came close to secession at the Hartford Convention of 1814. (You would really make a reader's day if you included this one!)
- Tecumseh, and his brother Prophet, of the Shawnee tribe attempted to unite all Indians east of the Mississippi River but were destroyed by General William Henry Harrison at the Battle of Tippecanoe. (What does this say about the Jeffersonian ideal of all men being endowed by their creator with inalienable rights to life, liberty, and the pursuit of happiness?)

The Monroe Doctrine

You pretty much have to mention the following:

- The Monroe Doctrine warned European nations not to interfere in the affairs of the Western Hemisphere and also claimed for us the right to intervene anywhere in our own hemisphere if we felt our security was threatened.
- The Monroe Doctrine smacked of bold nationalism and was applauded by the American public, though its full impact wasn't felt for quite some time, when it was later viewed as the cornerstone of our foreign policy. Nationalism signified quite a shift in Jeffersonian ideals and later took the form of economic growth and expansionism.
- The Monroe Doctrine, although issued under President James Monroe, was written by his secretary of state, John Quincy Adams. During Monroe's presidency, Adams helped to usher in a new wave of westward expansion, which was followed by our recognition of new nations in Central and South America.

Give yourself extra credit for mentioning the following:

- At the time of the Monroe Doctrine, the Republican Party was the only organized force in American politics, because the Federalists had ceased running candidates after 1816.
- Even though we proclaimed neutrality in the wars between Spain and its rebellious colonies, we were selling ships and supplies to the insurgents, and when Monroe established diplomatic relations with the Latin American countries, we became the first nation to do so.
- The Monroe Doctrine gave us the appearance of isolationism because we had "warned" European nations to stay out of our affairs, but in reality we had merely stated our nationalistic and patriotic fervor of the time.

About the Structure of Your Essay

Make sure you begin by exploring what is meant by Jeffersonian ideals and then explain how they changed during the three presidencies in question. Your introductory paragraph should elaborate on what Jeffersonian Republicans stood for and move on to discuss how circumstances made them change their views. You'll want to spend a paragraph on each of your category choices, explaining how your choice showed a shift in Jeffersonian policy. Make sure you discuss who was president at the time and how he differed from his predecessor. You should also compare the Republican philosophy to that of the Federalists and explain why the Federalists faded from politics at this time. And be sure to end with a strong conclusion.

Question 4—Foreign Policy in the 1920s

4. Explain how TWO of the following influenced U.S. foreign policy during the 1920s:

> Social and economic issues within the United States
> War debts and reparations
> Political ideology

This essay asks you to delve into U.S. foreign policy in the post–World War I period. You will need to be clear on what our foreign policy was and then select two of the choices to explain what influenced our policy. Remember: If you're asked to analyze two, then be sure to choose only two. The first thing you need to do in this essay is explain our foreign policy during the 1920s. Contrary to common belief, the United States was NOT isolationist at that time, although we did refuse to join the League of Nations. Yes, we were fearful of being pulled into another world war, but we did make arrangements with other nations that would advance our interests while also aiming for peace.

Social and Economic Issues Within the United States

You pretty much had to mention the following:

- The Red Scare—This was the time of the Palmer raids, rising nativism, a resurgence of the Klan, anti-unionism, and restrictive immigration laws.
- Fundamentalism—You should include the Scopes Monkey Trial and the Prohibition movement, and, of course, Harding's "return to normalcy" pledge, which kicked off the decade.
- Cultural modernism, including women getting the right to vote, a loosening of morals, and the Lindbergh flight
- In terms of the economy, you would have to mention the boom years (1922–1928), which were followed by the stock market crash and the Depression. You should also mention the concepts of consumerism and materialism.
- Because this essay asks you to concentrate on U.S. foreign policy, you need to be sure to connect all these aspects of the social climate with the views toward international involvement. The prevalence of xenophobia (fear of the foreign, especially immigrants) during this time obviously influenced the will to involve the United States in the affairs of other countries. The United States was, however, willing to deal with other countries for economic gain, rather than for political or social reasons.

Give yourself extra points if you mention the following:

- Attorney General A. Mitchell Palmer's raids on suspected radicals; his assistant, J. Edgar Hoover; the Red Scare; the bombs that went off in the spring of 1919; and the anti-union and anti-strike activities of the U.S. government during Palmer's tenure
- The attack on Industrial Workers of the World members, the attack on "radical" newspapers and literature, the 100 Percent Americanism movement, the rise in Klan membership and lynching, the stand taken against feminist demands, and the general xenophobia that gripped the nation
- The trial and execution of two radical immigrants, Sacco and Vanzetti; the Emergency Quota Act of 1921; and the Johnson-Reed Immigration Act of 1924
- Henry Ford and the automobile, leisure-time activities, sports, movies, the Jazz Age, and any other objects or activities that kept us from concentrating on the rest of the world

War Debts and Reparations

You pretty much have to mention the following:

- Before World War I the United States had been a debtor nation, and after the war it emerged as a creditor nation, having lent over $10 billion to the Allies.
- Under the Treaty of Versailles, Germany was required to pay $30 billion in reparations to the Allies, but was bankrupt and couldn't pay.
- The Dawes Plan of 1924 established a flow of payments from the United States to Germany and from Germany to the Allies.
- Tariff walls resulted in international and domestic economic distress.

Give yourself extra points if you mention the following:

- The Fordney-McCumber Tariff of 1922 created a high tariff barrier around the U.S. and resulted in economic dislocation here and abroad.
- Charles Dawes, an American banker, became Coolidge's vice president and was the mastermind behind the Dawes plan. He also won the Nobel Peace Prize for his efforts, even though the plan didn't solve the international economic crisis.
- The United States was not only lending money overseas, but also investing in European industry and in Latin American ventures as well.

Political Ideology

You pretty much have to mention the following:

- The three Republican presidents of the 1920s—Harding (1921–1923), Coolidge (1923–1929), and Hoover (1929–1933)—all had pro-business views.
- The Washington Conference of 1921 aimed to promote peace, cut military spending, and endorse world disarmament.
- The Kellogg-Briand Pact renounced war as an instrument of national policy.
- The Republican Congress refused to permit us to join the League of Nations and sign the Treaty of Versailles.

Give yourself extra points if you mention the following:

- The Nine-Power Treaty, the Five-Power Treaty, and the Four-Power Treaty that resulted from the Washington Conference and dealt with issues of territorial integrity and disarmament
- The Harding scandals and his unexpected death in 1923
- Harding's appointments of Hoover as secretary of commerce and Mellon as secretary of the treasury
- Coolidge's attitude toward the economy ("The business of America is business") and his belief in limited government
- Coolidge's refusal to pay World War I veterans their bonuses early
- Coolidge's veto of the McNary-Haugen Bill of 1928 to help farmers
- Hoover's work during World War I as head of the Food Administration and his campaign against Al Smith of New York in 1928
- Hoover's suggestion that poverty was eliminated and his belief in self-help
- The influence of Henry Cabot Lodge, chairman of the Senate Foreign Relations Committee, on U.S. foreign policy

About the Structure of Your Essay

You would have to begin with an explanation of U.S. foreign policy during the 1920s and follow with a discussion of what influenced this policy. Your essay would then include an analysis of the social, economic, and political pressures of the postwar period, focusing on the two categories you choose. In sum, your essay would outline the varying forces that defined our international relations in the 1920s.

Question 5—The 1960s

5. Discuss the ways in which TWO of the following changed both the social fabric and political structure of America during the 1960s:

> Social and economic issues within the United States
> The civil rights movement
> The Vietnam War
> The women's movement

This essay asks you to discuss that amazing decade, the 1960s. In it you should describe the politics and social fabric of the country, giving specific examples, and then choose which two issues had the most impact on this decade. The 1960s are often described as a turbulent decade, and the reasons for that turbulence are where you want to begin. The social upheaval that was brought about by domestic and international issues, combined with the generation gap that defined the era, as baby boomers went to high school and then college in the 1960s, needs to be discussed. Although both the civil rights movement and the war in Vietnam began in the 1950s, the 1960s were defined by a rising tide of change and resistance to what had been readily accepted during the decades before. In contrast to the 1950s, known for its conformity and Cold War jitters, the decade that followed, ushered in by the youngest president, John F. Kennedy, was one of the most mercurial in U.S. history.

You would have to begin with a solid description of the "stormy" sixties, with specific examples of the social changes that came about, and then move on to an in-depth analysis of two of the three categories listed. You would also be wise to mention the assassinations of the two Kennedys and King, and the difficult presidency of Lyndon B. Johnson.

The Civil Rights Movement

You pretty much have to mention the following:

- Martin Luther King Jr. and his "I Have a Dream" speech
- Malcolm X and the Black Muslims
- The Southern Christian Leadership Conference, CORE, the Student Nonviolent Coordinating Committee, the NAACP, and the Black Panthers
- The voter registration drives, the sit-ins in the South, and the Freedom Riders
- Johnson's War on Poverty and Great Society programs
- The desegregation attempts made by Kennedy and Johnson, compared with those made by Eisenhower and previous leaders
- The segregationist politicians and law "enforcers" in the South
- The Civil Rights Act of 1964
- The Voting Rights Act of 1965
- Urban violence, race riots
- The shift to a more militant movement after the death of King

Give yourself extra points if you mention the following:

- King's "Letter from a Birmingham Jail"
- The march from Selma to Montgomery, Alabama
- "Freedom Summer" in Mississippi
- The Greensboro, North Carolina, sit-ins at Woolworth's
- The assassinations of Medgar Evers and Emmett Till and the murders of the three civil rights workers in Mississippi (Schwerner, Chaney, and Goodman) and the four little girls at the 16th St. Baptist Church in Birmingham
- The integration of "Ole Miss" by James Meredith, and Mississippi Governor Ross Barnett, who tried to stop him
- Governor George Wallace (and his candidacy for president in 1968), police chief Eugene "Bull" Connor, and the use of police dogs and fire hoses in Alabama
- The Mississippi Freedom Democratic Party (MFDP) at the Democratic Convention of 1964
- Stokely Carmichael, H. Rap Brown, Huey Newton, Bobby Seale, Eldridge Cleaver, and the Black Power movement
- Robert Weaver, who became the first black cabinet member (secretary of housing and urban development)
- The 1967 Kerner Commission, which concluded that black riots were a result of poverty and lack of job opportunities

The Vietnam War

You pretty much have to mention the following:

- "Hawks" vs. "Doves"
- John F. Kennedy, Lyndon Johnson, Richard Nixon, Eugene McCarthy, Robert Kennedy
- Vietminh, Ho Chi Minh, South Vietnam, and Diem
- The Tet Offensive
- The war being broadcast on television to a national audience
- The Pentagon Papers
- Johnson's decision not to seek re-election
- The moratoriums and other demonstrations against the war
- The student anti-war movement

Give yourself extra points if you mention the following:

- The Berkeley Student Movement, hippies
- The Students for a Democratic Society (SDS)
- The Weathermen (and you can add two points if you mention the fact that they got their name from a line in a Dylan song: "You don't need a weatherman to know which way the wind blows.")
- Hubert Humphrey
- The Democratic National Convention in 1968, Mayor Daley, the Chicago Seven
- Laos, Cambodia
- "Vietnamization"
- The burning of draft cards and the draft resistance movement
- Anti-war music and Woodstock

The Women's Movement

You pretty much have to mention the following:

- Feminism and the women's liberation movement
- The Equal Rights Amendment and the Equal Pay Act
- National Organization for Women (NOW)
- Abortion rights controversy (though *Roe v. Wade* wasn't until 1973)
- The sexual revolution, the birth control pill, free love

Give yourself extra points if you mention the following:

- Betty Friedan's *The Feminine Mystique*
- The "glass ceiling"
- Sexual politics (and the book, by Kate Millett, that gave it its name)
- The Kinsey Report
- Gloria Steinem, Bella Abzug, Shirley Chisholm (Chisholm could be mentioned under civil rights also)
- Woodstock and the counterculture

About the Structure of Your Essay

You would need to describe the times by delving into the issues that caused the changes. But don't forget: The essays that look easy are often the most difficult. Don't forget to include lots of facts (don't let them go "blowin' in the wind…") that focus on how society and politics changed so dramatically in the 1960s.

HOW TO SCORE PRACTICE TEST 2

Section I: Multiple-Choice

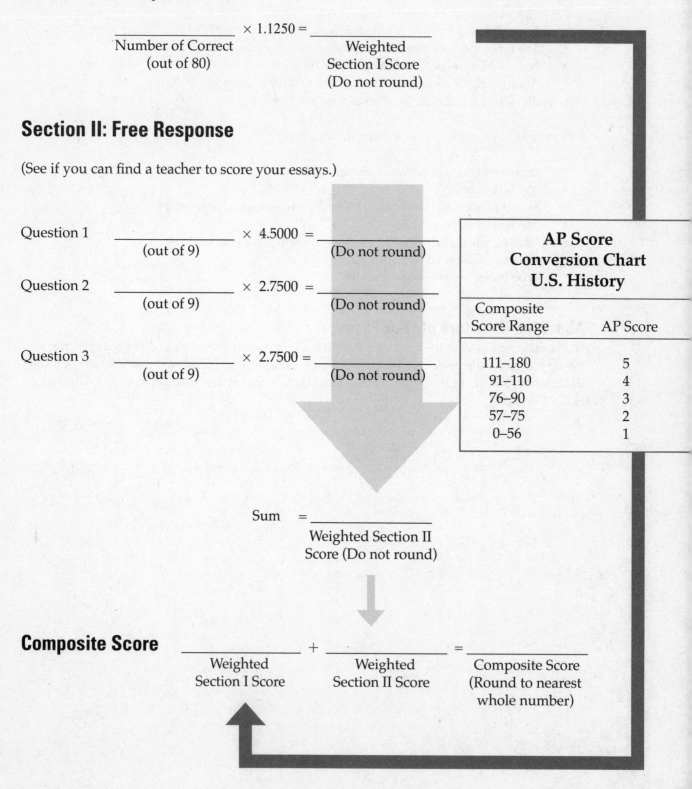

_____ × 1.1250 = _____
Number of Correct   Weighted
(out of 80)   Section I Score
                         (Do not round)

Section II: Free Response

(See if you can find a teacher to score your essays.)

Question 1 _____ × 4.5000 = _____
            (out of 9)   (Do not round)

Question 2 _____ × 2.7500 = _____
            (out of 9)   (Do not round)

Question 3 _____ × 2.7500 = _____
            (out of 9)   (Do not round)

AP Score Conversion Chart U.S. History

Composite Score Range	AP Score
111–180	5
91–110	4
76–90	3
57–75	2
0–56	1

Sum = _____
Weighted Section II
Score (Do not round)

Composite Score _____ + _____ = _____
                     Weighted   Weighted   Composite Score
                     Section I Score Section II Score (Round to nearest
                                                       whole number)

The Princeton Review®

1

YOUR NAME: _____
(Print)   Last   First   M.I.

SIGNATURE: _____ DATE: ___ / ___ / ___

HOME ADDRESS: _____
(Print)   Number and Street

_____
City   State   Zip Code

PHONE No.: _____
(Print)

IMPORTANT: Please fill in these boxes exactly as shown on the back cover of your test book.

2. TEST FORM

3. TEST CODE

4. REGISTRATION NUMBER

5. YOUR NAME

First 4 letters of last name | FIRST INIT | MID INIT

6. DATE OF BIRTH

Month	Day	Year
JAN		
FEB		
MAR		
APR		
MAY		
JUN		
JUL		
AUG		
SEP		
OCT		
NOV		
DEC		

7. SEX
- MALE
- FEMALE

The Princeton Review®

© TPR Education IP Holdings, LLC
FORM NO. 00001-PR

Start with number 1 for each new section. If a section has fewer questions than answer spaces, leave the extra answer spaces blank.

1 A B C D E   21 A B C D E   41 A B C D E   61 A B C D E
2 A B C D E   22 A B C D E   42 A B C D E   62 A B C D E
3 A B C D E   23 A B C D E   43 A B C D E   63 A B C D E
4 A B C D E   24 A B C D E   44 A B C D E   64 A B C D E
5 A B C D E   25 A B C D E   45 A B C D E   65 A B C D E
6 A B C D E   26 A B C D E   46 A B C D E   66 A B C D E
7 A B C D E   27 A B C D E   47 A B C D E   67 A B C D E
8 A B C D E   28 A B C D E   48 A B C D E   68 A B C D E
9 A B C D E   29 A B C D E   49 A B C D E   69 A B C D E
10 A B C D E   30 A B C D E   50 A B C D E   70 A B C D E
11 A B C D E   31 A B C D E   51 A B C D E   71 A B C D E
12 A B C D E   32 A B C D E   52 A B C D E   72 A B C D E
13 A B C D E   33 A B C D E   53 A B C D E   73 A B C D E
14 A B C D E   34 A B C D E   54 A B C D E   74 A B C D E
15 A B C D E   35 A B C D E   55 A B C D E   75 A B C D E
16 A B C D E   36 A B C D E   56 A B C D E   76 A B C D E
17 A B C D E   37 A B C D E   57 A B C D E   77 A B C D E
18 A B C D E   38 A B C D E   58 A B C D E   78 A B C D E
19 A B C D E   39 A B C D E   59 A B C D E   79 A B C D E
20 A B C D E   40 A B C D E   60 A B C D E   80 A B C D E

DO NOT MARK IN THIS AREA

The Princeton Review®

1

YOUR NAME: _____
(Print)   Last   First   M.I.

SIGNATURE: _____   DATE: ___/___/___

HOME ADDRESS: _____
(Print)   Number and Street

_____
City   State   Zip Code

PHONE No.: _____
(Print)

IMPORTANT: Please fill in these boxes exactly as shown on the back cover of your test book.

2. TEST FORM

3. TEST CODE

4. REGISTRATION NUMBER

6. DATE OF BIRTH

Month	Day	Year
⊂ ⊃ JAN		
⊂ ⊃ FEB		
⊂ ⊃ MAR	⊂0⊃ ⊂0⊃	⊂0⊃ ⊂0⊃
⊂ ⊃ APR	⊂1⊃ ⊂1⊃	⊂1⊃ ⊂1⊃
⊂ ⊃ MAY	⊂2⊃ ⊂2⊃	⊂2⊃ ⊂2⊃
⊂ ⊃ JUN	⊂3⊃ ⊂3⊃	⊂3⊃ ⊂3⊃
⊂ ⊃ JUL	⊂4⊃	⊂4⊃ ⊂4⊃
⊂ ⊃ AUG	⊂5⊃	⊂5⊃ ⊂5⊃
⊂ ⊃ SEP	⊂6⊃	⊂6⊃ ⊂6⊃
⊂ ⊃ OCT	⊂7⊃	⊂7⊃ ⊂7⊃
⊂ ⊃ NOV	⊂8⊃	⊂8⊃ ⊂8⊃
⊂ ⊃ DEC	⊂9⊃	⊂9⊃ ⊂9⊃

Test Code bubbles: ⊂0⊃ ⊂A⊃ ⊂0⊃... ⊂1⊃ ⊂B⊃ ⊂1⊃... ⊂2⊃ ⊂C⊃ ⊂2⊃... ⊂3⊃ ⊂D⊃ ⊂3⊃... ⊂4⊃ ⊂E⊃ ⊂4⊃... ⊂5⊃ ⊂F⊃ ⊂5⊃... ⊂6⊃ ⊂G⊃ ⊂6⊃... ⊂7⊃... ⊂8⊃... ⊂9⊃...

7. SEX
⊂ ⊃ MALE
⊂ ⊃ FEMALE

5. YOUR NAME

First 4 letters of last name				FIRST INIT	MID INIT
⊂A⊃	⊂A⊃	⊂A⊃	⊂A⊃	⊂A⊃	⊂A⊃
⊂B⊃	⊂B⊃	⊂B⊃	⊂B⊃	⊂B⊃	⊂B⊃
⊂C⊃	⊂C⊃	⊂C⊃	⊂C⊃	⊂C⊃	⊂C⊃
⊂D⊃	⊂D⊃	⊂D⊃	⊂D⊃	⊂D⊃	⊂D⊃
⊂E⊃	⊂E⊃	⊂E⊃	⊂E⊃	⊂E⊃	⊂E⊃
⊂F⊃	⊂F⊃	⊂F⊃	⊂F⊃	⊂F⊃	⊂F⊃
⊂G⊃	⊂G⊃	⊂G⊃	⊂G⊃	⊂G⊃	⊂G⊃
⊂H⊃	⊂H⊃	⊂H⊃	⊂H⊃	⊂H⊃	⊂H⊃
⊂I⊃	⊂I⊃	⊂I⊃	⊂I⊃	⊂I⊃	⊂I⊃
⊂J⊃	⊂J⊃	⊂J⊃	⊂J⊃	⊂J⊃	⊂J⊃
⊂K⊃	⊂K⊃	⊂K⊃	⊂K⊃	⊂K⊃	⊂K⊃
⊂L⊃	⊂L⊃	⊂L⊃	⊂L⊃	⊂L⊃	⊂L⊃
⊂M⊃	⊂M⊃	⊂M⊃	⊂M⊃	⊂M⊃	⊂M⊃
⊂N⊃	⊂N⊃	⊂N⊃	⊂N⊃	⊂N⊃	⊂N⊃
⊂O⊃	⊂O⊃	⊂O⊃	⊂O⊃	⊂O⊃	⊂O⊃
⊂P⊃	⊂P⊃	⊂P⊃	⊂P⊃	⊂P⊃	⊂P⊃
⊂Q⊃	⊂Q⊃	⊂Q⊃	⊂Q⊃	⊂Q⊃	⊂Q⊃
⊂R⊃	⊂R⊃	⊂R⊃	⊂R⊃	⊂R⊃	⊂R⊃
⊂S⊃	⊂S⊃	⊂S⊃	⊂S⊃	⊂S⊃	⊂S⊃
⊂T⊃	⊂T⊃	⊂T⊃	⊂T⊃	⊂T⊃	⊂T⊃
⊂U⊃	⊂U⊃	⊂U⊃	⊂U⊃	⊂U⊃	⊂U⊃
⊂V⊃	⊂V⊃	⊂V⊃	⊂V⊃	⊂V⊃	⊂V⊃
⊂W⊃	⊂W⊃	⊂W⊃	⊂W⊃	⊂W⊃	⊂W⊃
⊂X⊃	⊂X⊃	⊂X⊃	⊂X⊃	⊂X⊃	⊂X⊃
⊂Y⊃	⊂Y⊃	⊂Y⊃	⊂Y⊃	⊂Y⊃	⊂Y⊃
⊂Z⊃	⊂Z⊃	⊂Z⊃	⊂Z⊃	⊂Z⊃	⊂Z⊃

The Princeton Review®

© TPR Education IP Holdings, LLC
FORM NO. 00001-PR

Start with number 1 for each new section. If a section has fewer questions than answer spaces, leave the extra answer spaces blank.

1 ⊂A⊃ ⊂B⊃ ⊂C⊃ ⊂D⊃ ⊂E⊃   21 ⊂A⊃ ⊂B⊃ ⊂C⊃ ⊂D⊃ ⊂E⊃   41 ⊂A⊃ ⊂B⊃ ⊂C⊃ ⊂D⊃ ⊂E⊃   61 ⊂A⊃ ⊂B⊃ ⊂C⊃ ⊂D⊃ ⊂E⊃
2 ⊂A⊃ ⊂B⊃ ⊂C⊃ ⊂D⊃ ⊂E⊃   22 ⊂A⊃ ⊂B⊃ ⊂C⊃ ⊂D⊃ ⊂E⊃   42 ⊂A⊃ ⊂B⊃ ⊂C⊃ ⊂D⊃ ⊂E⊃   62 ⊂A⊃ ⊂B⊃ ⊂C⊃ ⊂D⊃ ⊂E⊃
3 ⊂A⊃ ⊂B⊃ ⊂C⊃ ⊂D⊃ ⊂E⊃   23 ⊂A⊃ ⊂B⊃ ⊂C⊃ ⊂D⊃ ⊂E⊃   43 ⊂A⊃ ⊂B⊃ ⊂C⊃ ⊂D⊃ ⊂E⊃   63 ⊂A⊃ ⊂B⊃ ⊂C⊃ ⊂D⊃ ⊂E⊃
4 ⊂A⊃ ⊂B⊃ ⊂C⊃ ⊂D⊃ ⊂E⊃   24 ⊂A⊃ ⊂B⊃ ⊂C⊃ ⊂D⊃ ⊂E⊃   44 ⊂A⊃ ⊂B⊃ ⊂C⊃ ⊂D⊃ ⊂E⊃   64 ⊂A⊃ ⊂B⊃ ⊂C⊃ ⊂D⊃ ⊂E⊃
5 ⊂A⊃ ⊂B⊃ ⊂C⊃ ⊂D⊃ ⊂E⊃   25 ⊂A⊃ ⊂B⊃ ⊂C⊃ ⊂D⊃ ⊂E⊃   45 ⊂A⊃ ⊂B⊃ ⊂C⊃ ⊂D⊃ ⊂E⊃   65 ⊂A⊃ ⊂B⊃ ⊂C⊃ ⊂D⊃ ⊂E⊃
6 ⊂A⊃ ⊂B⊃ ⊂C⊃ ⊂D⊃ ⊂E⊃   26 ⊂A⊃ ⊂B⊃ ⊂C⊃ ⊂D⊃ ⊂E⊃   46 ⊂A⊃ ⊂B⊃ ⊂C⊃ ⊂D⊃ ⊂E⊃   66 ⊂A⊃ ⊂B⊃ ⊂C⊃ ⊂D⊃ ⊂E⊃
7 ⊂A⊃ ⊂B⊃ ⊂C⊃ ⊂D⊃ ⊂E⊃   27 ⊂A⊃ ⊂B⊃ ⊂C⊃ ⊂D⊃ ⊂E⊃   47 ⊂A⊃ ⊂B⊃ ⊂C⊃ ⊂D⊃ ⊂E⊃   67 ⊂A⊃ ⊂B⊃ ⊂C⊃ ⊂D⊃ ⊂E⊃
8 ⊂A⊃ ⊂B⊃ ⊂C⊃ ⊂D⊃ ⊂E⊃   28 ⊂A⊃ ⊂B⊃ ⊂C⊃ ⊂D⊃ ⊂E⊃   48 ⊂A⊃ ⊂B⊃ ⊂C⊃ ⊂D⊃ ⊂E⊃   68 ⊂A⊃ ⊂B⊃ ⊂C⊃ ⊂D⊃ ⊂E⊃
9 ⊂A⊃ ⊂B⊃ ⊂C⊃ ⊂D⊃ ⊂E⊃   29 ⊂A⊃ ⊂B⊃ ⊂C⊃ ⊂D⊃ ⊂E⊃   49 ⊂A⊃ ⊂B⊃ ⊂C⊃ ⊂D⊃ ⊂E⊃   69 ⊂A⊃ ⊂B⊃ ⊂C⊃ ⊂D⊃ ⊂E⊃
10 ⊂A⊃ ⊂B⊃ ⊂C⊃ ⊂D⊃ ⊂E⊃ 30 ⊂A⊃ ⊂B⊃ ⊂C⊃ ⊂D⊃ ⊂E⊃   50 ⊂A⊃ ⊂B⊃ ⊂C⊃ ⊂D⊃ ⊂E⊃   70 ⊂A⊃ ⊂B⊃ ⊂C⊃ ⊂D⊃ ⊂E⊃
11 ⊂A⊃ ⊂B⊃ ⊂C⊃ ⊂D⊃ ⊂E⊃ 31 ⊂A⊃ ⊂B⊃ ⊂C⊃ ⊂D⊃ ⊂E⊃   51 ⊂A⊃ ⊂B⊃ ⊂C⊃ ⊂D⊃ ⊂E⊃   71 ⊂A⊃ ⊂B⊃ ⊂C⊃ ⊂D⊃ ⊂E⊃
12 ⊂A⊃ ⊂B⊃ ⊂C⊃ ⊂D⊃ ⊂E⊃ 32 ⊂A⊃ ⊂B⊃ ⊂C⊃ ⊂D⊃ ⊂E⊃   52 ⊂A⊃ ⊂B⊃ ⊂C⊃ ⊂D⊃ ⊂E⊃   72 ⊂A⊃ ⊂B⊃ ⊂C⊃ ⊂D⊃ ⊂E⊃
13 ⊂A⊃ ⊂B⊃ ⊂C⊃ ⊂D⊃ ⊂E⊃ 33 ⊂A⊃ ⊂B⊃ ⊂C⊃ ⊂D⊃ ⊂E⊃   53 ⊂A⊃ ⊂B⊃ ⊂C⊃ ⊂D⊃ ⊂E⊃   73 ⊂A⊃ ⊂B⊃ ⊂C⊃ ⊂D⊃ ⊂E⊃
14 ⊂A⊃ ⊂B⊃ ⊂C⊃ ⊂D⊃ ⊂E⊃ 34 ⊂A⊃ ⊂B⊃ ⊂C⊃ ⊂D⊃ ⊂E⊃   54 ⊂A⊃ ⊂B⊃ ⊂C⊃ ⊂D⊃ ⊂E⊃   74 ⊂A⊃ ⊂B⊃ ⊂C⊃ ⊂D⊃ ⊂E⊃
15 ⊂A⊃ ⊂B⊃ ⊂C⊃ ⊂D⊃ ⊂E⊃ 35 ⊂A⊃ ⊂B⊃ ⊂C⊃ ⊂D⊃ ⊂E⊃   55 ⊂A⊃ ⊂B⊃ ⊂C⊃ ⊂D⊃ ⊂E⊃   75 ⊂A⊃ ⊂B⊃ ⊂C⊃ ⊂D⊃ ⊂E⊃
16 ⊂A⊃ ⊂B⊃ ⊂C⊃ ⊂D⊃ ⊂E⊃ 36 ⊂A⊃ ⊂B⊃ ⊂C⊃ ⊂D⊃ ⊂E⊃   56 ⊂A⊃ ⊂B⊃ ⊂C⊃ ⊂D⊃ ⊂E⊃   76 ⊂A⊃ ⊂B⊃ ⊂C⊃ ⊂D⊃ ⊂E⊃
17 ⊂A⊃ ⊂B⊃ ⊂C⊃ ⊂D⊃ ⊂E⊃ 37 ⊂A⊃ ⊂B⊃ ⊂C⊃ ⊂D⊃ ⊂E⊃   57 ⊂A⊃ ⊂B⊃ ⊂C⊃ ⊂D⊃ ⊂E⊃   77 ⊂A⊃ ⊂B⊃ ⊂C⊃ ⊂D⊃ ⊂E⊃
18 ⊂A⊃ ⊂B⊃ ⊂C⊃ ⊂D⊃ ⊂E⊃ 38 ⊂A⊃ ⊂B⊃ ⊂C⊃ ⊂D⊃ ⊂E⊃   58 ⊂A⊃ ⊂B⊃ ⊂C⊃ ⊂D⊃ ⊂E⊃   78 ⊂A⊃ ⊂B⊃ ⊂C⊃ ⊂D⊃ ⊂E⊃
19 ⊂A⊃ ⊂B⊃ ⊂C⊃ ⊂D⊃ ⊂E⊃ 39 ⊂A⊃ ⊂B⊃ ⊂C⊃ ⊂D⊃ ⊂E⊃   59 ⊂A⊃ ⊂B⊃ ⊂C⊃ ⊂D⊃ ⊂E⊃   79 ⊂A⊃ ⊂B⊃ ⊂C⊃ ⊂D⊃ ⊂E⊃
20 ⊂A⊃ ⊂B⊃ ⊂C⊃ ⊂D⊃ ⊂E⊃ 40 ⊂A⊃ ⊂B⊃ ⊂C⊃ ⊂D⊃ ⊂E⊃   60 ⊂A⊃ ⊂B⊃ ⊂C⊃ ⊂D⊃ ⊂E⊃   80 ⊂A⊃ ⊂B⊃ ⊂C⊃ ⊂D⊃ ⊂E⊃

DO NOT MARK IN THIS AREA

ABOUT THE AUTHORS

Tom Meltzer, a Columbia University graduate, is the author or co-author of numerous Princeton Review books, including The Best 366 Colleges, Cracking the CLEP, and Illustrated Word Smart. He has developed materials and taught for The Princeton Review since 1988. He currently resides in Durham, North Carolina with his wife, Lisa.

Jean Hofheimer Bennett began her teaching career in 1973 after receiving her master's degree from New York University. She credits her life-long love of teaching and history to her high school history teacher, Eric Rothschild, who continues to inspire students and teachers all over the world. She serves as a faculty consultant for the College Board, along with other teachers and professors who read and score the AP U.S. History Exam. In 2001 she was awarded the AP Recognition Award for Excellence in Teaching from the New England Division of the College Board, and she has received special recognition by Tufts University for her work as a teacher.

She currently lives and teaches in Connecticut and extends her thanks to the many students who have brightened her classroom over the years by opening their minds, exploring new ideas, working hard, and being willing to learn the most important lesson of all: that by examining the many facets of our complex history, we determine how we live our lives and how we interact with our world.

She wishes to thank Tom Meltzer for his wit, creativity, and devotion to scholarship, and for bringing her in on this project. Special thanks to her colleagues at Weston High School, especially her visionary principal, Mary Monroe Kolek, and her spectacular social studies department Chair, Christopher Sidoli, for serving as examples and for believing that students can excel when given the chance. She also wishes to thank fellow teachers Wendy Cudmore, who got her started down this path, and Doris Fiotakis whose talents never cease to amaze. Most of all, she wishes to thank her family, Jim, Rachel, Michael, and Sarah, for their endless patience, cheerful encouragement, and loving support.

Susan Babkes began her teaching career in 1981 after earning a bachelor's degree in music and master's degrees in secondary education and history. She continued her education while teaching, earning two additional masters degrees. She holds an M.A. from the State University of New York at Stony Brook in European History, and an M.A. in Intellectual History from Washington University in St. Louis, where she was a teaching assistant and adjunct professor in the history department. She is currently the chair of the social studies department at John L. Miller-Great Neck North High School on Long Island, New York, where she has taught a variety of courses, including: AP U.S. History, AP European History, AP Psychology, and World History. She is also a member of the adjunct faculty in the history department at C. W. Post College. Ms. Babkes is the recipient of numerous grants and awards, including a Mellon dissertation fellowship, an NEH grant to study the Progressive Era at Hull House in Chicago, a Gilder–Lehrman award to participate in an international conference on the Cold War, and an Annenberg grant for alternative education. She has traveled extensively and has lived and studied abroad.

NOTES